Women of Westminster

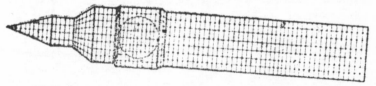

'To this day, astonishingly few books address the history of women in Westminster; luckily Rachel Reeves is not just helping to bridge that gap, but brings an insider's perspective to bear in telling the stories of these remarkable women. Rich with detail and original research, this highly readable history emphasizes the challenges women in Parliament continue to face, and the unexpected solidarity they often forged in meeting those challenges. A heartfelt, informative, and engaging read – highly recommended.' — **Sarah Churchwell**

'From household names like Nancy Astor to lesser-known, but equally pioneering, politicians such as Florence Horsbrugh and Mavis Tate, *Women of Westminster* tells the story of the female MPs who shaped parliament and the country. These women broke into Parliament's boys' club, rewrote the membership rules, and in the process set about transforming Britain. This is a glorious compendium of the manifold achievements they chalked up – and the sacrifices they made.

Rachel Reeves is perfectly positioned to tell their story, having experienced the slings and arrows of parliamentary prejudice first-hand. As she herself puts it, she "stands on the shoulders" of her pioneering forbears, and from that vantage point she can see not only all they achieved but also what more needs to be done.' — **Cathy Newman**

'There have been too few books chronicling the struggles and successes of women in Parliament. This volume goes a long way to address that, charting the hard-won progress made by female MPs of all parties and political views over the last 100 years. Much has been achieved and the UK has its second female Prime Minister. However, it is incredible that there have only been 491 female MPs since 1918 when some women got the vote for the first time. There is still much to do.' — **Jo Coburn**

'Our past isn't made up just of his stories, but her stories too. Rachel uncovers the best of them – the lives of those political women who wouldn't be stopped, who fought to make their way, and showed us all – household names and those who deserve to be.' — **Laura Kuenssberg**

Women of Westminster

The MPs Who Changed Politics

Rachel Reeves

BLOOMSBURY CARAVEL
LONDON · OXFORD · NEW YORK · NEW DELHI · SYDNEY

BLOOMSBURY CARAVEL
Bloomsbury Publishing Plc
50 Bedford Square, London, WC1B 3DP, UK

BLOOMSBURY, BLOOMSBURY CARAVEL and the Diana logo are trademarks of
Bloomsbury Publishing Plc

First published in Great Britain in 2019
This edition published 2020

A catalogue record for this book is available from the British Library

Library of Congress Cataloguing-in-Publication data has been applied for

ISBN: HB: 978-1-78831-220-2; PB: 978-1-4482-1785-4; eBook: 978-1-4482-1787-8

2 4 6 8 10 9 7 5 3 1

Typeset by RefineCatch Limited, Bungay, Suffolk
Printed and bound in Great Britain by CPI Group (UK) Ltd, Croydon CR0 4YY

MIX
Paper from
responsible sources
FSC® C020471

To find out more about our authors and books visit www.bloomsbury.com
and sign up for our newsletters

Contents

List of Illustrations

1. The first two women MPs to take their seats, Nancy Astor and Margaret Wintringham, on the terrace of the House of Commons in 1921. Courtesy of Time Life Pictures/Mansell/The LIFE Images Collection/Getty Images.
2. The first Labour women MPs assemble on the terrace in 1929 for a photograph to mark the first election following the introduction of equal suffrage in 1928. Back row, left to right: Dr Marion Phillips, Edith Picton-Turberville, Dr Ethel Bentham, Mary Agnes Hamilton. Front row: Lady Cynthia Mosley, Susan Lawrence, Margaret Bondfield, Ellen Wilkinson, Jennie Lee. Courtesy of National Portrait Gallery.
3. Labour MP Margaret Bondfield, the first woman to enter the cabinet, c.1930, on the steps of Number Ten. Courtesy of Bentley Archive/Popperfoto/Getty Images.
4. Conservative women MPs on the terrace in November 1931, celebrating shortly after a landslide that brought in a wave of Conservative women MPs. Back row, left to right: Nancy Astor, Helen Shaw, Mavis Tate, Thelma Cazalet, Sarah Ward, Ida Copeland, Florence Horsburgh. Front row: Norah Runge, Gwendolyn Countess of Iveagh, Katherine Duchess of Atholl, Irene Ward, Mary Pickford. Courtesy of Parliamentary Archives.
5. Labour MP Ellen Willkinson making a speech during her iconic leadership of the Jarrow Crusade in 1936. Courtesy of Popperfoto/Getty Images.
6. A portrait of Eleanor Rathbone, Independent MP and champion of family allowances. The portrait was originally the idea of four of Rathbone's friends. When it was suggested to her, she said 'I do not believe that I belong to the small class of people who justify public

portraits'. Courtesy of Julian Barrow after James Gunn/National Portrait Gallery/Curator's Office, Palace of Westminster.

7. The new intake of Labour women after the Labour landslide of 1945. Back row, left to right: Caroline Ganley, Edith Wills, Jennie Lee, Muriel Nichol, Leah Manning, Grace Colman, Lucy Noel-Buxton, Clarice Shaw, Florence Paton, Jean Mann and Lucy Middleton. Front row: Bessie Braddock, Mabel Ridealgh, Alice Bacon, Edith Summerskill, Ellen Wilkinson, Jennie Adamson, Peggy Herbison and Barbara Ayrton-Gould. Courtesy of Popperfoto/Getty Images.

8. Women MPs celebrating Megan Lloyd George's 20th anniversary in Parliament, 31 May 1949. Back row, left to right: Edith Wills, Lucy Middleton, Bessie Braddock, Jean Mann, Thelma Cazalet-Keir, Lady Grant of Monymusk (Priscilla Buchan, Baroness Tweedsmuir), Alice Bacon, Barbara Ayrton-Gould, Viscountess Davidson, Lucy Noel-Buxton, Leah Manning, Caroline Ganley, Grace Colman. Front row, left to right: Florence Paton, Margaret Herbison, Mabel Ridealgh, Megan Lloyd George, Edith Summerskill, Margaret Wintringham, Jennie Lee. Courtesy of Gerald Pudsey/Parliamentary Archives.

9. Conservative MP Irene Ward joins Labour's Barbara Castle and Edith Summerskill on Equal Pay Day, 8 March 1954, after presenting a petition of 80,000 signatures to the House of Commons. Courtesy of J. Wilds/Keystone/Getty Images.

10. Barbara Castle, Edith Summerskill and Alice Bacon striding along Scarborough's seafront just before the opening of the Labour Party conference, 1954. Courtesy of Reg Burkett/Keystone/Hulton Archive/Getty Images.

11. Key Labour MPs joining hands to sing the Red Flag on the platform of the Labour Party conference in Scarborough, October 1967. Left to right: Tony Benn, James Callaghan, unidentified, Richard Crossman, Barbara Castle, Alice Bacon, prime minister Harold Wilson, Jennie Lee. Courtesy of Rolls Press/Popperfoto/Getty Images.

12. Labour MP and secretary of state for employment and productivity, Barbara Castle (fourth from right) having tea with the Ford machinists to negotiate an equal pay settlement in 1968, prior to the Equal Pay Act in 1970. Courtesy of Wesley/Keystone/Getty Images.

13. Barbara Castle, a few months before the 1964 general election which saw a Labour landslide under Harold Wilson and her appointment to the cabinet as minister for overseas development. Courtesy of Walter Bird/National Portrait Gallery.

14. Margaret Thatcher in 1977, two years after having been elected as the first woman leader of the Conservative Party, and two years before making history as the first woman prime minister. Courtesy of Bern Schwartz/National Portrait Gallery.

15. Shirley Williams at a press conference in March 1981 to launch the Social Democratic Party (SDP) after having left the Labour Party with the 'Gang of Four', Roy Jenkins, David Owen and Bill Rodgers. Courtesy of Jacob SUTTON/Gamma-Rapho/Getty Images.

16. Labour's Harriet Harman found herself fighting the Peckham by-election campaign in 1982. She was heavily pregnant at the time. Courtesy of PA/PA Archive/PA Images.

17. Women MPs from various parties in 1988, including Margaret Thatcher, Diane Abbott, Betty Boothroyd, Joan Ruddock, Margaret Beckett, Edwina Currie, Clare Short, Mo Mowlam and Jo Richardson. Courtesy of Universal History Archive/Getty Images.

18. Labour MP Diane Abbott, the first black woman to be elected as an MP, in 1987. Courtesy of Peter Jordan/The LIFE Images Collection/Getty Images.

19. Labour MP Margaret Beckett in 1997. She later became the first woman foreign secretary. Courtesy of Steve Eason/Hulton Archive/Getty Images.

20. Labour's Betty Boothroyd, in 1994, two years after having been elected as the first woman Speaker of the House of Commons. She held the position for eight years. Courtesy of Anne-Katrin Purkiss/National Portrait Gallery

21. The infamous 'Blair's Babes' photo, taken shortly after the 1997 Labour landslide at which a record of 101 Labour women were elected. Courtesy of JOHNNY EGGITT/AFP/Getty Images.

22. Labour MPs Caroline Flint and Hazel Blears among others in their dance group, 'The Division Belles'. Courtesy of Hazel Blears.

23. Labour MP Tessa Jowell in 1998. Jowell oversaw the implementation of SureStart and the London Olympics in 2012. She tragically passed away in 2018 from brain cancer. Courtesy of Victoria Carew Hunt/National Portrait Gallery.

Acknowledgements

In 2016 I published my biography of Alice Bacon, Yorkshire's first woman MP. Alice's story inspired me to learn more about the pioneers who stood for Parliament in those early years after women gained the right to stand. So, my first thanks must go to Alice who got me started.

For the immense research help, I thank Mary Reader, recommended to me by my old friend Zosia Stemplowska, and Emma Lundin, who I found via Mari Takayanagi, curator at the House of Commons. We also benefitted from the help of Lisa Berry-Waite who is working on her PhD at Exeter university. This book couldn't have been completed without their forensic analysis, archive hunting and enthusiasm – I have enjoyed working with them and all that we have shared these past two and a half years.

From my office, hours of interviews have been transcribed by Stephanie Darlington, Beth Tye, Abby Bloomfeld, Joe dePaulo, Josh Molloy and Isabelle Agerback. I hope they enjoyed the stories of some amazing women past and present as much as I did.

For the historians' perspective, Jacqui Turner on Astor, Laura Beers on Wilkinson, Susan Pederson on Rathbone, Patricia Hollis on Jennie Lee, Alice Perkins on Castle and Julie Gottlieb on 1930s women in Parliament – you have all inspired and educated me.

For the stories from the floor of the House of Commons, the selection conferences and the political battles, my interviews with MPs from all parties, stretching back to the 1960s have, I hope, brought the book to life. Thank you to Shirley Williams, Shirley Summerskill, Betty Boothroyd, Gillian Shephard, Edwina Currie and all the former MPs for sharing your stories of the last fifty years. And to those serving today a special thanks to Harriet Harman who spent two and a half hours on a hot summer's day talking to me in her garden, to Diane Abbott, who I didn't know as well as I should, Jo Swinson, Jess Phillips and Amber Rudd who all tell of how their feminism inspired their political activism. And a huge thank you to Theresa May for finding time to talk to me about getting elected in 1997 and then her rise to the chairmanship of her party, cabinet and of course being Britain's second female prime minister.

Thank you to Seema Kennedy for helping to set up that interview and to Jo Cox, my friend and colleague who brought Seema and I together to take forward her work. The last chapter of this book is inspired by Jo Cox.

Thank you to my editor, Jo Godfrey and the team at Bloomsbury-IBTauris including Magdalene Abraha and Tia Ali. And to my agent Caroline Michel – you all believed in me and helped me meet a few deadlines. I am also grateful to the Leeds Literary and Philosophical Society, who provided a grant that helped make this book possible.

The book gets started with a marvellous foreword by Mary Beard whose own book *Women and Power* is a brilliant call to arms for women wanting to make the world a better place and to Harriet Harman for the epilogue – women transforming politics is still work in progress.

To the 494 women elected in the last 100 years, each of you have fought your own battles and overcome the odds. We don't agree on everything, but I hope this book tells the story of our collective history and the difference having women in Parliament has made.

On a personal level, thank you to my husband Nick. And, to my children, Anna and Harry, I hope by the time you are old enough to vote we will have equal representation of women and men in Parliament. I hope too that you will be champions of equality and call out injustices. And I hope you will understand why I spent many weekends and holidays reading and writing this history.

For my children, Anna and Harry

It is justice, not charity, that is wanting in the world – Mary Wolstonecraft

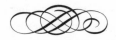

List of notable political 'firsts' for women in the House of Commons

1918	First woman MP elected (Constance Markievicz)
1919	First woman MP to take her seat (Nancy Astor)
1924	First woman minister (Margaret Bondfield)
1929	First woman cabinet minister/privy counsellor (Margaret Bondfield)
1936	First woman to move (introduce) the address in reply to the King's Speech (Florence Horsbrugh)
1948	First woman chair of committee of whole House (Florence Paton)
1953	First Conservative woman to be appointed to the cabinet (Florence Horsbrugh)
1961	First woman MP to ask a prime minister's question (Irene Ward)
1964	First woman parliamentary whip of the House of Commons (Harriet Slater)
1970	First woman deputy speaker of the House of Commons (Betty Harvie Anderson)
1975	First woman leader of the opposition (Margaret Thatcher)
1979	First woman prime minister (Margaret Thatcher)
1987	First black woman MP elected (Diane Abbott)
1992	First woman speaker of the House of Commons (Betty Boothroyd)
1997	First woman secretary of state for Northern Ireland (Mo Mowlam)
1997	First woman leader of the House of Commons (Ann Taylor)
1997	First full-time minister for women (Joan Ruddock)
1998	First woman chief whip (Ann Taylor)
2001	First woman secretary of state for Scotland (Helen Liddell)
2006	First woman secretary of state for foreign and commonwealth affairs (Margaret Beckett)

2007   First woman secretary of state for home affairs (Jacqui Smith)
2010   First woman secretary of state for Wales (Cheryl Gillan)
2016   First woman lord chancellor (Liz Truss)
2017   First woman black rod (Sarah Clarke)
2019   First woman secretary of state for defence (Penny Mordaunt)

Prologue to the Paperback Edition

The centenary of the first woman to take her seat in Parliament was reached in November 2019. In the last 100 years, more than 500 women have been elected. Each generation sees a rise in numbers, and new challenges.

In the most recent election, Boris Johnson has been returned as Prime Minister on his promise to 'get Brexit done'. Theresa May sits on the back benches. Record numbers of women stood down from Parliament. Jo Swinson lost her seat in Scotland and hence the leadership of her party.

While the new intake of women MPs includes plenty of 'rising stars' we have lost women from the House of Commons including Nicky Morgan, Luciana Berger, Heidi Allen, Caroline Flint and Seema Kennedy who all expected their parliamentary careers to have lasted longer. Many women have cited abuse for the reason they quit. We will never know what they could have gone on to achieve.

So you might think that women in Westminster were in a worse state than they were a year ago.

Yet I feel confident about the future. The two people who have caused the biggest problems for Boris Johnson since he became prime minister are Lady Brenda Hale, President of the Supreme Court, who forced Johnson back to Parliament after finding that the Prorogation was null, void and unlawful, and Gina Miller, who took the Government to court to argue that point.

In Parliament, a record number of women stood and were elected at the recent general election taking the number of women MPs to 220, just over a third of the total. More than half of Labour's depleted band of MPs are women. In the House of Commons chamber, Theresa May watches down on her successor from three rows behind the front-bench, occasionally giving withering looks from above, with the knowledge and experience of office.

In this parliament we should keep an eye on women MPs including Conservatives' Priti Patel and Victoria Atkins, Labour's Angela Raynor and Rosie Duffield, the Liberal Democrats' Leyla Moran and the SNP's Hannah Bardell – all rising stars in their parties.

Some people have asked whether Theresa May's failure to deliver on her own key promise will 'set back women in politics'. What an absurd proposition. Boris Johnson is hardly covering himself in glory in office, but would anyone seriously ask whether he might 'set back men in politics'? A salutary reminder that women have to jump a higher bar than men to succeed.

The last parliament was a fractious one, and we don't know what twists and turns we have ahead of us. Certainly in 2019 many women left their political homes to sit as independents or to join other parties – including the former home secretary Amber Rudd who quit the Tory party over Brexit and Luciana Berger who left Labour over anti-Semitism. Their absence from Parliament is a loss to our politics but shows that the women of Westminster cannot be taken for granted.

Following the election of Jo Swinson as leader of the Liberal Democrats – albeit only for a brief five months - Labour is now the only party in Westminster never to have been led by a woman. But at the time of writing, MPs Rebecca Long Bailey, Lisa Nandy, Jess Phillips and Emily Thornberry are all being tipped for the Labour leadership now that Jeremy Corbyn has stood down after a catastrophic defeat. There is no getting away from the fact that Labour needs to catch up. As Angela Rayner has said, having a woman lead Labour will be good for the party and good for the country. I agree.

One step forward has been on 'baby leave'. Proxy voting for MPs who have a baby or adopt is coming towards the end of its twelve month trial. It has helped MPs who are new parents better balance work and family life while ensuring our constituents are represented in Parliamentary votes. It didn't exist when I became a mother in 2013 and when I had my second child in 2015. I am pleased that this is now changing. I hope baby leave continues beyond the trial period and that some form of further maternity cover can be agreed on.

While Brexit continues to dominate our public debate and time in Parliament, hours in the chamber are long, uncertain and subject to change at short notice. When asked by my six and four year old children recently if I would be home for bedtime stories that night, I apologised and said that I wouldn't. 'Is it because of Brexit?' my daughter asked. It was.

It is not clear if and when politics and Parliament will 'get back to normal' (whatever that is) but I do hope that the divisions that have been so palpable can be mended and that mutual respect, tolerance and a desire to seek the common good can be re-kindled. It needs to be.

Hatred and anger have infected our politics inside and outside Westminster. Just down the road from my constituency office in Leeds, someone daubed the words "Hang traitor MPs" on the side of a building. The same slogan was painted on a wall by a bus stop. On Facebook, I have repeatedly been called a traitor and one person posted a message saying they 'couldn't wait' to 'run into me.'

A friend who isn't particularly political recently asked me how I cope with the attacks. It made me think. A few years ago I would have been horrified by the kind of abuse that is so regularly directed at me and many other MPs, particularly female politicians. But the reality is that this behaviour is now part of everyday life and we have had to become inured to it if we wish to continue as public servants. If I wasn't, I probably would have stood down at the last election. Although I want to stay, I understand why others have walked away.

Security around MPs has been tightened dramatically since the death of my friend and colleague Jo Cox who was murdered in 2016 as she carried out her work as an MP. Police now check in with my office every week. They will often come to events or maintain a presence nearby. Offensive graffiti is quickly painted over and abusive comments on social media reported. But they leave a mark and an impression of division and anger. In the aftermath of Jo's murder there was a determination to do things differently – to change the way we do politics. That resolve seems to have faltered. This toxic climate, fuelled by people's ability to easily cloak their identity online, is entirely different to 2010 when I left my job as an economist to become an MP.

With a new Parliament elected and with the Brexit issue seemingly settled, at least for now, I hope that our politics might become more civilised, less angry. All of us who care about the future of our democracy should hope for the same – because parliamentary democracy depends on good people being willing to serve and speak out.

Jo Cox's successor in Batley and Spen, Tracy Brabin, also worries about the political temperature. She told me that in terms of 'all that right-wing hate, misogyny, the way that she [Jo] died... Here we are again'. Jo's sister, Kim Leadbeater, even said that 'I think politics has, if I'm perfectly honest, become more toxic even than it was in the run-up to the referendum, and leading up to Jo's murder'. That must change.

As I hope you will discover in the chapters of this book, the history of women in Parliament is so often of working together across the political divide. All of us in Parliament can build on those endeavours as we try to work our way through what sometimes seem like enormous, insurmountable challenges – to both find policy solutions and bring the country back together. Perhaps it is too ambitious in today's climate. But I would say it is essential.

Rachel Reeves, December 2019.

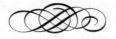

Foreword

Mary Beard

In 2010 the speaker, John Bercow, closed Bellamy's Bar in the Palace of Westminster and installed a nursery in its place. It is hard to understand how in the twenty-first century there could be any serious objection to the principle of on-site childcare for the benefit of Members of Parliament and staff. But it proved a controversial decision. In the press Bellamy's Bar was given the plaintiff adjective 'much missed' (as if there were not other bars in Westminster); and there was no end of blustering in the usual places about 'a waste of tax payers' money'. Nor was it just those on the right who raised objections. Some on the left also joined in, on the grounds that it was providing a perk for those who worked in Parliament that was not available to local residents. That may have been fair enough in a way, but I doubt if there had ever been much clamour to share the bar with Westminster's neighbours. The point is that nurseries tend to be seen as a perk for women, and as such more a privilege or a luxury than a basic essential. To listen to the complaints, you would think that men had nothing to do with the creation and care of children.

The architecture of institutions and their use of space (nursery or bar?) are often revealing guides to social hierarchy and exclusion. I remember vividly when the ladies' lavatories in most Cambridge colleges were located as inconveniently as possible, across several courtyards and down in some drab basement. The message was clear: this was not a place where women really belonged. As Rachel Reeves reminds us, even worse was true for the early women MPs. As soon as there was a prospect of female members in the House of Commons, there was the question of what facilities should be made available to them. When Nancy Astor became the first woman to take a seat in Parliament in 1919, she also became the sole denizen of the 'Lady Members' Room', uninspiring quarters located – predictably enough – in the basement: in fact so uninspiring that it was known as 'the dungeon'. When, over the next decade or so, a few more female colleagues joined Astor, the dungeon – with its seven desks and two couches – had far too little space to accommodate them all. It was standing room only, and (to judge from most descriptions) a terrible mess.

For someone of my age (I'm writing this aged 63), the experience of these early women MPs feels instantly recognizable. There were still 'male spaces' (by convention rather than rule) in the university in London where I had my first job. I can instantly feel the triumph of Ellen Wilkinson (Labour MP from 1924) when she walked into the House of Commons' smoking room. She said to the policeman who tried to stop her, with the 'sorry, not for ladies' line: 'I am not a lady – I am a Member of Parliament'. And all those bottom pinches that Shirley Williams and others reported in the division lobby are familiar to many of us in other contexts, from photo-copier to library or dance-floor. I like the story of the female MPs in the 1960s responding to this unwanted attention by stabbing their stilettos into the foot of the often unseen pincher, and looking out for who was limping later.

Things are a lot better now, though not quite as 'better' as we might hope. Most of the more than 200 women who are currently Members of Parliament have the same old stories to tell: being asked to get out of a lift that is for 'Members Only', or being assumed to be the MP's wife, not the MP. It is not unlike when I answer the telephone in my university faculty office and am regularly assumed to be a secretary: an insult both to our secretaries and to me! And, even if the women are no longer consigned to the Westminster dungeon, or kept out of the smoking room (which has ceased to exist anyway), the dispute over the nursery shows that the division of space is still an issue.

Some unexpected consequences, however, did come from putting the ladies in the dungeon in those early years. I am not for a moment suggesting that it is a good idea to give women worse accommodation than men (in fact I could make a pretty good case for systematically giving them the better). But it does seem that being thrown together in that way, under the often disapproving eyes of their male counterparts, helped them to create a rather different style of politics: much more collaborative, across the lines of party and class. It is wonderful to picture the extraordinary trio of the extremely posh Duchess of Atholl (MP between 1923 and 1938, sometimes as a Conservative, sometimes as an

Independent), Ellen Wilkinson, the working class hero of the smoking room triumph, and Eleanor Rathbone (Independent MP from 1929 to 1946 for 'the Combined English Universities', which then had their own parliamentary seat). They were all three strong supporters of the Republicans in Spain, went out there to see what was going on in 1937, and together were vociferous in their opposition to appeasement throughout the 1930s – a view that cost Atholl her parliamentary seat.

Of course, these early women parliamentarians did not always agree, even on 'women's issues'. Rathbone was a campaigner against what we would call female genital mutilation, a subject that did not cross the minds of most of them. Atholl meanwhile did not even think that suffrage should be extended to women on the same terms as men (the 1918 solution, which effectively restricted voting in general elections to propertied women aged over 30, was quite enough for her). But between them they introduced some of the most important reforms that we now take absolutely for granted as part of our social bedrock, from family allowances (which we now know as child benefit – the brainchild of Rathbone) to widows' pensions and the establishment of the fundamental principle that mothers and fathers had equal rights to the guardianship of their children (before 1924 women who separated or divorced had no rights to their children at all). In taking the lead in all this (including the dream of equal pay from the 1930s), they paved the way for the better-known names of the later twentieth century, from Barbara Castle to Margaret Thatcher, Shirley Williams to Diane Abbott.

I have lived through much of the revolution that Rachel Reeves charts in this book. My mother was born before any women had the right to vote in general elections and she lived to see a female prime minister (albeit one that she did not have much time for). When I was growing up in the 1960s only around 4 per cent of MPs were women; as a child I got the strong, and in some ways correct, impression that the country was governed by white men in suits. Currently just over 30 per cent of MPs are women. This is a big cause for celebration, not just because it is a victory for fairness, but it means that the country as a whole is no longer missing out on the political talents of half the population. And yet there is still a long way to go.

That is partly to do with the positions we entrust to women. Admittedly there have now been two women premiers, but not yet chancellor of the exchequer; we are still much more likely to find women in the 'caring' jobs. But it is even more to do with deeply embedded assumptions about the nature (and gender) of power. In our heads, I am afraid, politics is still often thought of as a man's world. Why else do female politicians, like Margaret Thatcher, get taught to lower their voices? And what do even *I* see when I shut my eyes and try to imagine a prime minister? Answer: a white man in a suit. The same thing happens, I confess, when I try to imagine a professor. Even though I *am* a female professor, it's a slightly batty-looking bloke in a lab coat that I see.

There could be no clearer glimpse of this than a tweet put out only last week by a prominent (Labour) politician in which he listed, from one to ten, his selection of the 'best politicians' of the last century. From Churchill at number one, via Aneurin Bevan and John Major and other assorted worthies, to Edward VII at Number Ten, every single one of them was a man. No Castle, no Thatcher – though Theresa May did scrape in at number ten of the parallel list of the 'most irresponsible & dangerous politicians' of the last century. This is the kind of mistake that it is, believe me, easy to make on Twitter. But it is revealing none the less. Even after two female premiers, the model of political power we offer ourselves remains resolutely male.

So how shall we know that the revolution has really worked? When we shut our eyes, think of a prime minister and see a wonderfully tough, eloquent and resplendent – *woman*.

Introduction

On 6 February 2018, I stood in the Central Lobby of Parliament with prime minister Theresa May, Harriet Harman and most of the other 208 women MPs in Parliament today. It was the 100th anniversary of the act of Parliament that finally gave some, but not all, women the vote. We were there to celebrate, reflect and mark that event in history. A couple of months later, a statue for Millicent Fawcett, suffrage campaigner and pioneer, was unveiled in Parliament Square – quite staggeringly the first statue of a woman in a square where people come to protest, see Parliament and witness political history.

That struggle for a voice was being celebrated. I took a rosette – in the purple, green and white tricolour of the suffrage campaign – home to my five-year-old daughter and tried to explain what it meant. It's harder than I thought it would be. How can a five-year-old understand that a century ago her dad would have had a vote but not her mum? Her granddads but not her grandmas? Her brother would have grown up to have rights – and opportunities – that she wouldn't have. So many inequalities that my daughter doesn't understand have been broken down. That is a wonderful thing.

The progress made by women and for women in the last one hundred years is remarkable. The opportunities available to girls and women today are infinitely greater than those available to my great-grandmother, born in 1900 in Swansea, South Wales, who I knew when I was a young girl. She would have voted for the first time in 1928 when men and women could vote on the same basis – aged twenty-one and with no property requirements. Women having the vote, but crucially, women in Parliament, helped make that progress possible.

One third of the MPs in Parliament today are women. When I was born, forty years ago, that proportion was just 3 per cent. I want my daughter – and my son – to grow up in a world where #MeToo is unthinkable, where women are paid the same as men, where women are not absent from the board room, where the number of women's refuges falls not because of cuts but because men don't batter their wives, where there is more than just one woman on our bank notes, where the United States of America has a woman as president, where the Labour Party elects a woman leader. Where Parliament looks like the country it is supposed to serve. Why not? We are more than half the population, and have the same proportion of the talent, the ideas, the energy, the passion.

This book tells the story of the women who have shaped our political history by being Members of the Mother of all Parliaments, the British Parliament, the House of Commons. It is a story of women across the political spectrum. It is a biography of Parliament told by the women elected to it. It is the story of the women who have advanced the rights of women – to equal pay, to the guardianship of children, to reproductive rights, to access to childcare, child benefits and maternity leave. Having women in Parliament has advanced the cause of women and has got onto the statute book crucial legislation that has transformed the lives and opportunities of women. Women in Westminster have changed the culture of politics and shown, through their leadership and example, that women can excel at the top and under pressure, so far including two female prime ministers. But apart from a few big names, these women who have shaped all our lives are largely unknown. These are stories that need telling and these are stories that all of us should know. This book is an alternative history of Britain in the last one hundred years, told through the stories of political women.

So, what was it like for those early women MPs? Whose shadow do I walk in as a woman in Westminster today? What difference have the 556 women elected to Parliament so far, made? And how was that difference achieved – collectively, or individually, or both? Did the role and status of women in Parliament change as the numbers increased? Are women MPs more likely to advance women's rights than men? Does it even make sense to describe a category of 'women MPs' today?

Over the last one hundred years there has been a vast quantity of legislation spearheaded by women which has hugely improved the lives of women outside Parliament. Through the chapters of this book we see that the vast majority of legislation that has directly and consciously benefitted women was fought for and legislated by women MPs – things that affect all of us, such as equal pay and childcare. The chapters that follow tell the story of how battles were fought and won – some quickly, some over decades – by women who weren't prepared to back down.

The change began in 1918 when Sinn Féin's Constance Markiewicz became the first woman to be elected as an MP. But it was only when the first woman MP took her seat in Parliament – Nancy Astor, who was elected in November 1919 – that women could make political change within the parliamentary system.

Legislation by women for women really started with Margaret Wintringham, elected as a Liberal MP in 1921. Working with Astor, she piloted legislation through Parliament which gave equal rights for the guardianship of children to mothers and fathers. Until then, fathers assumed guardianship of the children if parents separated, leaving mothers with no rights at all. This reform began to end the heartache of women losing access to their children on the breakdown of marriage.

During the Second World War, MPs from across parties formed the 'Woman Power' committee in an attempt to help direct the war effort of women. Woman Power was spearheaded by Conservative women Irene Ward and Mavis Tate working with Labour MP Edith Summerskill to help mobilize women in the campaign.

Equal pay will forever be associated with Labour's Barbara Castle, who introduced the Equal Pay Act in 1970 after intervening in an industrial dispute at the Ford works in Dagenham. But it was Conservative MP Thelma Cazalet-Keir who was the original pioneer. She championed the cause of equal pay for teachers and civil servants in the 1930s and 40s, much to the displeasure of prime minister Winston Churchill, who told Cazalet-Keir it was akin to 'trying to put an elephant in a perambulator'.

Fifty years after the Equal Pay Act, women are still paid less than men. To try to change that, the biggest employers now have to publish the gender pay gap in their workforces. This requirement was part of Labour MP and the party's deputy leader Harriet Harman's 2010 Equality Act, which was then taken forward by former Liberal Democrat leader and MP Jo Swinson when she was business minister during David Cameron's Coalition government. Family allowances and their successor child benefit and tax credits were also steered through Parliament by women. The Independent MP Eleanor Rathbone set out her vision of a family allowance in the 1920s, paid directly to the mother, based on the number of children in a household. It took almost two decades of formidable campaigning for Rathbone to realize her vision at the end of the Second World War, and it required Barbara Castle to take it forward with child benefit in the 1960s and the top-up benefit of family and child tax credits in the early 2000s, which were pushed for by Harriet Harman. Further reform, such as extensions in maternity leave and pay, childcare and SureStart centres were at the heart of the New Labour vision for family policy. However, it is unlikely that these policies would have been pursued with the same vigour without the election of 101 Labour women MPs in 1997. As home secretary and prime minister, Theresa May has prioritized tackling modern-day slavery and the exploitation of women and girls, working with a new and growing cohort of women on the Conservative benches. The raft of legislation over the last 100 years reminds us that getting the vote was about having women's voices heard. Women MPs gave a voice, a sisterhood of cheerleaders, to the causes that had been neglected by a cosy all-male club at Westminster. I believe that every woman in the country has had her own life affected in some way by the women in Parliament. I also believe that the effect has been profoundly positive and empowering.

But you have to look beyond the acts of Parliament to see the many other changes that having women in Parliament has helped to bring about. Women in Westminster have changed the culture of politics and the perception of what women can do. Parliament today is still male-dominated and its culture is institutionally oriented towards middle and upper class men. The hours that parliamentarians sit better suit a private male dining club than a modern workplace; until recently there were hooks in the members' cloakroom designated for you to hang your sword, and the debating chamber sometimes gives the impression of men engaging in a chivalrous duel of words. But there has been considerable change over the past hundred years.

In 1918 there were no facilities for women in Parliament. A gallery for 'ladies' to watch the proceedings of Parliament was shielded by a metal grille so the men in the Commons couldn't see the women watching them. When women won the right to stand for office, the Lady Members' Room was created. The first women parliamentarians nicknamed it 'the Dungeon' because of its location in a dingy basement on the parliamentary estate. Labour MP Ellen Wilkinson noted that 'if all the women MPs happened to be in the room together they would not even have a chair apiece to sit on'. Gradually, the facilities were updated – and women were given the space to work, think and represent. The hours of Parliament today are still long and late, but the all-night sittings, prevalent right up until the early 2000s, have now almost vanished. Labour MP Joan Ruddock can take a great deal of the credit for those reforms, which make combining work and family life for MPs, including me, a little more manageable.

The culture of Parliament has also changed as women have called out harassment, inside and outside Parliament. The work of feminist campaigner Caroline Criado-Perez on the portrayal of women by the media and her campaign to get a picture of Jane Austen on the ten pound note, as well as Laura Bates' campaign against everyday sexism, are today's incarnation of campaigns and issues that go way back in time. Astor physically struggled to get to her place in the chamber as her male colleagues tried to block her from taking her seat. Women were not expected to be parliamentarians – they were wives, mothers, home makers, society hostesses, shop and mill workers. Not in positions of authority, certainly not in their clubs. Labour and then SDP MP Shirley Williams has written of how women MPs were regularly pinched on the bottom in the packed voting lobby. Labour MP Dawn Butler tells of being mistaken for a cleaner in Parliament as her gender and her race made her appear a very unlikely MP, while Labour's MP Stella Creasy was told to get out of the lift when the division bell was ringing for a vote in the Commons as the lifts were reserved for Members. She *was* an MP, she told a rather surprised male colleague. When I was elected as the Labour MP for Leeds West in 2010 I was told I could have a 'spouse's pass' for my then fiancé. I went to collect it and the man in the pass office remarked that I must be very excited. The prospect of my fiancé being able to come to Parliament wasn't hugely exciting but I smiled. The man went on – 'did your husband just get elected?' 'No, *I* have just been elected', I corrected him. 'You're an MP?' he looked at me rather taken aback. 'Yes, of course', now he corrected himself, looking at the application form in front of him and re-gaining his composure. 'And, how are you finding it, Miss Reeves?' Fine, I thought, but attitudes are still a bit backwards.

The difficulty in conceiving of the fact that a woman – particularly a young woman, or a BAME woman – could be an MP is beginning to change and certainly women MPs are not pointed at like 'some sort of giant panda' as Conservative MP Thelma Cazalet-Keir felt she was when she was an MP. While terms like 'Blair's Babes' and 'Cameron's Cuties' continue to define women by their male leaders rather than taking them on their own merits, it is clear that with more women MPs occupying the green benches the culture of politics is changing. The resignation of cabinet ministers accused of sexual harassment towards women is the latest evidence of this cultural shift, in Parliament and in society.

Having more women in Parliament has also changed the perception of what women are capable of and how they should be treated. In the public eye women have shown that they can take on leadership roles and operate at the highest levels of pressure and responsibility. In doing so they have changed people's attitudes and assumptions about women and power.

Labour MP Margaret Bondfield said on her appointment as the first woman cabinet minister in 1929 that she knew her position was 'no sinecure' and that she went into the role with her eyes open. But she also declared that she was doing this not just for herself but for all women. From Bondfield onwards, prime ministers have felt they needed a woman in the team, paving the way for the Duchess of Atholl, Susan Lawrence, Ellen Wilkinson and Florence Horsbrugh in the following decades.

I was just three months old when Margaret Thatcher became prime minister in 1979. Aged eight, I knew I didn't agree with Thatcher – I was an early convert to the Labour cause – but I never doubted that a woman could lead and be prime minister. Thatcher fundamentally challenged assumptions about women and power. A woman as PM may have been a challenge to our notions of power, but there she was (handbag, blow-dried hair and all) with her clear sense of purpose, phenomenal capacity for hard work on very little sleep and probably the most reforming prime minister this country has seen for a long time – at least since Clement Attlee.

I first voted in 1997, and as well as being delighted that we had a Labour government for the only time in my memory, I also recall vividly the pictures of all these new women in newspapers, magazines and on the television. It was the greatest advance for women's political representation that this country had ever seen – 'women of all ages, shapes and sizes, left and right' (as Clare Short put it). They were women I related to and I remember feeling very excited about the future as I started my adult life. I am sure it helped me think that politics might be for me.

This book tells the story of the positive difference women have made, but we must also acknowledge the sacrifices made to break those glass ceilings and get women's voices heard. Of the early women pioneers in Parliament, most didn't have children. Many were also unmarried. This was particularly true on the Labour benches. Of the first women to serve in the cabinet – Bondfield, Wilkinson, Horsbrugh and Castle – none had children and only one (Castle) ever married. But it is unclear how women could have combined a family and a political career in the first forty or fifty years; the idea of a father bringing up the children or running the household was still a long way off. Thatcher's children were at boarding school while she was an MP, and by the time she was prime minister they had left home. The sacrifices made by the early women in Parliament are ones that my generation don't have to make. And for that, too, I certainly am very grateful.

Those women who did have young children while being MPs have often spoken of the guilt that they felt when fulfilling their parliamentary duties. Harriet Harman has spoken about how difficult it was to have a young family as an MP in the 1980s. Diane Abbott, who received a barrage of criticism when she sent her son to a fee-paying school, says that this was the one time that she felt she put her son first, so used was she to being out late at night voting, on international delegations, or at the weekends campaigning. For those MPs with constituencies out of London (like mine in Leeds), that challenge is harder still, as you are either away from your children during the week if they are in the constituency, or frequently at weekends if they are in London. It is part of the job, but it is a difficult part of it for parents – and particularly for mothers, who are still expected by society to bear most of the responsibility of bringing up children. The first woman to have a baby while serving as an MP was Labour's Helene Hayman. Elected in 1974 when she was just married, she had her first child two years later. Politically, it couldn't have been a worse time. Labour's majority was wafer thin and falling, and pairing had been suspended. Just ten days after giving birth, Hayman went to Westminster, driven by parliamentary colleague Lena Jeger, with buggy and baby in tow. The press was teeming outside Hayman's house, hoping to snap a photo. When Hayman lost her seat as Labour lost office in 1979, she did not have a desire to return, in part because she wanted another child and didn't see how she could combine the two roles.

Fast forward to 2010, and the House of Commons speaker John Bercow decided to close a bar in Parliament to install a nursery. 'The Houses of Parliament had a shooting gallery', Bercow told me, 'but not a nursery. I thought that was wrong.' For the first time MPs could bring their babies to Parliament and not have to leave them with a friend, a member of staff or a doorkeeper – or smuggle them through the voting lobby as Harriet Harman was wrongly accused of doing. Certainly, the nursery, the sitting hours, the change in the rules so that parents can take young children through the voting lobbies (Liberal Democrat couple Jo Swinson and Duncan Hames were the first to do this in 2014) have made a big difference. Probably the biggest advance is a change in societal attitudes. More men now do more of the childcare, more women are the primary earners, and it is more common that two parents work and balance everything together. This is my experience, as I've had two children while serving as an MP. It's not always easy, but I know I have a much easier ride than Hayman, Harman and the other wonderful women pioneers who have made it a little bit easier for my generation of women in Parliament.

But, of course, challenges remain. When I was on maternity leave with my first child, the campaigning group 38 Degrees contacted my constituents telling them I had abstained on a crucial vote – but I had been paired, so my absence was cancelled out by a Conservative who didn't vote either, and my baby was just a few weeks old. They asked my constituents on their email list: 'Where was Rachel Reeves?' One of my constituents contacted them saying I was on maternity leave and 38 Degrees promptly apologized. But it shows the need to change the procedures in Parliament so that MPs don't look like they just aren't turning up. My Labour colleague, Lucy Powell, was labelled by a tabloid newspaper as the 'second laziest MP in Westminster' after she was elected in a by-election and had her second child shortly afterwards. Lucy is anything but lazy, but the newspaper again forgot to check the facts.

In 2015 Labour were just ahead in the opinion polls and the general election was weeks away. As shadow work and pensions secretary I did an interview where I said the first thing I would do if Labour won would be to bring forward legislation to abolish the hated bedroom tax. I would do this before my second child was born (he was due about six weeks after polling day). Conservative MP Andrew Rosindell told the *Daily Mail* that as an expectant mum I shouldn't be appointed to the cabinet if Labour won the election. I have never been totally clear what his precise objection was, but presumably he worried that I wouldn't be able to cope with two things at once, or because maternity cover wasn't compatible with the job. Men who became fathers while MPs or ministers are never told they couldn't do the two. Blair, Brown and Cameron all had children born while they were prime minister. I don't remember anyone ever saying that they should step back from the front line as screaming children and changing nappies would render them incapable of political leadership.

Today, Parliament is progressing towards 'baby leave' for MPs who have children so that we can take time off in those first few weeks and months. It is a system which did not exist at all until recently, as absence from votes could only be granted at the discretion of the whips in a 'pairing' arrangement. This informal arrangement was far from satisfactory, as your voting record was blank if you were not in Parliament to vote, and you had to rely on staff or a friendly councillor to run your constituency surgeries and engagements. However, this year a twelve-month trial of proxy voting was introduced, enabling MPs who have had a baby or adopted to nominate another MP to vote on their behalf for six months. Later this year, it was announced that the parliamentary authorities would fund a 'locum MP' for Stella Creasy, who is pregnant after having suffered multiple miscarriages in the past, to cover the other responsibilities of an MP in the constituency. However, proxy voting is still under trial, and there is no guarantee that Creasy's securing of a 'locum MP' in her constituency will be extended to others. Baby leave is not yet a formal or permanent arrangement.

My Labour colleague and friend Jo Cox had two young children when she was elected. She often cycled back to the house-boat on the Thames where she lived with her family to read bedtime stories before returning to the House of Commons to vote. Like many MPs, combining politics and family was a careful juggling act. In her maiden speech she said that 'we have far more in common and are far more united than that which divides us'. Jo helped me learn that lesson too. Jo followed in the footsteps of women MPs who worked across party lines to achieve political change. After Jo died, I took forward her work on loneliness, a campaign that Jo started with Conservative MP Seema Kennedy. In some ways I feel that I am following in the footsteps of Jo and a long history of political partnerships between women across the political spectrum. I am proud to be doing that. While most evenings women walk through the division lobbies on party, not gender, lines – and the occasional entreaties from Astor to form a women's party (and indeed Christabel Pankhurst and others standing as women party candidates) fell on deaf ears – women certainly have a long and distinguished track record of cross-party collaboration.

I asked at the beginning whether it is still sensible or possible, with a third of MPs now female, to talk about women MPs. I think it is. The barriers that women face – on pay, on sexual violence and in carrying the greater responsibility for caring duties – mean that there are still distinct issues that women face. Women in Parliament are often still championing those causes. But more and more, women are also ignoring the advice that former Labour deputy leader Herbert Morrison gave to new MPs in 1945, to 'stick to women's issues'. Two prime ministers, one speaker, three home secretaries, two Northern Ireland secretaries, one foreign secretary (although still no chancellor of the exchequer). They are still far too unusual, but women now speak and campaign on all issues, not just within the narrow confines of so-called 'women's issues' (and as many women MPs past and present have reflected to me, women's issues are increasingly mainstream ones as women are giving them a voice and making them so). Women don't agree on everything, and women MPs don't either. But most women in Parliament identify themselves with the women's and often the feminist cause. And they work across the traditional political divide to achieve their goals.

I wrote this book to celebrate the women who transformed Parliament and politics, while also reflecting on my time so far as an MP and my impressions of Parliament as a woman trying to combine being a good mother and a good MP both at once. This is the book of women who dared to put themselves forward, often to endure ridicule and often at the sacrifice of family life, but for a cause – to take a stand and make their voices heard. Some of them are household names – Barbara Castle, Margaret Thatcher, Shirley Williams, Harriet Harman and Theresa May. Some of them, like Eleanor Rathbone, Nancy Astor, Ellen Wilkinson and Margaret Bondfield, should be known by every girl and woman, but aren't. Too many have largely been forgotten from our history. I hope that this book writes some of them back into our history – women like the Duchess of Atholl, Mavis Tate, Irene Ward, Judith Hart, Susan Lawrence and Jo Richardson. These pioneering women should be part of our history syllabus and national story. We should know their stories and this book tells them – bringing these fabulous women pioneers to life.

I stand on the shoulders of all the women I have written about in this book, and the shoulders of many others too. We all do – women and men. And we are taller and stronger because of them.

Seats For Women:
1919–31

*We can never forget the pioneers, the women who first dared – ours
is such an easy task compared to theirs.*

LADY NANCY ASTOR, 1928[1]

Shortly after 2pm on 28 November 1919, a tram conductor in Plymouth
made an announcement to his passengers. 'She's in!' he shouted, having
heard the decibels of an ecstatic crowd in the distance. Lady Nancy Astor
had been elected to serve as the Member of Parliament for Plymouth
Sutton in Devon.

This book begins in 1919 with the first woman to take her seat as an
MP, Nancy Astor. But her election would never have happened without
the women who had campaigned and championed female suffrage, equal
rights and representation over the previous decades – the Pankhursts and
Millicent Fawcett among others.

Before 1918 women could not vote or stand for Parliament; they could
only observe the proceedings from the Ladies' Gallery, where they were
separated not just from the floor of the Commons but also from
gentlemen visitors. A metal grille with small holes was designed to
prevent the ladies from being seen by Members of Parliament. Fawcett
said that 'it was like using a gigantic pair of spectacles which did not fit',
because the holes were not large enough for you to see through them
with both eyes.[2] Although they couldn't vote, women lobbied ministers,
signed petitions, went on strike, organized rallies, participated in acts
of civil disobedience, endured imprisonment, went on hunger strike
and suffered force-feeding, all because the basic channel of achieving
change – voting – was unavailable to them.

In protest at their physical exclusion from politics, Muriel Matters and Helen Fox from the Women's Freedom League (WFL) chained themselves to the Ladies' Gallery grille in October 1908. Two sections of grille had to be unscrewed from the stonework before a smith was called to file off their padlocks and free them from the grille in a committee room. After this, the galleries were closed. Another incident occurred in April 1909 as suffragettes chained themselves to statues in Parliament's St Stephen's Hall, in protest at their inability to enter Central Lobby. A porter's bolt clipper was used to free them, and it is still in the office of the principal doorkeeper today, ready for any future cases of 'chaining'.

Votes for women was partly a reward for women's work during the First World War, but predominantly due to the work of the suffrage movement. The end of war, and the political necessity of extending the franchise to working-class men who had made such sacrifices during the conflict, meant that voting reform more generally was possible, and increasingly necessary. The government was also wary of the inevitable return of militancy should they refuse to grant women's suffrage. Fawcett ensured that prime minister Asquith considered women's suffrage along with extending the vote to working-class men, when the Speaker's Conference – a cross-party committee made up of MPs and peers – on electoral reform was established. In February 1917 the Speaker's Conference recommended a limited form of women's suffrage. Six months later, a motion was passed to spend the sum of £5 (now just under £400) to remove the grille to the Ladies' Gallery. The barriers between women and Parliament were gradually coming down.

The recommendation of the Speaker's Conference was implemented in February 1918 when the Representation of the People Act gained Royal Assent, giving the vote to all men over the age of twenty-one, as well as to women over the age of thirty who satisfied minimum property qualifications. 8.4 million British women were enfranchised, but this only amounted to two-thirds of the total female population.

The famous suffragette demand of 'Votes for Women' was now a reality. The next task was to achieve *seats* for women in the House of Commons. This battle was won remarkably quickly. Between February and November 1918, there were a series of tests to see whether women were now eligible to become MPs. When Nina Boyle forwarded her candidacy for the Women's Freedom League (WFL) for Keighley in April 1918, it was rejected by the returning officer. It was not (allegedly) due to her gender, but the fact that her nomination papers were out of order – although whether this is to be believed is open to interpretation. There were fears that women MPs would lower the quality of legislation and increase the number of 'capricious', 'emotional' laws. There was even speculation that they might legislate for a national bedtime for children.[3] The ambiguity as to whether women could now be MPs was only clarified on the day that Parliament was dissolved (21 November 1918), just three weeks before the general election when the Parliament (Qualification of Women) Act was passed. Many former anti-suffragists including Asquith had come to feel that if women had the vote, they might as well be allowed to stand for election to Parliament – in part fearing a backlash from new women voters. As Asquith put it: 'You have the camel; you ought not to strain at the gnat.'[4] It was now official that, like men, women aged twenty-one or above could stand for election as MPs, even though to vote as a woman you had to be over thirty.

Just before the 1918 election, the Lady Members' Room was made ready, eagerly awaiting its first occupants. But it was an empty vessel until Lady Astor arrived in 1919. The prominent suffrage campaigners who had led the women's movement in 1918 failed to be elected that year, although seventeen women stood as candidates. Most of them had been heavily involved in the suffrage campaign, and the group included prominent figures such as the co-founder of the Women's Social and Political Union (WSPU) Christabel Pankhurst, and the General Secretary of the Women's Trade Union League (WTUL) and co-founder of the National Federation of Women Workers (NFWW), Mary Macarthur. In a trend that continues today, many of these women candidates were nominated for unwinnable seats. Many also chose to stand as Independents, instinctively sceptical of the male-dominated structure of the main political parties, which made it more difficult to be elected.

The only woman to win a seat in the 1918 election was a Sinn Féin candidate, Countess Constance Markiewicz. However, in keeping with the Sinn Féin position, she refused to take the parliamentary oath and did not take her seat in the Commons, in protest against British policy in Ireland. It is also not clear that she would have been allowed to take her seat had she wanted to, since she was in prison for treason at the time. Nevertheless, Constance Markiewicz was the first woman to be elected as a Member of Parliament, ending 600 years of only men being elected to the Commons. The only trace of her within Parliament was a nameplate inscribed beneath her coatpeg. It is said that she visited it once incognito.

A one woman show: Nancy Astor

Although Constance Markiewicz's seat in the Commons was unoccupied, another woman would soon take her seat, initially acting as a 'warming pan' for her husband's seat in Parliament. When Conservative MP Waldorf Astor reluctantly inherited his father's seat in the House of Lords in October 1919 upon the death of the first Viscount Astor, it was agreed that his wife Nancy would serve as a stop-gap candidate in the November by-election for his constituency in Plymouth. The idea was that Viscount Astor would divest himself of the viscountcy and his place in the Lords as soon as possible, returning to his seat in the Commons. But Nancy became a success in her own right; in the by-election she polled more than the Labour and Liberal candidates combined and she remained an MP until 1945.

As her train chuffed into Paddington Station en route to take her seat in Parliament, Nancy was moved greatly when she was greeted on the platform by a small gathering of veteran suffragettes. One of the suffragettes presented her with a badge, saying 'It is the beginning of a new era. I am glad to have suffered for this.' Astor had been famous before her election, but she now entered the cult of celebrity, with Madame Tussauds installing a wax figure of her in their collection.[5]

Yet Nancy Astor was a somewhat surprising cause-célèbre for the women's movement. Of American heritage and a divorcée with strident views on temperance, she had not been involved in politics except through her husband and the Primrose League (a national organization spreading Conservative principles) in Plymouth. She was certainly not active or even particularly interested in the women's suffrage movement. She had primarily become known as a 'Queen Bee' or society hostess at Cliveden, the family home in Berkshire, rather than as a political campaigner. The Astors frequently held illustrious gatherings at Cliveden, where the visitor books are strewn with noteworthy signatures belonging to Winston Churchill, Amelia Earhart, members of the royal family, the Kennedys and Charlie Chaplin. In her by-election campaign, she seemed at pains to emphasize that she would not just be a women's MP: 'I am not standing before you as a sex candidate. I do not believe in sexes or classes.'[6]

But in many ways, this lack of suffrage history was exactly what Astor needed as the first woman MP; she was perhaps perceived as less of a threat to male MPs than Christabel Pankhurst would have been. She emphasized this in a Panorama interview in 1959, saying that 'it was a jolly good thing that I was the first'. Her wealth enabled her to have a big team to support her with casework, speeches and questions in Parliament, and her ambivalent attitude towards political parties meant she worked easily with MPs and campaigners from across the political spectrum. As part of the establishment, she knew how the parliamentary process worked, and could count on the loyal support and knowledge of her husband, Waldorf, whom she had previously supported. She was uniquely positioned in her access to and influence over the press: the Astors owned the *Pall Mall Gazette* and *The Observer*, and her close friend Geoffrey Dawson was editor of *The Times*. As she herself put it, 'I knew everybody'. As a Conservative, she also had more access to power than she would have enjoyed as a Labour MP, given that at the time, Labour was a relatively small party and the Liberals were rapidly diminishing as a political force.

Being the first was a difficult and untrodden path, requiring someone thick-skinned enough to survive the parliamentary thickets of misogyny and condescension. As Astor later reflected, 'Pioneers may be picturesque figures, but they are often rather lonely ones'.[7] Astor was certainly tough, with inexhaustible reserves of pluck, dogged determination, and a touch of Virginian pertness. Indeed, being a Virginian gave her more than a penchant for Virginia hams, chewing gum and peanut brittle (of which she received frequent deliveries from the States); it gave her a sense of directness, temerity and non-stuffiness, to which both Plymouth and the country responded. Baroness Trumpington, a close friend of Lady Astor's, told me that she was 'an institution of her own'. In the early days, she needed to be. The very act of physically taking her seat was a challenge: since it was in the middle of a row, male MPs who didn't want women to have the vote let alone to be MPs, often physically obstructed her from getting through. One way or another, she squeezed past them, to the sound of jeers and shouting. As Astor put it, the other members 'would rather have had a rattlesnake than me' in the Chamber.[8] Even supposedly close friends, such as Winston Churchill and Neville Chamberlain, would blank her in corridors. Often, she returned home at the end of the day in tears. Winston Churchill later told Astor that 'we hoped to freeze you out'. But Nancy Astor was made of stronger stuff.

When Astor took her seat for the first time, MPs packed themselves into the Chamber like sardines, standing in gangways and peering over each other's heads. It was a terrifying and paralysing experience for her to sit in the House of Commons when surrounded by so many men poised for the attack. She later admitted that although she had given the appearance of composure, on her first day she had been absolutely terrified and sat in the House 'for five hours without moving'.[9] Characteristically, she rounded off the day by hosting a dinner party, with guests including the prime minister David Lloyd George and his ministers.

Lady Astor did not take long to settle in. Her relentlessness in the Chamber expressed itself in a mixture of infuriatingly persistent interruptions, banter with her male colleagues (especially Churchill) and more serious verbal fisticuffs (with Sir Frederick Banbury, who became something of a nemesis). Astor had been a compulsive giggler at school, and in the Commons it was not unusual for her to be called to order by the speaker. During one debate, she was asked to apologize for having called John Remer, Conservative MP for Macclesfield, 'a village donkey'. One male colleague likened her to a 'bottle of sparkling champagne', brimming with energy and effervescence.[10] It was because of this energy and playfulness, combined with steely determination, that so many grew to love, or at least admire, Nancy Astor. Such admiration could be seen among those women who would later join her in the Lady Members' Room. When I spoke to Norah Runge's granddaughter (Runge was a Conservative MP from 1931), she said that Runge tried to emulate Astor and always wanted to behave as badly as her, but 'didn't quite dare!'[11] Irene Ward, who also entered Parliament in 1931 as a Conservative MP, later commented that Astor had a 'great sense of humour'. Sometimes, Astor would peremptorily place herself on the front bench, put in artificial teeth and bow to the Labour opposition. Ward also said that Astor 'couldn't have been kinder' to the new women who entered Parliament; she congratulated every new woman who was elected, regardless of party, and sought to make them feel at home.[12]

Yet simultaneously, Ward noted that Astor 'was really no asset politically to the Tory party', and that 'she could have done a great deal more politically'. At times, Astor's manner in the Chamber was counter-productive. Her interruptions originated from a combination of a lack of restraint and a myopic focus on certain issues. George Bernard Shaw, a close friend of Astor's, said that she could never 'think consecutively for sixty seconds', while Harold Nicolson stated that debating with Astor 'was like playing squash with a dish of scrambled eggs'. As Astor scholar Dr Jacqui Turner describes, 'if nothing else, Nancy was a politician of conviction.'[13] She often gave the impression of being impractical, obsessive in her devotion to Christian Science and dogmatic in her loathing of liquor: she once insisted that the English cricket team lost the Ashes because it drank to excess (despite the Australian team's well-known enthusiasm for alcohol). This had a noticeable impact on male perceptions of women's proficiency within the public sphere. Even Lord Winterton, an MP who was in love with Nancy for a long time, wrote that her quarrelsome nature supplied him 'with another example of the fatalness of the policy of giving women votes'.[14] Nevertheless, her determination and obdurate style in the House ultimately forced Parliament to notice her and to take her seriously.

In her Panorama interview with Lady Astor, the ex-suffragist interviewer Mary Stocks explicitly pointed out that women's organizations were underwhelmed at Astor's election. Yet within two weeks, they adored her. They quickly realized that she intended to represent neither her husband, nor her party, but the millions of women across the country whose needs had been neglected by Parliament until now. Most women MPs felt some sort of obligation to represent women, but Astor felt it particularly strongly because she was the first (and for eighteen months, the only) woman in the Commons. She felt that 'the most important thing for a woman member of Parliament is to be first of all a woman'.[15] Her postbags were full to the brim with 1,500–2,000 letters a week from women across the country, many of which she responded to and kept. On the morning after she took her seat for the first time, she received more than 600 letters in her mailbag.[16] Astor decided that as the only woman in Parliament she had to prioritize women's concerns. On 15 June 1920, she wrote to Millicent Fawcett asking her to tell her when 'you think I am doing wrong'.[17] Astor also collaborated with key women's organizations through her 'at homes', held once a month at her London house on St James's Square, enabling leaders of women's organizations to meet with key MPs. This gave the women's movement unprecedented access to those in power, as well as a sympathetic ear.

According to Ellen Wilkinson, who was elected in 1924, Astor worked 'like a terrier' to voice the concerns of women and children in a male-dominated chamber.[18] Not long after taking her seat in December 1919, Astor asked the food controller about the price of milk, a commodity whose price had a direct impact on women managing household budgets.[19] She also agitated for more house-building, which she saw as a woman's priority: 'If they [men] thought as much of housing as public-housing [pubs], we should have had the houses long ago,' she conjectured.[20]

Anthony Masters, Nancy's biographer, wrote that Astor made 'little impact' in her political career and 'only technically advanced the feminist cause by virtue of being the very first woman MP'.[21] This is unfair: there were campaigns, such as equal franchise in the 1920s, for which Astor was one of the most central actors. The significance of her being the first woman MP within the context of the women's movement should also not be underestimated, nor should her longevity (1919–45), which forced the men to hear her voice and demonstrated that women could be popular with the voters.

But it was impossible for Astor to do it alone: more women were needed in the Commons, a fact she recognized keenly. As one woman, it was impossible 'to try and express what women thought on all the complex matters relating to public affairs, and I began to feel impatient for the arrival of women of every shade of political thought into the House of Commons', she reflected.[22]

Warming pans and male equivalence

Less than two years after her own election, Astor was joined by a woman who, though of a different temperament, and party, would come to be a close friend and colleague. On the unexpected death of her husband, the Liberal MP for Louth Thomas Wintringham, Margaret Wintringham stood as his replacement in the by-election. Still in mourning, her campaign was minimal: she made no speeches and was known as 'the silent candidate'. With a strong Conservative campaign against her, she held little hope of success, so was pleasantly surprised at her victory on 22 September 1921 (albeit with a slim majority of 791). The press did not hesitate to interpret her election as an advance for the women's cause, a headline in *The Times* reading 'Louth Reduces Sex Prejudice'.[23] There was a fizz of excitement: Parliament was to have its first British-born woman MP.

Seeds of solidarity were sown between the two women MPs when, despite representing different parties, Astor expressed support for Wintringham's campaign and sent her a telegram of congratulation when the results were in. Once elected, Astor insisted that Wintringham should use the Lady Members' Room as her office, since Astor had her own office in her London house. They became both close political partners and good friends who were able to work together because they were both progressive, non-partisan and firm believers in women's equality. Astor declared herself an 'ardent feminist', and Wintringham had been an active member of Fawcett's National Union of Women's Suffrage Societies (NUWSS).[24] They helped each other with constituency work, and campaigned together for nursery education, women police officers and the equal guardianship of children. Wintringham even persuaded the Liberal party headquarters to refrain from forwarding a candidate in Astor's seat in 1923 and 1924.[25] Writing to each other on a regular basis for the rest of their lives, Astor addressed Wintringham affectionately as 'Fi' in her letters.[26] 'I loved Mrs Wintringham, she was good and solid,' Astor said fondly.[27] This description accords with Wintringham's own view of their partnership: she described Astor as a 'prancing pony', while she herself was a solid, reliable 'cart-horse' trotting along beside.[28]

The two women balanced each other out: Wintringham was calm and reasoned in her arguments; Astor was fiery and volatile. While Astor explicitly stated that her role did not include economic affairs, Wintringham made her maiden speech on the economy. She challenged the stereotype that economics was a male sphere, saying that 'the question of economy appeals very much to women ... They feel that the best investment for the nation at the present time is good education and good health.'[29] In April 1923, Wintringham criticized Stanley Baldwin's budget as a 'man-made Budget', on grounds that he reduced the tax on beer but maintained the tax on tea and sugar, disproportionately benefitting men to the detriment of housewives.[30]

But although they were politically active and had established themselves as representatives of women, unfortunately neither would have made it into Parliament in the first instance without the association with their husbands. This also applied to a string of subsequent women MPs, including Mabel Philipson (elected in May 1923), Lady Terrington, the Duchess of Atholl (both December 1923), and the Countess of Iveagh (November 1927). 'It is curious how Conservative voters prefer to accept a woman representative only if she is ... stepping into the discarded shoes of her husband,' the *Manchester Guardian* commented in 1927, although the Liberals also succeeded in getting women into Parliament via this route.[31]

Of the thirty-eight women MPs returned before 1945, 'male equivalence' – women standing as MPs to represent men who could not fill the role themselves – accounted for the election of ten.[32] To a certain extent this was inevitable in the early days, as women were only likely to be selected by their local party organizations if they were well-respected

within the community, and illustrious husbands were a useful vehicle
for that. As Baroness Jenkin, granddaughter of Lady Joan Davidson
(Conservative MP from 1937 to 1959) told me, 'because of her background
(her husband, father, grandfather and great-grandfather had all been
MPs), the local party asked Davidson to stand in 1937 when her husband
moved to the House of Lords.' She added, 'They were all family in those
days'.[33] Although it was frustrating that women were not being elected as
individuals, male equivalence did facilitate a gradual introduction of
women into Parliament. It also put pressure on the fledgling Labour party
to catch up and elect women MPs.

Labour women

In 1923 the Labour Party did just that. The general election of that year
brought in three experienced, hard-working and passionate women MPs
on the left: Margaret Bondfield, Susan Lawrence and Dorothy Jewson.
When joined by Ellen Wilkinson, who was elected the following year,
these four Labour women had an impressive total of eighty years of
political experience between them at the time of their election. The first
Labour women constituted a challenge to male domination within the
Labour party, with its industrial trade union roots being heavily male-
oriented. They also undermined the precedent of male equivalence, since
they were all single. The 1923 election was heralded as a success for
women as the total number of women MPs swelled to eight, albeit
condescendingly dubbed 'eight little peaches on eight little perches' by
the press. Leaflets published in celebration by the Women's Election
Committee (a women's organization dedicated to increase the number of
women MPs) were entitled 'See How They Grow!'

Margaret Bondfield, a working-class woman from Somerset, had
worked as a shop assistant and trade union organizer before becoming an
MP. Never married, Bondfield was in many senses married to her politics
and to her causes: in her autobiography she declared that she had 'no
vocation for wifehood or motherhood' but 'the dear love of comrades'.[34]
However, she lived with Mary Macarthur – a prominent trade union
organizer – for most of her life. Bondfield's Labour colleague from 1929
to 1931, Mary Hamilton, wrote biographies of both Bondfield and
Macarthur and suggests that they had a romantic relationship.[35]
Bondfield's political career had begun when she first read about the Shop

Assistant's Union in a newspaper wrapped around her supper of chips, a dinner which changed her life forever. She joined the union and eventually became its Assistant Secretary. Later, Bondfield stood as an MP and survived her election campaign, during which she spoke on average six times a day, on simple meals of onions stewed in milk, which she called 'the ideal candidate's supper'.[36] On polling day, 'Bondfield flew round the constituency in the red Ford that had been lent to her for the campaign, decorated with scarlet streamers and adorned with a fuzzy black cat'.[37] But despite her talent and experience, this was her third attempt at election: Labour women candidates were generally allocated Conservative or Liberal safe seats, and Northampton had a Conservative majority. During her unsuccessful campaign in 1922, she asked George Bernard Shaw to speak for her, and he asked: 'Why Northampton? You are the best man of the lot, and they shove you off to a place where the water is too cold for their dainty feet ... and keep the safe seats for their now quite numerous imbeciles'.[38] Yet on this occasion Bondfield won with a stunning result in Northampton, turning a 5,000 Conservative majority into a 4,036 Labour majority. In her memoirs, Bondfield recalls: 'The constituency went nearly crazy with joy, and they insisted on taking me round the town perched on the high seat of a big charabanc, men hauling the ropes for two hours around the wards and ending up in the Square'.[39]

The fact that Labour women such as Bondfield, Lawrence and Wilkinson won seats that had only elected Conservative or Liberal MPs before was a testament to their ability and determination, albeit in the context of a national swing to Labour. Their presence in Parliament also injected into the House a strong dose of female aptitude. Bondfield's maiden speech was described by a press correspondent, in rather back-handed terms, as 'the first intellectual speech by a woman the House had ever heard'.

Susan Lawrence was Bondfield's opposite physically: Lawrence was tall with a masculine bob-cut and a touch of the bluestocking, while Bondfield was small and round-faced with long hair pulled back into a bun.[40] Unlike Bondfield, Lawrence was from a wealthy family. She had been a Conservative London county councillor until she gained an insight into the shockingly low wages of cleaners at the council in 1912. This stimulated a political conversion: without state intervention to prevent economic injustice, she concluded that voluntary local initiatives were powerless. Lawrence resigned from the council, joined the Fabian Society and was re-elected as a Labour councillor in 1913. Lawrence was

serious-minded and intimidatingly intelligent. Having studied
mathematics at University College London and Newnham College
Cambridge, she had an aptitude for precision which translated into her
political work. In the words of her admiring parliamentary private
secretary (PPS) Ellen Wilkinson, Lawrence possessed 'a mind which
drank in facts as some men drink whisky'.[41] Yet this ability to scrutinize
issues up-close – Lawrence would often go through a bill seventy times to
ensure there were no loopholes – was complemented by the passion with
which she spoke on political matters.

1924: 'The orphans of the storm'

The 1923 election had brought in a minority Labour government. But less
than a year later, in October 1924, a vote of no confidence was passed, and
prime minister Ramsay MacDonald was forced to dissolve Parliament
and call a general election. It was a devastating election for the new intake
of Labour and Liberal women MPs. The storm had struck.

Wintringham, Bondfield, Jewson, Lawrence and the Liberal MP Lady
Vera Terrington were all swept aside in a Conservative landslide. The
Conservatives Nancy Astor, Mabel Philipson and the Duchess of Atholl
retained their seats. The Liberals Wintringham and Terrington never
returned, nor did Labour's Jewson. Regretting the loss of Margaret
Wintringham, Astor wrote: 'I know that she will be desperately missed as
she was loved and respected by all Members – no one more so.'[42] The only
Labour woman to be elected that year was Ellen Wilkinson, who referred
to the remaining women MPs as the 'orphans of the storm' in her maiden
speech.[43]

Wilkinson had grown up in a working-class community with slum
housing in Manchester where, she later remembered, even the leaves were
grey from the soot. She was exposed to gruelling poverty from an early
age and she quickly developed a passion for social justice. Having won a
scholarship to Manchester University to study history, she was one of few
working-class women to go on to higher education, an impressive and
unusual achievement. Before being elected, Wilkinson had worked as a
trade union organizer, suffragist campaigner for the NUWSS and
councillor for Manchester city council. She was a socialist, feminist and
internationalist on the left of her party, having left the Communist Party
only shortly before being elected to Parliament. Standing at less than five-

foot, she became known as 'The Fiery Particle' and attracted the epithets 'Red Ellen' and the 'Pocket Pasionaria' (the latter for her campaigning during the Spanish Civil War). Her secretary was nearly six-foot tall, so they made a rather comical duo together.

The seat for which she was elected, Middlesbrough East, was so poor she described it as 'a book of illustrations to Karl Marx'.[44] But this didn't make it an easy seat for Wilkinson to win. An industrial town that had never been in Labour hands before, Middlesbrough's municipal politics was dominated by owners of the steel mills. But, 'exceptional[ly]', she managed to gain sponsorship from the male-dominated trade unions, who rarely funded women candidates.[45] Her victory was a surprise, especially given that it bucked the national trend of a swing to the right. Despite the press's 'Red Scare' campaign, which discredited a swathe of Labour candidates including the incumbent Labour women MPs, Wilkinson won the seat and became the only Labour woman in Parliament.

It was a lonely experience – similar to being dropped 'like a stone into a quiet pond'.[46] Later, Wilkinson said that she had been wary of becoming 'a sort of pet lamb' as the only Labour woman and being expected to speak on prescribed issues.[47] But she did not let it dim her enthusiasm. Unhindered by marriage or family commitments – as was true also for the other early Labour women MPs – Wilkinson threw herself into politics. Despite being advised by the speaker to wait to make her maiden speech, she was itching to get started and, invigorated by the debate after the King's Speech, went home to prepare herself for a speech the next day. After apologizing to the speaker for not having followed his advice, she lambasted the King's Speech for its failure to mention equal franchise. Despite intermittent ill health, she filled more column inches in Hansard and attended more divisions (votes) than any of her fellow women MPs.[48] From railing against Churchill's tax on tea and silk in 1925 and its impact on the cost of stockings, to vociferous campaigning on widows' pensions, she often 'sat through the night wrapped in her cloak and munching chocolates from her handbag'.[49] When she rose to speak, her listeners would sit 'transfixed at the sound of the searing, scorching words that poured from her lips in a torrent of dynamic oratory'.[50]

Wilkinson's feminism and socialism were for her intertwined. In an impassioned plea to steer women away from apathy and encourage them to vote Labour, in 1929 she wrote an article for the *Daily Herald*, 'Why women should vote Labour'. She emphasized the power of politics to transform lives within the domestic sphere: for women workers, she spoke of Labour's commitment to 'put[ting] the strong arm of the law between her and the sweating employer'; for housewives, she spoke of investing in health and education, and ending tuberculosis and rickets (still prevalent in poor communities) through the provision of free school milk.[51]

Wilkinson's analysis of gender inequality was rooted in class conflict and the way in which capitalism pitted the interests of the rich minority against the interests of the working class. In Parliament she was able to describe poverty and exploitation that had not been witnessed by most MPs. In 1926, in her column for the socialist paper *Lansbury's Labour Weekly*, she reported that in Somerset, when the seams in the mines were too narrow for pit ponies, the men had to pull the coal, attaching a rope around their waist and a chain between their legs hitched to a wagon. The article was illustrated by a photograph of a naked Somerset miner harnessed to a tub (the collieries were so hot and poorly ventilated that men often wore minimal clothing). A male Conservative MP alleged that this was a fake photograph. In response, one June day in the Chamber, Wilkinson dramatically brandished a rope and chain similar to the one featured in the photograph, declaring: 'This was worn, not 60 years ago, as stated by certain coal-owners, but on 30th April of this year by a miner.' She gave the name and address of the person who took the photograph, the colliery at which it was taken, and produced pay checks to provide evidence for her statements about low wages. In doing so, she calmly and convincingly rebutted her critics, and made an indictment of the government's attitude towards miners: 'It is abominable, and those who vote for these longer hours ought not to sleep in their beds until they themselves have done what these men are doing every day in their work.'[52]

Wilkinson was like none of the women in Parliament before her: she was a strong feminist and socialist, yet she did not let those categories get in the way of building bridges, making reform and achieving progress. She was well-loved in Parliament, even by her opponents: a group of Conservative MPs, worried about her domestic arrangements, clubbed together to buy her an electric cooker, to help her look after herself better.[53] She was one of the new generation of modern women, with her love of colourful outfits, the political spotlight, and more controversially, her various love affairs with married men. Her secretary, Diana Hubback, commented that Wilkinson was rumoured to have 'broken many hearts'.[54]

In turn, the love of her life – Frank Horrabin – broke her heart when he left her for a secretary that they both shared in Parliament.[55]

After eleven months in Parliament, Wilkinson's time as the only Labour woman came to an end, as Susan Lawrence returned in the East Ham North by-election in May 1926. Margaret Bondfield also returned that summer in the Wallsend by-election. Step by step, women were making their mark on Parliament. But it was slow progress in those early years.

The Lady Members' Room

'I find a woman's intrusion into the House of Commons as embarrassing as if she burst into my bathroom when I had nothing to defend myself, not even a sponge,' Winston Churchill famously quipped to Lady Astor. She rebuffed him with a wry smile: 'You are not handsome enough to have worries of that kind.' Yet Churchill's attitude was typical of male views towards women in Parliament.

Westminster was, and remains today, a male-dominated institution. Charles Barry, who designed the Houses of Parliament, had designed a number of male-only private members clubs; in many ways Parliament was just another club with a debating chamber appended to it. The physical barriers to women's acceptance within Parliament were particularly pronounced in those early years of women's representation. The scarcity of the new women MPs, combined with institutional sexism, meant that they were often made to feel unwelcome in the Commons. There were numerous cases of women MPs being mistaken for secretaries, as well as generally being treated with distrust and a continued sense of disbelief at their very existence.[56]

The Lady Members' Room, a designated room where women MPs could respond to correspondence and dress themselves, served as an office for all women MPs. Known as 'the dungeon', it was a small, stuffy room in the basement of the Palace of Westminster. Mark Collins, Parliament's estates archivist and historian, described it as 'a dark place with wooden panelling.'[57] When Wilkinson first entered the House in 1924, the nearest ladies' toilet to the debating chamber was a quarter of a mile walk, along three long corridors and two flights of stairs.[58] In 1929, the Lady Members' Room was moved down the corridor to accommodate the larger pool of women, but it was still small and lacked a changing room or an annunciator to alert MPs as to what was happening in the debating chamber. It wasn't until the 1970s that the facilities were improved.

Meanwhile, male MPs had a much greater purchase on the space of Westminster. Unlike women, male members had access to baths (particularly useful during all-night sittings) and dining rooms. Ministers (almost exclusively male) had their own offices, and not even Nancy Astor dared to enter the smoking room, 'where a whispered word may sometimes have more effect than an hour's speech thundered in the debating chamber', as Ellen Wilkinson described it.[59] The physical infrastructure both facilitated, and was facilitated by, elite social networks. In almost a physical extension of the parliamentary estate, male members would go to their private male-only clubs (including the Athenaeum, the National Liberal Club, the Garrick and the Carlton) to discuss politics.

Ellen Wilkinson was the first woman MP to enter the smoking room. As she bounded up to the door, she was stopped by a policeman who informed her that ladies did not usually enter. 'I am not a lady – I am a Member of Parliament,' she responded peremptorily as she opened the door. Wilkinson continued to push the boundaries of Westminster convention. In 1928 she used her position on the Kitchen Committee (a select committee dedicated to the domestic arrangements of the House of Commons) to initiate a campaign for women to be admitted to the Strangers' Dining Room. As it stood, while male parliamentary secretaries of ministers and opposition leaders could eat in this cheaper dining room, women had to eat in the more expensive Harcourt Room. Despite opposition to Wilkinson's campaign from others on the committee, including her only other female colleague (Mabel Philipson), the motion passed. The speaker decided that a lady guest could be admitted for dinner, but not for lunch, on the dubious grounds that there was a shortage of accommodation. Astor intervened, saying: 'Do not women need luncheon, too?' Nevertheless, this was primarily a moment of celebration and Wilkinson entertained a party of female guests in the Strangers' Dining Room (a meal which was, interestingly and unusually for the time, a vegetarian and non-alcoholic affair). But she continued to push forwards, and when appointed to the committee once more in 1930, she was active in the campaign to admit women for lunch as well. In October 1931, Labour MP Edith Picton-Turbervill made a request for a women's dressing-room, which was granted in the next Parliament. Women were beginning to 'take up space'.

Dull little frocks and fur coats

Women also made their presence known in their choice of outfits, which became a prominent feature of press coverage of women MPs – a tradition which continues until this day. For women MPs, the issue of what to wear posed a dilemma: they didn't want to appear too feminine or frivolous, and yet they didn't want to fulfil the stereotype of being 'sexless' bluestocking suffrage campaigners. Nancy Astor set the tone when she decided that she did not want to be trivialized by the press and chose to wear a simple women's suit: white satin blouse and black skirt, jacket and tricorn velvet hat, with a white gardenia in her buttonhole. She was going to dress like a respectable woman in her Sunday best, with a touch of the seriousness of a uniform. But the way Nancy dressed mirrored her approach to the physical space of Westminster: she kept herself to herself, especially in the early days. Later on, influenced by the colourful attire of Ellen Wilkinson, Astor indulged in a red hat and dress in 1928, and even a ball gown in the Commons in 1931. Like Astor in the early days, Susan Lawrence wanted the focus to be on content rather than image, and so she took a minimalist approach. She sent round to a department store for half a dozen inexpensive dresses to be sent to her office, 'briefly raising her head from her papers to select one by pointing with a pencil'.[60]

As the number of women increased, the necessity of obeying those unspoken conventions diminished. Women began to relish the notion of difference and rebel against conformity in Parliament. A clothing controversy was sparked in December 1923, when just three days before Lady Terrington's election to Parliament, the *Daily Express* featured a headline 'The best dressed woman MP. Lady Terrington's aim if elected'. The article misquoted Terrington from an interview as saying: 'I shall put on my ospreys and my fur coat and my pearls. I do not believe in a woman politician wearing a dull little frock with a Quaker collar, and keeping her nicest clothes for social appearances. It is all humbug.' She later sued the paper for libel, denying that she had said this. However, a year later (shortly after she lost her seat in the general election) the jury concluded that the dress of women MPs was a subject of public interest after all, and that the report had not injured her. If the incident demonstrated the press's appetite for sensationalizing and trivializing women's representation, it also indicated a means by which women could gain publicity for their politics through their appearance. This was particularly helpful for working-class women, since they could not be accused of materialism or elitism in the way Terrington could. When Parliament reassembled in the new year of 1925 after Christmas, just two months after Wilkinson's maiden speech, she shocked the House by wearing a vivid green dress. Astor advised Wilkinson to dress more soberly, but it was to no avail. In fact, Wilkinson relished the press attention, and gave an interview on her inability to pull off the colour red. When a secret admirer sent her a puppy (an Airedale called 'Ginger'), she posed for photographs before sending it up north to live with her brother, making a plea to her other fans not to 'develop the idea of sending me more pets – a giraffe or something like that!'[61] Wilkinson embraced the novelty factor and the ability to draw in interest through appearance and theatre, as a way of promoting her brand of socialist politics.

There was also the persistent 'Hat Question'. The usual convention in public meetings was that women showed their respect by their heads being covered. Before Astor took her seat, *The Times* speculated that 'No doubt she will wear her hat in the House, as she would do in a church or chapel.' But, it asked, 'if she wears a hat, should she remove it when she rises to speak, as male M.P.s are bound to do?'[62] It was a dilemma, permeated with a sense of annoyance that the rules of the chamber were being challenged by the inappropriateness of the presence of women. A *Daily Express* headline screamed 'HAT PROBLEM STILL UNSOLVED'. It remained unsolved well into the 1920s: in February 1925, when Wilkinson rose to ask a question, Conservative MP Colonel Applin asked Speaker Whitley whether it was appropriate that she was addressing the Chair without a hat. Whitley reported that it was fine, eliciting jibes against Applin 'there's a gentleman!' and 'what a snob!' from the Labour MPs. In 1929, Susan Lawrence's usual sobriety saw a brief interlude when, wishing to speak after a division had been called, but having no hat with her, she placed an order paper over her head. Speaker Fitzroy ruled that in future, women could remain uncovered when speaking in the Chamber. The hat problem, at least, was settled.

Collaboration and conflict

The early women MPs represented all shades of political opinion, not to mention 50 per cent of the population, and were a diverse group of people. Nevertheless, there were many cases of solidarity and collaboration between them. In December 1928, when Margaret Bondfield put forward her 'Boots for Bairns' bill to provide footwear for children in distressed areas, she received the support of all six women backbenchers. The only female MP who didn't support the bill was Atholl, who was by this point a minister.

There were notable friendships rooted in close physical proximity within Westminster, and proximity of policy interests as women. Despite their opposing ideologies, Astor and Wilkinson became close friends. They shared strong, sparky temperaments and a deep commitment to women's issues. When Astor spoke after Wilkinson during the second reading of a bill to reform the law on married women's nationality in 1930, Astor said, 'I only want to say "ditto" to every word she said.'[63] In 1929, when Wilkinson was in severe need of rest due to ill health and overwork, she asked Astor if she could lend her Rest Harrow (the Astors' seaside cottage) for some respite. Astor responded that unfortunately she had already lent it to future prime minister Harold Macmillan, but generously offered to book a room for Wilkinson at a nearby hotel where she would have a good rest.

There was also disagreement among the women about their representative duties: were they representing their constituency alone, or women more generally? In the early years, it was customary and even *expected* that women MPs should focus on 'women's issues' and the domestic sphere, which Astor's work reinforced. Ellen Wilkinson's tireless work on widows' pensions attracted significant correspondence from widows, and she joked that 'I feel sometimes that I am the Member for widows rather than the Member for Middlesbrough'.[64] But other women MPs doubted whether they had a duty to represent the interests of women over men. Such women could, broadly speaking, be broken down into two groups: anti-feminist women (including the Duchess of Atholl and Mabel Philipson) who were sceptical about the very notion of distinct 'women's interests', and socialist women (such as Bondfield and Lawrence) who were sceptical of middle-class feminists ignorant of the class struggle and indeed of the particular challenges working-class women faced. Atholl denied that she had an obligation to represent women generally and spoke belittlingly of the 'charming habit' of those thinking that women MPs did have such an obligation.[65] She was also the only woman MP not to support equal franchise and 'absented herself' from the final vote on the bill. This was the source of a great deal of resentment among the women MPs, notably from Astor, who felt that other Conservative women working cross-party were overlooked for promotion whereas loyalists like Atholl were promoted. Meanwhile, working-class women like Bondfield and Wilkinson emphasized that Labour women should not lose sight of their duties to represent the working classes. On 8 September 1931, Ellen Wilkinson bitterly shouted 'Just like you middle-class people!' when Labour colleague Edith Picton-Turbervill said she would abstain in the National Government's confidence debate, rather than vote against the drastic cuts in unemployment benefit. Despite their personal friendship, there is a distinct note of frustration in Wilkinson's description of Nancy Astor, who cared 'little for party ties and is very aggravating in her outspoken scepticism of those to whom party is a reality'.[66] For the Labour women, especially those from a working-class background, socialism and class were very concrete categories that could not be jettisoned with appeals for gender solidarity. Hence it was no surprise that Astor's calls for a 'Women's Party' were greeted with little enthusiasm by the Labour MPs: they could not support working-class women without supporting working-class families, their men included. Soon after Bondfield's election in 1923, she received a telegram from a Conservative newspaper asking if she would cooperate with Lady Astor and Mrs Wintringham. She replied: 'Emphatically, no.'[67]

There was also class-based division in terms of who could become an MP in the first place. In 1937, Wilkinson pointed out that it was impossible for an MP to live on a £400 salary (which had only been introduced in 1912) unless she/he had either 'unearned income, or the professions of law, journalism, or something "consultant" which can be fitted in to suit'.[68] It was rather difficult for women to bolster their income through entering other professions, because the workload of a woman MP was considerably more than for a man, due to greater demand to sit on committees, as well as the additional representative function towards women. It was no coincidence that the first few women MPs were wealthy. If they were not, they either received trade union funding (Bondfield and Wilkinson) or had inherited money (Eleanor Rathbone). Those with more funds had a greater chance of being able to employ good staff, which helped with the unusually high workload; Astor was able to employ three excellent secretaries from the start.

From words to deeds:
legislating for reform

Despite these inter-party tensions, it was not long before the presence of women in Parliament had a concrete impact on legislation, as women brought a new perspective and focus on a range of issues which had previously been ignored or marginalized. As Ellen Wilkinson reflected in the Chamber in 1928, 'Women have worked very hard. They have starved in prison, they have given their lives, or have given all their time, in order that women might sit in this House and take part in the legislation of the country.'[69] The women MPs were certainly ready to take part, and legislation was one of the most powerful means through which they could represent women's interests.

Astor had always believed that temperance was an issue to champion on behalf of women and children. She frequently emphasized the impact of alcohol misuse on women and children in terms of domestic abuse and the draining of household income. 'I do not want you to look on your Lady Member as a fanatic or lunatic. I am simply trying to speak for hundreds of women and children throughout the country who cannot speak for themselves,' she emphasized to the House in her maiden speech.[70] Astor's own experiences of drunken and allegedly near-abusive male family members were interfused with the discipline she cultivated through Christian Science, and temperance quickly became her pet cause. She 'could no more drop it than drop a baby', Astor used to say. In 1923, Astor introduced the first private member's bill sponsored by a woman MP, to ban the sale of alcohol to children under eighteen (thus upholding wartime restrictions on alcohol). The legislation is still in effect today, but in 1923 there was a great deal of opposition on grounds that restrictions on alcohol would be a 'slippery slope' towards prohibition (which the US had introduced in 1920). But Astor's tireless campaigning and solidarity from her partner-in-crime Wintringham pushed the bill through the parliamentary process. Astor showed particular determination during the third reading, when her nemesis, Sir Frederick Banbury, threatened to thwart the bill, declaring it a 'silly Bill'.[71] Their rivalry had begun in June 1920, when he had attempted to filibuster a private member's bill that Astor supported to reduce shop hours. Now, three years later, Banbury rose to move an amendment against Astor's own bill just before 4pm, when she had been sat in the House from 11am 'on a boiled egg and a glass of water'. In response, she walked up to him and thundered: 'I have tried kindness, I have tried rudeness, now I shall try force. I shall hold on to your coat-tails and you shall not rise.' She clung onto him, but Banbury was too strong and ended up talking out the bill, so that Astor had to wait another fortnight for a third reading. It passed on 13 July with only ten noes at the division (vote).

Then there was Margaret Wintringham's campaign for equal guardianship. Under the Guardianship of Infants Act of 1886, parental authority for children was vested in the father. Hence, if a wife left her husband she could stand to lose access to her children; a husband would even be able to put them up for adoption. 'Mrs Wintringham's Bill', which became law in 1925, granted mothers an equal right to apply to court for the custody of her children. In addition, the bill stipulated that if a court granted custody to the mother it could require the father to pay maintenance to the mother. Women could also apply for separation orders while still living with their husbands, which would come into effect after they had left. This gave women the confidence to leave unhappy marriages without fear of retribution by their husbands. Wintringham's lobbying on this issue is a perfect example of how the presence of women within Parliament forced men MPs to consider women's interests. She said to the Commons: 'I realise I am addressing men chiefly, and I want them for a few minutes, in considering the position of the law as it stands at present, to take a mental somersault. I want them to view it from the standpoint of the woman who passionately desires the guardianship and the ownership of her own child.'[72] Although the bill was halted by the fall of the Labour government in the autumn of 1924, there was enough momentum for the Conservative government to re-introduce the bill. It was supported by all the women MPs, with the exception of Mabel Philipson, who had reservations about how the bill would work. In the Lords, the spouses of women MPs (Viscount Astor and Lord Terrington) also spoke up for the bill.

Their efforts were rewarded on 31 July 1925 when the Equal Guardianship Act was passed. A victory had been won for mothers that was both substantive and symbolic in significance. Substantively, applications by mothers to magistrate courts for equal guardianship rose steadily over the next twenty years. Symbolically, the act was the culmination of five years of legislative attempts in the form of private member's bills, six years of lobbying from the National Union of Societies for Equal Citizenship (NUSEC, the successor of the NUWSS), tireless parliamentary work by Margaret Wintringham, and consistent contributions from women MPs in Parliament. Wilkinson suggested in her speech on the matter that further guardianship reforms would be possible when more women were elected to Parliament, 'when it will not be completely taken for granted that women have to be satisfied with any crumbs that fall from the table of the Right Hon. Gentlemen on both sides.'[73]

Mothers were not the only demographic of women who particularly suffered at the hands of the male-centric political and economic system – it was a similar situation for widows. Before 1925, the only support for widows was the Poor Law, which either provided relief payments covering subsistence, or took the whole family (or just the children) into the workhouse. But in 1925, the Widows, Orphans and Old Age Pensions Act introduced a contributory insurance scheme in which widows with children were given the amount paid to old-age pensioners for the rest of their lives. Susan Lawrence helped pilot the bill through the House from the backbenches and it received a great deal of support from women MPs. But while Wilkinson welcomed the legislation, she thought it did not go far enough: it should not be restricted to the widows of insured men. She tabled an amendment to include widows who were insured but whose husbands were not. Despite the passion of her argument, the amendment was voted down at about 2am. But Wilkinson was not finished with the bill. She went for a nap at 3am in the Lady Members' Room, along with Mabel Philipson. She woke at 6am and returned to the Chamber to point out the injustice that while an unmarried man or woman in an insured trade was eligible to draw a pension from the age of sixty-five, a married woman forfeited her right to draw her own pension when she stopped working. She made this point incisively and clearly, but the House was not receptive. Although Astor did not support Wilkinson politically on this issue, she continued to support her personally. After a second night of debate ending at 5.39am, Astor rushed through the departing MPs to find an exhausted Wilkinson and offered to drive her home.

Perhaps the most significant legislation that women MPs lobbied for in this period was equal franchise. Since the 1918 suffrage act was restricted to propertied women over thirty, it left 5.6 million women without a vote. It was not until the Representation of the People (Equal Franchise) Act of 2 July 1928 that women were given the vote on the same terms as men. Equal franchise bills had been proposed every year from 1919 to 1927. Astor was supportive from the outset and persistent in lobbying the government. In 1924, a bill presented by Labour MP William Adamson came very close to success, receiving support from Astor, Wintringham, Lawrence and Jewson. Nevertheless, the Duchess of Atholl opposed the bill and asked for a conference to be held on the issue (she doubted whether women really wanted it and had concerns about the role of women in public life). Atholl's amendment was defeated on a division 288 to 82. It was in this vote that women MPs acted as 'tellers' for the first time, counting MPs as they made their way through the division lobbies, Atholl for the 'noes' and Jewson for the 'ayes'.

Although Adamson's bill was not successful, progress was made when the Conservative prime minister Stanley Baldwin pledged commitment to equal franchise during the 1924 election campaign. He did so in a letter to Dame Caroline Bridgewater, the chair of the Women's Unionist Organisation, which was subsequently published in the press. The letter committed Baldwin to forming an inter-party conference on the issue if he was re-elected. When there was no government equal franchise bill forthcoming in the autumn, the women's movement was disappointed.

It was at this moment that Wilkinson used her 'excellent' maiden speech to express dismay at the failure to mention equal franchise in the King's Speech.[74] She then seconded Labour MP William Whitley's equal franchise bill in February 1925. It was quashed by the home secretary William Joynson-Hicks, who stated that equal suffrage would be disruptive if passed at such an early stage of Parliament. However, he revealed his own progressive opinion when he said that the government would bring in legislation before the end of the term. This amounted to a promise, which women's organizations repeatedly cited and used as leverage. Astor pressed Joynson-Hicks further, asking whether he meant votes for all women at twenty-one. He conceded that equal suffrage would mean 'that no difference will take place in the ages at which men and women will go to the poll at the next election'.[75] In doing so, he committed the government to act before the next election, much to the chagrin of his Conservative colleagues – including Churchill – who felt Joynson-Hicks had spoken unwarrantedly on behalf of a divided cabinet.

Wilkinson and Astor ensured that Baldwin and Joynson-Hicks didn't forget their promises. At prime minister's questions on 10 February 1926, Wilkinson asked when the government intended to introduce a bill on equal suffrage. She asked again in November and December. Meanwhile, Astor acted as a conduit between women's organizations (notably NUSEC), the Conservative Party, and even with individual members of the cabinet, including Baldwin. Feeling the pressure, on 13 April 1927, Baldwin announced on behalf of the government that a bill would be introduced during the next session for equal franchise at twenty-one.

When the government bill was debated, women MPs made forceful contributions. Wilkinson drew attention to women over thirty who did not have the vote – those without husbands or property. Bondfield reinforced this powerfully, lamenting that 'Since I have been able to vote at all, I have never felt the same enthusiasm because the vote was the consequence of possessing property rather than the consequence of being a human being.'[76] The equal franchise bill passed its second reading with only ten votes against.

In the twelve years before women had the vote, only five pieces of legislation were passed on women's issues. From 1918 to 1928, twenty pieces were passed.[77] Women MPs were already making their mark on policy within Parliament and making a difference to the lives of women outside of Westminster.

The end of an era

As NUSEC's 1928 annual report emphasized, the equal franchise act marked 'the close of a momentous ten years in the history of the women's movement'.[78] This sense of watershed was heightened by the deaths of the two leading lights of the suffrage movement: Emmeline Pankhurst in June 1928 and Millicent Fawcett in August 1929. In a demonstration of how far the women's movement had come, in 1930 Baldwin unveiled a statue to the once law-breaking Emmeline Pankhurst in the Victoria Tower Gardens next to Parliament, where it remains to this day.

The late 1920s was an era in which a new generation of young women, shaped by the suffrage movement, were coming of political age. The force of the 'flappers' (a derogatory term used to refer to young women of the 1920s with their distinctive and modern style of dress) had begun to make political waves. On 30 May 1929, the first general election with an equal franchise for men and women took place. It became known as the 'Flapper Election', with five million new young female voters' names having been added to the electoral register. Candidates and parties were desperate to appeal to this newly enfranchised demographic: parties targeted posters and events at young and working-class women, particularly those who were mothers. They were also keen to make use of women's voices in the campaign: Mrs Baldwin broadcast a message to women voters for the Conservatives, as did Lloyd George's daughter

Megan for the Liberals. Just like in 1924, the 1929 election resulted in a hung Parliament with a minority Labour government under Ramsay MacDonald. It also brought in a raft of new women MPs: Ethel Bentham, Mary Hamilton, Megan Lloyd George, Cynthia Mosley, Marion Phillips, Edith Picton-Turbervill and Eleanor Rathbone.

Two months previously in a by-election, one of these new young women voters had achieved something remarkable when she was elected as an MP at the tender age of twenty-four. Since equal franchise was not to come into effect until the next month, she was not yet able to vote; but she was able to stand for Parliament. Jennie Lee, who would go on to become minister of the arts in Harold Wilson's government in the 1960s and establish the Open University, was elected for Labour in March 1929 in North Lanarkshire. She quickly captured the press's attention with her beauty, her youth and the stridency of her left-wing politics; it was noted in typically gendered language that, with 'the assurance of a Bond-Street mannequin', she 'took the Speaker's breath away' as she walked up the floor, sporting an emerald dress 'of a clinging variety'.[79] When Charlie Chaplin visited Parliament, there was only one woman MP he wished to meet: Jennie Lee.[80] Lee, like many of the women of her generation, had been shaped by the suffrage movement. She recalled how the suffragette Helen Crawford was a regular visitor at her childhood home, and used to tell Lee tales of 'window-breaking adventures and prison exploits', which caused her to wonder 'ruefully if anything at all would be left to do by the time I had finished with school'.[81] Lee soon found that there was plenty still wrong with the world, and plenty left to do to conquer inequality. Having overturned a Conservative majority of 2,000 and winning a majority of 6,000 for Labour, she announced that her victory 'should be taken as a declaration of war on poverty'.[82]

When Jennie Lee arrived at Westminster, she was warmly welcomed by the women MPs, headed by Nancy Astor who was 'almost hidden by an enormous bunch of Parma violets'.[83] After Lee took her oath, the press reported that the women MPs, 'smiling like a bevy of aunts ... swooped upon her and carried her to tea'.[84] A few days later, during Astor's speech on equal franchise, She reflected back to 1919, when 'they thought that I was rather a freak, a voice crying in the wilderness'.[85] By 1928 she was one of seven female voices in Parliament who, diverse in background and politics, had begun to make their mark both individually and collectively on the policy and culture of Westminster.

Women in government

By the mid-1920s, women MPs were beginning to chip away at the walls of government and the cabinet. In the ten-month Labour government from January 1924, Margaret Bondfield was appointed parliamentary secretary to the Ministry of Labour and became the first woman minister. This appointment was by no means tokenistic, but a reward for tireless, loyal and impassioned political work which was viewed as bearing the mark of political leadership. Astor thought that Bondfield deserved a cabinet post, and George Lansbury's biographer suggests that she was actually made a cabinet offer but turned it down.

When the Labour government fell later that year, the Conservatives felt they should follow MacDonald's example and appoint a woman when forming the new government. Baldwin decided upon Atholl and made her parliamentary private secretary (PPS)[86] to the Board of Education, since at this time she was a loyalist unlike Astor and her mind was 'pre-Raphaelite in its careful accuracy of detail', according to Ellen Wilkinson.[87] Atholl was a traditional party loyalist who was sceptical about equal franchise, yet she was dedicated to women's issues and to making a mark in Parliament. She was an illustrious presence in the Lady Members' Room, with her luxurious furs, her fluency in several languages, and her love of classical music. The president of the Board of Education, Lord Eustace Percy, took every opportunity to express his disgruntlement at the notion of having a woman as his parliamentary secretary. During a meeting with the permanent secretary and members of the department, Percy ignored Atholl's contribution and, after she had finished speaking, turned away to the permanent secretary and said, 'You were going to say?' Other members of the department were angry on Atholl's behalf, but she herself was too polite to show her distress.[88]

In 1929, when MacDonald's Labour Party was back in power, Susan Lawrence was made parliamentary secretary to the Ministry of Health. From May 1930, Wilkinson was, in turn, PPS to Lawrence. This partnership was incredibly formative for Wilkinson. Lawrence's maturity, her calm attention to detail and political *nous* taught Wilkinson a great deal about how to be radical within the parliamentary system. Lawrence also held Wilkinson in great esteem and praised her ability to 'leap instantaneously to the heart of the problem', no matter how complicated.[89]

Labour also made history by appointing Margaret Bondfield as the first woman cabinet member – minister of labour – in its 1929 government.

As the first female privy counsellor, sworn in by King George V, she was the first woman MP to take the title of 'The Right Honourable'. Bondfield's biographer and fellow MP Mary Hamilton comments that Bondfield's ascent to the cabinet 'was received with universal acclaim and intense interest throughout the world'.[90] Labour's foreign secretary Arthur Henderson had emphasized that it was 'a matter of principle' that a woman should be in the cabinet given the advances women had made since 1918.

But 1929 was a difficult year to take office following the Wall Street Crash, amid falling tax revenues and an increasing demand for unemployment relief. Bondfield recognized the challenges immediately. Being minister of labour at a time of a severe economic crisis 'was no sinecure', she wrote in her memoirs. 'The urgency, the difficulty, the complexity of the work puts this ministry high among those that require not only intelligence but courage; and this was particularly true at the juncture at which I took up office in 1929'.[91] After an international liquidity crisis, leading to a drain on foreign currency reserves, the government had a choice between devaluing the pound and asking for an external loan to maintain levels of spending. Despite key economists such as John Maynard Keynes advocating the former, many members of the cabinet – including chancellor Philip Snowden – were reluctant to abandon the gold standard, so the government turned to the USA for a loan. To be eligible for such a loan, the cabinet concluded that Britain would have to balance its budget deficit, necessitating £20 million in cuts and a 10 per cent reduction in unemployment relief. A family means test was imposed on all those who had been unemployed for more than six months. 'How can you means-test someone without any means?', Ellen Wilkinson objected angrily.

Margaret Bondfield was responsible for administering these cuts at the Ministry of Labour, and in doing so she signed the death warrant of her own parliamentary career. But if the cuts provoked criticism from the left, the right accused her of being fiscally irresponsible. Economic circumstances forced her to raise borrowing powers for the insurance fund incrementally from £40 million in March 1930 to £115 million by June 1931. Churchill lambasted the Labour government for failing to establish checks on the abuse of benefits, misleadingly claiming that an unemployed person could 'sit and smoke his pipe until an offer of employment is actually brought to him'.[92] This criticism drove Bondfield to clamp down on benefit abuses or 'anomalies'. In the Anomalies Act of July 1931, Bondfield proposed a clause disqualifying 180,000 married women from benefits on the grounds that they were not seriously looking for work. This was opposed vehemently by many women MPs, including Wilkinson and the newly elected Independent MP, Eleanor Rathbone. Divisions within the Labour Party between right and left, pragmatists and idealists, began to take hold.

With pressure on the currency, and a cabinet torn between the ideals of supporting the vulnerable and the need for economic stability, the cabinet split with eleven members – including Bondfield – supporting MacDonald, and nine opposing the cuts. The cabinet resigned on 23 August 1931 and the next day MacDonald announced his intention to lead a National Government backed by Conservative and Liberal support. Facing opposition from even those on the right of the Labour Party, MacDonald was expelled from the party. Figures on the left, including Wilkinson and the fresh-faced Jennie Lee, were incandescent; they loathed MacDonald for his willingness to abandon the unemployed and vulnerable. The cuts seemed all the more futile when the National Government was eventually forced to devalue the pound regardless, leaving the gold standard in September 1931.

In the October 1931 general election, Labour was obliterated in a Conservative landslide, leaving the National Government Conservative-dominated. No Labour women MPs survived; many, including Cynthia Mosley, Edith Picton-Turbervill, Susan Lawrence, Marion Phillips, and notably, Margaret Bondfield (who was defeated by the Conservative's Irene Ward) never returned to Parliament. Bondfield's defeat was a tragic end to the political career of an outstanding woman who had much more to offer in Parliament and in government.

Although Bondfield decided to support unemployment benefit cuts and the withdrawal of benefits from married women, she ultimately refused to follow MacDonald into the National Government. Bondfield had successfully infiltrated a male-dominated political party and gained a well-earned place in the cabinet. In her own quiet, understated and administrative way she transformed attitudes towards women in leadership. In her autobiography, she wrote: 'When I accepted the Ministry of Labour, I did so knowing well it touched much more than merely my own self – it was part of the great revolution in the position of women which had taken place in my lifetime and which I had done something to help forward. Some woman was bound to be the first. That I should be was the accident of dates and events.'[93] It was also, to a certain extent, an accident of dates and events that she was unelected.

In 1931 the storm clouds of the Depression, European fascism and war were looming. And for women the left in Parliament it was a sorry state of affairs: no female Labour MPs were elected between 1931 and 1935. But women had come a long way since 1919, with thirty-two women taking their seats in twelve years. And in the immediate years to come women MPs – including Ellen Wilkinson, Irene Ward and Eleanor Rathbone – were about to shape the course of history.

2

Women at War:
1931–45

One must get rid of the idea that women are still weak, gentle
creatures who must be protected . . . Hon. Members may think that,
but the modern enemy does not.

EDITH SUMMERSKILL, 1940[1]

With the arrival of equal franchise in 1928 and the deaths of Pankhurst
and Fawcett, a void was left at the heart of the women's movement. The
central aims of the cause – the right to vote and the right to stand as an
MP – had now been fulfilled, and there was a growing debate about the
direction of feminism. Increasingly, the movement was splitting into two
factions. While the 'equal rights' feminists (or equalitarians) campaigned
for women's legal equality, including equal pay for equal work, the 'new
feminists' thought that equality before the law was not enough. The needs
of women were different from men, and therefore protective legislation
was an important way of safeguarding women from exploitation. The
tension between these two factions simmered throughout the 1930s and
1940s, as the forces of war recast the status of women in society. By 1945,
women were significantly more empowered than they had been in 1931,
due to the dramatic increase in women's labour market participation
during the war and a growing consensus around the need to fund a
welfare state to reduce poverty, particularly among women and children.

The 1930s were the prelude to world war, a decade of 'economic blizzard',
Depression and unemployment. With the Labour Party divided over reducing unemployment benefit, the October 1931 general election almost wiped
out the Party. MacDonald, expelled from the party, led a Conservative-
dominated National Government promising to take the country 'From

Chaos to Confidence'.[2] The swing to the right in 1931 ushered a fresh group of Conservative women into Parliament, including Florence Horsbrugh, Irene Ward and Mavis Tate. '[W]hat visions of white gloves, and chains, and pearls, and shining heads of freshly waved hair!', the *Evening Standard* exclaimed.[3] Nancy Astor held a celebratory lunch on 10 November 1931 and sent a jubilant telegram to Irene Ward which read, 'I rejoice at last that we have plenty of the right kind of women' – namely, Conservative women.[4]

Slowly but surely, women MPs were gaining respect in Parliament. In 1932, the *Sunday Chronicle* reported that women MPs were 'working harder than the men'.[5] Of a possible 135 divisions in the parliamentary session, Norah Runge, the newly elected Conservative MP for Rotherhithe, voted in 129 divisions while men averaged 76 divisions each. All the while, women were attending diligently to constituency work: Mavis Tate set up one of the first constituency 'surgeries' and Norah Runge sat in a different pub every lunchtime during her election campaign to hear the concerns of dockworkers. According to Runge's family, it was the only time they remember her going to the pub. The 1931 intake also proved resilient in the face of tough all-night sittings. On 16 December 1933, the *Daily Mail* reported that six women (Horsbrugh, Tate, Runge, Shaw, Graves and Ward) braved an all-night sitting of twenty-two hours and forty-five minutes, wrapped in their furs. To sustain the members through thirty-four divisions (amounting to four miles of walking), the House consumed a hundredweight (50kg) of bacon. At 4.30am, Labour MP Joe Tinker rose to plead for an adjournment, expressing concern for the women's welfare, whom he described as resembling 'washed-out rags'. But the women were undeterred, and the sitting continued.[6]

In 1936, Florence Horsbrugh, one of the new Conservative MPs, became the first woman to move (introduce) the address in reply to the King's speech as a reward for her loyalty to the Conservative Party. When Horsbrugh had been elected in 1931 for a two-member seat in Dundee, it was the culmination of a long battle to enter Parliament. Straight-laced and proficient, she quickly gained respect in Parliament and impressed with her maiden speech, which was made impromptu. She saw her invitation to make such a prominent speech as 'a compliment not only to the women Members of this House but to the vast number of women electors'.[7] The familiar debate about what to wear was intensified by the novelty of the occasion. Traditionally, men wore court dress. On consulting the government's chief whip, it was decided that Horsbrugh should wear a long evening dress in raisin-coloured velvet, with a train and long white gloves, to pair nicely with the black diplomatic uniform of Harold Nicolson MP, who was to second the address.

The speech was praised in the press, with the *Morning Post* describing it as 'a better speech than the prime minister, the leader of the opposition, or any other member, front bench or back bench'.[8] Meanwhile, *The National* named Horsbrugh 'Woman of the Month' and observed: 'As she spoke one forgot she was making history, that she was a woman. It was a model speech.'[9]

Horsbrugh was in the ascendant within the Conservative party and was recognized as such the next year. One hot day in July, she was working in the Commons Library when the prime minister's PPS, Lord Dunglass (later Sir Alec Douglas-Home) told her that Neville Chamberlain wanted to see her. Horsbrugh thought it was about the amendments she had written to the government's proposals for a members' pension fund. 'Oh, Alec, say you can't find me', she responded dismissively. But he insisted, 'You must come, Florence. It isn't about your amendments, I promise you.' She was offered the job of parliamentary secretary to the Ministry of Health, a post she held until 1945. Two years later in June 1938, Conservative Thelma Cazalet-Keir was made PPS (a role Atholl had previously held) to Kenneth Lindsay MP at the Board of Education.

But this chapter is not just a story of women in power and government; it is a story of women in opposition, in campaign, and in collaboration. Many women MPs put their parliamentary careers on the line by pitting themselves against the orthodoxy of the day on a range of issues, including economic policy during the Depression, family allowances, appeasement, women's participation in the war effort and equal pay. This chapter tells the story of some of these campaigns.

Ellen Wilkinson and the Jarrow Crusade

A prime example of the crusading, campaigning woman MP was Ellen Wilkinson, who lost her Middlesbrough seat in 1931 but was returned for the seat of Jarrow in the 1935 general election. Her resilience was fuelled by her hatred of inequality and her passionate desire for social justice. She told Parliament: 'I loathe poverty. I don't just mean being hard up and having to do without things for a bit. I mean poverty as an institution, the deep grinding health-destroying poverty in which 70 per cent of the people in this country live.'

The closure of Jarrow's steelworks in 1931 and the demolition of its shipyard in 1934 'cut the throat of Jarrow', with unemployment increasing to an astounding 70 per cent. Malnutrition made Jarrow's young men 'just like eggshells. They looked all right on the outside, but when they were faced with the infection and cold of the winter they just cracked like eggshells,' Wilkinson said.[10] Despite the specific plight of Jarrow as a town reliant upon steel and shipbuilding, Wilkinson emphasized that 'Jarrow's plight is not a local problem ... it is the symptom of a national evil.'[11]

To raise national awareness and stir consciences, in October 1936 Wilkinson helped organize a hunger march – the Jarrow Crusade. Some 200 local unemployed men marched the 290 miles from Jarrow to Westminster over twenty-six days. Wilkinson, not in the best of health, marched for most of the journey, only stopping briefly to attend the Labour Party conference, where she thundered, 'Our people shall not be starved ... If we cannot do this, what use are we as a Labour Party?'

And starved they were. One helper recalls a marcher taking the ham from a sandwich he was given and placing it in an envelope to send home, as his family had not had meat in six weeks.

Although there had been hunger marches before Jarrow, they had attracted a strong Communist presence and the Labour Party were reluctant to get involved as a result. Aware of this, Wilkinson strategically engineered the march. It was named a 'crusade' rather than a 'march'; it even opened with a church service to emphasize its uprightness. The Communist Party were banned from taking part and the traditional colour of the Left (red) was avoided, with banners sporting blue lettering on a white background instead. Wilkinson deliberately kept a low profile, leaving most of the organization to Jarrow Town Hall. Behind the scenes, she encouraged the marchers to look smart to eschew the stereotype of shabbily-clothed hungry marchers. The 200 men were selected and vetted by the Medical Officer to ensure that they were fit to march (Wilkinson knew what the cost of a tragedy would be), and they were cleanly shaven with ties and polished boots. As a result of these efforts, the crusade was widely supported across the country. The Edgware Mayor and Rotary Club paid for a room at the White Hart Hotel to be reserved for the marchers and provided them with a hearty free meal of tomato soup, steak and kidney pie, followed by apple pie. In Barnsley, the municipal baths were opened specifically for the marchers. In Leicester, Wilkinson persuaded the Co-operative Society's boot repairer to provide materials and work throughout the night to repair the many worn-out boots.

But if the nation was warm and supportive towards the marchers, Westminster proved as nonchalant and insipid as the cold wind and heavy rain that greeted them on the last leg of their journey. On 1 November, the day after the crusade reached Westminster, they gathered in Hyde Park for a demonstration, but it was sparsely attended. Three days later, Wilkinson and the marchers attempted to present to Parliament their petition of 11,000 signatures, held in an oak box with gold lettering, but prime minister Stanley Baldwin refused to meet them. The government's cold response was exacerbated by a timid apology and lack of support from the Labour Party. All Wilkinson's efforts had come to nothing. She felt profoundly abandoned by her party. Margaret Bondfield recalled seeing Ellen 'sobbing broken-heartedly' in a quiet street near Oxford Circus on her way home to her flat in Bloomsbury on the evening after the Commons debate on the Jarrow Crusade.[12]

The men took the train home to their hungry families in Jarrow. As if to rub salt into the wound, the Unemployment Assistance Board (UAB) denied assistance to the marchers' families on grounds of the men's month-long absence. Wilkinson made it her new mission to ensure payment of the men's allowances. She made a cogent and reasoned argument, rightly pointing out that the marchers had remained in touch with the council and that they would have been able to return to work if employment were available. Persistent in challenging the minister of labour on the issue, she asked the same parliamentary question on 12 November and again on 19 November.[13] Her protestations fell on deaf and unsympathetic ears. But despite the cold response, in 1937 a much-harangued Oliver Stanley, president of the Board of Trade, announced plans for a new steel plant in Jarrow. Wilkinson cheered as she rose to thank him, though she added that employment in the industry would only be secure when it was under public ownership.

The crusade shaped the historical perception of the 1930s as a period of economic depression, hunger and unemployment. It also gave the marchers a sense of purpose and political participation. When Wilkinson returned to Jarrow, she was nearly trampled by the cheering and adulating crowds.

Eleanor Rathbone and family allowances

If there is a woman MP who most defines the era of this chapter, it must surely be Eleanor Rathbone. Raised in a wealthy family in Liverpool steeped in the Liberal tradition, Rathbone was a fiercely intelligent woman who developed an early awareness of political injustice and identified unapologetically as a feminist. From previous work as a social investigator in Liverpool to a suffragist campaigner, she sought to implement her family's motto of 'What ought to be done, can be done'. When she was elected as an Independent MP in 1929, she became a lobbyist for women's economic independence, a persistent critic of appeasement, and a passionate voice on behalf of refugees all at the same time. She personified the non-partisan activism that this period often facilitated.

In the divide between 'equal rights feminists' and 'new feminists', Rathbone aligned herself with the latter. From 1919 Rathbone replaced Millicent Fawcett as President of NUSEC, signifying a major shift in its programme. With suffrage having been achieved, NUSEC focused on substantive causes to improve women's status in society (such as equal guardianship and equal pay for equal work), as well as equal franchise. The senior NUSEC organizers – Eleanor Rathbone, Eva Hubback, Elizabeth Macadam (who lived with Rathbone as her companion for most of her life) and Mary Stocks – epitomized the 'new feminism'. They supported the creation of family allowances to support wives and mothers who stayed at home to bring up their families.

Rathbone's philosophy was underpinned by the argument that getting the vote was not just a matter of principle; it was a means of achieving substantive changes for women. She also articulated the importance of having women MPs in Parliament: in her election campaign, Rathbone stated: 'I am standing as a woman, not because I believe there is any antagonism between men's and women's interests but because I believe there is need in the House of Commons for more women who can represent directly the special experience and point of view of women.'[14] She also emphasized that women MPs should not be relegated to domestic policy: 'those who expect women's contribution [to Parliament] to be something completely sui generis, utterly different from the contribution of men, will be disappointed.'

As an MP, Rathbone utilized her political power to campaign for family allowances, weekly payments made directly to mothers to help them provide food and clothing for their children. It was a recognition that they bore the burden of most childcare, and that work ought to be rewarded with an income. For Rathbone, this signified 'the idea of treating each family as though every man, woman and child in it had a separate stomach to be filled, back to be clothed, individuality to be developed and respected'.[15]

Paying family allowances directly to the mother amounted to a kind of remuneration for the work they did in the home to which most men did not contribute – the cooking, the cleaning, the laundry, the childcare. Since men's incomes were dependent on their wives' domestic support, Rathbone argued that women were 'disinherited' from the family income because domestic labour was not recognized as valuable. This translated into political disenfranchisement: women's underrepresentation in the political realm was the result of gender roles within the institution of the personal family.

Family allowances were not popular among all feminists. Many women were concerned that the campaign for family allowances would reinforce traditional gender roles and jeopardize the campaign for equal pay. Rathbone rebutted that women's dependence on men was often used to justify their lower rates of pay, and therefore reducing dependence would galvanize the campaign for equal pay. Other opponents, like Nancy Astor, suspected that family allowances could be easily abused. Astor and Millicent Fawcett also worried that they might weaken the bonds of parental responsibility.

In the face of opposition not only from other feminists but also from male politicians and trade unions, the achievement of family allowances in 1945 was a testament to Rathbone's steely determination, intellectual sharpness and political lobbying. Rathbone earned respect from across the political spectrum for her intellectual ability, which the press felt could only be described in terms of the 'masculine solidity' of her mind.[16] Labour MP Edith Picton-Turbervill likened Rathbone to a 'sledge-hammer' driving her points home in argument.[17]

It had been a long struggle, as Rathbone's campaign for family allowances had begun towards the end of the First World War. In 1924 she published her iconic book, *The Disinherited Family*, outlining how women's rightful share in the family income had become 'disinherited'. The book was reviewed widely and positively, catching the attention of William Beveridge, then the director of the London School of Economics, who professed himself a convert to the cause, and who in 1944 published the Beveridge Report setting out a framework for post-war social reform. After writing her book, Rathbone started recruiting other well-regarded figures to the cause, including the social investigator and chocolate manufacturer Seebohm Rowntree.

Being an Independent MP helped Rathbone in her cause: she was not bound by party ties, could not be accused of trying to score party political points, and could work with Liberals, Conservatives and Labour MPs alike. Her lobbying techniques were such that ministers would duck behind doorways when they saw her coming. Gradually she rallied wide parliamentary support and built up pressure through her writings and parliamentary bills (culminating in a select committee on the issue). In May 1942, a government white paper was drawn up looking at the cost of allowances. It should have been a day for Rathbone to celebrate, but the proposal was for the allowance to be paid to the father, with the qualification that it would be 'natural and appropriate' for him to delegate his wife to cash it. This was despite widespread popular support for payment to mothers.[18] Rathbone was fuming and led a deputation consisting of twenty-five women's organizations in protest.

One month later, in June 1942, Rathbone's motion urging immediate consideration of a national scheme of allowances passed easily in the Commons despite hardened and often personal attacks from its opponents. An Independent Labour Party (ILP) MP, Andrew Maclaren, made a personal jibe at Rathbone's spinsterhood, claiming that she had wasted her life on family allowances and he supposed that it was 'a good enough substitute for the absence of a family'.[19] Such blatant sexism provoked Mavis Tate and Nancy Astor to come to Rathbone's defence. In the debate Labour MP Edith Summerskill, a strong supporter of family allowances, drew attention to the 'long-term' preventive power of family allowances in shielding families from want and disease. She urged: 'Let us ensure to-day that the child receives a bottle of milk before he receives a bottle of medicine.'[20] The debate was a success for Rathbone, and although the chancellor did not promise to introduce family allowances, he expressed sympathy with the idea.

In November of that year, William Beveridge published 'Social Insurance and the Allied Services', which came to be known as the Beveridge Report, laying the foundations for the welfare state set up by Labour from 1945. Beveridge later declared that family allowances were 'the greatest of all the revolutions' advocated in his seminal report.[21] His specific proposal was for a non-contributory fund, provided by general taxation, giving a family allowance of eight shillings a week per child. Endorsement by Beveridge was a major step forward for Rathbone's campaign. Subsequently, the minister for education R.A. Butler (commonly known as 'Rab') made government proposals for a new scheme of social insurance loosely based on Beveridge's recommendations. But despite Rathbone's best efforts, the government bill published in February 1945 made the family allowance payable to the father, although either could technically cash it. Butler defended this decision, explicitly stating that 'it is not the business of the Government to resolve differences within the family, and say who will cash it'. The general sentiment in the Commons was to the contrary. The most popular argument was one of practicality: since the woman would be the one spending the money, it made sense for her to draw it. But for Rathbone it was so much more than this. In her words, 'This precious gift of family allowance without payment to the mother, is like an egg without salt. An egg to-day is a precious morsel, but it is savourless without salt.' Women MPs were resolutely in favour of payment to the mother, with the notable exception of the anti-feminist Conservative Lady Apsley, the first woman MP to use a wheelchair, who feared the creation of a matriarchy and held that it was 'very important to do nothing to undermine the position of the father in the family'.[22]

But Rathbone was determined and organized an all-party deputation demanding payment to the mother. By a combination of substantial backbench opposition and the prospect of Labour tabling an amendment, the cabinet decided to allow a free vote, although it did not omit mentioning that this was due to the presence of 'unnecessarily strong views'.[23] Payment to the mother was hence achieved by will of Parliament rather than government, and Rathbone's cross-party lobbying was key to gaining this support. So too was her ability to stay on the right side of the line between persistence and dogma. She had become increasingly involved in foreign affairs and the refugee campaign during this time, which benefitted her family allowances campaign because she was no longer viewed as an esoteric feminist 'warrior'. For instance, Rathbone's biographer, Susan Pedersen, has suggested that Churchill voted with Rathbone for family allowances as a reward for her anti-appeasement stance in the 1930s. In the final debate, Rathbone, Summerskill, Tate and Astor all spoke in favour of payment to the mother, with Rathbone even threatening to vote against the bill without the amendment. She said, 'If the Bill goes through in its present form I cannot vote for the Third Reading, although I have worked for this thing for over 25 years. It would be one of the bitterest disappointments of my political life if the Bill did not go through.'[24] These debates were extremely stressful for Rathbone, exacerbated by the fact that she was by now in bad health and, at seventy-three, the oldest woman MP. Having injured her leg, she attended the third reading in a wheelchair. Her efforts finally paid off when the bill was quietly amended at the committee stage so that the payments were indeed made to mothers.

Family allowances were a victory for the independence of women by 'A Most Independent MP'.[25] Rathbone's legacy as a woman MP was outstanding, and the first family allowance payments were made to mothers on 6 August 1946, eight months after she sadly passed away. Her legacy continues today, both in terms of the principle behind family allowances and the women MPs she inspired. Today, family allowances have been superseded by child benefit, a policy introduced by Labour MP Barbara Castle in the 1970s and championed by Harriet Harman in the 1990s.

The prophetesses and the gathering storm

The most important backdrop to the 1930s was Germany's re-militarization and the growing threat of war. World War I had left Europe in ruins and Germany plunged into economic paralysis under the weight of reparation charges set out in the Treaty of Versailles. If prime minister Stanley Baldwin refused to address concerns about unemployment and hunger at home, in Europe there were political figures who made their campaigns off the backs of the unemployed. As Conservative MP Marjorie Graves pointed out in May 1935, Hitler was 'the first of the rulers in Europe' to discover 'that the putting into uniform of the unemployed [was] a cure for unemployment'.[26] In Germany, Italy, Spain and Eastern Europe the spectre of unemployment was being spirited away by yet more sinister forces of fascism, rearmament and nationalism.

Many women MPs across the political spectrum demonstrated an astute awareness of the threat that fascism posed and persistence in their opposition to appeasement. In a speech on malnutrition, Wilkinson emphasized that the rise of fascism and economic depression were inextricably linked, and she stressed that Britain needed to nourish the population as well as rearm to oppose fascism. 'We must build up the nerve, sinew, and muscle of our people now,' she urged the House.[27] But there was a great deal of annoyance expressed by the press that women MPs were straying from domestic women's issues. A *Daily Mirror* article in 1935 entitled 'These women MPs: The questions they ask' lamented that the suffrage 'spirit of 1913 is very hard to trace in Westminster these days'.[28] This demonstrated a complete misunderstanding of why women fought for suffrage. It was not so that they could be 'women's MPs' campaigning on gendered issues; it was so they could be treated as political equals with an influence and interest in all areas of policy. The article signified a wider reluctance on the part of the press and male politicians to treat women as equals, with individual interests that extended beyond the sphere of the home and family.

'Guilty Women'

Although appeasement typically has been considered with exclusive reference to male politicians – reinforced by the powerful indictment of the 'Guilty Men' by 'Cato' in 1940 when Churchill came to power – women MPs were also heavily invested in the foreign policy debate. Appeasement was widely supported until Hitler's invasion of Czechoslovakia in March 1939 and Nancy Astor was one of the key MPs supporting Chamberlain's strategy of doing deals with Hitler. In 1936, the left-wing journalist Claud Cockburn alleged that there was a 'Cliveden Set' who met regularly at the Astors' family home, and that Nancy Astor was using her wealth to influence foreign policy in the direction of appeasement. The Cliveden Set was reputed to include the influential figures Lord Halifax (foreign secretary 1938–40), Philip Kerr (the Marquess of Lothian), Geoffrey Dawson (editor of *The Times*) and J.L. Garvin (editor of *The Observer*).

Astor's support for disarmament, affection for Chamberlain, opposition to Soviet Russia and openness to divergent political opinions combined to create an enthusiasm for appeasement and a failure to understand the threat that Hitler presented. Astor was far from alone; the vast majority of politicians and the public were extremely wary of rearmament. However, she attracted particular attention from the press and the public due to distrust of her American heritage, of her impulsive and socialite tendencies, of her wealth and connections, but also of her gender. She rashly shouted 'Nonsense' at Churchill's prescient observation that 'we had sustained a total and unmitigated defeat' in the Munich Agreement of 1938.[29] But perhaps most misjudged was Astor's invitation of German foreign secretary Joachim von Ribbentrop to her London house in 1936 after the invasion of the Rhineland. It is alleged that they played musical chairs and Astor whispered to her guests that they must let the Germans win. However, there were many senior male politicians at this event who held more influence than Nancy did as a woman MP and backbencher. When Ribbentrop gave Astor the 'heil Hitler' salute she curtly responded, true to character, 'Stop that nonsense with me!'

At one of her lunch parties, Chamberlain controversially stated that he would not rule out the secession of the Sudetenland to Germany as a solution to the crisis. It was not long before the news reached the press, with a headline in New York claiming: 'Britain preparing land sacrifices for Reich accord'. When Chamberlain was questioned in the Chamber on the matter, Astor shouted that there was not a word of truth to it. Chamberlain had been backed into a corner. In a letter to his sister, Chamberlain wrote that the incident would 'not have mattered, if Nancy had not shouted that there was not a word of truth in it. The consequence is that she has got to make a personal statement on Monday to explain that in fact it was all true! Heaven save me from my friends.'[30]

Increasingly, the Astors' endorsement of appeasement was interpreted in terms of fascist sympathy. Nancy Astor received reams of angry letters on the subject from both the UK and America.[31] One woman wrote urging Astor to reconsider her recognition of the annexation of Abyssinia by Italy. It read: 'Think again, Lady Astor. Your attitude is undoing much of your great work for children in this country. It is unworthy of you.'[32]

Although Astor was undeniably naïve in her belief that appeasement could deter Hitler from aggression, she received more bad press than was perhaps deserved. Her anti-war stance was complex, rooted less in pro-German or anti-Semitic feelings than in her belief that the Treaty of Versailles had been unnecessarily punitive, and her distrust of Churchill for being too right-wing on issues from the General Strike to Indian independence. Although she was committed to disarmament and peace in Europe, Astor was clear that *unilateral* disarmament was out of the question.[33] Her grandson, Viscount William Astor, told me that Nancy was anxious to avoid the loss of life of young men seen in World War I, and that Waldorf Astor felt the criticism even more keenly than his wife.[34] Perhaps most of all, Nancy Astor was one of many with pro-appeasement views: the general population were enthusiastic about Chamberlain's approach, as were many members of the Conservative party.

Just as the press vilified Nancy Astor, those opposed to appeasement often gender-coded appeasement as a 'feminine' approach to foreign policy and cast Chamberlain as effeminate. In November 1938, anti-appeaser and former diplomat Harold Nicolson MP blamed British women for their putative lack of courage and their tendency towards pacifism. In an unfounded generalization, he stated that 'while men had been resolute women had only been afraid'.[35] While many 'Munich mums' preferred the 'umbrella-yielding peaceable gentleman' Chamberlain to the 'cigar-chomping imperious Churchill', the fact is that, with the exception of Nancy Astor and loyalists such as Florence Horsbrugh, women MPs were active and outspoken anti-fascists who opposed appeasement.[36]

A 'Feminine United Front' against fascism

The unsung heroines of the anti-appeasement movement included Independent MP Eleanor Rathbone, Conservative MP the Duchess of Atholl and Labour MP Ellen Wilkinson, who have been omitted from the Second World War history books. In Churchill's iconic account of the failures of appeasement, *The Gathering Storm*, women make almost no appearance. They were also excluded from meetings of the male anti-appeasement clubs, known as 'The Old Guard' in the case of the Churchillians and the 'Glamour Boys' in the case of the Edenites.

Wilkinson was well-known for her anti-fascism: in 1937 when Sir Nevile Henderson, the British ambassador in Berlin, suggested to Hermann Göring that he should visit England, Göring replied: 'If I came to London all your Ellen Wilkinsons would throw carrots at me'.[37] But Wilkinson did a great deal more than throw carrots. Despite her previous pacifist sympathies and involvement with the Women's International League for Peace and Freedom (WILPF), she came to believe that non-intervention was powerless in the face of fascist aggression. Fascism was the antithesis of everything she believed in and she devoted every ounce of her energy to resisting it. When she visited Germany during the Reichstag elections in 1932 and campaigned for the Social Democratic Party of Germany (SPD) against the Nazis, she went around the city chalking the SPD's symbol (three downward arrows) over Nazi swastikas on the city walls. Five days after the Reichstag fire in February 1933, she flew to Germany and heard stories of mass arrests, torture and violence against Jews and socialists, as well as the expulsion of women from the civil service. When she returned to Britain she was determined to publicize the horrors she had seen. She co-wrote *Why Fascism?* with Edward Conze and joined the World Committee for the Relief of the Victims of German Fascism, raising awareness and fundraising for the relocation of refugees. In 1936 Wilkinson published a ground-breaking scoop on Nazi military developments in the *Sunday Referee*. She had gained intelligence from a contact in the SPD student movement, who had become a member of the Nazi administration, that Germany was preparing to advance on the Rhineland. As she reported the story to her editor over the phone from her hotel room in Berlin, she spoke in hushed tones and hid under the bedcovers, to avoid being overheard by any lurking Gestapo agents. Afterwards, she quickly packed her bags and left, knowing that her status as an MP would not protect her if she were caught. The paper published her story on the front page, which read: 'Hitler Prepares to March on Rhine: "WE CAN MOBILISE IN 24 HOURS."' The government questioned the German ambassador in vain, since Hitler had not informed him of the plan. Three weeks later, Germany invaded the Rhineland. Yet, as Lord Lothian blithely remarked, at this stage most British people felt Hitler was merely marching into his own back garden. The public appetite for war was non-existent, and the Conservative government and press were eager to reinforce this.

Meanwhile, 'Cassandras' such as Wilkinson, Rathbone and Atholl were calling for rearmament and emphasizing the importance of Britain taking a stand against fascist forces before it was too late. The three women MPs were united by the experience of the Spanish Civil War when Wilkinson, Rathbone and Atholl supported calls for Britain to arm the republicans against General Francisco Franco's Falange forces.[38] For these three women (the 'Spanish Lobby'), the Spanish Civil War highlighted how non-intervention and appeasement were futile in the face of fascist expansionism and aggression. It also served as a rallying point for cross-party collaboration. Wilkinson found little support within the Labour Party, who were opposed to rearmament and wary of becoming associated with communist republicans in Spain. Wilkinson instead turned to non-partisan women such as Rathbone and Atholl, who shared her concerns about the rise of Franco as well as Nazism in Germany.

In April 1937, Wilkinson, Rathbone and Atholl visited Spain together to witness the political and military situation first-hand. They were shelled one evening in Madrid while having dinner.[39] On their return to Britain they were determined to raise awareness and launch a campaign. They published two papers, one of which secretly compiled evidence on how the German and Italian navy were helping Franco and was subsequently sent to Churchill. To disseminate pro-republican information about the Spanish situation, they also set up a Parliamentary Committee for Spain. This committee was dominated by women MPs with Irene Ward, Megan Lloyd George and Thelma Cazalet-Keir joining Wilkinson, Rathbone and

Atholl. Rathbone and Wilkinson constantly asked parliamentary questions about the Spanish situation. The women also kept up a stream of written propaganda. In 1937, Rathbone wrote *War Can Be Averted*, outlining how appeasement had only strengthened the Nazis, and that it might even now be possible to avoid war if there was a complete reversal of foreign policy. The following year, the Duchess of Atholl wrote a book on the Spanish situation, entitled *Searchlight on Spain*.

On 1 April 1939, the Spanish Republican government surrendered to Franco. Chamberlain recognized Franco's government as legitimate almost immediately. In doing so, the British prime minister largely ignored the efforts of the women MPs, although they did successfully persuade the government to allow nearly 4,000 Basque children to come to Britain as refugees. Wilkinson also set up a Milk for Spain fund, supported by some of the trade unions, whereby customers at Co-operative shops could buy a sixpence token to help buy cost-price condensed and powdered milk for children in Spain. The fund served 33,000 glasses of milk and a biscuit every morning for school children in Barcelona.

The press and political elite mocked and patronized these women campaigners. Wilkinson, at 4'11, was labelled the 'Pocket Pasionara'; Atholl, in a smear intended to associate her with Communism, as 'The Red Duchess'.[40] When the women were speaking in the Chamber, the Tories seemed 'to take peculiar delight in jeering at their two women opponents, Ellen Wilkinson and Eleanor Rathbone'.[41] Such circumstances often pushed them to their limits. In May 1937, after the German bombing of Guernica the previous month, Wilkinson broke down and sobbed during a debate on Spain in the Commons. But their efforts were beginning to gain traction. Wilkinson was gradually generating support for the cause in the Labour Party: at the October 1937 conference, the party opposed non-intervention. The party also re-elected Wilkinson onto its National Executive Committee (NEC) and named her secretary of the executive's new Spain Campaign Committee (SCC).

Rathbone, meanwhile, proved to be a passionate defendant of the right of refugees fleeing Nazi terror to be allowed into Britain. She led the Parliamentary Committee on Refugees from November 1938 and gathered the support of 200 MPs, as well as heading the National Committee for Rescue from Nazi Terror in 1942. Refugee issues came to dominate in the latter part of her career. When she visited a camp in England for interned refugees, one detainee recalls that she spoke four simple words to him with immeasurable significance: 'You are not forgotten.'

The Duchess of Atholl, a Conservative MP whose anti-feminist, pro-colonial convictions were at odds with Rathbone and Wilkinson's progressivism, was a rather unexpected critic of appeasement. Yet from 1933, Rathbone and Atholl corresponded about the dangers of German rearmament.[42] On 5 November 1936, Atholl made her first speech on foreign affairs, stressing Britain's obligations under the League of Nations towards the 'Little Entente' countries (Czechoslovakia, Yugoslavia and Romania). In thanks for the speech, she was invited by Princess Cantacuzene on behalf of the Romanian National Council for Women to visit the country. Atholl asked Rathbone to accompany her and they set off in February 1937. Atholl was a useful asset to the anti-appeasement campaign because she eschewed the stereotype of a left-wing feminist, and she served as a good link to the anti-appeaser Churchill and the Conservative Party.[43] Fluent in German, Atholl publicized aggressive sections of Hitler's *Mein Kampf* that had been omitted by German authorities from the English version, and briefed Churchill on them in 1935. By 1937, even Conservative MP Thelma Cazalet-Keir, who was originally sympathetic to appeasement, had become 'fully disillusioned', to the extent that she sent a telegram to President Roosevelt during the Munich Crisis, urging him to fly to Europe to help preserve peace.[44]

Yet despite all the evidence of Hitler's intentions, Chamberlain stuck with his strategy of negotiation and containment. Wilkinson likened Chamberlain, firmly entrenched in Number Ten, to 'an old widow in a boarding house, jabbing at critics with knitting needles'.[45] Rathbone grew to detest Chamberlain and everything he stood for. In February 1938, when he suggested the press should exercise 'restraint' in reporting foreign affairs, she mordantly asked whether they should set up 'a concentration camp for British journalists'.[46] Wilkinson shared Rathbone's distrust of Chamberlain, seeing him as an upper-class, simpering fool who was too pally with the German elite. In her view, von Ribbentrop had been reassured in his dealings with the British elite that 'the real feeling of the upper classes in this country was that the Nazis had at last learned how to keep their working classes quiet'.[47] On 24 August 1939, Wilkinson made a damning indictment of Chamberlain in what was described as 'perhaps the most impressive speech by a woman M.P. on foreign policy to date'.[48] She called for Chamberlain to stand down, saying that he had put 'the narrow interests of his class . . . and of the rich, before the national interests'.[49]

Rathbone and Wilkinson knew who should take Chamberlain's place. Winston Churchill, although diametrically opposed to the two women's progressive politics, was a leader. In the midst of the Munich Crisis, Rathbone wrote to Churchill urging him to consider taking on the premiership. 'There is a great longing for leadership,' she wrote, 'and even those who are far apart from you in general politics realize that you are the one man who has combined full realisation of the dangers of our military position with belief in collective international action against aggression.'[50] Churchill thanked her for her letter, but didn't include her in his 'Old Guard' of male colleagues who opposed appeasement.

After the *Anschluss* in March 1938, Hitler's eye turned to Czechoslovakia. In September 1938, Wilkinson and Rathbone were key speakers at a rally at Trafalgar Square in support of Czechoslovakia, whose audience was dominated by women. When the Czech Sudetenland was annexed by the Germans under the Munich Agreement in October 1938, Chamberlain's reluctance to take a stand was crystal clear.

The photograph of Chamberlain waving a piece of paper as he left the plane returning from Munich has become an iconic symbol of false hope and failed brinkmanship. But at the time, it was heralded as the advent of a new kind of politics that would avoid the horrors of war as experienced just two decades earlier. Nevertheless, some described the Munich Agreement as being as 'poisonous as Snow White's apple' (the Disney film was being screened at cinemas at the time). Rathbone saw appeasement in this light. She astutely described Chamberlain's policy as 'a clever plan of selling your friends in order to buy off your enemies – which has the danger that a time comes when you have no friends left, and then you find you need them, and then it is too late to buy them back.'[51]

The Duchess of Atholl put her neck on the line by opposing appeasement. In November 1938, she resigned as an MP and forced a by-election on the issue. It came to be known as 'the dirtiest by-election in history' and one of the first in a series of by-elections that were seen as 'miniature referenda' on the question of appeasement.[52] Atholl stood as an Independent, endorsed by a 'motley coalition' of Eden and Churchill within the Conservative Party, as well as the Liberal and Labour parties.[53] Rathbone sent Atholl her car to help with the campaign; the socialist suffragette Sylvia Pankhurst sent her a telegram of support, which read: 'every woman who prizes her vote should vote for you.' Atholl wanted people to be able to support her 'without voting against their several parties', and she emphasized that 'It is through co-operation of this kind that I believe we can best attain the national unity that we all desire in this time of danger.'[54] But although Churchill tacitly supported her and rang her every evening to check in with her progress, he did not risk making his support public. In this respect Atholl took 'political risks that no male anti-appeaser would run'.[55] The Conservative Party thought that a victory for Atholl would be embarrassing, so they invested a great deal of time and energy on defeating her, employing the loyalist Florence Horsbrugh in their campaign. It paid off, and Atholl was defeated by the Conservative candidate, William Snadden. She was devastated by the news, not only because of the loss of her seat, but also because of its significance for international affairs. She consoled herself by playing Beethoven's *Moonlight Sonata* on her piano.

However, in the same month an anti-appeaser woman Labour candidate, Jennie Adamson, won a tight by-election in Dartford. Adamson declared that her victory showed 'Mr Chamberlain that he had not got the people of this country behind him and he must go'.[56] Seven months previously, another woman who vocally opposed appeasement, Labour's Edith Summerskill, had won her by-election in West Fulham.

In March 1939, Hitler invaded Czechoslovakia. Wilkinson accused Chamberlain of employing futile 'smooth words' of sympathy for the suffering in Austria, Czechoslovakia and Spain, 'but you sell them to Hitler every time.' [57] Similarly, Rathbone berated the government and Chamberlain in particular for allowing the 'rape of Czechoslovakia'.[58]

Just five days later, Germany made an ultimatum to Lithuania demanding the restoration of the Klaipėda territory controlled by the Germans prior to the Treaty of Versailles. In response, Britain made an Anglo-Polish military alliance pledging assistance to Poland in case of German invasion. But this didn't stop Hitler from turning on Poland, galvanized by a Nazi-Soviet Pact signed in late August. On 1 September Hitler invaded Poland from the West. Finally, Chamberlain was forced to act: two days later Britain and France declared war on Germany.

Now at war, Chamberlain was viewed as weak and ineffective; he 'was not the man to lead the country', Wilkinson said.[59] Women MPs played a vital role in the downfall of Chamberlain's government in May 1940. Conservative Mavis Tate informed Wilkinson that both she and Astor were intending to resign the whip if there was a division. Wilkinson reported this to Herbert Morrison (future Labour home secretary) who rallied Labour support against the Chamberlain government.[60] Meanwhile, Megan Lloyd George helped persuade her well-respected Liberal father, ex-prime minister David Lloyd George, to attack the government in the debate. In the end, Astor (who had only recently been accused of being a fascist sympathizer) and Tate were among thirty-three Conservative rebels in the National Government who defied the three-line whip and voted against Chamberlain in the motion of confidence.

At the end of the war, Mavis Tate was the only woman in a parliamentary delegation visiting Buchenwald concentration camp. Tate narrated moving video footage produced by British Pathé to raise awareness about the Holocaust that had taken place at the hands of the Nazis. 'Let no one say these things were never real,' she said solemnly.[61]

Woman power

One might be forgiven for thinking that the demands of war would lead to the marginalization of women MPs and their campaigns. Indeed, war and foreign policy were often gendered as masculine, and women MPs were sometimes criticized in the press for their intrusion into these policy areas. But from 1940 to 1943, women overtook men in their average annual contribution to debates.[62] The women MPs continued to take active positions in government and sat on influential select committees, making an observable impact on people's lives during the war.

Women in the wartime coalition

Once installed as prime minister, Winston Churchill formed a national government with Labour's Clement Attlee as his deputy. As Churchill proudly declared, his wartime cabinet was diverse and spanned the political spectrum 'from Lord Lloyd of Dolobran on the Right to Miss Wilkinson on the Left'.[63] The wartime government included three women MPs: Jennie Adamson, Florence Horsbrugh and Ellen Wilkinson. In October 1940 Labour's Jennie Adamson was made PPS to the Ministry of Pensions, dealing with pension claims affecting women and children, including war orphans. Conservative Florence Horsbrugh, who was in charge of casualty service, evacuation, billeting and day nurseries as parliamentary secretary to the Ministry of Health, was described by *The Telegraph* as one of the most 'remarkable' of the women MPs.[64] However, much to the distaste of Astor and Summerskill, Horsbrugh defended unequal pay in civil defence and celebrated the government's creation of a lower pensionable age for women as a victory for 'tired women' workers.[65]

Horsbrugh also argued that children were the responsibility of mothers, not the state, defending the government's tardiness in installing state day nurseries – an early form of childcare to help the women now expected to work in factories or on farms as part of the war effort.[66] Horsbrugh did not necessarily promote 'feminist' issues or women's interests in government. But she received unfair and misogynistic criticism: Nancy Astor, although a defender of the childless Ellen Wilkinson and Eleanor Rathbone, unfairly declared that Horsbrugh was unfit for her post because she was a spinster and therefore allegedly not interested in children.[67] Horsbrugh always sought to be a member of government on her own merit without reference to her gender: 'I want to forget that I am a woman in doing my job ... It doesn't help for people to emphasize that somebody doing a certain job is a woman.'[68]

The third woman in Churchill's government was Ellen Wilkinson; once a critic of the government machine, she was now a cog in the wheels of the wartime coalition. Churchill felt indebted to Wilkinson for her work undermining Chamberlain and the appeasers, and awarded her with the job of parliamentary secretary to the Ministry of Pensions. She was put in charge of hardship tribunals, which she declared a position 'after her own heart'. Any qualms she may have had about Churchill's right-wing politics were quashed by the urgency of the situation. As she wrote in *Tribune*, 'We are fighting for our very lives'.[69] If it was a time of crisis for the nation, it was a time of opportunity in Wilkinson's political career. She benefitted from exposure to the realities of government, just as the government benefitted from her contribution. On 25 June during a debate on Ministry of Pensions estimates, she made the case for war service grants from the despatch box and deflected an onslaught of questions with a hardiness and a confidence that belied her small stature. Not tall enough to stand behind the despatch box (where ministers stand to make speeches and answer questions) she stood beside it instead.

Throughout the 1930s, Wilkinson had an extra-marital affair with the future home secretary, Herbert Morrison. Although Morrison's biographers have doubted whether their relationship was sexual, Wilkinson's biographers (Laura Beers and Matthew Perry) maintain that it was more than a platonic affair. The secretary of state for war, P.J. Grigg, stated that Wilkinson and Morrison were almost 'living together', having 'met them once broken down in Morrison's car coming back from a weekend with all their luggage in a ditch'.[70] As their affair progressed, Jennie Lee increasingly distanced herself from Wilkinson, as she was deeply suspicious of Morrison's position on the right of the party.[71] In October 1940, a month after the start of the Blitz, Herbert Morrison made Wilkinson responsible for the provision of air raid shelters within the Home Office. Nine months of aerial bombing of London – 'the Blitz' – left 20,000 dead and approximately 70,000 wounded. Fifteen other major cities had also been raided. Wilkinson quickly became known as the 'Shelter Queen'. On the first evening of her new job, she visited the East End to listen to people's concerns. At that time, more than 15,000 were sleeping at 'Nightmare Arches', a shelter off the Commercial Road, where the floor soon was covered with urine and faeces. Wilkinson spent the vast majority of her time on her own visiting shelters from London to Liverpool, often at night during the black-out, in her little Austin Seven car (which, much to the delight of the press, she maintained herself). The morning after the catastrophic bombing of Plymouth, she stayed overnight with Nancy Astor and they inspected the damage together.[72] Newspapers commented on the morale-boosting effect of Wilkinson's visits to the East End, one stating that her 'womanly sympathy carried further than mere words'.[73]

The inadequacy of home shelter provision lured people into tube stations to sleep at night, in hope of better rest and protection. Wilkinson was deeply concerned about this, both on grounds of safety and morale. The government ordered London Transport to ban the use of the tube stations as accommodation, but it was forced to abandon this position when large numbers ignored the rules. By the end of September 1940 nearly 200,000 people were sleeping in the tube. Wilkinson's warning that the use of tube stations was 'inviting tragedy' was realized in March 1943. When one person slipped while running into Bethnal Green tube station, a panicked stampede resulted in the deaths of 173 people, including 84 women and 62 children.

Wilkinson knew that drastic measures were required to make shelter provision effective. She developed a new scheme to improve provision, promising 'Safety, Sanitation and Sleep'. She made it a reality through the tactics she had learnt so far in her political career: she 'chivvied and bullied, encouraged and threatened, ordered and charmed'.[74] To replace the old outdoor Anderson shelters, which were cumbersome and difficult to use, she helped organize deliveries of new Morrison shelters. Named after her boss and lover, Morrison shelters were flat-topped, easy to make, and could accommodate a family of two adults and two children, with a steel frame and wire mesh sides that didn't crumble if the house was bombed. They could even be used as kitchen tables and were provided free to those earning less than £350 a year. Wilkinson also requisitioned 500 private cellars for Londoners to use, revamped existing official shelters and established a ticketed system of entry to the underground shelters. Her work led to the installation of 200,000 bunks, canteen facilities, chemical lavatories, ventilation, lighting and running water. Some shelters even provided night classes and film screenings. While the government had requisitioned and refurbished the unused Down Street tube station for its own use (complete with bathrooms), Wilkinson refused to use it on principle: she belonged with the people, not a government elite.

In January 1941, Morrison introduced compulsory unpaid fire-watching and put Wilkinson in charge of implementing it. Each fire-watcher was given a bucket of sand, a bucket of water and a stirrup pump to help put out small fires caused by bombing and to ease demand on the National Fire Service. In April 1942, fire-watching was made compulsory for women too, provoking a negative reaction from both men and women, and huge numbers of exemption claims. In response, Wilkinson urged that the only substitute for 'man power' was 'woman power', a theme which became a motif throughout the war.[75] When women complained about balancing fire-fighting and domestic duties, she boldly suggested they should get their husbands to help with the housework instead of going to the pub.[76] Although the scheme was unpopular, her efforts were not in vain: during the 'Little Blitz' on London in February 1944, fire watchers extinguished 75 per cent of fires caused by incendiary bombs, without requiring the assistance of the fire service. Wilkinson was a hands-on minister who worked incredibly hard. As Nancy Astor recognized, 'if you think women cannot stand the strain of war, let one of you try to do what Miss Wilkinson is doing'.[77]

The strain of the war on Wilkinson was sharpened by a tension between principles and pragmatism that marked her political life. As a member of the wartime government, she had to make difficult decisions that she might otherwise have argued against. She did so because she thought that the defeat of fascism was a pre-condition for any socialist principles or ideals. Under the Emergency Powers Act 1939, the government gained the right to direct and control labour, and strikes were banned. Many unions resented this and ignored the ban: in 1944 there were over 2,000 strikes. Much of the time Wilkinson was successful in acting as a sympathetic buffer, with her trade union background being an asset. In August 1941, she persuaded 2,000 skilled men in the North-East to resume work, saying 'If you want a fight, fight Hitler'. When an old comrade asked her 'Are you still uncompromisingly a Socialist?', she responded, 'Much more so than ever.'

'Women Fall In'[78]: The wartime mobilization of women workers

At the outbreak of war, there was a massive increase in demand for man power, with acute shortages pushing many women into jobs that were traditionally seen as 'men's work'. Although there were mixed feelings from both men and women, one part-time woman war worker reflected on the emancipation that this brought at the time: 'I thoroughly enjoy my four hours working in the afternoon. I'm all agog to get here. After all, for a housewife who's been a cabbage for fifteen years – you feel you've got out of the cage and you're free.'[79] Yet despite the enormous increases in 'woman power', the war was still directed predominantly by men, and women MPs were becoming restless at both the inappropriateness and the incompetency of the situation. Three Conservative women MPs were at the forefront of the campaign to work towards equal opportunities for women in the workforce. Irene Ward, Mavis Tate and Thelma Cazalet-Keir had all been elected in the landslide for the Conservative-dominated national government of 1931, and all three lost their seats in the Labour landslide of 1945. But while in Parliament they were at the heart of a wartime select committee initiated by Irene Ward. Named the Woman Power Committee (WPC), it was designed to serve as an official advisor to the Ministry of Labour on the question of employing women in industry.

Irene Ward had won her Wallsend seat in 1931 by defeating Margaret Bondfield. As was common for women, Ward was selected as a candidate primarily because the seat was considered impossible for the Conservatives to win. At one point during the election campaign, Bondfield and Ward were both asked to kick off a football match. Ward recalled that she had never kicked a football before so she did it very badly, while Bondfield was more assured. Yet the election reversed their fortunes. Ward described Bondfield as 'very patronising' and arrogant in her belief that she would keep the seat. Ward, meanwhile, utilized her prior experience fighting a tough campaign in the Labour safe seat of Morpeth, as well as the popular surge towards the Conservatives, and won. A former private secretary of coal owner Cecil Cochran, Ward was an expert on coal and used her knowledge to great effect in the Commons. She had a sensitivity to the needs of mining communities not often found on the Conservative benches. In her northern constituency of Wallsend, she was able to relate to the miners in a way that most Tories would have been unable to, as a self-described 'very left-wing tory'.[80] She even used to dance with the miners and was known as the best ballroom dancer in the north. Impressively, she passed four private members' bills in 1938, 1954, 1961 and 1962. Her close friend and colleague Thelma Cazalet-Keir said that 'if she were not in private the sweetest and tenderest of characters the title of "battle-axe" might well have been made for her. She gets things done'.[81] Like many of the women on the Labour benches, Ward remained unmarried for her whole life and was utterly dedicated to her politics.

Thelma Cazalet-Keir later described Ward as 'one of the few really dear friends, as distinct from acquaintances, who survive from my time at Westminster'.[82] The daughter of a wealthy socialite, Cazalet-Keir benefitted heavily from her connections, much like Astor had before her. Her brother, Victor Cazalet, was already an MP when she was elected in 1931, and she was family as far as the Lloyd Georges were concerned. After seven years as a Conservative councillor on the London county council, in 1931 she stood unsuccessfully in a by-election in Islington East. Yet at the general election later that year, she stormed home in the same constituency, displacing Labour's Leah Manning with a majority of more than 14,000. During the war, Cazalet-Keir was very active on the issue of woman power. When Attlee announced an all-male committee to consider women's services, she asked him whether he would consider setting up an all-female committee to investigate men's services. In the end, Attlee's committee featured five women and three men, with Mavis Tate in the chair.

Just as victory in 1931 had been a surprise for Ward and Cazalet-Keir, so it had been for Mavis Tate in West Willesden, a seat previously held by Labour. Plucky, serious-minded and hard-working, Tate refused to be confined to 'women's issues', speaking in Parliament on a range of subjects including overseas trade and civil aviation (on which she was an expert). Although she didn't originally identify as a 'feminist', throughout the 1930s and the wartime period Tate became increasingly vocal on issues of women's equality. In 1935, she presented a petition for equal nationality rights for women, and during the war she was very active on the issue of providing equal compensation for wartime civilian injuries.

With Mavis Tate in the chair, the Woman Power Committee had its first meeting at Eleanor Rathbone's home on 28 June 1940. Remarkably, the WPC then met every two weeks throughout the war. It was dominated by Conservative women with the core trio of Ward, Cazalet-Keir and Tate; with the exception of Edith Summerskill, Labour women were reluctant to cooperate with the WPC, seeing it as a top-down organization that sought to push middle-class, inexperienced women into work without regard for the impact on men's wages.[83] Jennie Adamson and Ellen Wilkinson preferred to address the problem of woman power by encouraging women workers to join unions. Their forum was the Standing Joint Committee of Working Women's Organisations (SJCWWO), a massive women's organization founded in 1916, which also met regularly during the war and reported regularly to the Labour Party NEC. The wartime minister of labour Ernest Bevin and the government saw the SJCWWO as the reasonable alternative to the WPC. As such, the government was reluctant to cooperate fully with the WPC, fudging the issues and diverting attention wherever possible. Much to the frustration of the WPC, the government refused to give it official status as an advisory body.[84] Instead, it established a new Women's Consultative Committee (WCC) in March 1941 at the Ministry of Labour, mostly made up of trade union and professional women, as well as three women MPs – Irene Ward, Edith Summerskill and Megan Lloyd George.

One key decision for the government was whether to introduce industrial conscription for women as a means of utilizing woman power. In late 1940, reports by the Manpower Requirements Committee of the Production Council recommended an increase in compulsory direction of women into industries such as munitions and engineering. By January 1941, Bevin had secured permission from the war cabinet to introduce industrial conscription for women. It was now compulsory for all women in the narrow age range of 20–21 to register with their local Ministry of Labour office, so that they could be allocated to appropriate war work.

Bevin consulted the WCC, who were divided on whether to extend women's conscription. On the one hand, conscription would push women out of the domestic sphere, giving them a taste of working life and economic independence. It would also give them status and a chance to show their abilities. On the other, conscription might devalue the kind of work traditionally performed by women in the home, such as childcare and housework. It risked creating a division between married and single women, as well as the exploitation of women workers as 'cheap labour' by employers undercutting men's wages. Eventually the WCC agreed to conscription, on the proviso that married women would not be wholly exempt, and that conscripted women would receive equal pay for equal work.

Meanwhile, the WPC lobbied for parliamentary debates to encourage further discussion on the issue of woman power. Ward and Summerskill approached the whips for their respective parties, and a debate was scheduled. The WPC were divided on the issue of conscription, as became apparent through the debates. While figures such as Rathbone and Summerskill thought conscription was essential and that equal citizenship demanded equal responsibilities, Labour's Agnes Hardie and the Conservative's Lady Davidson felt that women should not be driven away from their traditional domestic responsibilities.

Irene Ward introduced the woman power debate in March 1941.[85] It was the first comprehensive discussion of women's employment to take place in the Commons and it was directed by women MPs: the WPC planned individual speeches and assigned each woman to a topic on which to focus. Edith Summerskill noted that it was perhaps 'unprecedented' for her to say that 'having listened to all my women colleagues, I find myself— strangely—entirely in agreement with all of them'. As Shirley Summerskill, Labour MP from 1964 to 1983, told me, 'these issues, along with equal pay brought women together, whatever party'.[86] The consensus was that although the women MPs welcomed the government's greater enthusiasm to employ and direct woman power, it had to be respected as equal to man power. Megan Lloyd George pointed out that the under-utilization of woman power was not due to a lack of enthusiasm on the part of women to participate in war work, but a lack of demand by employers for women workers. To help the situation, she suggested a publicity scheme to raise public perceptions of women's capabilities.

Towards the end of 1941, conscription was extended to women between the ages of twenty and thirty. But even this failed to satisfy the country's need for woman power, and so the Lord President John Anderson asked the war cabinet to approve compulsory national service for all women between eighteen and sixty. This was highly controversial, and although Bevin was in agreement, prime minister Churchill and the minister of supply Lord Beaverbrook were less enthusiastic. The reluctance to include women in the war effort was a source of great frustration for many women MPs: 'I wonder', Summerskill said, 'what the country would say if the whole question of man-power were dealt with by women ... I am beginning to feel that the war is being prosecuted by both sexes but directed only by one.'[87] Eventually, the war cabinet agreed in November 1941, and the National Service (No.2) Act was passed the next month. The resultant mobilization of women far exceeded that of World War I and that of other countries fighting in World War II.

There has been some debate about whether women were emancipated through war work and the utilization of woman power. While it gave them a taste of economic independence, this was countered by a powerful 'cult of domesticity' in the post-war period, strengthened by the withdrawal of day nurseries which had been set up to allow mothers to work during the war. This made it much harder for women to combine work and family in the post-war years. Nevertheless, the marriage bar was abolished in teaching and the civil service in 1944 and 1946 respectively, empowering married women to take up, and stay in, work. Overall, the war and the efforts of women MPs to mobilize woman power did make a significant difference to the empowerment of women, and to the war effort.

'Four-fifths of a man': Equal pay

By April 1943, the government had finally relented to parliamentary pressure from women MPs on the subject of equal compensation, reversing the situation in which different rates of compensation were provided for civilian men and women who were injured during the war. This was entirely due to the efforts of Mavis Tate's Equal Compensation Campaign Committee (ECCC) and the women on the Equal Compensation select committee. In August 1941, Edith Summerskill asked the minister of pensions 'why a woman's arm or leg is not of the same value as a man's?'[88] When that battle was won, women MPs began to turn their attention towards an interlinked injustice – the absence of equal pay.

The argument for unequal compensation had been that since a woman earned less than a man, if she was injured she would be losing less in the form of wages and therefore be owed less in compensation. Once equal compensation was established, however, the logical implication was that women should be paid the same as men for equal work. The WPC consequently shifted its focus to the campaign for equal pay, one which permeated the women's movement throughout the twentieth century and continues to be pressing even today.

Mirroring the ECCC, the Equal Pay Campaign Committee (EPCC) was established with Mavis Tate as chair, with the goal of achieving equal pay in the civil service. Equal pay was more divisive as a campaign than equal compensation, at both ends of the political spectrum. On the left, there were concerns that expanding the workforce to include women on equal pay would place downward pressure on male wages, making it difficult for them to provide for their families. On the right, there were fears that equal pay would push women out of the home and lead to the dissolution of the traditional nuclear family.

Before the war, women received four-fifths of men's pay in both the public and private sector.[89] The campaign to abolish these pay differentials had begun in earnest during the 1930s. In 1936, Wilkinson had persuaded all the Conservative women apart from Atholl to vote against the national government in a successful division calling for equal pay in the civil service. But the prime minister, Stanley Baldwin, effectively threatened that the government would resign if it was implemented, calling a vote of confidence in the government which he won. Although equal pay did not make its way into law, this was a victory indicating parliamentary support. But by the end of the 1930s, with high levels of unemployment and downwards pressure on wages, equal pay seemed unachievable and the campaign had waned.

The wartime expansion of woman power gave the equal pay campaign a new impetus. In 1941, women MPs expressed frustration that industrial conscription of women was not accompanied by equal pay. As with equal compensation, there were Labour MPs (such as Wilkinson and Adamson) who thought pay was an issue for trade unions to negotiate with employers, not for Parliament to interfere with. Consequently, the equal pay campaign bifurcated into the trade unions representing industrial women workers, and the WPC representing other women workers. On the trade union side, there was an echo of the suffragette days with a rise of militancy in 1943 and multiple wildcat strikes. In Hillington near Glasgow, 16,000 men and women workers at a Rolls-Royce aircraft engine plant went on strike for ten days, protesting the absence of equal pay in their wage agreement. Bevin was concerned about unrest and sponsored a national women's conference in London. But this sticking plaster tactic failed to conceal the gulf between the treatment of men and women in the workforce, antagonized by the feeling familiar to the women's movement that the government was all 'words not deeds'.

Nevertheless, in March 1944 the WPC formed a deputation to the chancellor, John Anderson, demanding equal pay in the civil service. In the same month, Thelma Cazalet-Keir tabled an amendment to the Education Bill for equal pay for women teachers. When the government opposed the amendment, they embarrassingly lost the division by one vote. It was the only defeat of the Churchill wartime government and a great source of irritation to Churchill.[90] As Irene Ward emphasized, it was 'very courageous' for Cazalet-Keir to vote against Churchill. Ward, who was close to Cazalet-Keir, stated that she would have voted with Tate, but her mother was tragically killed in an accident on the day of the vote and therefore she was unable to attend.[91]

As Baldwin had done eight years earlier in response to Wilkinson's victory, Churchill turned Cazalet-Keir's amendment into a matter of confidence in the government, a vote which he won resoundingly. Although implementing equal pay had been dodged, publicity and support for the cause had increased. Churchill was aware of this fact; hence he gave some pretence of enquiry and consideration, whilst stalling any legislative action.

The government was advised that there should not be a debate or a select committee (as had been established with equal compensation), but instead a royal commission which was limited to fact-finding, not policy advice. It took the government five months to appoint members and announce the terms of reference, and the final report took more than two years to emerge, published eventually in October 1946. Ellen Wilkinson had commented on the ineffectiveness of commissions back in 1935 in relation to Jarrow and unemployment, saying 'If my constituents could live on commissions they would be the best fed people in the world.'[92]

A couple of weeks after VE Day in May 1945, the wartime coalition government was dissolved and Churchill appointed a national caretaker government which lasted three weeks. When he offered Thelma Cazalet-Keir the position of parliamentary secretary to the Ministry of Education in his government, he warned her, 'now, Thelma, no more of that equal pay business.'[93]

By 1945, women MPs had collectively chipped away at the edifice of opposition to equal pay, but it was not until 1970 that Labour MP Barbara Castle could capitalize upon her senior cabinet position to achieve legislative action.

Into a brave new world

On 1 December 1944, Nancy Astor celebrated her silver jubilee of twenty-five years in Parliament. She marked the occasion with a lunch in the

Commons attended by twenty-eight women MPs, past and present. 'I do not say we have been brilliant or glamorous, but we have been useful,' she reflected. She also announced that she would retire at the next general election. The reasons cited for her retirement were ostensibly Waldorf's poor health and that she could not continue without his assistance. But more importantly, Waldorf and their family thought she would be defeated in the election: the allegations of a Cliveden Set had taken their toll on her popularity, and she was becoming increasingly disruptive and unfocused in the Chamber. But Astor wanted to go on, and she made no secret of her reluctance to stand down. 'My Lord and Master has made the decision, and I am obedient as ever,' she said dolefully. She expanded further in the Chamber, bitterly suggesting that her resignation was 'a triumph for men'.[94] Waldorf's drafted letter of her resignation is covered with Nancy's defiant staccato corrections in red marker.[95] During a speech by Waldorf Astor at a dinner for female businesswomen, he demonstrated a lasting and deep affection and respect for Nancy, as well as an appreciation of how much she had achieved in her parliamentary career: 'When I married Nancy, I hitched my wagon to a star. And then when I got into the House of Commons in 1910 I found that I had hitched my wagon to a shooting star. In 1919 when she got into the House I found I had hitched my wagon to a sort of V2 rocket.'[96]

In early 1945, Rathbone too considered standing down due to poor health and old age. In the end, she was too preoccupied with refugee issues to abandon her seat. She won with a large margin but died following a stroke on 2 January 1946. It was the end of an impassioned, dedicated and principled life of political service which ranged from pioneering family allowances to helping rescue refugees from Nazi terror. Wilkinson described Rathbone as 'a great public institution'.[97] In the debate on family allowances, Astor had also paid tribute to Rathbone. 'It is very difficult', she said, 'when we look at the hon. Lady the Member of the English Universities (Miss Rathbone), to think of her as a revolutionary, but she is, and it is her work, and her vision and courage, that have really brought us where we are to-day.'[98] During her memorial service, Sir Arthur Salter, a fellow Independent MP, poignantly expressed the respect and affection that Rathbone had attracted in Parliament over seventeen years: 'There must be many of us who, when we reassembled yesterday, looked at that second bench below the gangway and realized with a pang that we should not again see that small, gallant figure, clutching the big black bag with bulging papers, in recent months frail and stooping, but never for an instant flagging in courage or persistency, watching for every chance of pressing her case by supplementing question or intervention in debate.'[99]

If the end of the war saw two of the boldest and most determined women MPs leave the Commons, it also saw the birth of a new era emboldened by the state planning necessitated by the war and continued in its aftermath. The war had raised public awareness that the personal matters of the family were inextricably linked with the political matters of the state. It had been a people's war, with the British people witnessing civilian bombing on a grand scale, and a systematic re-haul of domestic life including conscription, rationing and evacuation. The horizon above the bomb-blasted cities of Britain had been changed irrevocably. When the British people looked towards this horizon, they saw a new future and a new era waiting for them.

3

Let Us Face the Future: 1945–59

The people won the war, now let them win the peace.
LEAH MANNING, 1945[1]

On the morning of 5 July 1945, the British people awoke to news of a shock Labour landslide. Churchill, the national wartime hero, had been swept aside by a landslide majority of 146, making way for a radically progressive Labour government headed by Clement Attlee. This Labour government irrevocably shaped the course of British modern history, with the creation of the National Health Service (NHS), education reform, the introduction of comprehensive national insurance, and nationalization in industry as a means to achieve full employment.

The manifesto that took Labour to victory in 1945, *Let us face the future*, was written by Ellen Wilkinson, Michael Young, Herbert Morrison and Patrick Gordon Walker. Now chair of the Labour National Executive Committee (NEC), Wilkinson presided over the Labour Party conference in Blackpool at which the party agreed the contents of the manifesto. In what she described as the proudest moment of her life, Wilkinson made the opening speech – a call to take up cudgels and expose the empty Conservative rhetoric on social justice. For the first time in history, Labour had a real opportunity to forge the future, building a world free of fascism and poverty. The Fiery Particle was burning bright: 'we fight for power ... not for any Party advantage but because we believe that in this programme which we are putting forward lies the one hope of building in Britain, this beloved island of ours, the type of civilisation which we so passionately desire,' she rallied.[2]

But if the post-war period was one of political idealism, it was also one of economic austerity and scarcity. With the impending end of lend-lease – the US's loan of critical aid and supplies to Britain during the war – and the start of repayments, the full toll of the war weighed heavy on the government's shoulders. While many thought that the end of the war would bring about the end of economic hardship, rationing continued until the early 1950s and was even extended for some goods. With the return of men from the war, women were gradually displaced from their wartime jobs and their gendered role as homemakers was re-entrenched, with a potent 'cult of domesticity' emerging into the 1950s. For many women it was a backwards step to return to the role of the housewife. They had to contend with the challenges of stereotypes as well as the continuance of rationing well after the war was won. Such gendered power dynamics were reflected in the politics of the era: the Conservative Party in particular began to realize the power of the women's vote and capitalized upon housewives' discontent in the 1951 and 1954 elections. Meanwhile, women in Parliament played a crucial role both in constructing the Attlee consensus, and in critiquing it. In doing so, they were formative in the sculpting of twentieth-century British history.

Parliamentary culture, chocolates and cancans

By 1945, the days of Ellen Wilkinson sitting alone as a woman on the Labour benches were a distant memory. 1945 was a ground-breaking election for the left and for women MPs, whose number trebled between 1935 and 1945 from eight to twenty-four (twenty-one of whom were Labour), and the number of women candidates swelled by almost 25 per cent. All but one (Lady Davidson) of the Conservative women either lost their seats or retired. Of the defeated MPs, Irene Ward and Florence Horsbrugh returned to the Commons in 1950, but Mavis Tate and Thelma Cazalet-Keir never did.

The Lady Members' Room brimmed and bustled with new Labour women, including Barbara Castle, Alice Bacon, Bessie Braddock and Jean Mann. The three youngest women MPs – Alice Bacon, Peggy Herbison and Barbara Castle – were elected on their first attempt, a remarkable feat for women candidates. Herbison, who was elected for Jennie Lee's old North Lanarkshire seat, was known as 'the miners' little sister'. After her father, a miner, was tragically killed in the pit, the miners' lodge asked her to stand as the Labour candidate in North Lanarkshire as a way of marking his memory and pushing for change in the terrible conditions faced by miners.

She initially refused and said to them 'I'm sure you can find a man'.[3] When they came back and told her that they couldn't, she said yes. Like many of the Labour women, Herbison had an intimate knowledge of, and sensitivity to, the concerns of working people and the struggles that they had experienced. According to Baroness Patricia Hollis (biographer of Jennie Lee), Herbison became the 'unofficial leader' of the group of Labour women MPs.[4]

One of the new women MPs, Barbara Ayrton Gould, had been a suffragette and was imprisoned for window-smashing back in 1912. And although it was only her first attempt at election, Barbara Castle later remembered that her campaign was fought 'on gin and nerves'. Most of the Labour women 'had borne the brunt of long battles, many defeats, much victimisation and bitterness', which infused the Lady Members' Room with a sense of sisterly solidarity – a political mission but also joviality.[5] Chocolates were liberally shared to keep the women going through the all-night sittings, and it is said that Jennie Lee and Barbara Castle once danced a cancan on the desks.[6]

Such bonds of friendship extended beyond the Labour Party. Although at this point Megan Lloyd George was a Liberal MP – 'petite, dark-haired and bright-eyed, with a great sense of fun' – she was embraced by the Labour women as one of their own.[7] She and Leah Manning – who had now returned to Parliament after her previous, brief stint in the 1930s – were good friends and often went to cinema matinees together.[8] In 1950, with Megan Lloyd George having been made deputy leader of the Liberal Party the year before, the women MPs hosted a birthday party for her with a presentation to mark her twenty-one years in Parliament. By 1956, Megan Lloyd George had converted to Labour and taken the seat of Carmarthen with her, out of the hands of her previous party. She explained her decision in a letter to Attlee, writing that 'in the changed situation of today it is only in the Labour Party that I can be true to the Radical tradition'.[9] Her collaboration and contact with the twenty-one Labour women during the 1940s is likely to have influenced this decision.

Among the other non-Labour women MPs, Eleanor Rathbone was quite content keeping herself to herself, and Lady Davidson cut a rather lonely figure at first. But even Davidson was welcomed into the fold gradually. It helped that she was a relatively moderate Conservative and that her father, the MP Willoughby Dickinson, had been a prominent Liberal devoted to women's suffrage. One day she came home and told her family, 'Darlings, I've finally broken through. Bessie Braddock offered me a chocolate.'[10]

If the Lady Members' Room boasted a larger-than-life atmosphere during this era, it was anything but in terms of physical space. Despite significant increases in the number of women MPs, Westminster still felt 'a little like a boys' school which had decided to take a few girls', as Edith Summerskill put it.[11] The women remained in the 'dungeon'; with just seven desks and two couches to accommodate twenty-four women. With no wardrobe and no pegs for hats or coats, the Lady Members' Room quickly descended into chaos with scattered belongings and 'littered desks, overflowing wastepaper baskets ... newspapers half-opened, half-read, strewn around the room'.[12] When pegs were installed, the lack of space meant that the pegs were too close together and the hats too big, so that the room 'looked like the hour before the Jumble Sale opened'.[13]

After piling pressure on the parliamentary authorities, over the next ten years the women were granted an additional small room on the bend of a stairway with facilities for four women MPs, and one room behind the Speaker's chair, which Edith Summerskill and Megan Lloyd George adopted. The congestion in the main Lady Members' Room was also ameliorated by the appointment of three women – Wilkinson, Summerskill and Adamson – to ministerial office, when they acquired offices of their own.

As the composition of the women MPs changed and more Conservative women entered the Lady Members' Room in the 1950s, the sense of post-war euphoria and socialist sisterhood dissipated. The 1950 general election was something of an anti-climax for women in Parliament; despite a field of 126 women candidates, only 21 were elected. With Labour's overall majority reduced to six, Conservatives Florence Horsbrugh and Irene Ward reunited with Lady Davidson in Parliament, accompanied by new Conservative MPs Patricia Hornsby-Smith and Eveline Hill. A number of Labour women lost their seats. In 1951, when another general election led to the return of Churchill's Conservative government, the atmosphere in the Lady Members' Room changed further. Only seventeen women MPs were re-elected and no new women MPs entered the House that year.

Confined within such a small space, the flames of tension were fanned even within parties. Leah Manning recalled that in the early days Barbara Castle aroused a lot of jealousy as a young, successful and attractive woman and 'did not have an easy time'. Manning would often find Castle 'vulnerable and in tears in the Lady Members' Room'.[14] And as the number of women MPs grew, it was inevitable that party allegiances trumped the gender allegiance, even when the women were close. There were a few rows between women MPs, notably between Labour's Bessie Braddock and the Conservative's Edith Pitt. Once in the Chamber, Pitt argued that retirement pensions should not be increased and maintained that pensioners were not facing absolute poverty. Bessie Braddock retorted defiantly, challenging Pitt to visit Braddock's own constituency to witness pensioner poverty and starvation for herself (an invitation which Pitt did not accept). In a biting critique of Conservative policy, Braddock drily commented, 'if you starve them quickly enough, you will not have to keep them.'[15] Both rose to their feet and engaged in a shouting match.

More attention was drawn when women MPs had arguments compared to their male colleagues. When the *Yorkshire Post* commented on Barbara Castle's attempt to introduce a bill to extend protection of common law to sex workers, it noted that 'the House likes her best when she gets a bit waspish with Dr Edith Summerskill', who was less inclined to the reform.[16] As Jean Mann wrote in her memoirs: 'I have always noticed that men can attack one another sometimes venomously but if two women do so the alleged dominant sex whisper "bring out the saucers of milk" or they quote: "My dear, if ever you become a mother, please can I have one of the kittens?"'[17]

In 1953, a particular piece of gossip was relished by the press. When newly-elected Patricia Ford published a piece on her impressions of the House for the *Sunday Express*, she alleged that she had spied Bessie Braddock and Edith Summerskill sprawled across a settee and snoring in an unladylike manner, in the new retiring room. Braddock objected to this assertion and denied it. Alice Bacon had been a witness and said that the four occupants of the room were Ford and herself, with Summerskill and Davidson (not Braddock) on the couches. 'It is a particularly unobservant person who would mistake Mrs. Braddock for Lady Davidson,' she joked; for while Braddock was of large stature, Davidson was willowy in her physique.

Such focus on gossip, conflict and trivia was a demonstration that women's status in Parliament remained secondary to that of men. On Barbara Castle's first day as an MP, she was accompanied to the entrance by Michael Foot. He was stopped by a policeman who, with a gesture towards Castle, informed Foot that he was not allowed to bring in any guests. When Foot informed the guard that his 'guest' was the Honourable Member for Blackburn, the guard's face clouded over with amazement.

The press, and male MPs, continued to shine a spotlight on the clothing of women MPs rather than their political contribution. The endless newspaper columns about women MPs' fashion obscured the columns of Hansard that they filled with their speeches in the chamber. When Conservative MP Lady Tweedsmuir was elected in a by-election, she was treated as the 'Glamour Girl for Parliament' and attracted wolf whistles from male MPs as she was introduced to the Chamber. Leah Manning, dressed for a Buckingham Palace garden party, drew applause when she entered the Chamber in her fine attire. And when Jean Mann once rose to ask a question in a brown velvet outfit, comments echoed round the Chamber that she was 'dressed like a bride'. As minister of education, Ellen Wilkinson tried to answer questions next to the despatch box, wearing a hat with 'a green feather perched on her head', only to be held up for several minutes by opposition cheers.[18] But like some other women MPs, Wilkinson revelled in this sense of theatre and celebrity, and utilized it as a means of making herself seen and heard. On the election of the first woman MP for Northern Ireland, Ulster Unionist Patricia McLaughlin told the press she needed a fortnight after the election to prepare her wardrobe for the House. Labour MP Lena Jeger, who was elected in 1953, returned to the Chamber after a dinner at the speaker's house 'in a very low plunging neckline', causing the press gallery to put down their pens and peer over to get a better view. Unintimidated by the noticeable ogling, Jeger 'rewarded them by slowly rising from her seat and taking the longest way out, right down the centre of the Chamber'.[19] Labour's Elaine Burton took to wearing bareback plunge dresses even in winter, despite Jean Mann's concerns about her catching cold. A year or so later, fashion writers in the press announced bareback dresses as the 'new fashion'. Women MPs were beginning to enter the cult of celebrity.

Although some women MPs were becoming household names, the speaker of the Commons often saw them as a homogenous group. During the debate on the Berlin air-lift of 1948–9, Barbara Castle, Leah Manning and Jean Mann all wanted to speak. But the government whips approached Mann, whispering to her that the speaker could not tolerate three women in the debate, and could she arrange with the other women about who should be allowed to speak. When Mann relayed this to Castle and Manning, Castle refused; they all had unique lines of argument that couldn't be essentialized with reference to their gender. The women informed the speaker that they all wanted to speak. In the end, the speaker only called on Manning and Mann. Sending such negative messages to women MPs hardly encouraged political participation. In Jean Mann's memoirs, she wrote that the excitement and novelty of a woman speaking in the Chamber was so great that when one quiet woman MP rose to catch the speaker's eye, she 'electrified' the House with anticipation. The Chamber deflated as it became apparent she was only requesting for the lights to be turned on; she timidly uttered, 'I was only asking for candles', and sat down abruptly.[20]

Local party selection committees continued to ask questions of women interviewees that would never be asked of their male colleagues. How do you intend to balance your commitments as an MP with your commitments to your children? How does your husband feel about you standing as a political candidate? Why have you not had children, and do you intend to in the future? When selected, women often found themselves fighting unwinnable seats – the view being that the safe or marginal seats could not be jeopardized by a risky woman candidate. Typically, women had to interview for more constituencies than men before being selected: Barbara Castle did six interviews (and applied for even more) before being elected for Blackburn, while James Callaghan was selected on his first attempt and Harold Wilson on his second. Every time a woman stood for selection or election without success, she sacrificed a great deal of money and time, a commodity which was simply not available to most women. It was therefore no surprise that standing as a candidate remained an unattainable career option for most women. In 1945, of 1,600 candidates, only eighty-seven were women and only twenty-four of those were elected. Without increasing the number of women candidates, there was little hope of having more women MPs.

In early 1952, a group of Conservative women MPs sought to improve women's prospects for selection within their party. In a letter to the Conservative associations, Lady Davidson, Eveline Hill, Lady Tweedsmuir and Irene Ward demanded that the party should consider fielding more women candidates in winnable seats. 'Far too often, women fight the hopeless seats over and over again,' they wrote. However, they clarified that they were not seeking positive discrimination: 'Women candidates ask no favours, only to be considered on their merits.' In an essay entitled 'The Missing Women', Labour's Lena Jeger noted the 'appalling habit' of Conservative Party selection committees asking to interview the wives of male candidates, which inevitably disadvantaged women candidates who could not boast wives to help with constituency work, go to tea parties or accept bouquets at hospital fêtes.[21] But this was not a problem exclusive to the Conservative Party. Labour women, particularly those without partners at all, were also affected by the precedent of 'political wives'.

Edith Summerskill recalled that in her first few days in Parliament, Ellen Wilkinson exhaled a deep sigh as she trundled into the Lady Members' Room, laden with her briefcase and a pile of letters collected from the Post Office, exclaiming 'Oh! For a wife. If I had a wife, she might have collected these, drafted answers and finally typed them. She would help with the women's section, give a hand with the bazaar and, when I get home fagged out, have a delicious meal ready for me.'[22] A couple of decades later, Lena Jeger, who took her husband's seat in 1953 when he died, also commented how she could do with a wife to help, and wrote of the 'dark hole at the bottom of every day' without a partner to return home to.[23]

When women MPs had husbands in Parliament, it was often assumed that they were proxies for them. During the 1950 election campaign, an American woman reporter asked Jennie Lee whether her husband Nye Bevan helped write her speeches. Lee snapped with indignation: 'I'm not the soft underbelly of the axis.'[24] Attitudes towards the Bevan-Lee political partnership and marriage were permeated with sexism. Bevan was given credit when Lee said anything of merit, and Lee took the flak whenever Bevan said anything worthy of criticism. She was demonized as the Lady Macbeth or 'dark angel at his shoulder', pushing him to the left and towards picking battles with his colleagues. When Bevan informed the shadow cabinet that he would resign after the Easter recess in 1954, Dalton distastefully commented, 'Clearly he slept with his politics last night', in a reference to Lee.[25] Yet as Lee's biographer, Baroness Patricia Hollis, told me, Bevan was volatile with or without Jennie. The only cure for such attitudes was to normalize women MPs – to see them as individuals in Parliament in their own right. This could only happen by increasing numbers in the hope that they might one day achieve a 'critical mass'. The Labour NEC-member and future MP Barbara Ayrton-Gould recognized this at the Labour conference of 1943: 'The more women they could get into Parliament the sooner they could eliminate women's questions as women's questions and they would all become universal questions.'[26]

On Labour's NEC, four places were reserved for women, and six women MPs served on the NEC between 1945 and 1959. Yet they were often treated with disrespect. Many grew particularly disillusioned with Nye Bevan, who, when heckled by Jean Mann, responded: 'Contain your bile, woman.' Even Edith Summerskill, who enjoyed spending time with Bevan and respected him greatly, found him difficult to work with.

During the women's conference in early 1948, Bevan was criticized by delegates, including Bessie Braddock, for making changes to the composition of boards in the NHS so that local authorities could no longer nominate representatives. Bevan grew defensive: 'I'm not going to be dictated to by a lot of frustrated females.' Braddock did not respond in public, but the next day she asked to see Bevan and she gave him a piece of her mind. Jennie Lee came to see Braddock afterwards, demanding to know what she had said to Bevan and saying that she had never seen Bevan look so upset. Braddock refused to tell Lee, commenting that it would serve him right to tell his wife himself.

'From the cradle to the grave'

When William Beveridge published his report on social insurance in December 1942, he envisaged a new system establishing 'freedom from want … from the cradle to the grave'. His report diagnosed five 'evils' of British society that needed to be tackled: want, disease, ignorance, squalor and idleness. It was hugely popular: a survey by the British Institute for Public Opinion found that 90 per cent of the public had heard of the report, with a majority supporting its recommendations. It was also supported by the Conservative Reform Committee, although Churchill was nonchalant. At the end of the war British bombers dropped copies of the Beveridge Report across Europe as propaganda about the future they might build. When Beveridge was briefly elected as a Liberal MP in 1944 and made his maiden speech, he referred to his report as a 'large and noisy baby' which he 'laid on the doorstep of His Majesty's Government in Whitehall', and had been kindly taken in. But it had been more readily welcomed by Labour than the Conservatives. Despite many Conservative MPs being told that 'unless we swallowed the Beveridge medicine we would suffer political extinction at the next general election', many refused to do so.[27] The warning proved accurate.

After the 1945 landslide, Attlee's government set to work to transform British society with the blueprint of Beveridge's report in hand. The 1945 manifesto had criticized the way in which after World War I the 'great men who did well out of the war' were given free rein by the government to profiteer, driving people into poverty, hunger and unemployment. As Wilkinson colourfully described it on a BBC party political broadcast, families' 'nest eggs' were turned into 'scrambled eggs'. In an explicit reference to the failure of Conservative appeasement, Labour's manifesto demanded that peace 'must not be regarded as a thing of passive inactivity, it must be a thing of life and action and work.' It had, after all, been unemployment, hunger and despair that drove people, like moths to the flame, to fascism and remilitarization. Two women MPs in particular – Ellen Wilkinson and Edith Summerskill – played a crucial role in pushing for reform, within education and health policy respectively.

Ellen Wilkinson vs. 'ignorance'

Ellen Wilkinson became the first woman minister of education and the second woman in the cabinet on 3 August 1945. Although Attlee initially offered her the minister of health portfolio, she asked if she could take on education instead, and Attlee agreed. Education was a labour of love for Wilkinson, as it was at the epicentre of two things she longed for: social equality and world peace. In April 1945, she had been the only woman to accompany Attlee, Eden and Lord Halifax on an official visit to San Francisco to set up the United Nations (UN) – a new cooperative group of 'allies in a new war on hunger, ignorance and want', an ambition infused with the language of Beveridge. In 1945, she served as the president of the United Nations conference to establish its Educational, Scientific and Cultural Organisation (UNESCO) with the aim of promoting world advances in education and understanding.[28] Recognizing the importance of technological education in a nuclear age, she warned: 'it's a race between education and extinction.'[29] Such ideas could be seen in Labour's 1945 manifesto, which proclaimed that 'the great purpose of education is to give us individual citizens capable of thinking for themselves'.

Before 1944, most children were educated up to fourteen in 'all-age' elementary schools, with only 20 per cent receiving specialist secondary education. The reforms of the 1944 Education Act guaranteed free specialist secondary education until the age of fifteen for all children. It also specified a selective tripartite education system, based on an eleven-plus exam which streamed students into grammar schools, secondary moderns and technical schools. Labour took these reforms further, pledging in their manifesto to raise the school leaving age to sixteen 'at the earliest possible moment'. But once in government, with resources limited, Wilkinson found many of her colleagues reluctant to prioritize education spending. While trying to implement the raising of the school leaving age (ROSLA), Wilkinson faced constant undermining and opposition from cabinet colleagues. Home secretary Herbert Morrison was particularly concerned that, if proper provisions could not be made before the start date, there would be overcrowding in schools and a shortage of teachers.[30] When Morrison suggested delaying ROSLA during a cabinet meeting, Wilkinson responded firmly, 'If we stick to it we can do it. If you *first* ask whether it can be done the answer will probably be no.'[31] Wilkinson's recent affair with Morrison had probably petered out by the end of the war, according to Wilkinson's biographer Laura Beers. Given this, his hostility and aggression towards her plans caused her pain and disappointment, both personally and politically. Civil service staff, too, were sceptical about the possibility of implementing ROSLA before the proposed start date of 1 April 1947 and suggested pushing the date behind the Tories' provisional timetable. Edith Summerskill suspected that the civil service did not respect women ministers; this was almost certainly the case with Wilkinson and ROSLA.[32] But Wilkinson was determined to avoid 'procrastination' on the issue: 'those to suffer most by deferment will be precisely those working-class children whose education has already been so seriously interrupted by the war,' she told the cabinet.[33] All this took place at a time when Wilkinson's health was deteriorating; she had suffered from bronchial asthma all her life, and it was beginning to escalate.

To make matters worse for Wilkinson, even Bevan, a known sceptic of compromise and cuts, supported postponing ROSLA. When he suggested that they should prioritize house-building over education, Wilkinson snapped at him, 'you can't build houses without schools'. After heated cabinet exchanges such as these, Attlee decided to put the question to the Lord President's Committee, and within a month Wilkinson's case was won. On 28 September, she announced that ROSLA would be implemented on time, for 1 April 1947. Richard Tawney, an historian and Christian socialist of huge influence within the Labour Party, wrote to Wilkinson congratulating her on her persistence, without which the 1944 act 'looked as though it were drifting into the doldrums. Your bold and decisive announcement will tune things up all round.'[34] When Attlee asked Wilkinson what Tawney's thoughts on ROSLA were, she enclosed his complimentary letter to Attlee.

Wilkinson's success didn't prevent her ex-lover Morrison from making further attempts to postpone ROSLA, but she now had the support of the prime minister, chancellor Hugh Dalton, and by now even Bevan. In rebutting Morrison, Wilkinson emphasized that education had all too often 'been the first casualty of an economic blizzard' and that it was time to prioritize it for once.[35] She was right – Morrison frequently targeted her department for cuts, despite the fact that in 1946 education spending made up only 1.8 per cent of total government spending. Wilkinson's persistence on ROSLA demonstrated that although she was willing to compromise on certain issues, there were red lines.

Wilkinson was determined to ensure not only the quantity of children educated (through ROSLA), but the quality of their education: 'secondary education shall be secondary and not elementary with frills on,' she insisted.[36] To avoid overcrowded classes, she pushed for huge building and recruitment programmes to remedy the shortage of schools and teachers. With many schools having been bombed during the war, she advocated the short-term mass building of 'huts' and prefabricated classrooms to deal with increased demand. Meanwhile, she created an emergency training scheme for teachers, consisting of a one-year crash course to boost teacher numbers in advance of ROSLA. She also sought to improve social service provision for children as part of the educational system by introducing free school milk. As a child, she had personally felt the effects of malnutrition on health and development, standing at under five foot in her adult years. When Wilkinson met Edith Summerskill's eleven-year-old son, who was tall for his age and taller than Wilkinson, she looked up at him and said dolefully: 'If only I had been given the opportunity to drink fresh milk every day I would be as tall as you.'[37] In February 1946, Wilkinson issued a joint memorandum to Morrison's Lord President's Committee recommending that free school milk should be provided to complement family allowances when introduced in August 1946, and free school dinners as soon as local authorities could make the necessary arrangements. The committee accepted the recommendation for free school milk but referred the decision on free school dinners to the cabinet, resulting in another battle between Wilkinson on the one hand, and Morrison and Dalton on the other. Despite Dalton's concerns that such spending would set an undesirable precedent, Wilkinson passionately argued that if the exchequer didn't foot the bill, local authorities would drag their heels. In the end, it was left to local authorities to decide about school meals provision. Her concerns proved to be right: while 84 per cent of schoolchildren were drinking free school milk, only 49 per cent were eating free school meals by 1951.[38]

While these were progressive reforms, Wilkinson's implementation of what was a selective system of education is ripe for criticism from the left by modern standards. Wilkinson genuinely believed that not all children had the same needs, and that some needed to be pushed intellectually more than others, but this does not detract from the fact that selective education was deeply divisive along class and gender lines. And while selective education was broadly accepted in 1944, there were voices within the Lady Members' Room – such as those of Alice Bacon and Peggy Herbison – calling for a more comprehensive system. By 1956, Labour's Anthony Crosland indicated that the tripartite system was 'the most divisive and unjust and wasteful of all the aspects of social equality'.[39] Wilkinson had her work cut out even with her own backbenchers. Once, after a barrage of hostile questions from her own benches, Wilkinson came down to the Lady Members' Room 'shaking and upset'.[40] Although she could have been more radical on the issue of comprehensive schools, she did push for short-term remedies to ameliorate the inequality of the selective system. First, she advocated multilateral schools to cater for children of all abilities. Second, she thought that there should be a late-transfer window so that gifted children who didn't pass the eleven-plus could still go to grammar school later on. Third, she sought parity of esteem between grammars and secondary modern schools.

Two months before the implementation of ROSLA for which Wilkinson had worked so hard, tragedy struck. One cold February night in 1947, amid the harshest winter of the century, Ellen Wilkinson died of an overdose of medinal, one of many medicines she was taking for her increasingly poor health. In a British Pathé video making a tribute to her life, her friend and colleague Ernest Bevin held back tears as he said: 'Ellen all her life had been a very great fighter, a fighter for the common people. She would never accept the inevitability of poverty. She fought through it as an individual herself . . . Farewell Ellen, great little courageous soul. We will carry on your work.'[41] The next cabinet meeting was suspended for a few moments as a mark of respect.[42] Wilkinson had made an inestimable impact upon perceptions of women in Parliament, inspiring many women to walk in her footsteps. When Jean Mann was clearing out her own possessions from the small chest of drawers in the Lady Members' Room before leaving Parliament in 1959, she came across Wilkinson's cosmetic box in the bottom drawer. She showed it to Jennie Lee. 'We stared at it for a moment, then Jennie said: "You take it, Jean."'[43]

It must have been a poignant moment. Jennie Lee had, after all, lived opposite Wilkinson for many years in Dolphin Square in Pimlico, and Wilkinson was the only woman MP with whom Lee had been friends.[44]

Although Lee was generally more stubborn and sceptical of compromise than Wilkinson, the two women felt a similar frustration with party moderates during the 1930s, being on the left of the party, and they had both been through tumultuous love affairs with married men (both of whom happened to be called Frank). In 1980, when Lee was asked on Woman's Hour if there were any women MPs she had admired, she quickly answered, 'Oh yes, Ellen Wilkinson. Ellen was older than me ... she was so kind to me; she could have been jealous of a younger woman who was taking part of the limelight, you know, but Ellen was a very good friend and I loved her.'[45] When Frank Wise, the first love of Lee's life, died suddenly and left her utterly bereft, Wilkinson pushed a note under Lee's door which read: 'I feel sick every time I think of E.F.W. [Frank Wise] but I am glad to know that he was happy at the end. That is a big thing. There are certain miseries you are spared my dear.' Wilkinson had in mind the misery of rejection, which she herself had felt keenly from the loss of Frank Horrabin, her former lover, who had left her and married someone else.

But after twenty years as an MP, Wilkinson was cut down in her prime at the age of just fifty-five. It was a huge loss to Parliament, and it was not until the 1960s that Labour women surpassed the heights that she reached.

When the Conservatives returned to power in 1951, Florence Horsbrugh followed in Wilkinson's footsteps as the second woman minister of education. However, while Churchill felt obliged to appoint a woman, he refused to give her a seat in his cabinet, despite the precedent of all ministers of education having been cabinet ministers since 1931. He claimed that he wanted to keep the cabinet small, but he also undoubtedly disapproved of the notion of having a woman in his inner circle. Consequently, Horsbrugh had to mark out her territory and assert herself within a Conservative government whose leadership was incredibly hostile towards her. In September 1953, Churchill relented, and she became the first Conservative woman appointed to the cabinet. This didn't stop Churchill from making her feel isolated: he often used strong language, apparently forgetting she was there, and then drew attention to his embarrassment given the presence of a lady in the room. If Horsbrugh dared to express an opinion on anything except education, he humiliated her in front of the whole cabinet, exclaiming: 'Fancy the minister of *education* taking an interest in foreign affairs.'[46] During her time at the Ministry of Education, Horsbrugh faced the challenge of providing primary education with limited resources during a baby boom.

Her approach was to encourage cuts in spending while attempting to maintain 'the essential fabric of education'. In early 1952 she sent a circular to local authorities asking them to reduce spending by 5 per cent.[47] This provoked significant opposition from a range of Labour MPs, notably future schools minister Alice Bacon, who used her experience as a school teacher to critique Horsbrugh's policy. In doing so, Bacon defended Labour's record on education from 1945 to 1951, giving a resumé of its (and Wilkinson's) achievements in office compared to the cuts under the Conservatives:

> Let me remind the House of some of the things which were accomplished. We raised the school-leaving age. Fees for secondary schools were abolished. We trained more teachers. The emergency training scheme alone was responsible for the training of 4,000 teachers. More students were admitted to universities. There were more students with scholarships—scholarships which were adequate for the proper maintenance of those students who entered universities ... October, 1951, saw the return of a Conservative Government, and they pursued a policy of economising at the expense of the children.[48]

Horsbrugh came to be regarded as a very successful woman politician, although her ability was noted in the press in sexist terms. In 1952, the *Sunday Times* reported that: 'To the sympathy and warm heart of a woman she adds a solid good sense and ability to get things done which is rarer in politicians of her sex.'[49] In becoming the first Conservative woman in the cabinet, she stood on the shoulders of those before her, notably Wilkinson, who had made huge sacrifices to break through the thick walls of government.

Edith Summerskill vs. 'disease'

Edith Summerskill, a middle-class mother of two, doctor and MP, was in many ways the polar opposite of Ellen Wilkinson and many of the Labour women before her. Summerskill relished her dual role as a homemaker and breadwinner, emphasizing that marriage and politics were not incompatible. Tall, elegant and well-spoken, she starred in a British Pathé film in 1945 entitled 'Mrs, Dr, MP: Pathé Close-Up of Dr Edith Summerskill'. It shows a day in her life as she walks her dog in the idyllic countryside at first light, completes her morning rounds as a GP, undertakes her domestic chores and shopping, and finally heads to the House of Commons with a briefcase in hand. The film demonstrates how hard-working and impressive Summerskill was, and that women MPs were gaining respect and prestige. Edith's grandson, Ben Summerskill, told me that when he was at school, all the dinner ladies knew who Edith was; she was admired not only as a politician but as a glamorous woman in the public eye.[50] It was clear that women could have roles within both the private and public spheres (if their circumstances allowed it): 'a woman who does three man-sized jobs' was proving that women's capabilities were just as strong as men's, the Pathé news reel remarked.

In Parliament, one of Summerskill's most passionate campaigns was for accessible healthcare as a means of vanquishing Beveridge's evil of 'disease'. As a doctor, Summerskill had come to believe that most ill health and disease was caused by economic inequality, poverty and squalor. Every week, forty-five women died in childbirth in insanitary and cramped conditions at home without experienced medical help.[51] Malnourished children experienced stunted growth and development. The inaccessibility of vaccinations meant that thousands of children died every year from diseases such as whooping cough, tuberculosis, polio and diphtheria. Ellen Wilkinson had watched her mother die slowly and painfully from cancer in 1916, when she was unable to afford proper medical care. Summerskill came across copious examples such as these, and they motivated her to become an MP. When in Parliament she didn't miss an opportunity to champion proactive, progressive methods of reducing disease. Given Labour's new policy of free milk for schoolchildren, Summerskill's long-standing campaign for the pasteurisation of milk to avoid the spread of tuberculosis became all the more salient. Clean milk had been advocated by Astor and Wintringham in the 1920s, but it was Summerskill who resolved to eradicate the problem. In October 1939 she pointed out that a daily dose of tuberculous-infected milk was more dangerous to health than an air raid. After continual lobbying through the 1940s, in 1949 she successfully piloted through legislation enforcing the pasteurisation of milk. She called it her 'finest hour'.

Edith Summerskill once told her grandson that the reason Nye Bevan didn't want her to become too involved in the health portfolio was because she would upstage him on the day of the introduction of the NHS.[52] Mervyn Pike, who became a Conservative MP in 1959, often said to Ben Summerskill that his grandmother had been a target for a kind of sexism that many other women didn't encounter: her triple role as a housewife, MP and doctor compounded the jealousy caused by her beauty and sense of style.[53] This hostility and prejudice has resulted in the virtual erasure of Summerskill's role from history and from her role in campaigning for universal free healthcare.

Back in 1911, the Liberals had legislated for the provision of free GP healthcare to all insured workers. However, this excluded those in work who could not afford insurance contributions, and housewives. While presenting her Cancer Bill in 1938, Summerskill pointed out the unfairness of a housewife with a limited income having no right to free medical treatment, and often being forced to delay seeking medical help. Berating the minister of health for having gone to sleep in her speech (he jumped to his feet and denied the accusation), Summerskill went on to say that the only long-term solution to the problem was 'a State medical service in the country so that the people can have a free health service just as they have free education'. In a prescient foreshadowing, she declared that such an idea 'is a kind of Utopia but we know that that Utopia will probably come during the next ten years'.[54] In 1939, during a debate on tuberculosis, she again emphasized the importance of a comprehensive national health service to cover women and children as well as male breadwinners. Summerskill moved several resolutions at Labour Party conferences for a state-run healthcare system as well as urging for all voluntary hospitals to be abolished and for all medical schools to accept women students.[55]

During World War II, a National Emergency Medical Scheme was introduced, giving an impression of what a comprehensive health service might look like. However, after the war the British Medical Association (BMA) withdrew its support and remained resistant to the idea of an NHS. Faced with a BMA strike, health minister Nye Bevan granted concessions to the medical profession, including the ability of GP surgeries to operate like small businesses, the ability for consultants to maintain private patients, and an increase in nurses' pay to prevent shortages. The BMA relented just five weeks before the first NHS patient was seen. 'I stuffed their mouths with gold,' Bevan boasted. Within two months, 95 per cent of the population were covered by the health service, and 90 per cent of GPs had joined. The first patient to be treated on the NHS was a thirteen-year-old girl, Sylvia Beckingham, who was admitted to a hospital in Manchester for a liver condition. Summerskill's utopia had been realized.

But problems of course remained. A central point of contention in the NHS was the extent to which private services and health charges should be maintained. A limited number of pay-beds were provided in hospitals, to the fury of Labour MP Bessie Braddock. During an NHS debate on the potential of health charges, Braddock complained to the speaker that she had been punched (or at least pushed heavily on the shoulder) by Conservative MP Arthur Colegate on her way from the division lobby and asked whether this was in order. 'It is certainly not in order for any member to punch another member,' the speaker responded. Colegate denied the allegation. Braddock quipped that if such a thing had occurred outside the House, the Honourable Gentleman would not have been on his feet for two seconds, which everyone agreed with (given her burly stature and enthusiasm for boxing). The speaker advised Colegate to apologize, which he refused, and for Braddock to forgive him, which she did.

At first, the NHS covered charges for optician and dentist prescriptions. This was a liberating prospect for many: by 1950, 17 million people received glasses and 9 million were given false teeth. Dentures and spectacles were very difficult to obtain without the NHS. Jennie Lee recalled her husband Nye Bevan bringing home a blue and white cotton handkerchief, crocheted with a blue border (to symbolize the NHS) by an old lady who had received free dentures. '[N]ow I can go into any company,' she wrote excitedly. But by 1950, with the UK obligated to dispatch troops to fight in the Korean War, the balance of payments was straining under the pressure of a £2.4 billion increase in defence spending. Within months of the NHS's birth, chancellor Stafford Cripps was urging Bevan to make health cuts of £75 million. Prescription charges on spectacles and dentures were the most feasible option. Bevan was incandescent at the suggestion. On Budget Day in April 1951, the new chancellor Hugh Gaitskell announced that the implementation of charges would be deferred for six months to see if they were needed. When he later announced them, Jennie Lee shouted 'shame' and stormed out of the Chamber. Lee urged Bevan to resign, and on 23 April he did. After a parliamentary labour party (PLP) meeting, he was joined by Harold Wilson and John Freeman.[56] Ironically, the defence spending came in under budget and such deep health cuts were not required.

When a Conservative government was returned in 1951, it was Patricia Hornsby-Smith who was tasked with implementing further health prescription charges when she was made parliamentary secretary to the Ministry of Health, becoming the youngest woman to achieve ministerial rank.

'Jam tomorrow'?
The housewives' revolt

Back in 1943, a young Barbara Betts made her first speech to the Labour Party conference as a constituency delegate from St Pancras. As she took to the platform of Central Hall in Westminster, glimpses of her future reputation as a 'fiery redhead' were seen as she accused the Conservative-led coalition of trying to delay the implementation of Beveridge's proposals in the face of economic uncertainty. In a reference to Lewis Carroll's White Queen in *Alice in Wonderland*, she summarized the leadership's attitude as 'Jam yesterday, and jam tomorrow, but never jam today!'[57] Ted Castle, night editor of the *Daily Mirror*, was in the audience and was blown away by her speech, which featured on the front page of the paper the next morning. Barbara and Ted married in 1944. Barbara Castle – as she had now become – was elected as a Labour MP in 1945.

Although Attlee's government did seek to bring 'jam today' in terms of implementing Beveridge's recommendations and achieving a more equal distribution of wealth through full employment and the nationalization of industry, rationing was beginning to grate. Two-thirds of middle-class housewives felt that they were not getting enough essential foodstuffs, according to a Mass Observation survey in 1949.[58] Even bread and potatoes, neither of which were rationed during the war, were now rationed due to poor harvests and a shortage of foreign currency to import wheat. In May 1948, Castle asked the minister of food for more soft fruit and sugar to be allocated directly to housewives rather than manufacturers, so that they could make their own jam, which was cheaper and better.[59]

Castle was not the only woman MP who raised concerns about shortages of food and the squeeze housewives were facing. While seconding the address in reply to the King's speech in 1947, Peggy Herbison emphasized: 'We have the right to ask much from them, but they ask much from us in return.'[60] Jean Mann was particularly persistent in defending housewives against shortages and high prices; she asked questions about the cheese ration, the lack of beef in the meat ration, the sale of decayed fruit and vegetables by greengrocers, and the price of tea.[61] When she asked the Conservative minister of food, Derick Heathcoat-Amory, about the latter in 1955, he implied that she had poor housekeeping skills. 'I have had reason before now to doubt whether the

Hon. Lady is as skilled in buying food as she has indicated,' he goaded, 'I do not think she finds the best markets.'[62]

When Labour was still in power, it was often Edith Summerskill who had to answer such questions in her role as parliamentary secretary to the Ministry of Food. Jean Mann believed that Summerskill's 'prowess under fire at question time' was proof that as a woman MP you had to be better than a man.[63] Her exposure to the difficulties of government at the Ministry amounted to, in Summerskill's words, 'a form of political immunisation against attack', which 'would last as long as my parliamentary life'.[64] When bread was rationed, Summerskill said that 'The jeers and the counter-jeers drowned my voice time after time'.[65] During a debate in 1947, Barbara Gould requested an increase in the sugar and bacon ration, Barbara Castle expressed concern about the potato ration's impact on vitamin intake, and Alice Bacon criticized the rationing of bread and the reduction of the bacon ration. As historian Pamela Brookes has pointed out, 'the index of Hansard under her [Summerskill's] name might be mistaken for that of Mrs Beeton's cookery book'.[66]

In her job Summerskill toured shops to study queues, received deputations from housewives, and gave speeches urging the population to be resourceful. In 1949, she famously addressed the Oxford University Club to argue that you couldn't tell the difference between butter and margarine. But perhaps Summerskill's greatest challenge was to pitch to the British population an unappetising tinned fish from South Africa – snoek – which was imported from 1948 as a solution to food shortages and malnutrition. Summerskill jovially invited the women MPs to visit the ministry buildings to taste the delicacy. Like most British housewives, the MPs were unimpressed. Jean Mann expressed her dissatisfaction freely: 'it tasted to me like the Dead Sea, then dragged thro' the Red Sea to lend it a false colour'.[67] Despite a mass advertising campaign to persuade housewives that it was a delicious alternative to herring and salmon, snoek was a catastrophic flop. Jean Mann snapped at Summerskill in the Chamber: 'Is the hon. Lady aware that as far as snoek is concerned the rest of Scotland could not care less?'[68] In the end, tonnes of snoek were left uneaten and sold as fish bait and cat food.

Another political issue for Labour was the rationing of clothes, which stayed in place until March 1949. When Christian Dior sparked a trend for long skirts, the new Labour MP Mabel Ridealgh urged Harold Wilson at the Board of Trade to take a stand against the fashion. Herbert Morrison also joined in: 'the longer you have your skirts, the fewer there'll be of them,' he warned. Meanwhile, Bessie Braddock emphasized the challenges faced by larger women under clothes rationing, demanding that they should be eligible for more coupons. Braddock and Leah Manning, both of whom were on the large side, were good friends with a habit of going everywhere together, arm-in-arm. Asked by another MP 'What do you think you are – a couple of tanks?' Braddock replied, 'We are much more dangerous than tanks. Our point of view is that the workers should be able to obtain the fruits of their labour, and that is a more dangerous argument than the tank could ever be.' They even attracted the derogatory label of the 'United Dairies', owing to their 'ample bosoms'.[69] Yet Braddock ignored such abuse and embraced her size. She also sought to encourage other women to feel comfortable in their bodies, even posing as a mannequin at one point. When the Conservative MP and clothing manufacturer Sir William Darling was making a speech on clothing purchase tax and defending the current sizing system, Leah Manning bounded into the Lady Members' Room and persuaded Braddock to come along for a jaunt. When they peered through to the chamber, Sir William was commenting that 'he liked a woman who went in like this and came out like that', articulated by hand gestures. While he drew his hourglass figure in the air, Braddock and Manning strode down the chamber, 'very erect and very sedate', before bowing to the speaker together.[70] Sir William, stunned at their parade, stopped speaking and joined in the roar of laughter that erupted from the House.

To compound growing anger regarding shortages of food and clothing, the winter of 1946 to 1947 – the winter in which Ellen Wilkinson died – was the hardest of a century. In January, snow made coal reserves inaccessible and production ground to a halt. Power stations closed and street lights went out. Restrictions on domestic power and fuel increased. Although the situation started to improve in 1947 when Britain became a beneficiary of American Marshall Aid, which Ernest Bevin described as a 'lifeline to sinking men', there was a growing bitterness about the relentlessness of austerity – a fact that the women in Parliament seem to have understood better than the men.

The 1951 election was fought on rationing, shortages, and the cost of living. While Labour issued warnings of 'sixpenny eggs' if price controls were abandoned, the Conservatives made a strategic bid towards disillusioned middle-class housewives, promising to 'set the people free' from controls. In a *Daily Mail* cartoon depicting queues of housewives, Labour's slogan 'Ask your Dad!' (referring to 'the hungry years' of the

1930s under the Tories) was countered with 'Ask their Mums!' by the Tories. This focus on housewives became a trope in Conservative propaganda: one of their pamphlets alleged that Labour 'forgot to ask about Mum'.[71] The party regularly published a short magazine, *Home Truths*, targeted at housewives featuring the character Winnie Welcome, who agonized over what to cook her husband for dinner.[72] This campaign created a powerful narrative aligning post-war scarcity with socialism, compared with future abundance under Conservative rule. The strategy worked: the Tories won the election and their women's vote share shot up.

But the abandonment of controls and rationing did not make things significantly easier for housewives, particularly those of the working class. Under rationing, working-class calorie consumption fell only slightly and protein intake increased during the 1940s. Meanwhile, middle-class calorie consumption and protein intake had reduced significantly from previously high levels.[73] Shortages could not be magicked away and, without price controls, the cost of living increased. Wilkinson had warned of the dangers of dropping controls 'like hot bricks' in her 1945 conference address: 'The housewife of to-day hardly realises the extent to which the controls have kept down the prices of the necessities of life. Let me warn her that she will know it the moment any of these controls are taken off.'[74]

At midnight on 4 July 1954, rationing on meat and bacon was lifted, marking the end of fourteen years of controls for housewives across the country. It was a moment of joy and relief, signifying that the days of the war were firmly in the past. Much of the impetus behind de-rationing came from the Conservative Party's astute acknowledgement of the difficulties housewives faced as maintainers of the home. What was more, women MPs were crucial in bringing those difficulties and concerns to the fore in Parliament. When Conservative MP Patricia Ford's question about the end of rationing elicited a specific date from the minister of food, she expressed her gratitude and declared that it would 'give great pleasure to the housewives of Great Britain and Northern Ireland'.[75] The London Housewives' Association held a ceremony to celebrate in Trafalgar Square on Derationing Day, and ration books all over the country were cast onto bonfires in a moment of jubilation.

However, the 1950s were not all milk and honey for housewives: in 1955, chancellor Butler announced his 'pots and pans' budget, which aimed to curb inflation by raising purchase tax (known today as VAT) to 30 per cent on basic household items. This provoked opposition from women MPs from both sides of the House. Among the Labour women,

Jean Mann compared the budget with the time 'when the Chancellor went a'wooing and when the women of this country accepted his luscious promises about doubling the standard of living'.[76] She requested that Butler should exclude baths, washtubs and washboards from the increase in purchase tax, on grounds that they were mostly bought by the very poorest who could not afford bathrooms and washing machines. Meanwhile, Eirene White and Freda Corbet asked for pot scourers, pastry boards, rolling pins and coal sieves to be exempt. Butler refused all the requests. Bessie Braddock raged against Butler: 'I should like to be told how pot scourers can interfere with inflation. If anyone can tell me how rolling pins, bread boards, pots and pans can affect such a situation, I should be interested.'[77] Among the Conservative women, Ward called the budget 'barren and abominable', and again emphasized the repercussions it would have for those on fixed incomes.[78]

Defending the vulnerable: the beginnings of social reform

It was not just housewives that women MPs sought to defend in this period: they made impassioned individual lobbying efforts to help a range of vulnerable women.

From 1952, Summerskill tried to get a bill through the House requiring husbands who had deserted their wives to pay them maintenance. Under the current system, when husbands defaulted on their debt and fell into arrears with maintenance payments to deserted wives, they could choose to go to prison instead of paying. When this happened, the deserted wives and their family were forced to rely on the meagre provisions of the National Assistance Board. Summerskill's bill set out to make it possible for deserted wives to have arrears of maintenance deducted from their husband's income. It also divided housekeeping funds equally between husband and wife and asserted the wife's right to certain goods or furniture. However, facing huge opposition from lawyer MPs, her bill was talked out. In 1957, Conservative MP Joan Vickers took up Summerskill's cause and put forward her Maintenance Orders (Attachment of Income) Bill, which similarly made it possible for maintenance payments to be taken directly from a man's earnings. The second reading of the bill was carried without a division, but at standing committee Vickers met the same opposition that Summerskill had earlier in the decade. This time, the lawyer MPs boycotted the standing committee so that it had to be adjourned due to lack of quorum. Vickers was forced to withdraw the bill. Nevertheless, the fact that the issue had persisted and was now advocated by a Conservative meant that the government was more sympathetic. In late 1957, the government put forward their own Maintenance Orders Bill, which they allowed Vickers to pilot through the House.

In 1951, Barbara Castle helped protect sex workers from abuse and abduction by forwarding her Criminal Law Amendment Bill. When it passed the third reading and passed into law, the Association of Moral and Social Hygiene sent her a letter of congratulation, writing that 'you have done what we have attempted to do for 50 years', and giving a lunch in her honour. Eight years later, women MPs worked as a group to protect the welfare of sex workers, in recognition that often it was the poorest and most unfortunate who were forced into the trade. In 1959 Rab Butler had introduced a Street Offences Act which made it illegal for a 'common prostitute' to loiter or solicit in public, with increases in penalties. Although some women MPs such as Jean Mann supported the act, most – including Braddock, Lloyd George, Summerskill, Jeger and Lee – opposed it, on grounds that it merely 'swept the crumbs under the carpet'.[79] It was a source of particular concern that the bill criminalized women sex workers without referring at all to the male clients who bought their services. As Lena Jeger passionately argued, 'I consider that this House, and society in general, has no right to condemn a woman without also condemning those who pay her.'[80] Jeger also objected to the degrading use of the antiquated term 'common prostitute' in the legislation.[81] In a lighter moment of the debate, she relayed a story in which her colleague, Patricia Hornsby-Smith (then joint under-secretary of state for the Home Office) was mistaken at a bus stop as being a sex worker by a woman who was herself a sex worker. 'If one prostitute can mistake the hon. Lady for a prostitute, how can any young police officer be expected to know the difference?' she asked the House.[82]

*

Forty years on from the first woman taking her seat in Parliament, by 1959 seventy-four women had taken their seats and twenty-five women were currently sitting in Parliament. Major progress had been achieved for women's rights, including the achievement of equal compensation for injury, equal nationality and family allowances, as well as developments towards equal pay. But women were still very far from achieving equal representation in Parliament, with women MPs making up just 3.9 per cent of the Commons. Despite their achievements, this was no time to over-indulge in reflection and congratulation; it was time to act on the words of Wilkinson and 'face the future'. With second-wave feminism and 'women's lib' on the horizon, the cosy nostalgia of the 1950s was dissolving into a kaleidoscope of social reform and the breaking down of boundaries that encapsulated the swinging sixties.

4

Stilettos and Springboards: 1959–70

Would any man have worked as hard for family allowances as Eleanor Rathbone, for clean milk as Edith Summershill, for equal pay as Barbara Castle? Perhaps not.

LENA JEGER, c. 1970[1]

From 1959 to 1964, the Conservative government clung onto power by its fingernails as the old order slowly crumbled under the weight of a new progressive era. The tremors of the Suez Crisis, the scandal of the Profumo affair and the premiership of the aristocratic Sir Alec Douglas-Home in 1963 gave an impression of a rigid, old-fashioned establishment, at odds with the increasingly open-minded, counter-cultural and cosmopolitan zeitgeist of the sixties. By 1964, a general election had ushered in a brand-new Labour government led by Harold Wilson – a grammar-school educated Yorkshire MP who had made it to Oxford and became symbolic of a new, meritocratic social order. Simultaneously, the total number of women MPs rose from twenty-five to twenty-nine (eighteen Labour; eleven Conservative). Although 1964 brought about a symbolic sea-change in political and cultural direction by seeing an end to thirteen years of Conservative governance, numerically the Wilson government was skating on thin ice, with a fragile majority of just four seats. In 1966, when Wilson took the country to the polls to bolster his majority (successfully, with ninety-two more seats won), the total number of women MPs fell to twenty-six. It hovered around this figure right up until the 1990s, before being turbocharged in 1997 by the advent of all-women shortlists in the Labour Party.

During this period, several women of importance were elected for the first time. In 1959, Margaret Thatcher, who within twenty years would go on to become Britain's first woman prime minister, was elected as Conservative MP for Finchley. In 1967, Winnie Ewing became the first woman to be elected as a Scottish National Party (SNP) MP in an electoral watershed moment for the party. Twenty years later, she was elected president of the SNP and had become known as 'Madame Ecosse' for her fierce advocacy of Scottish interests and European cooperation. Later, Ewing would also go on to become a mentor to, and political heroine of, SNP first minister Nicola Sturgeon. There were other notable figures in the 1964 intake: 33-year-old Shirley Summerskill, the new Labour MP, joined her mother Edith, who had recently been made a life peer in the House of Lords when she stood down from the Commons in 1961. Edith and Shirley Summerskill are the only mother and daughter to have both served as MPs. Throughout Edith Summerskill's career in the House of Commons, she used to write to her daughter, giving commentary about her parliamentary activities as well as pieces of life advice. Shirley Summerskill recalled to me that her mother would write to her every other day when she was at Oxford University, letters mostly composed while she was sitting late in the Commons. The letters were later published in *Letters to my Daughter*. Edith was clearly a role model for Shirley, and she followed in her mother's footsteps by becoming both a GP and an MP. Shirley Summerskill entered Parliament with her contemporary from St Paul's Girls' School, Shirley Williams. Williams was the daughter of the author Vera Brittain, and later went on to forge an impressive parliamentary career as secretary of state for education before becoming one of the 'Gang of Four' forming the breakaway Social Democrat Party (SDP) in 1981. In her autobiography, Williams recalls being introduced to Nancy Astor as a teenager by her father. When he declared that Shirley wanted to become an MP, Astor responded brusquely, 'Not with that hair!'[2] Yet here she was, hair and all, making history and making her mark on Parliament in ways of which Astor simply couldn't have imagined back in 1919.

Building Barbara's Castle

In 1962, *The Times* commented that there had only been seventy-six women MPs in forty-three years, and it was 'still a man's world for women politicians ... On any view, the women politicians have all the big cards stacked against them when they take the high road to Westminster and so it will continue.'[3] The wife of the speaker, Lady Hylton-Foster, expressed her thoughts on women becoming MPs in the *Sunday Express* in 1960: 'I cannot think why they do it. I just do not understand them. Women do not have enough education to become politicians.'[4]

The undermining of the intelligence of women went hand-in-hand with their over-sexualization and objectification. When walking through the division lobby to vote, Shirley Williams would often find herself being pinched on the bottom by male MPs. When she relayed such experiences to other women MPs, they said it happened to them all the time. Like a 'coven of witches', they plotted a plan of revenge: when walking through the division lobbies, they would be sure to wear stiletto heels, so that they could dig them into the foot of any male MP who made untoward advances.[5] When one of the culprits hobbled into the tearoom later that day, several stiletto-clad women gathered around him, fussing and feigning concern. He pretended it was gout. Shirley Summerskill recounted to me a story of walking along an empty corridor when she bumped into a fellow MP who spoke to her and then stroked her hair. When she asked him not to do so, he said it was only a gesture of friendship. 'Do you stroke Harold Wilson's hair?' she replied. When I asked whether she had ever told anyone, she said she could hardly have reported it to the whip's office, as the culprit was the chief whip Bob Mellish.[6]

The lack of 'symbolic' space available to women MPs continued to be matched by a lack of physical space within the Palace of Westminster. As the number of women increased, the overcrowded confusion that infused the Lady Members' Room worsened to the extent that it gained the attention of some male MPs. In a debate on Commons accommodation, Conservative MP Robert Cooke informed the House that he had peeked into the room recently, to find himself 'horrified at its state':

> It was not their fault. They have a room which was meant originally for rest and relaxation, but the whole space is smothered with books and papers, and telephone cubicles open straight off the room. They are not allowed to have any of the refreshment facilities of the House brought to them. If they want a cup of tea there is some impediment which prevents it being taken there. I think that could be remedied almost overnight.[7]

Cooke suggested that the Lady Members' Room should be moved away from the Terrace level, so that larger accommodation could be provided on the Chamber level. It was not received with great enthusiasm by the House. However, the women's facilities were improved somewhat thanks to a determined campaign by Barbara Castle. While male MPs had an easily accessible lavatory in the corridor behind the Speaker's chair, the nearest Ladies' toilet was a long walk away. As Castle had recently become a member of the shadow cabinet and had to spend long hours on the frontbench, she became particularly aware of the problem and campaigned to resolve it. However, the parliamentary authorities insisted that building a closer Ladies' lavatory was impossible, due to the plumbing. Eventually, Castle's persistence culminated in the installation of a new retiring room for Lady Members in 1961. She was very proud when it acquired the name 'Barbara's Castle'.

As shadow minister of works, Castle was in a prime position to combat overcrowding and expand facilities for MPs, especially women. Parliament was, in Castle's words, 'a relic of the days when government was run by wealthy amateurs', with no desks or offices, and storage limited to narrow lockers lining the corridors.[8] She hounded the minister of works on the matter: how many desks were there in the Palace for the exclusive use of MPs and their secretaries? Would it be possible to avoid 'perch[ing] like a bird of passage to do a bit of writing?'[9] She demanded improvements in the library as well as more telephones and copying machines in convenient places (in short, the same resources that would be available to any businessman). 'This palace is not a club,' she pre-emptively rebutted, 'in which we want to install a few more armchairs in which we can have a comfortable snooze. This Palace is a very important workshop, and in approaching the question of accommodation we ask for the elbow room, equipment and tools to do the job of work that a modern Member of Parliament ought to do.'[10] Castle also lobbied for what became known as 'Centradict' - a system of centralized dictation whereby any MP could dictate a letter by going to any intercom phone. The idea was that it would increase flexibility for those MPs who couldn't afford secretaries and facilitate a 'continuous flow of efficient office output for a very little expense'.[11] In 1961, a Centradict machine was installed in Parliament.

From 1959 to 1964, the progress in terms of ministerial appointments of women MPs slowed. While Conservative MP Mervyn Pike became assistant postmaster-general, two other junior ministers - Edith Pitt and Patricia Hornsby-Smith - were just shuffled around. This provoked Irene Ward to write a letter to the *Telegraph* protesting against

Macmillan's 'unimaginative decision to appoint women in his Government merely to do the chores of administration'.[12] Later when Labour was in power, Edward Heath, Conservative leader from 1965 to 1975, chose Mervyn Pike as his 'statutory woman' in the shadow cabinet because the other option was Margaret Thatcher, to whom he objected because 'we'll never be able to get rid of her'.[13] Little did he know that, without his help, Thatcher would rise through the Commons and the party to usurp him as leader in 1975.

Within the Labour Party there was a tendency to play women MPs off against one another when deciding ministerial appointments. In the 1960 Parliament, the talented Barbara Castle was disappointed not to have made it to the shadow cabinet, though party leader Hugh Gaitskell did give her a frontbench job as shadow minister of works. Gaitskell disliked Castle, and he seems to have hidden behind other women in his reluctance to promote her on the frontbenches: 'Why should I annoy Alice Bacon for the sake of Barbara?', he once objected to Harold Wilson.[14]

In 1961, Patricia Hornsby-Smith resigned her post as under secretary to the minister of pensions (though retaining her seat in Parliament) to become a director of a large industrial company, leaving Margaret Thatcher to replace her. At thirty-four, Thatcher now became the youngest ever woman to join the frontbench. A year previously, she had impressed the House by taking 'two bites at a cherry' with her maiden speech also introducing her first private member's bill.[15] Her Public Bodies (Admission to Meetings) Act was the first private member's bill to be sponsored by a woman in both Houses – by Thatcher in the Commons and Baroness Eliot in the Lords – and reached the statute book within the year. Thatcher's maiden speech on the bill was heralded as 'outstanding', having been delivered without the assistance of notes, 'with very considerable clarity and charm, and ... introducing a piece of by no means unimportant legislation in a manner that would do credit to the Front Benches on either side of the Chamber'.[16]

Meanwhile, Conservative leader Edward Heath remained blinkered and quietly hostile to women in Parliament. In 1966, he was asked whether he wanted more women in politics. 'Yes, I would,' he responded with resignation, 'so long as they are providing what women can and not just duplicating what men can do, which probably would lead to them not making a women's contribution anyway.'[17] Such notions were still commonplace: the assumption was that women couldn't possibly emulate the performance of a man in normal political affairs, and that they could only hope to have an impact and role within the sphere of 'women's issues'. Such attitudes gradually faded as the number of women MPs increased, and their varied interests became apparent. By 1972, Jeger was able to note that women MPs could now 'acceptably take a more unisex attitude' – 'partly because of the persistence of the early nagging females who first brought the problems of their sisters, as well as their constituents, into Parliament.'[18]

This increasingly 'unisex' attitude didn't prevent women MPs from continuing to take a keen interest in domestic social reform. From 1964 with Wilson in power, legislation for social reform tumbled through the division lobbies, with the abolition of the death penalty in 1965, and the legalization of abortion and the decriminalization of homosexuality in 1967. Women MPs played a key role in lobbying on these issues. Conservative women Evelyn Emmet and Margaret Thatcher voted against their party to implement the Wolfenden Report's proposals to decriminalize homosexuality, alongside their Labour sisters Alice Bacon, Barbara Castle, Harriet Slater, Edith Summerskill and Eirene White. In addition, Alice Bacon, who was minister of state at the Home Office, was an early proponent of abolishing the death penalty – another key social-liberal reform in the 1960s.

Meanwhile, Labour MPs Lena Jeger and Renée Short raised awareness about the dangers of backstreet abortions and campaigned for abortion reform. Lena Jeger, like her late husband whose seat she now occupied, was profoundly concerned about the damage that illegal abortions could inflict upon vulnerable women. She first became involved in the campaign during the 1950s, when she encouraged the Abortion Law Reform Association (ALRA) to embark upon a parliamentary strategy. She also liaised with barristers defending doctors who had performed abortions and lobbied the home secretary, Rab Butler, on the matter.[19] After she temporarily lost her seat in 1959, Jeger published a series of influential articles on abortion for the *Woman's Sunday Mirror*.[20] In 1964, she returned to Parliament and when David Steel forwarded his eventually successful Abortion Bill in 1967, she sat on its standing committee. Renée Short also prodded the government towards abortion reform. In February 1966, Short asked the home office minister and Leeds MP, Alice Bacon, in the Chamber how many prosecutions and convictions there had been for illegal abortion over the last five years. Bacon responded that from 1960 to 1964, 296 people had been convicted for provision of illegal abortions.[21] While Bacon was never explicit about her support for abortion reform, she was on the Abortion Law Reform Association (ALRA)'s list of MPs 'known or believed to be in support of abortion law reform'.[22] However, it should be noted that women MPs were not as vocal on abortion reform as they were on campaigns for equal pay or sex discrimination, possibly because abortion was such a contentious issue that they could not risk their already-precarious parliamentary positions on the issue. In fact, David Steel's Abortion Act is arguably the only piece of feminist legislation not to have been forwarded by a woman. Yet once the act had been passed, Short described it as 'the greatest step in the emancipation of women that the Government took'. Within just six years, the number of women who died from having an abortion was reduced by half.[23]

Alongside transformative waves of legislation came shifts in attitudes towards women's status within Parliament. In stark contrast with Heath, prime minister Wilson demonstrated an enthusiasm to promote women to office and the 'barriers to ministerial promotion' came 'tumbling down in the sixties'.[24] To Barbara Castle, Wilson came across as 'an instinctive feminist' and someone who 'rejoiced in their success and was always trying to promote them to new opportunities'.[25] Leah Manning opined that he had 'given more chances to women to prove their ability than any other prime minister in history'.[26] From 1964, Peggy Herbison, Alice Bacon and Barbara Castle became ministers, with Castle promoted to cabinet rank. In 1966 Judith Hart and Eirene White also reached ministerial rank. Women were gaining confidence in the Chamber: in 1961 Irene Ward became the first woman to ask a prime minister's question, and in 1968 she was even kicked out of the Chamber. In protest against the government's control of the order of business in the Commons, she had stood in front of the mace (a silver ornamental club representing royal authority, without which the House cannot meet or make laws) and refused to move, preventing a vote from being announced. When the sergeant forcibly moved her, she shouted at him 'Parliament no longer exists. It has become a dictatorship.' She also famously threatened to 'poke' Harold Wilson when he evaded her parliamentary question: 'I will poke the prime minister,' she warned. 'I will poke him until I get a response.'[27]

Being appointed to the cabinet in 1964 marked the beginning of a long and productive ministerial career for Barbara Castle. She was 'overjoyed' to have been made minister for overseas development, a policy area for which she had a keen interest. She had grown hopeful of some kind of position when, at an election evening rally, Wilson asked her when she would be back in London. By the end of the day after the election, she still hadn't heard from Wilson. Disgruntled and despondent, Castle sought refuge in her cottage in Buckinghamshire. At 9am the next morning, her lie-in was abruptly interrupted as the phone rang. It was the prime minister's secretary, informing her that Wilson would like to see her. Churlishly, she replied 'Does he? Why?' It was decided that they would meet for lunch and in the meantime she spent her morning agonising over what to wear. A few hours later, she emerged from the steps of Number Ten, a huge smile beaming from underneath her straw hat. She had not only been appointed minister for overseas development but had secured a seat in the cabinet (a novelty for the post). It had been worth the wait.

This was just the beginning of the challenge that lay ahead for Castle, as a woman pushing the boundaries of political possibility. As the minister for the smallest and newest department in the cabinet, let alone as a woman on the left of the party, she found it difficult to gain the respect of figures such as George Brown and Roy Jenkins. Perched at the end of the cabinet table, she was distant from the epicentre of power around Wilson (Roy Jenkins, George Brown, Richard Crossman among others). Even Wilson, who was fond of her, referred to her condescendingly as his 'little minister'.

When the cabinet photo was taken, Wilson insisted that Castle was seated in the middle (unlike Ellen Wilkinson in 1945, who had been perched on the edge of Attlee's cabinet photo). A cynic could describe this as 'window-dressing', but nevertheless women were now visible in government.

A tiger in my tank

Back in the 1930s, Labour MP Susan Lawrence, who was by no means prone to overstatement, had her eye caught by a young, fervent and engaging Barbara Betts making one of her first speeches. At its conclusion, Lawrence informed the audience, 'You have just listened to one of the future leaders of the Labour Party.'[28]

Lawrence's intuition proved to be right in the steady and inexorable rise of Barbara (now Castle), from her ebullient 'Jam tomorrow' speech at the 1943 party conference, to her position as secretary of state. At the height of her success, she was regarded by many as the most likely

PLATE 1 The first two women MPs to take their seats, Nancy Astor and Margaret Wintringham.

PLATE 2 The first Labour women MPs assemble on the terrace in 1929 for a photograph to mark the first election following the introduction of equal suffrage in 1928.

PLATE 3 Labour MP Margaret Bondfield, the first woman to enter the cabinet, c.1930.

PLATE 4 Conservative women MPs on the terrace in November 1931.

PLATE 5 Labour MP Ellen Willkinson making a speech during her iconic leadership of the Jarrow Crusade in 1936.

PLATE 6 A portrait of Eleanor Rathbone, Independent MP and champion of family allowances.

PLATE 7 The new intake of Labour women after the Labour landslide of 1945.

PLATE 8 Women MPs celebrating Megan Lloyd George's 20th anniversary in
Parliament, 31 May 1949.

PLATE 9 Conservative MP Irene Ward joins Labour's Barbara Castle and Edith Summerskill on Equal Pay Day, 8 March 1954.

PLATE 10 Barbara Castle, Edith Summerskill and Alice Bacon striding along Scarborough's seafront just before the opening of the Labour Party conference, 1954.

PLATE 11 Key Labour MPs joining hands to sing the Red Flag on the platform of the Labour Party conference in Scarborough, October 1967.

PLATE 12 Labour MP and secretary of state for employment and productivity, Barbara Castle (fourth from right) having tea with the Ford machinists to negotiate an equal pay settlement in 1968.

PLATE 14 Margaret Thatcher in 1977, two years after having been elected as the first woman leader of the Conservative Party, and two years before making history as the first woman prime minister.

PLATE 13 Barbara Castle, a few months before the 1964 general election.

PLATE 15 Shirley Williams at a press conference in March 1981 to launch the Social Democratic Party (SDP).

PLATE 16 Labour's Harriet Harman found herself fighting the Peckham by-election campaign in 1982.

candidate to become the first woman prime minister, and today many regret that she was not.

Like Ellen Wilkinson before her, Barbara Castle understood the power of publicity, fashion-sense and the cult of celebrity in politics. 'Plums don't fall in plain girls' laps,' she used to say. Castle disregarded the convention that redheads should wear quiet colours and wore large ostentatious accessories with attention-seeking hats. She made her twice-weekly visit to the hairdressers with religious dedication and would send her secretaries all over London to pick up clothes from dressmakers and drycleaners, or to buy her cigarettes or a new lipstick. Unlike many of the Labour women before her, she embraced her role as a housewife: in the 1945 election she posed for photographers curled up in an armchair, darning one of her husband Ted's socks. When in cabinet, she complained that her stockings were becoming laddered from her chair at the table, so she requested that it should have a special cover placed on it.

If Castle wasn't short on style, neither was she short on substance. She put in the hours and did her homework: unlike Roy Jenkins who prided himself on ten-hour days with long lunchbreaks, Castle 'would beaver away for hours amassing and digesting facts and statistics'. She always woke up early, with a quick breakfast of yoghurt and fruit, ate her lunch at her desk and finished late.[29] Jenkins, somewhat bitterly, regaled that Castle 'made a political virility test (if that is the right phrase) out of being continually on the brink of exhaustion'.[30] In her diary she described a particular mammoth of a day, when she attended an NEC meeting, prepared for a session on the Transport Bill, prepared for and answered questions in the Commons, sat in on the Transport Bill committee, gave three television interviews, and topped it all off with an all-night sitting of the Transport Bill committee. Admittedly, she fell asleep during a cabinet meeting the next day.

Where her style and substance collided, the result was a housewife-superstar aesthetic later emulated by Margaret Thatcher. Castle even posed for a picture for a Top of the Pops piece in the *Mirror*, mounted on a pony and wearing tight-fitting pedal-pushers. Wilson commented to her that it was the sexiest thing he had seen in years and that he had stuck a cut-out of it on his shaving mirror. Comparisons flew around between Castle and Marilyn Monroe or Zsa Zsa Gabor. In an interview for *John Bull*, the scene was set by the image of her padding around in her pink mules, with her long cigarette holder poised in her well-manicured hands.

Although Castle's sex appeal was an asset in terms of publicity, it also exposed her to objectification and condescension. First, she had to weather out several sexual advances from male colleagues. In the Commons, Tories would pass her lewd notes. Even among the cabinet, many men had made passes at her, including 'an enormous pass from Bevan', 'occasional overtures from Hugh Dalton' and 'a rather fumbling kiss from Wilson'. Second, her close working relationship with Wilson attracted speculation, it being suggested that they may have had an affair. It was allegedly impossible for a woman to hold the political influence that Castle did with the prime minister, without sex being involved. As Crossman suggestively put it, 'She got under his [Wilson's] skin in a quite extraordinary way.'[31] This seemed to generate considerable political jealousy within the cabinet, which was perhaps the source of the rumours: Wilson recalled one minister as saying to him, 'She only has to waggle that bottom of hers and she gets it all her own way.' But as Castle herself accounted for it: 'He liked a little flirtation, but it was verbal rather than physical.'[32]

Underneath this femininity lay the 'tiger' and 'fiery redhead' she became renowned as. Interestingly, in interviews, Castle emphasized that she was surprised when people thought of her as angry or 'tigress-like'; she suspected that it was an over-compensation resulting from the terrible nerves she experienced in public speaking. More generally, she was the frequent victim of what would today be called 'impostor syndrome'. In October 1971 she wrote in her diary: 'I really ought to be able to do it on my head, but as always self-doubts are creeping in . . . just because I can't rattle off effectively disguised platitudes like the chaps can . . . go to bed muttering to myself: "I know I am a second class mind trying to do first class things. It's agony but I believe it is better than to be a first class mind doing second class things."'

This subtle combination of steely determination and self-conscious vulnerability ensured Castle was a major source of attraction for the press. And she knew it: she mastered the art of publicity and became a perfectionist to the extreme about her public image. She ensured that press stories were constantly streaming throughout the week, and when her staff made mistakes with timing, angry memos would land on their desks.

Her rise through the cabinet started to gather momentum when she became Wilson's 'tiger' at the Department of Transport in late 1965. When Wilson suggested the role to her, Castle was reluctant to leave her beloved

Department of Overseas Development, but slowly she came to be optimistic about the potential of transport to revolutionize a whole set of socio-economic issues. Wilson recognized Castle's unique potential to take the role to a new level: 'I must have a tiger in my transport policy and you are the only tiger we've got.'[33] He was referring to the 1960s petrol advert slogan – 'Put a Tiger in your Tank' – which gained iconic status as car ownership swelled in the sixties. It was clear that Wilson wanted Castle to have a central role in his vision of social progress forged in the 'white heat of the technological revolution'.

After Wilson's offer, Castle returned home, sullen and unconvinced, until she thought of an excuse: she couldn't drive.[34] The next morning she bounced into Number Ten, saying '"prime minister, of course I want to help you, but you don't realise–" he interrupted me. "I know", he said. "You don't drive," adding with a twinkle, "I think that is a good thing. We cannot have ministers of transport knocking down people on pedestrian crossings."'[35] Eventually, just before Christmas, Castle acquiesced and accepted the job. Among her Christmas cards, letters of congratulation flooded into her postbags. One woman wrote a note to her saying it was 'the most heartening of messages since our struggling suffrage days'.[36]

Yet predictably, the press was flooded with commentary to the effect that 'her inability to drive a vehicle was of more importance than her manifest ability to drive a ministry'.[37] Once, a BBC interviewer tackled Castle explicitly on the issue of whether she was up to the job – 'You're only a woman, you don't drive, what do you know about it?'[38] Yet at the same time, there was a kind of fascination with Castle in her new role. On her first day in the department, she was trailed by paparazzi. She relished the attention, calling in the press while she presented her ideas, sporting a scarlet dress with eye-catching gold jewellery.

When Castle took her transport portfolio, nearly 8,000 people were dying a year on the roads, with hundreds of thousands injured. Her mission, in response to the surge in car ownership, was to make the roads safe and to integrate road use with public transport services. She exceeded expectations with her revolutionary Road Safety Bill of 1967, which made the 70mph speed limit permanent and institutionalized the breathalyser for police use. Previously, police had relied on the inaccurate method of asking drivers to walk steadily down a white line to determine whether they were too drunk to drive. Now, breathalysers provided a simple and effective deterrent with an 80mg blood alcohol limit per 100ml of blood. She put her stamp on the bill in two respects: she insisted on the abandonment of random breathalyser tests (which she thought would alienate road users); and she demanded that the penalty for drink-driving should be increased from a fine to a ban on driving for twelve months. The latter 'brought a tonne of bricks' on her head, but she weathered the opposition with characteristic determination.[39] She also managed to pass legislation requiring all new cars to be fitted with seatbelts and campaigned for it to be compulsory for all passengers to wear them – an idea which was ahead of her time and only became a reality in 1983.

The reception to Castle's transport reforms was mixed, but it often parted along gendered lines. She received reams of angry letters from male pub-goers and drivers defending their right to freedom from 'Barbara's snoopers'. One anonymous letter, signed off by '3 Regulars', read 'You've ballsed our darts matches u, so get out you wicked old B'.[40] She even received a death threat, of sufficient concern for Scotland Yard to arm her with a bodyguard overnight. But simultaneously she received letters from grateful wives, who thought her policy would reduce drink-driving and casualties. One such letter declared that 'No-one but a determined woman – a single-minded woman – could have done it.'[41] The reception was less warm from quarters of the Commons, and Castle was often treated with condescension: notably, and despite her vigorous knowledge and preparation, Conservative MP Peter Thorneycraft alleged that Castle didn't understand her own bill.[42]

In the final analysis, the bill revolutionized road safety like nothing since. According to a speech in 1997 by Professor Brian Prichard, the Chairman of the Institution of Alcohol Studies, the act may have prevented over 62,000 people from being killed in road accidents over thirty years – roughly the number of people in an average MP's constituency.

By 1967, Castle was approaching her political prime and had demonstrated potential as a future leader. Her railways minister, John Morris, told her, 'I wouldn't be married to you for any money, but you will be prime minister one day if your health holds out.'[43] She was increasingly valuable in the cabinet, often serving as a left-wing sounding board for Callaghan and Jenkins. Meanwhile, Wilson utilized his closeness with Castle to out-manoeuvre the right of the cabinet. She was now at the centre of the political action and held her place within the cabinet as a politician in her own right: she had become much more than a 'statutory woman'. 'I always thought of myself as an MP, not as a woman MP,' she maintained.[44] The *Telegraph* proclaimed that 'she has smashed the sex barrier'; others described her as 'the only woman who met the men on their own terms'.[45] Such compliments made her particularly happy: she glowed coquettishly with a touch of the Monroe about her, 'Now I wouldn't feel the same pleasure if my husband or anyone else paid me a compliment about a new hat or suddenly said that I looked pretty'.[46]

Not another Maggie Bondfield!

By March 1968, industrial unrest had undermined the Labour government's credibility and it was reeling from three bad by-election defeats. During 1967, wage disputes had accounted for 2.7 million working days lost; by 1968 the total was 4.6 million. Senior cabinet member, MP and fellow left-winger Richard Crossman recommended to Wilson that he should undertake a major cabinet reshuffle. Both Crossman and Wilson were keen for Barbara Castle to take over trade union relations as minister of labour in the reshuffle. Castle was an attractive candidate for the role; she had a natural rapport with the left and good relations with the trade unions. Crossman informed Castle that Wilson was going to speak to her about it. But by the time she met with Wilson, Roy Jenkins had interfered, and Wilson had changed his mind. When Wilson suggested that she should instead become leader of the house (a significantly inferior role), Castle stormed out.

Late that night, as she was preparing for bed, she was summoned to Downing Street, and Wilson offered her minister of labour as well as leader of the house. Castle was still unconvinced, knowing full well that this was no promotion and that the position had historically been a poisoned chalice. In Wilson's memoirs, he recalled her concerns to avoid becoming 'Margaret Bondfield Mark II', who had become an 'ogre of the left' since 1931.[47] Wilson even resorted to asking her husband, Ted, to come in from the car and persuade her to accept. But Castle was categorical about the Bondfield issue. At this, Wilson proposed changing the name of the department. When Castle suggested the department of labour and productivity, Wilson jokingly warned 'that with a lady minister this might lead to bar-room ribaldry'.[48] By the end of the meeting, a stalemate had emerged.

Eventually, Castle accepted Wilson's offer of the somewhat grander sounding secretary of state for the Department of Employment and Productivity. It was an historic moment; as her colleague Harriet

Slater wrote to her, it was 'a great achievement for you and for women generally'.[49] In the press she was hailed as the most powerful woman in British history.

The big question now arose – could she make it all the way to the top and become prime minister? A congratulatory letter to Castle from a retired civil servant spinster read: 'Why not? You deserve it. What a wonderful day that could be, for women?'[50] Crossman, Castle's cabinet ally and friend, knew full well that as Wilson's political partner-in-crime, she was the most powerful person in the cabinet regardless of her ranking, and wrote: 'Already she's a natural number two and if she weren't a woman she would be a natural number one: she could quite conceivably be the first lady prime minister.'[51] In the end, the accolade of secretary of state was a pyrrhic victory, the consequences of which extinguished her chances of being prime minister.

The task she had been allocated was gargantuan: she had to reduce union disputes and build economic stability without undermining the trade union base of her own party and movement. In response to a letter from Leah Manning, Castle demonstrated the self-doubt which often motivated her and underlay her bulldozer-like attitude: 'I know I have let myself in for a job on which I am almost bound to fail but it is important to try and you know I always believe in having a bash!'[52] In her diary, she wrote: 'I am under no illusions that I may be committing political suicide. I have at least moved from the periphery of the whirlwind into its very heart.'[53] This was more than a metaphor; quite literally, she was now at the centre of the whirlwind of the cabinet, seated opposite Wilson and chancellor Roy Jenkins.

Castle's predecessor, Ray Gunter, described the position of minister of labour as a 'bed of nails'. When asked by the press how she would describe the role, Castle quickly replied, 'a springboard'.

In her role, she quickly and adeptly crafted a prices and incomes policy leading to a giant ninety-seven-clause Industrial Relations Bill. The sensible aim of the bill was to reduce unconstitutional strikes but simultaneously strengthen the unions' position as an advocate for workers' rights. Her preparation for the presentation of her bill was meticulous. She would record sections of her speech, listen back to them and make alterations in content or tone accordingly. Wilson declared it 'the most important speech ever made in Parliament by a woman'.[54]

Yet the reaction to her bill was overwhelmingly negative. 'No Smiles for Mrs Castle's Toothless Bill,' pronounced the *Daily Telegraph*.[55] She found herself straddled between three powerful blocks of resistance – from both the left and right wings of her own party, and from the Conservatives. The left of the party declaimed Castle's policy as a boost for employers. The right of the party, dominated by trade-union-sponsored MPs, saw it as an assault on the unions. The Conservatives snubbed it as a charter for the unions. Castle pointed out the absurdity of the situation in the Commons when presenting the paper: 'According to some of my Hon. Friends' – in other words, the trade-union-sponsored MPs – 'I am not the first woman in history to offer a poisoned package to those whom I would seduce. To the Opposition, on the other hand, I am not a temptress offering a poisoned chalice, but a capitulator waving a white flag.'[56] It was opposition from her own party that proved most destructive. She was gradually drifting from her friends on the left (Judith Hart, Ian Mikardo and Michael Foot in particular) who opposed the bill. Ian Mikardo put it to her: 'You are a marvellous woman and we love you dearly, but even you can't make us think a cesspool smells like roses.'[57] Embittered, Castle rebuked her once-close left-wing friend Michael Foot for having 'grown fat on a diet of soft options because he had never had to choose'. The demands of government entailed the politics of priorities, and untrammelled trade union freedom was incompatible with those priorities. The trade-union-rooted right wing of the party were even more critical: the Trades Union Congress (TUC) denounced the bill, as did most of the trade-union-sponsored MPs including James Callaghan and Douglas Houghton. Vic Feather, general secretary of the TUC and Castle's main opponent in negotiations, dismissed her policy as contrary to the interests of working people: 'This is no revolutionary bill,' he declared. Feather had been a protégé of Barbara's father, Frank Betts, who had asked Feather to write for his local socialist journal, the *Bradford Pioneer*. Now, he sought to undermine Barbara and used his personal links with her father to undermine her publicly: he said of her to Bernard Ingham, 'I knew that girl when she had dirty knickers'. Behind the scenes, Callaghan and Houghton – both of whom held influential positions as chancellor and chairman of the Labour Party respectively – machinated with Vic Feather to quash Castle's bill.

The opposition to Castle's bill expressed itself in the form of vicious personal attacks, nearly all of which were gendered. It drove Castle to the point of resignation on several occasions, but she reminded herself that it would only strengthen the Callaghan wing of the cabinet. Ray Gunter, whom Castle had usurped at the Ministry of Labour, was incandescent that he had been replaced – not only by a left-winger but a woman. Spitefully, he referred to her as 'leather knickers'. People made snide comments about the time and effort she invested in her appearance: some male cabinet members complained that she left meetings early to go to the hairdressers, which was certainly false: her habitual twice-weekly appointments were always first thing in the morning. In a recurrent form of criticism for women MPs, her voice was the source of a great deal of mockery. Castle had always found speaking in the chamber a challenge: quite unlike any other kind of public speaking, it involved 'trying to keep the attention of several hundred men who wolf-whistled and jeered and heckled'.[58] The *Daily Herald* once reported of Castle 'in a white frock [standing] undaunted for 20 minutes in the House of Commons last night against the concerted attempt of 200 Conservative men MPs to shout and laugh her down.'[59] If she shouted back, she was accused of having a shrill, coarse voice. Even Wilson once quipped at Castle's expense that 'she went on and on like a mechanical drill' during cabinet meetings.[60] He also joked that he had to change his private number to stop her calling him incessantly and accused her of behaving 'like a little bitch' when she insisted on standing as deputy leader in 1970. But Crossman seemed to understand the challenges faced by a woman MP, especially one in government: 'If you are little and can only just see over the top of the despatch box, if you have a high-pitched woman's voice and if you are trying to still the post-prandial, alcoholic clouds of noise you are at a terrible disadvantage, especially if you are a bit schoolmistressy and try to hector and lecture them at the same time.'[61] Despite these challenges, Castle was determined to have the last word. When an elderly member of the Lords opined that it was inappropriate for there to be women in politics, she retorted that she thought it inappropriate for there to be unelected peers in politics.

Castle's vocal critics drowned out a huge swathe of grassroots support for her approach. In a *Sunday Times* poll of trade unionists, it was revealed that there was substantial support for her policy within the rank-and-file trade-union membership. Castle even featured on the front page of *The Economist* – an unlikely supporter – which granted that her ideas were 'some steps towards the right policy'. Labour MP Joan Lestor, who was friends with Castle, wrote her a letter of reassurance: 'However down you may feel on the reaction to the White Paper it is not a personal opposition and your personal standing is still high.'[62] Another woman MP – Peggy Herbison – was a source of comfort when, after a PLP meeting in which

Castle was shot down from all quarters of the party, Herbison came up to her and said supportively: 'You're right, Barbara. Stick to your guns.'[63]

Wilson had given up negotiating with the TUC, but Castle was determined and busied away behind the scenes trying to find a compromise. The final drafted proposal to which the TUC agreed was prepared completely by herself, long after her officials had given up. Wilson accepted the settlement, 'but,' as he bitterly remarked, 'only because, under the catalytic action of our legislative proposals, they [the TUC] had "moved forward forty years in a month".'[64] It was Barbara Castle who had pushed them forwards.

From an historical perspective, Castle came out of the process in a better position than Wilson and became characterized as 'Battling Barbara'. History and the power of hindsight has been kind to her in a way it has not been to Margaret Bondfield (and, to a certain extent, with justification). As Castle had predicted, trade union reform without legislation was inadequate: in the first six months of 1970, 5 million days were lost to strikes. After the Winter of Discontent of 1978 to 1979 and Callaghan's failure to check the power of the trade unions, the advent of Thatcherism and the decimation of the trade unions, many have speculated that if Castle's industrial reforms had been passed, it may have prevented this chain of events from occurring. Castle may not have made it to Number Ten, but 'Maggie Bondfield Mark II' she was certainly not.

The reason Castle didn't become leader of the Labour Party or prime minister is rooted in her role as secretary of state and the impossible nature of her brief. She had to clear an untrodden path, with the stubborn weeds of malice and sexist opposition, but she also failed to take her colleagues with her on what would always be controversial reforms – especially for a Labour government – thus blocking her from the highest echelon of power. In many ways, Castle had cleared the path for Margaret Thatcher by the time she became prime minister in 1979.

'Minister of the future': Jennie Lee, the Arts and the Open University

On 6 July 1960, Jennie Lee's husband Nye Bevan – founder of the NHS and deputy leader of the Labour Party – passed away after having been diagnosed with stomach cancer. Suddenly, the light in Lee's world went out. She had always been prone to bouts of depression, but when Nye died she fell into an abyss like no other time in her life. Harold Wilson, a friend of Bevan and Lee's, was clearly concerned about her. Four years later, when Labour was back in power with Wilson at its helm, Lee received a call from Number Ten offering her a newly-created job as minister of the arts. 'I've got a job for you to do,' Wilson told her, – 'Find a desk and pack your handbag'. It was, as many observed at the time, 'a wreath for Nye'. But Lee took control of her post with an alacrity and a determination that transformed her parliamentary career and legacy. As Lee's biographer Patricia Hollis put it, she became 'the first, longest serving, the best known and the most loved of all Britain's ministers for the arts'.[65]

Lee loved her new job. She declared with dramatic pride: 'All the others deal with people's sorrows . . . the tidal wave of past neglect. But I have been called the minister of the future'.[66] In an article for *Socialist Commentary*, Lee gave a vision of her aims at the ministry: although she could not give children a loving home through legislation, she *could* give them an education that was infused with the arts, and a society in which theatres and libraries were easily accessible.

Wilson told Lee that if she produced a white paper defining her arts policy that gained cabinet approval, he would back her ambitions and the new position of 'minister of the arts' would continue in the future.

Lee drafted her transformative white paper for the arts – *A Policy for the Arts, the First Steps* – in February 1965, published under Wilson's name so as to give it more authority. Its content sketched the central aims of her new policy: to make arts accessible to all without lowering standards, to 'diffuse excellence without diluting it'.[67] Yet Lee emphasized that it was essential for the government not to interfere in the way in which the Arts Council spent its money: 'My function is simply a permissive one,' to make 'living room for artists to work in'.[68] The best thing Lee could do to encourage the arts to thrive was to support artists by giving them audiences, and the best way to do this was, as Wayland Young (then Lord Kennet) thought, 'money, policy and silence'. She did, however, influence funding distribution and, remarkably considering the traditionally centralized nature of the arts, ensured that most of it was distributed not in London but across Scotland, Wales and other regions. Lee managed to treble Arts Council funding in just six years. But there were many challenges Lee had to face.

No sooner had she entered the Department of Education and Science (DES) in 1965, than she had to deal with the pressing issue of the future of the National Youth Orchestra, the most esteemed orchestra for young musicians aged 13–19. Anthony Crosland, as secretary of state for education from 1965, was unconvinced that it was a priority within the Department of Education and Science (DES) and refused to provide sufficient funding. Jennie never forgave him for it. In the end Lord Goodman 'magicked the money from private funds', so that when Irene Ward asked Lee about the orchestra in the Commons, she was able to reassure Ward that 'we are determined to save this orchestra' and that a grant of £20,000 had been sourced.[69]

Having carefully watched Lee as she began to blossom in her new arts portfolio, Wilson decided to give her further responsibility for engineering what was then just a figment of his imagination – a 'University of the Air' as he called it. His idea was to create an educational trust offering distance learning by commissioning broadcasts literally 'over the air' via television, which provided diplomas and degrees for people at any stage in their life, regardless of their qualifications. Interestingly, Ellen Wilkinson had proposed the broadcast of lectures back in 1945 when she took over as minister of education, but the idea was too ahead of its time to be considered.[70] At the 1963 Labour Party conference, Wilson proposed his iconic idea of a 'University of the Air' in a speech outlining his vision of social progress forged within the 'white heat of the technological revolution'.

Jennie Lee – whom Nye Bevan called his 'ILP lassie' – had been born and bred in the ILP heartlands of Fife, Scotland, in a family with a high regard for the power of education 'as a kind of lamp to light the feet of their children'.[71] Lee soon gained an appreciation that adults also needed a lamp to light their feet at times, when facing the darkness of unemployment, poor social mobility and family poverty. During her time studying for bachelor's and master's degrees at the University of Edinburgh, Lee became disillusioned with both the accessibility and the standards of traditional higher education. The notion of an 'open' university which upheld excellent standards yet maintained open entry was a remedy for her two concerns about higher education.

First, in terms of accessibility, pre-existing full-time courses were by no means accessible to those engaged in work or in raising a family. Yet Lee thought that if the power of education could be widely harnessed for the social good, it could offer opportunities for those entrenched in a cycle of poverty. This belief was reinforced by her husband's educational and social background. Nye Bevan had not had the opportunity to go to university and had worked as a miner. But, having received two years of adult education at the Central Labour College in London funded by the South Wales Miners' Federation, he managed to work his way up to become one of the most respected politicians of his time.

Second, Lee felt that in terms of standards, all too often the incumbent system of higher and adult education encouraged the cramming of facts instead of the fostering of a deep understanding of one's subject. In Lee's eyes, education should be more than 'dowdy and mouldy . . . old-fashioned night schools ... hard benches'; it should offer the capacity for self-expression, inspiration and enhanced understanding of the world.[72] Wilson's vision of a vocational, interactive and voluntary educational institution was therefore appealing to Lee.

She soon became immersed in the project. In 1964 she established an Advisory Committee to consider the possibility of a 'University of the Air' along the lines outlined in Wilson's 1963 speech. Further to her white paper on the arts, Wilson asked Lee to produce a white paper on the University of the Air before the next election (which was likely to be soon, as Wilson desperately needed to increase his wafer-thin majority). When the DES drafted proposals for her, she dismissed the lot, much to the irritation of her officials, and started over.

By 1966, Lee had produced a white paper, and after the election, with an increased majority, Wilson had the power to implement it. Coming before the cabinet two days after the 1966 election, she was grilled about costs and brazenly said she hadn't a clue – 'but then no one knew how much a tank or Concorde really cost either'.[73] In the Commons she was more specific and complained that 'in some quarters the cost of this project has been grossly exaggerated'.[74]

Wilson was a clever operator and knew that the role he had allocated Lee was uniquely tailored to her political strengths. Creating the Open University required someone who was single-minded and determined to the point of stubbornness, and Lee was certainly all of those things. Lee's characteristic idealism and aversion to compromise was not a problem for this project: the role was limited and self-contained, separate from the overall educational budget. She ended up founding the Open University 'against almost universal hostility by steely political will'.[75] At a meeting between the cabinet and the NEC at Chequers prior to the 1966 election, Wilson recalled that at the end of the afternoon, when there was an open invitation for anyone to speak on anything, 'Jennie got up and made a passionate speech about the University of the Air. She said the greatest creation of the previous Labour government was Nye [Bevan]'s National

Health Service but that now we were engaged on an operation which would make just as much difference to the country. We were all impressed. She was a tigress.'[76] She also championed the idea of a fourth channel to broadcast its lectures, despite the increased costs it would entail; but the cabinet rejected her proposal and she had to amend her white paper.

Lee's determination did not preclude her from feeling the strength of the hostility towards the project. As she acknowledged, 'the press was against us, the cabinet was indifferent or hostile, the opposition totally hostile ... [and the civil servants were] snobs.'[77] Even Richard Crossman, once a good friend of Bevan and Lee's, was unsupportive. But, aided by chief whip Ted Short, Jennie persuaded Crossman in late 1965 not to publicize his objections. Tony Crosland, who headed the DES as secretary of state, was particularly hostile to Lee's efforts: he felt that the funds should be redirected towards other aspects of education, namely schools and the raising of the school leaving age. But luckily for Lee, her brief was narrow and the hypothecated budget excluded other educational alternatives. Lee didn't have to think in the language of priorities: the priority had already been chosen for her by Wilson, and it was the Open University. If anything, the opposition pushed her further. In 1967 when nothing had been settled, Lee assured her senior civil servant that the 'little bastard that I have hugged to my bosom and cherished, that all the others have tried to kill off, will thrive.'[78]

Many members of the opposition were dismissive of the power of television to replace a university degree; they doubted its ability to foster intellectual rigour and bonds of community in the way that traditional universities did. Although Renée Short was not an opponent of the OU, she did ask for clarification from Lee about facilities for practical work for science students, so as to prevent 'do it yourself' science experiments in the backyard.[79] Such concerns prompted Lee to emphasize the idea was not confined to television, and to rename Wilson's idea 'The Open University'. Lee also became concerned that television was expensive and could impair her goal of accessibility. It was therefore decided that most of the teaching should be carried out via correspondence with tutors operating in local study centres.

Amid a run on sterling in 1966 and a package of spending cuts advocated by Callaghan, the OU came under further attack. But Lee didn't blink, keeping focused on positive developments and the eagerness of the BBC to start planning. Meanwhile, she dodged questions in the Chamber and promised she was going to make a statement 'soon' on the formation of the OU. Finally, in a clever bargaining strategy, Wilson pledged to support Callaghan in his package of spending cuts, in return for Callaghan's support of the OU. Callaghan begrudgingly accepted, and in July 1967 the Treasury gifted the funds stipulated by Lord Arnold Goodman (Chairman of the Arts Council, an old friend of Wilson's and member of the planning committee of the OU) for the exclusive purpose of setting up the OU. Further opposition was dispersed in April 1968 when Crosland moved to the Board of Trade and Lee's ally, Ted Short, replaced him. Along with steady support from Tony Benn (then postmaster general, with responsibility for broadcasting policy), things were beginning to come together for Lee and for the OU.

As the 1970 election loomed, Lee was increasingly aware that her fledgling OU could be swept away by a Conservative majority. Shortly after the general election, she wrote to Frank Soskice (then a life peer): 'of course it is bitter to think that all one cares about is at risk, but I am an incorrigible optimist and feel that much of what we were able to achieve in the Arts will be maintained.'[80] To ensure the longevity and sustainability of the OU, it became necessary to win over Margaret Thatcher (as shadow secretary of state for education), a rising star in the Conservative party but hardly a political soul mate of Lee's. At first, Thatcher dismissively assumed that the OU would only offer hobby-based courses in flower-arranging and the like. Meanwhile, shadow chancellor Ian MacLeod described it as 'blithering nonsense' which he would scrap when the Tories were in power. Yet eventually, Thatcher came to see the value of the OU within the framework of her emergent ideology. Perhaps surprisingly given the overwhelmingly left-wing inclinations of those who created it, the OU was compatible to a certain extent with Thatcher's philosophy of 'pulling yourself up by the bootstraps', of self-betterment and aspiration. She even sought to trial the OU with a cohort of eighteen-year-olds to see whether it could serve as a cheaper, outsourced alternative to traditional universities. Eventually, Thatcher fought to save the OU in the cabinet against MacLeod's attempts to scrap it.

At the 1970 election, Lee lost her Cannock seat, having neglected constituency politics for some time. But although she lost her seat, she didn't lose her national legacy. The Open University survived, albeit with reduced grants and increased fees under the Conservatives. In January 1971, it enrolled its first 24,000 students. During her time in the Lords, Lee remained fiercely protective towards the OU, railing against increases in fees and reduced grants: '[T]he very essence,' she inveighed, 'of the OU is that it should not be for the rich or the poor, for black or white, for men or for women, but it should be judged on its academic standards and be available to all.'[81]

The OU was a source of immense personal pride to Wilson: as Tony Benn recalls, it was 'the one' achievement of his premiership 'for which – above almost anything else in his career – he most wished to be remembered'.[82] But in reality it was Jennie Lee who not only delivered it, but who defined Wilson's vision and put it into practical terms. As Michael Young, the sociologist who helped generate a blueprint for the OU and coined the term 'meritocracy', wrote, 'The OU was built by one person – though she had many able lieutenants and one ace card … the direct support of the prime minister … It was a stunning performance.'[83]

Ultimately her performance was sustained by her deeply-rooted belief that such an institution was necessary both for 'private pleasure' and 'to promote [people's] usefulness in society and their jobs'.[84] As she effusively put it, '[the OU] is not a dream … is not a luxury: it has become an urgent necessity.'[85]

After Jennie Lee's time as minister for the arts, theatre audiences would applaud her when she entered the building. Today, the Open University is the largest academic institution in the country. Although its teaching methods have changed with the advent of digital technology, the OU retains the principles that Lee intended. In tribute to her work, two of the buildings on its campus have been named in her honour.

Equal pay: Made in Dagenham

The last piece of legislation to be squeezed into the parliamentary session before the 1970 election was Barbara Castle's iconic Equal Pay Act. The legislation was largely a response to a strike by women machinists working at a Ford car factory in Dagenham in June 1968, the event that inspired the film *Made in Dagenham*, with Miranda Richardson playing Castle. The machinists, bearing 'equal rights' placards, were striking in protest against a new job evaluation scheme which undervalued their work. Although there is a debate about whether their demands were explicitly gender-based, it was quickly transformed into an equal pay issue, and Castle approached it as such.

Women MPs taking a stance on equal pay was not new. In 1944, Conservative MP Thelma Cazalet-Keir had tabled a successful equal pay amendment against her own government only for it to be quashed by Churchill in a confidence vote. While previous governments had 'paid lip service to the principle of equal pay for women', action had been confined to the civil service, and even then, only in selected areas.[86] In principle, equal pay had been a TUC objective ever since the matchgirls' strike in 1888, but it was far from being a priority. As Lena Jeger pointed out, in 1970 the average wage for a full-time woman industrial worker was half that of a man.

Despite this, equal pay faced opposition from both Labour and the Conservatives. Essentially, both parties believed that equal pay was desirable, but that it could wait until the economic situation was suitable. Jeger disagreed, stating that, 'The more [equal pay] costs, the more has been women's compulsory subsidy to the wages bill of this country over the years'.[87]

The internal equal pay debate within Labour was encapsulated by a debate between Barbara Castle and Jennie Lee. Lee thought that until men's wages had reached sufficient levels, the notion of 'equal pay for equal work' was futile. 'Barbara, we cannot ask for equal pay when miners' wages are so low,' she pleaded. 'In that case, we will wait forever,' Castle responded. After the 1947 party conference, at which MP Eirene White persuaded conference by a ratio of four to one votes to support equal pay, Lee wrote a provocative article in *Tribune* entitled, 'Are Women a Priority?' Lee was undoubtedly an example of a socialist who found it difficult to identify with the feminist movement. Yet she was swimming against the tide, with increasing support among Labour politicians for equal pay.

Equal pay was also becoming increasingly popular in the Conservative party. After the 1945 election – known as the Conservatives' 'Waterloo' – the party identified that they had missed out on a core women's vote and sought a method of engaging it. Committing to some measure of equal pay was increasingly seen as a means of targeting working women. In spring 1948, the party set up a Committee on Women's Questions and commissioned it to produce a Women's Charter. *A True Balance* was published a year later. Thelma Cazalet-Keir played a huge role in making sure that the charter was truly committed to equal pay. In the original draft, it was pledged that the next Conservative government would 'begin' to implement equal pay. Cazalet-Keir wrote to Churchill in protest, demanding that 'begin' was replaced with 'proceed'.[88] She succeeded. Cazalet-Keir also expressed frustration at the ambiguous wording of the

1950 Conservative manifesto, which stated a 'hope that during the life of the next Parliament the country's financial position will improve sufficiently to enable us to proceed at an early date with the application' of equal pay for equal work in the civil service.[89] Even after the 1951 election, the Conservatives were dragging their heels on implementation, falling back on the fear that equal pay would be inflationary. But as the Equal Pay Campaign Committee (EPCC, founded in 1943 by women MPs) pointed out, in his 1952 budget, chancellor Rab Butler went ahead with £229 million of tax cuts, while only £29 million was needed to introduce equal pay in the civil service. Women MPs were at the forefront of the campaign to highlight Butler's procrastination.

Butler's final wake-up call came on 7 January 1954, when the Labour Party committed to the immediate implementation of equal pay in public services if it won the next election. The next month, Butler met with advisers to ask for 'definite proposals' for gradual implementation. On 9 March 1954 a coordinated day of campaigns inside and outside of Parliament – 'Equal Pay Day' – was coordinated by women's organizations and women MPs. Conservative women Irene Ward and Patricia Ford, along with Labour's Barbara Castle and Edith Summerskill, drove together with an EPCC petition in an open-horse-drawn carriage to Parliament. The carriage was intended to draw a parallel with the days of the suffrage campaign, emphasizing the anachronism of the government's attitudes. Summerskill recalled stepping out of the carriage with Irene Ward 'to the flash of many photographers' bulbs'.[90] On the same day, twenty-five questions were put down on the subject in the Chamber (from Barbara Castle, Elaine Burton, Alice Bacon, Edith Summerskill and Irene Ward among others) and a ten-minute rule bill was introduced. Butler responded defensively to the women's questions, repeating that the government would implement equal pay when in an economic position to do so, and denying that equal pay was at the 'back of the queue'.[91] But he also unintentionally undermined the integrity of his economic concerns by stating: 'There is no precise criterion by which to judge whether the financial and economic situation of the country is such as to justify the step desired.'[92] In other words, equal pay was at the mercy of Butler's whim.

This made cross-party pressure on the government incredibly important. Unlike the Labour women Alice Bacon and Elaine Burton who opposed collaborating with Conservative women, Castle was keen to emphasize the importance of cross-party work and she paid tribute to the role of Irene Ward during a debate on equal pay in 1954. Castle was right that Ward had done a huge amount for the cause. On 2 November 1950, Ward had raised the issue of equal pay for the first time since the war, during her intervention in response to the King's speech. She reminded the Labour government of the royal commission's report in favour of equal pay: 'women are very tired of promises without performance,' she warned them. She also took her support to an individual level within Parliament by lobbying for Mrs Winder, the Hansard recorder in the House of Commons, to be paid at the same rate as the men. Initially hired on a temporary basis, when Mrs Winder was given a permanent contract she was promised that she would receive equal pay. When this didn't materialise, she contacted Irene Ward, who pursued the financial secretary of the treasury (John Boyd-Carpenter) on the matter. After one and a half years of constant pressure, Ward secured full compensation for Mrs Winder including all arrears owed to her. Vast amounts of correspondence poured into Ward's postbags from women and women's organizations, thanking her for the work that she had done for the cause.

Facing overwhelming support for equal pay, in 1954 Butler viewed that it was wise to placate the campaigners by announcing the restricted implementation of civil service equal pay. Before putting it to cabinet, Butler told Florence Horsbrugh: 'If we don't move (on equal pay), someone will.'[93] That 'someone' was Labour MP Douglas Houghton, who in March 1954 introduced a private member's bill for equal pay which was more radical than Butler would tolerate. Butler wrote to a fellow cabinet member, 'If we don't play *with a mute* others will without.'[94] Butler knew he needed to act.

In his budget speech just before the second reading of Houghton's bill, Butler announced plans to proceed with the gradual implementation of equal pay. Ironically, the announcement was made so cautiously that most people didn't even notice it. An embittered Irene Ward dismissed it as a 'crumb', while the EPCC was even unsure whether to welcome the move.[95] Nevertheless, the announcement proved to be a step in the right direction (albeit a small one). In January 1955, a plan was agreed whereby equal pay would be granted for 155,000 of the 210,000 non-industrial female civil servants, through six annual increments until 1961. Those groups not doing work interchangeable with men, such as the 27,000 civil service typists, were not included. Although it was not a stunning victory, it was nevertheless cause for celebration, if nothing else for signifying that major political parties were vying for women's votes. In 1955 Thelma

Cazalet-Keir organized a milestone dinner to celebrate, with Butler as a guest of honour.

It was within this context that the striking machinists of 1968 were viewed as part of a history of women protesting against low pay. Castle was determined to fulfil the 1964 Labour manifesto's commitment to introduce legislation on equal pay. Her women MP colleagues ensured that she kept her eye on the matter. Jeger repeatedly fired questions on equal pay – three times in 1967 and three times in 1968. In addition, Joyce Butler, Edith Summerskill and Renée Short all asked questions of Castle on the topic in 1968–9.

In June 1967, Castle was taken aside by Lena Jeger, who had tabled an amendment for equal pay which the whips thought was likely to pass. At this point, Castle was piloting through the relevant bill on prices and incomes, a bill which had been written by her predecessor and with which she was distinctly uncomfortable. Jeger was determined on the issue of equal pay: 'Pay should reflect the value of the work, not the shape of the worker,' she wrote in an article.[96] During the debate, chancellor Roy Jenkins sat down on the frontbench next to Castle. She turned to him and whispered, 'We're going to be defeated on this amendment, unless you allow me to announce that I am drawing up proposals to phase in equal pay over the next five years.' Jenkins, rather surprisingly, acquiesced. Castle managed to dodge the amendment by promising in her speech to initiate immediate talks about legislation on equal pay. She cited seven years as a period of adjustment and implementation for companies, across all industries and sectors, as a possible timeframe. The tactic worked, and Jeger's amendment was narrowly voted down. Yet, as Castle recognized in her autobiography, legislation 'was only made possible' due to the parliamentary pressure engineered by Jeger and other women MPs through their support for the amendment.[97]

A year after this debate in Parliament, the Dagenham machinists went on strike. In Castle's position as secretary of state, every major wage dispute went through her office so that she could decide whether the government should intervene. When Castle heard about the machinists, she demanded that the women should be invited for tea in her office, despite the protests of her officials. Castle was under huge pressure to get the women back to work, or she risked bringing the whole of Ford's production to a halt and exacerbating the balance of payments crisis. According to Wilson, Castle 'worked all hours of the night to settle [the strike] ... Night after night, until 2.00a.m. and later, Barbara chaired the attempts to settle.'[98] At the beginning of her meeting with the machinists, Castle allowed the photographers in; once they had left, she cleared away the tea and made 'a real drink' for the machinists. When the women first sat down, they were intransigent and insisted that they would not return to work until their full demands had been met. In the face of this, Castle changed tack and adopted a more relaxed persona. According to the Ford managing director present at the meeting, 'She kicked off her shoes and tucked her legs under her, on the settee. She was brilliant!'[99] In the end, Castle managed to persuade the women that although she couldn't change the grading system, she could make them a good offer in terms of pay differentials between men and women. She proposed an increase from 80 per cent of men's wages to 92 per cent, as well as instituting another court of inquiry. She also promised them that she intended to introduce legislation on equal pay. The machinists proved sceptical about the latter. 'We'll be old ladies by then!' they said. Yet within just two years, Castle's Equal Pay Bill was on the statute book.

For the first time, it was proposed that equal pay should be legally enforced across all forms of employment and industry. There were inevitably points of debate, and Castle settled for the language of 'equal pay for equal work of the same or broadly similar value'. This included 'not only the situation where men and women do identical work but also the situation where there are differences between the work of women and men but the differences are not of practical importance.'[100] For instance, typists' work was different to 'men's work', but that didn't warrant unequal pay according to Castle's bill. The act also brought into effect a ban on discrimination, so that women's and men's rates could no longer be negotiated separately.

In her speech presenting the Equal Pay Bill, Castle referred to the history of the campaign for equal pay, and the 'great moment' when Thelma Cazalet-Keir had engineered a rebellion on the issue in 1944.[101] Castle's bill received support from a wide range of the women MPs, including Conservative women Margaret Thatcher, Jill Knight and Mervyn Pike. Thatcher undertook an in-depth analysis of the costs of equal pay, in which she emphasized that as women's wages went up, so too would tax revenue. Jill Knight did, however, temper enthusiasm for the bill by her concern that it would prevent women from being hired; so long as women were in receipt of benefits like maternity leave, they would face discrimination at the hiring stage with equal pay in place.

When the bill passed through Parliament before the election, Castle was hailed as a feminist icon. This was ironic in many ways; after all, she felt a disconnect with the 'women's lib' movement and thought it was overly focused on self-analysis rather than pushing through political change. Lena Jeger shared those concerns, and often complained of the 'non-politics' of women's lib. It is also arguable that Castle's legislative action stemmed less from an alliance with the women's movement, and more from her need to quell the Dagenham strike and get the women back to work. Historian Sheila Cohen is quite disparaging about Castle's handling of the strike: she argues that Castle twisted what was essentially a class-based strike into an equal pay issue because she was unwilling to truly reform the system of grading within industry. While there is an element of truth in this, it is easy to overstate Castle's pragmatism. Ultimately, she was a proponent of social justice to her core, and was infuriated by backwards attitudes towards women, having campaigned for equal pay since the 1950s. In her autobiography, she wrote of her 'determination to force the macho male chauvinists in the Treasury to accept the principle of equal pay'.[102] She would also certainly not have been uninterested in the class-based demands made by the Dagenham workers. She realized the importance of the intersection between class and gender: 'It may not seem overtly so, but this is above all a Socialist Bill,' she declared, 'because it is about poor women. It is about . . . working women who earn less than 5s. an hour. There has been equal pay for some time for clever, articulate, professional women. Today we are talking about poor women.'[103]

The act was by no means the end of the disparity between pay for women and men. Despite equal pay for equal work having been achieved in law, today a gender pay gap persists of 18.4 per cent, due in part to occupational segregation between 'men's' and 'women's' work. But the Equal Pay Act was a momentous milestone in women's history, which eclipsed all previous efforts. In 1970 women's wages were a paltry 63.1 per cent of men's; by 1977 they had risen to 75.5 per cent.[104] During Shirley Summerskill's speech in the equal pay debate, she paid tribute to both Barbara Castle and the Ford machinists: 'Like the early pioneers for women's suffrage,' she reflected, 'they faced abuse, misrepresentation and ridicule.'[105]

Castle's many lives

Castle's final role in the cabinet was secretary of state at the Department of Health and Social Security. Yet, when Harold Wilson stood down as

Labour leader in 1976, Barbara Castle's days as a minister were numbered. Once Jim Callaghan (with whom she had never seen eye to eye) was elected leader, Castle was fired. Shirley Williams sent her a note in which she wrote that while the two had differed on some very important political questions, she admired and respected Castle for her courage, vitality and intelligence. 'No woman in Britain since it became a democracy has achieved so much politically as you. The cards are still stacked against women, as we both know.' Williams added that she had always voted for Castle in the elections to the shadow cabinet, although Castle assumed she hadn't. 'Whatever the party groupings, I always did,' Williams wrote. 'You were simply too good to exclude.'[106]

Before leaving the House of Commons, Castle saw in the introduction of ground-breaking legislation. The 1978 State Earnings-Related Pension Supplement (SERPS) was a pension related to earnings used to supplement the basic state pension, and its introduction did much to alleviate the pension poverty of women workers. It remained in place until 2002, the year Castle died.[107]

Like the Equal Pay Act, the introduction of SERPS saw Castle championed as a women's rights activist. In reality, Castle had been very sceptical of the women's movement. In 1972, she had come into contact with women's activists on a lecture tour in the United States and wrote in her diary that she was 'surprised how seriously they took it: they just can't see how funny words like "consciousness raising" are.' *The Times*' US correspondence quoted Castle on the same trip as saying: 'If I had bothered about whether I was called Mrs, Miss or Ms, I would never have worked up to the good neuter title of Minister. (. . .) Women should find a cause bigger than themselves.'[108] Jack Straw, who worked for Castle in the 1970s, later compared her to Margaret Thatcher, saying that 'she had an extraordinary sense of herself as a woman in a male world. She was contemptuous of women who wanted special treatment. She was very feminine, but she knew how to operate in a masculine world. She was very competitive with her peers, as Margaret Thatcher was, and contemptuous of them.'[109] Like Thatcher, Castle also refused to see how her own path to power – as a remarkable woman within a male-dominated political party – had been closed to so many others. But as she reached the last decades of her career, Castle began to think differently about feminism and the gendering of women in political life. She felt erased from the history of women's activism and recorded her anger when she was almost completely overlooked in an exhibition on the fiftieth anniversary of women's suffrage. 'Damn it all,' Castle wrote in her diary. 'I have done more than any other Minister to carry forward the work the suffragettes began: equal pay, equal pensions, child benefit.'[110] The latter reform, prepared by Castle, had run into trouble before becoming law as her successor at the Department of Health and Social Security, David Ennals, announced that it would be postponed indefinitely. Using her position on Labour's NEC, Castle fought to save it and finally succeeded in 1978 by threatening a backbench revolt during the budget debate. The child benefit bill merged family allowances – first introduced in 1945 after decades of lobbying by Eleanor Rathbone – and child tax credits (which benefit the breadwinner, often the father, through their pay check) and would now be paid directly to the mother.[111]

Expectations of what a woman MP could achieve in Parliament had shifted irrevocably by 1970. This was partly due to the combined efforts of a range of women MPs to defy convention and stamp down (quite literally in some cases) against sexism within the Commons – with the stiletto-stamping efforts of Shirley Williams and others. But it was mostly due to the legacy of one woman – Barbara Castle – for she was quite simply unprecedented in the scope of her contribution to politics as a woman MP. In using the precarious 'springboards' presented to her, she launched herself through the labyrinth of cabinet hierarchy, to the point at which it was no longer inconceivable that a woman could become prime minister. And in doing so, Castle lay the foundations for those women to come, including Margaret Thatcher, who would further those expectations.

5

Leaders and Losses: 1970–79

*All of us owe you an immense debt for proving that a woman can
do what used to be thought of as men's jobs better than a man.*
**LETTER FROM SHIRLEY WILLIAMS TO
BARBARA CASTLE, 17 APRIL 1976**[1]

The 1970s saw women becoming more visible in British public life. The
second-wave feminist activists claimed space and made demands in an
attempt to force change. The decade had begun with the publication of
Germaine Greer's *The Female Eunuch* – a book calling for the disruption
of nuclear family life – and the much-publicized protests at the Miss
World contest in London, and ended with a woman elected prime
minister. The Equal Pay Act, the Sex Discrimination Act and the
Employment Protection Act all took effect in 1975, during the United
Nations' International Year of Women. The gender bar had been abolished
in several professions, including at the London Stock Exchange, where
women gained access to the floor for the first time in 1973. These visible
changes were accompanied by the activism of women MPs; individuals
who often sacrificed their every waking hour to secure nominations and
support, who had to withstand condescension and organized campaigns
against them, and who rarely got the credit or job titles that they deserved.
This chapter tells the story of a few of them.

Throughout the 1970s, the number of women in the House of
Commons remained stable and low. Just twenty-six women were elected
in 1970; by the time the decade ended, only nineteen MPs were women,
a drop from the twenty-seven who had been elected in October 1974.
When the Conservatives' Betty Harvie Anderson became the first woman
to serve as deputy speaker in 1970, parliamentary procedure was slow to

adapt to a female speaker: Harvie Anderson is referred to as *Mr. Deputy Speaker (Miss Harvie Anderson)* in Hansard.[2]

As the decade began, it seemed as though the successful passing of the Equal Pay Act in 1970 could still be a stepping stone on Barbara Castle's path towards party leadership and becoming the first woman to cross the threshold into 10 Downing Street as prime minister. That honour instead went to a Conservative woman MP, Margaret Thatcher. When the Conservatives swept to a surprise victory and Edward Heath formed his first government in 1970, Thatcher replaced Castle as the only female cabinet minister. Thatcher had held six shadow posts when in opposition, and her final posting – as shadow minister of education and science – was now translated into the same role at the Ministry of Education. Like Castle, Thatcher had a seemingly endless capacity for hard work and was always meticulously prepared, organized and presented.

Becoming the Iron Lady

Thatcher had been born Margaret Roberts in the Lincolnshire market town of Grantham in 1925. She grew up in a small house where her parents ran a grocery shop on the ground floor, and her childhood was her great political inspiration. Thatcher was relentless in her pursuit of candidate selection for the Conservative Party, and stood for Dartford in the elections of 1950 and 1951. She was unsuccessful – the constituency sent a Labour MP to Westminster as predicted, although Thatcher made a dent in Norman Dodds' majority – but in the process of selection and campaigning, she met both her husband – Denis Thatcher – and future party leader, Ted Heath. She married Thatcher at the end of 1951 and qualified as a barrister while pregnant with twins in 1953. Specializing in taxation law and hiring a nanny, Margaret Thatcher then returned to her quest to become an MP. She had decided that family life would not stop her ambitions, writing in the *Sunday Graphic* in 1952 that it was 'a great pity' that so many women 'have cut short their careers when they marry'. Thatcher's article coincided with the accession of Elizabeth II to the throne, and Thatcher called for women to 'play a leading part in the creation of a glorious Elizabethan era'.[3]

Thatcher's gender and background set her apart among candidates standing for election for the Conservative Party in the 1950s. She was, like many others, an Oxford alumnus, though she had studied chemistry at

Somerville College in the late 1940s, where she was described as a second-class student who threw herself into her work with much enthusiasm.[4] But Thatcher's father, Albert, was a self-made man who had left formal schooling at the age of thirteen. He was a Rotary man and a Methodist preacher, whose Victorian values Margaret would later celebrate. Unlike most Victorian patriarchs, Albert had great plans for his two daughters and encouraged their education and ambition to an unusual degree. He also inspired her antipathy towards the labour movement: Margaret could never forgive Labour for throwing her father off the Grantham town council after thirty years of service in 1952 (he had been the mayor of Grantham 1945–6).[5] Less is known about Margaret's mother, Beatrice Roberts, and her influence – Margaret's sister Muriel spoke of Beatrice as 'a bigoted Methodist'[6] – but Thatcher's later celebration of femininity, homemaking and housewife skills certainly came from her childhood home. It was also at home that Thatcher's hardworking ethos was honed. The Roberts daughters went to school and worked in the shop during the week, and spent Sundays in church. Church taught her the art of public speaking, as she listened to her father's sermons. She also had elocution lessons while at grammar school.

The historian David Cannadine has described the young Margaret as 'serious, intelligent, competitive, and hard-working', adding that she 'possessed great powers of concentration, and was already hyperactive and seemed able to get by with very little sleep'.[7] These were characteristics that defined her throughout life. At Oxford, she made the most of opportunities to enjoy dinners and dances; always proud of her appearance, she dressed well and had boyfriends. While she may not have dazzled her contemporaries with her scientific mind, she became the president of the Conservative Association at the University of Oxford. It gave her an opportunity to attend national Conservative gatherings, and inspired her ambitions to become an MP, although she – as a woman – was not allowed to speak at the Oxford Union.

At the end of 1954, Thatcher called the Conservative Central Office, expressing her wishes to stand in the selection for a parliamentary candidate in Orpington in Kent. She lost to the local party chairman Donald Sumner but, encouraged by John Hare, Conservative MP and later chairman of the Conservative Party, she tried again in 1957 setting her sights on Beckenham and Hemel Hempstead. Both attempts were unsuccessful. In 1958, Thatcher attempted to win the nomination in Maidstone, where the local association report had her as having a fine brain and great appeal, but that she needed to think more about how to approach life as an MP as a woman rather than a politician. Asked about how to cope as a Member of Parliament with a young family, Margaret Thatcher had explained that she had a good nanny and that she would have mornings free. It left the local association unimpressed: MPs had committees in the mornings. For once, Thatcher seemed unprepared, but she had come up against an issue that was keeping the number of women running for the Conservatives low. That was the belief in traditional family values, the idea that women best served their country by staying at home to look after their children and husbands. Some constituencies were more traditionalist than others and Thatcher's Maidstone interview was not the first time a female candidacy fell apart. Research has shown that women, especially those who were married and had children, were more often viewed as potentially unreliable and therefore less likely to win selection.[8] As a result, women involved in Conservative politics held traditional roles – they hosted parties, supported their partners and planned events and catering – and they were often among those most critical of women running for Parliament.

Party planning was never enough for Margaret Thatcher. In 1958, she put herself forward for selection in Finchley, a prosperous borough in north London and a safe Conservative seat, which proved to be the perfect fit. She impressed the local association with her modern outlook and political ethos, and came first in the first round of voting. In the second round, she beat the Second World War veteran and local man Thomas Langton by forty-six votes to forty-three. Despite her winning, five members of the association's executive refused to endorse Thatcher as the candidate because of her gender. The man responsible for the count later told his son that he had '"lost" two of [Langton's] votes and gave them to [Thatcher]', a claim that cannot be verified.[9]

In the general election, Thatcher campaigned hard and won over 50 per cent of the vote. Over the next decade, she worked out of the Lady Members' Room in Parliament and kept to herself; she generally chose not to build allegiances or alliances with members of her party. In 1961, she was appointed parliamentary under-secretary for pensions and national insurance, an office she took very seriously and kept during the spell of three ministers (John Boyd-Carpenter, Niall Macpherson and Richard Wood) and three Conservative prime ministers (Anthony Eden, Harold Macmillan and Alec Douglas-Home). Thatcher lost her position when Labour swept to power in 1964 but held on to Finchley. She also managed to hold on to Denis, who had suffered a nervous breakdown and travelled on a one-way ticket to South Africa shortly after the election. He came back to sell the family business, which allowed him to better fulfil his role as an MP's husband.

In 1965, Margaret Thatcher supported Heath's leadership campaign following Alec Douglas-Home's resignation. She believed Heath could better challenge the Labour prime minister Harold Wilson than his opponent, former chancellor Reginald Maudling. It could have made a great partnership: Heath had a background that resembled Thatcher's. Nine years older than her, Heath was the son of a Broadstairs builder, who had gone to Oxford via a grammar school and graduated with a second-class degree and was also president of the Oxford University Conservative Association. In 1950, Heath was elected MP for Bexley, having run his campaign next door to Margaret Thatcher's in Dartford. Nevertheless, the two were not friends. Thatcher held several shadow cabinet positions during Heath's time as leader of the opposition from 1965 to 1970, but it was generally acknowledged that 'he promoted her only belatedly and grudgingly'.[10] In 1967, she was appointed to the shadow cabinet, responsible for fuel and power; she was moved to transport a year later, and to education at the end of 1969.

As secretary of state for education from 1970, Margaret Thatcher was, as always, hard-working and enthusiastic. Within a couple of weeks of taking office, she scrapped the previous Labour government's commitment to pressurize schools to become comprehensives. This was one of the first times that she promoted her own childhood influences in government: she was unflinching in her support for grammar schools and elite universities. She was rebuked by Heath, who felt cabinet should have been consulted. Thatcher complained about the lack of loyalty from her civil servants and wrote in her memoirs that the atmosphere in her department was 'self-righteously socialist'.[11] Her biographer Charles Moore has argued that the tension between Thatcher and her members of staff had more to do with culture and politics than her gender. Department of Education officials were struck by the fact that their boss 'never for a second considered sending her own children to state schools'. John Hedger, Thatcher's private secretary who discussed schooling with her on a trip to Cambridge, found that 'she assumed (a) that one's son would go to a private school, (b) that he would board and (c) that there was no need to mention one's daughter'.[12] Carol and Mark Thatcher were sixteen when their mother became a cabinet minister; Carol went to St Paul's Girls and Mark to Harrow.

It was at the Department of Education that Thatcher weathered her first political crisis. In an effort to make short-term savings to the budget, she decided to run with the proposal to cut milk given to school children, and to allow authorities to sell it to those who had previously received it for free (thus reversing a policy first introduced by Ellen Wilkinson twenty-five years previously). It was a highly unpopular move that saw Thatcher dubbed 'the milk-snatcher' and roundly condemned in the press. Snapping under pressure, she asked the *Guardian*: 'why, why? Why are you doing it?' only to be rebuked by Jean Rook in the *Daily Mail* who stated that Barbara Castle would have come 'back at critics like a blow-lamp'.[13] The scandal was enough to leave Thatcher mulling over the idea of leaving politics altogether.[14] In the end, she went back to work, paid her way into popularity by working with the unions to increase teachers' salaries, and remained in her post until 1974.

The Conservative gains at the election in 1970 had been lost over the space of the following three years as Heath's government ran into financial trouble. Strikes and government bailouts continued, despite the fact that Heath had promised to combat both. In February 1974, Margaret Thatcher held on to her seat, but her majority in Finchley almost halved. Out of office as Harold Wilson formed his cabinet, Thatcher told the *Daily Mail*, not entirely convincingly, that 'It is easier for a woman than a man to give up power because you are not so lost. I can fill the time by spring-cleaning the house.'[15] It was not long before she would campaign again: this time to lead the party.

Conservative women and feminism

When the Conservatives had been in power, Margaret Thatcher had supported the rights of women by supporting the implementation of the Equal Pay Act, but she was not a vocal champion of gender equality and far from a self-defined feminist. She, like many other Conservative women, supported women's right to equality at work while also supporting their right to be housewives. They argued that women's status should be elevated, but that their femininity should not be threatened, a view that Conservative MP Sally Oppenheim-Barnes advocated when she appeared on the BBC's Argument in 1974. The programme was dedicated to a discussion about the merits of women's fight for equality and Oppenheim-Barnes's opponent was the radical feminist and academic Juliet Mitchell. Mitchell argued that laws could only go so far; society itself needed to be radically reformed to change patriarchal culture and attitudes before equality of the sexes could be achieved. Oppenheim-Barnes, on the other hand, argued that the women's liberation movement harmed the cause of women as it denigrated those fulfilled as housewives and mothers. She argued that most women were not looking for a fundamental change in their role in society, but sought an elevation of status. The way to get there, Oppenheim-Barnes suggested, was through friendliness (so as not to confirm the prejudices of opponents to the women's liberation movement) and legislation. While agreeing that girls are born disadvantaged because of their gender, she called the demands made by Mitchell's side of the argument 'extreme' and 'counter-productive'.[16]

Yet, Oppenheim-Barnes had done her bit to keep equality legislation on track: in July 1972, she asked the secretary of state for employment, Robin Chichester-Clark, to make a statement on the progress towards the implementation of the Equal Pay Act. It finally came into effect in December 1975, alongside the Sex Discrimination Act.[17] The two acts, alongside the Employment Protection Act (which gave pregnant workers the right to reinstatement and paid maternity leave) of 1975 and the Race Relations Act of 1976, helped raise wages, improve employment rights and make discrimination against women and minorities illegal. They became law once Labour was back in power, but despite its supposed challenge to the traditional dependent housewife and male breadwinner system that many within the Conservative Party favoured, the Heath government carefully guided the Equal Pay Act into practice. The laws had a great impact on British women's lives, visible for example in the 22 per cent increase in the employment rate of married or cohabiting mothers between 1974 and 2000.[18]

More women on the benches

The mid-1970s was a hectic time for the electorate. In early February 1974, Ted Heath asked the Queen to dissolve Parliament ahead of a general election on 28 February. He was hoping to be re-elected to Number Ten and the polls were marginally in the Conservatives' favour, but the result was a hung Parliament in which Labour took the greatest number of seats. Harold Wilson became prime minister when talks between Heath and Jeremy Thorpe, the leader of the Liberals who had gained fourteen seats, broke down. Shirley Williams took over Thatcher's desk and portfolio as secretary of state for education and science, and Barbara Castle became the secretary of state for health and social services. Before the year was out, Wilson called another election, and on 10 October Labour gained a three-seat majority. It was not much, but it was enough.

The consecutive elections of 1974 were hard work, particularly for voters whose enthusiasm waned. It was also tough on some MPs who had spent over a year campaigning. In 1973, Betty Boothroyd had finally become an MP after decades of trying. She stood successfully for Labour in West Bromwich after the incumbent, Maurice Foley, resigned to take a post with the European Commission. Born in 1929, Boothroyd had been beaten by Conservative candidates in elections in 1956, 1957, 1959, 1968 and 1970, and had lost selection for Labour seats in 1962 and 1965. She was determined to make 1973 her final campaign if she lost again: 'I had had enough of failures,' she later wrote in her memoirs. 'I felt qualified for the *Guinness Book of Records* for the number of seats I had fought and lost.'[19] Instead, she won three elections in sixteen months between May 1973 and October 1974 and remained the MP for West Bromwich for twenty-seven years, including serving as the first female speaker of the House of Commons between 1992 and 2000.

Boothroyd was a working-class daughter of two mill workers, who failed her eleven-plus examination. But the Boothroyd family were better off than many who lived on her street in Dewsbury: Betty was an only child and her father was in his forties when she was born. He still suffered long stretches of unemployment in the 1930s, and rumour had it that his involvement in the trade union movement had left him blacklisted. Betty's mother, meanwhile, found work more easily but had to contend with being paid a lower wage on account of her gender. Boothroyd's mother took her to Labour Party meetings from an early age, and she later described being weaned in the women's section of the party where she encountered leading Labour women like the Leeds MP Alice Bacon and Liverpool's Bessie Braddock, both of whom she described to me as 'inspirational'.[20] After a stint as a semi-professional dancer in London – the press was always making references to her past as a Tiller Girl throughout her career – Boothroyd came to Parliament as a secretary for Barbara Castle and Geoffrey de Freitas in the mid-1950s. Castle and de Freitas were at opposite ends of the party. Castle was considered a Bevanite, and de Freitas a member of the party's right wing. Boothroyd was happy to work for them both, saying that they 'were gregarious intellectuals in a party where sober suits and tribal loyalties still held sway'.[21] She enjoyed her work but called the working conditions for MPs' secretaries in the House of Commons 'primitive, to say the least'. The secretaries worked in an open office in Westminster Hall where there was no privacy for them or their MPs. Each secretary had one shelf and two drawers of a filing cabinet, which were checked once a week to ensure that they had not expanded into more space, and there were only four telephones in the room. Boothroyd's job was to handle Castle and de Freitas's correspondence and help them chase ministers and government departments on behalf of their constituents. 'Barbara had been a wartime civil servant and was tenacious at badgering Whitehall,' Boothroyd later wrote. 'I learned a lot from her, tackling everything that came my way. All the time, I was learning how Parliament works, from the bottom up.'[22] Decades later, Boothroyd told me that 'Barbara was a great personality, speaker and orator. She was also a workaholic and always turned herself out to look fantastic.' Once, Boothroyd relayed, when Castle was doing a media interview, she insisted that there be a make-up artist available. '"It's radio, Barbara!", I said'.[23] Having worked for Castle, Boothroyd had an insight into the hard work behind the scenes in the Commons. 'Although my Tiller days cured me of my show-business ambitions, the daily routine of synchronized high kicks and co-ordinated teamwork taught me much about the need for rigorous preparation,' Boothroyd wrote in her memoirs. 'Politicians, like Tiller Girls, are public performers – they forget it at their peril.'[24]

While Margaret Thatcher had found the selection process difficult on account of her being a married woman with children, Betty Boothroyd, who was single, found that too proved to be a hurdle to be overcome. 'Having political ambitions was hard enough for a young woman in the days when men dominated public life; I was doubly suspect because I was unmarried. In that respect, the Labour Party was little different from the Conservatives.' Like Thatcher, she would not take no for an answer: 'I grew up in a family whose convictions were set in Yorkshire granite, and I would not be beaten.'[25] Finally installed as an MP, in October 1974 Boothroyd won her third election and saw her majority soar to 15,000.

Within just a few months, she became the first woman to be recruited to the Whips' Office, as a regional labour whip. The work was hard: during her first year as a whip, Boothroyd reckoned that she was never home before midnight. She was also not as strict as she should have been, allowing MPs under stress to go back home to their families against the rules. She had been recruited by Bob Mellish, who 'told me he knew I was a very feminine woman, but it was toughness that mattered in the whips' office. "Tough?" I replied. "I chew tobacco for breakfast."[26] Serving as a whip for two years gave Boothroyd a taste for the disciplining of MPs that is a hallmark of a speaker. She had a front row seat when Labour MP John Stonehouse faked his own death in the US in November 1974 only to be discovered living with his mistress in Australia a month later. He was one of the thirty-two Birmingham and Midlands MPs under Boothroyd's responsibility, and she was particularly incensed about his refusal to resign as an MP and his defection to the English National Party before his conviction for fraud in 1976. Stonehouse left his constituents unrepresented for two years, though Boothroyd and other nearby MPs stood in for him as often as they could manage.[27]

One of Boothroyd's closest friends in the House of Commons was Jo Richardson, who started her career in Parliament as a secretary to Ian Mikardo in 1945. Born in 1923, she became a key collaborator of Mikardo's, sharing his ideas about the importance of nationalization and public ownership. She was also a strong advocate for women's rights, a founding member of the Campaign for Nuclear Disarmament in the 1950s and a supporter of the Greenham Common Women's Peace Camp. Richardson served on Hornsey borough council and stood as Labour's candidate in Monmouth and then Harrow East before finally being elected MP for Barking in February 1974. In the Chamber, she made her name as a champion of ordinary women, saying: 'I am not interested in the high-achieving women, I am concerned about all the women with expertise and women who never get to first base, they're poor, they've got kids, their lives are a drudgery. It is about women getting a greater share of the cake, it is not just about changing the recipe.' Later in her career, Richardson was a key opponent to Liberal Democrat MP David Alston's attempt to reduce the legal limit for abortions from twenty-eight to eighteen weeks (it was subsequently reduced to twenty-four weeks), and in 1989 she ensured the defeat of Ann Widdecombe's private member's bill that sought to curb abortion rights. Within the Labour Party, Richardson was a staunch women's activist: when she was elected to the National Executive

Committee (NEC) in 1979, she became the first chair of its brand-new Women's Committee and was one of the first advocates for the use of quotas to ensure a fair share of women candidates in general elections.[28]

Like Boothroyd, Margaret Jackson – later to be known under her married name of Beckett – was another new recruit in the Labour whips' office during the Wilson administration. Born in 1943, Beckett became the MP for Lincoln in the October election of 1974, and a whip in 1975. She had been selected as the Labour candidate for Lincoln in 1973 but lost to the incumbent MP Dick Taverne, who had resigned from the Labour Party over its left turn in the early 1970s. Before her successful election, Beckett was employed as a special advisor to Judith Hart at the Ministry of Overseas Development. Once she too was an MP, Beckett became Hart's PPS. Working with Hart, Beckett learned that 'people always assume that a woman is not the minister, and so, although it's right to be friendly and approachable, don't you forget you're the minister, or else they certainly will.' She also realized that ministers can write their own white papers, and that the Civil Service is not always right.[29]

It was the start of a long and illustrious political career: Margaret Beckett was the deputy leader of the Labour Party under John Smith and the acting leader of the opposition following his death in 1994. She ran for leadership in 1994, but lost to Tony Blair. She served in Blair's cabinets as lord president of the council and leader of the House of Commons, secretary of state for environment, food and rural affairs and foreign secretary, and for Gordon Brown as minister for housing and planning. In the 1970s, however, Beckett was in her thirties and finding her feet in the Westminster system. She was used to being a woman among men, having worked as an engineer before running for Parliament. She had grown up in a politically aware home, but neither of her parents had been members of the Labour Party, and Beckett spent two years trying to become a member while at university. 'This was in the old days, when [Labour was] very much a voluntary organisation,' she later told Peter Hennessy. 'Our letters and phone calls went unanswered, and then eventually we got a response.'[30]

In March 1976, Margaret Beckett became a junior minister of education after her predecessor – Joan Lestor – resigned over spending cuts. Beckett, who also belonged to the party's left wing, did not agree with the cuts but decided, in consultation with her constituency party in Lincoln, that it was better for Lestor to be replaced by someone with the same views.[31] She was also not certain that education was for her.

'Everybody in my family were teachers,' Beckett told me. 'I'd been determined not be a teacher, and then they wanted me in the Department for Education, which is not what I had in mind at all.'[32] Once she accepted the post, Beckett worked for Shirley Williams, who was not always impressed by her junior's loyalty: Beckett, Williams wrote in her memoirs, silently sided with opposition to the green paper in which Williams proposed a core curriculum of fundamental subjects to take up half the time a child spent in school.[33]

Making a difference

Judith Hart

In 1959, Judith Hart had been elected MP for Lanark, a Labour-voting constituency in Scotland. She had grown up in a working-class home in Burnley with easy access to the arts; her father, who had run away from home because he wanted to play the piano in pubs, used to go to hear the Hallé orchestra in Manchester. Hart, whose mother died when she was eleven, went to a grammar school and became politically active after seeing the blackshirts marching. While her head teacher advised her to become a teacher, Hart had other ideas: she applied to the London School of Economics to study sociology, got in, and got a First. Born Constance and called Connie by her family, she changed her name to Judith on the train to London, and dropped her accent. 'That was always a contrast between her and Barbara Castle,' Hart's youngest son Steve later told me, 'Barbara was her senior, but was always seen as the working-class darling because she kept her Yorkshire accent. No one appreciated what my mum's background was because of her plummy accent.'[34]

When she arrived in Westminster, Hart was a 35-year-old mother of two. Her husband, Tony Hart, was a chemist and former member of the Communist Party whom she had met at the Association of Scientific Workers in Portsmouth. They lived in Poole after the war and Hart stood for Labour in Bournemouth East in 1951, losing to the Conservative candidate. After moving to Glasgow, Hart stood against Lady Tweedsmuir in Aberdeen in 1955, a contest dubbed the 'battle of the housewives'. Ahead of the 1959 election, both Hart and her husband were selected as candidates for Labour; he withdrew his candidacy when Judith was selected for Lanark. Their son Steve – whose earliest memory is the flaming torches of the rent strike in 1957 – remembers 'driving all around the constituency, spending all afternoon sitting outside the Miners Welfare Club playing with my dad when she made speeches inside'. Hart's determination and organization paid off: having arranged postal votes for miners who had been moved to Ayrshire, she won the election by 700 votes.

Hart spent her first years in Parliament on the backbenches. Two years after winning in Lanark, the Harts relocated. Steve Hart remembers meeting his mum off the steam train in Glasgow, but that ultimately moving to London was the 'only decision'. With her marriage under strain and a lonely existence 400 miles from her family, the Harts moved to Barnes in south London. For a short time, Hart was able to see her children for bedtime before going in to vote. Once she became a minister of state for commonwealth affairs in 1966, that changed. Steve Hart remembers being lonely, with his dad at council meetings and his mum in Parliament. Like many families with demanding jobs, the wider family played a key role in holding things together, and Hart's mother-in-law moved in to help. Hart's election leaflets told voters that her mother-in-law lived with the family – presumably to reassure her constituents that they were not neglected. A year later, Hart became minister of social security, just as her oldest son was receiving unemployment benefits 'from his mother' after having graduated from university without a job to go to.[35]

Hart was appointed to the cabinet as the first female paymaster-general in 1968, but it was as minister for overseas development in 1969–70, 1974–5 and 1977–9, a role previously held by Barbara Castle, that Hart made her greatest contribution. Her determination, ability and organization set her apart, as did her radical left-wing ethos, which were visible in several articles she published while in office (one of the most famous was *Aid and Liberation: A Socialist Study of Aid Policies*). Hart was actively engaged in supporting Chilean refugees fleeing Augusto Pinochet's military junta; having led the Labour deputation there in 1972, Hart met with the democratically-elected president Salvador Allende, who was killed in the 1973 coup. Refugees and exile politicians were always welcome in her home. 'Anti-apartheid people were going in and out of our house,' Steve Hart said when I interviewed him. 'It was a normal part of life.'

But Judith Hart's work was often controversial. When she launched the Labour Party's Southern African Liberation Fund, she was roundly denounced. In 1972, she was sent a bomb in the post for the same reason.[36] Having been the shadow minister for overseas development during

Labour's term in opposition between 1970 and 1974, she almost lost out on being appointed the same role when Wilson became prime minister in April 1974. He called her into his office and told her that he could not appoint her as he understood she had Communist connections. She retorted that she had never been a Communist (although her husband, Tony, had been), but that she had called the secretary of the Communist Party to tell him she would not speak at a Chilean solidarity meeting alongside a member of the Communist Party. A few hours later, Wilson went ahead and appointed her. Yet, while she could attend cabinet she never became a cabinet minister after her stint as paymaster-general (when, Steve Hart has pointed out, he was 'the first person in history who could say to his school mates that his mum was a cabinet minister'), partly because of MI5 concerns about her Communist connections. In his diaries, fellow left-winger Tony Benn later wrote: 'It is significant that the security services decided to pick off Judith Hart, very significant. And it is significant that Harold decided to take it up, having known her since 1959; he would have to pitch his judgement against the security service's judgement. It shows the sort of thing we are up against.'[37] In the 1987 election, Hart stood down from Parliament. She died six months later from bone cancer. According to her son, Hart was essentially a functional alcoholic, who – like a lot of people in Parliament at the time – would drink a lot at times of high stress. She also smoked sixty cigarettes a day.[38]

Shirley Williams

Others had more luck getting appointed to the cabinet in the 1970s. Shirley Williams had been a minister of state at the Home Office just before the 1970 election, and she was promoted to secretary of state for prices and consumer protection in 1974. As a home office minister, it had been Williams' job to handle 'the three Ps' – prisons, probation and pornography. She developed 'a quick inspector's eye for sadism' as she worked her way through a pile of porn magazines to decide which ones were to be banned. 'The inescapable conclusion I reached,' she wrote in her memoirs, 'was the extraordinary intensity of the hatred some men feel for women – and the inexplicable willingness of some women to play up to that hatred.'[39] She was no stranger to the sentiment that some jobs were not for women: having wanted to see prisons from the inside, she arranged a twenty-four-hour incognito stay as an offender in Holloway

Prison. In the guise of a jailed sex worker, Williams discovered poor washing and toilet facilities, and was surprised by her high regard for the prison officers, despite the fact that some of them thought the appointment of a woman as minister of state for prisons was absurd.

Williams was aware that being a woman could make her work difficult, but she also realized that it gave her a certain visibility. She benefitted from working for Harold Wilson, who – she has argued – deserves more credit for being the first prime minister to appoint women to cabinet positions beyond the 'family' departments. Wilson appointed women to the Foreign Office, the Home Office, the Ministries of Transport and Overseas Development. But despite his record, Williams does not think that Wilson was promoting women on account of their gender: 'He simply appointed whoever he thought would be best for the job.'[40] Her own appointment, Williams told Peter Hennessy in 2013, was a result of Wilson wanting 'to make a point, that "I'm open to young people of ability regardless of their sex". And that was quite an important part of it. I think he would have probably promoted me somewhat slower if I hadn't been a woman. It was an advantage, not a disadvantage.'[41] Shirley Summerskill concurred, telling me: 'In my day, if you were a woman you were noticed, which is probably a good thing in a way; provided it *is* in a good way.'[42]

In 1970, Shirley Williams was negotiating losses and wins. Labour lost the election, but she won a place both in the shadow cabinet and on the party's NEC. Yet, she was not in the mood to celebrate as her marriage to the academic Bernard Williams – with whom she had a child – disintegrated, and her mother, the writer Vera Brittain, died. Williams was spoken about in the press as one to watch and was in demand for comments and interviews, and she learned during times when life was hard that being in the public eye helped her to keep going. 'The eyes and the ears of the media are everywhere; there are few hiding places,' she wrote in her memoirs. 'So one learns composure, to keep hand and eye steady, to never let go except with the most trusted friends. That discipline helps, acts as a lifeline when the foundations themselves crumble away. The show must go on.'[43]

Despite her popularity, Shirley Williams argued that her appointment as shadow home secretary in 1972 was due to 'one of those vagaries of chance that sometimes derail political fortunes'. Unlike three other members of the shadow cabinet on the right of the party, she had not resigned in opposition to a referendum on the UK's entry into the European Common Market that spring. Williams' appointment was an attempt by Wilson to heal the rifts within the parliamentary labour party (PLP), by appointing a pro-European to a senior role. After a year in the position, she was moved to social security. Williams calls this a clear demotion, but adds that she 'deferred to Roy [Jenkins, a fellow right-winger who replaced her as shadow home secretary, having previously resigned from the government] as the more senior and prestigious figure'.[44] On Labour's election win in 1974, Shirley Williams was appointed secretary of state for prices and consumer protection, heading a brand-new department that was intended to address the economic crises that had cost the Conservatives the election in February. In her new role, she sought to enable consumers to find the best deals by forcing the prices of essential goods to be transparent. Following Harold Wilson's resignation in the spring of 1976 and Roy Jenkins' departure in September to become president of the European Commission, Shirley Williams became the minister of education and science in Jim Callaghan's cabinet. At first, she had refused: Labour's policy of rolling out comprehensive schools was not popular with fellow parents at her daughter's grammar school, a few of whom had sworn and spat at Williams. In the end, she agreed to take the position, aware that Callaghan could not be expected to 'leaf his way through every possible vacant cabinet post'.[45]

The press, hostile to Labour's plans to introduce comprehensive schools, continued to target Williams. In 1976, she visited striking workers at the Grunwick film processing factory in north London, who were predominately first-generation female Asian immigrants. They were members of APEX, the union that sponsored Williams, so she went along to give them support and publicity. Three weeks later, there was a clash between militant trade unionists and the police at Grunwick, and Williams was accused of inciting violence. She later wrote: 'Failure to anticipate what the Tory press might make of my intervention was one of the biggest mistakes of my career'.[46] The accusations were doubly frustrating as Williams was a well-known and core member of Labour's moderate Manifesto group, and ran for the deputy leadership of the party in 1976. Her opponent was Michael Foot, and Manifesto were anxious about ending the 'accelerating lurch to the left'. Foot won with 166 votes, just 38 more than Williams.[47] It would take another sixteen years before a woman – Williams' junior minister, Margaret Beckett – was elected deputy leader of the party. But on the Conservative benches in the House of Commons, one woman went further than that. In 1975, Margaret Thatcher challenged Ted Heath for the leadership of their party, and won.

Prime Minister Margaret Thatcher

Disillusioned about the ideological path of the Conservatives while in opposition, Margaret Thatcher had become involved in and inspired by the Centre for Policy Studies (CPS), a think-tank set up in 1974 to lobby for economic liberalism. It was now that Thatcher's personal political ideology was formulated, and she began to lose her appeasing tone towards her party. She read Friedrich Hayek and Milton Friedman, and found a new camaraderie with her colleagues at CPS.[48] When the need to run a leadership contest to depose Heath, who was refusing to stand down, became apparent, she first supported one of them, Keith Joseph. But his position as a challenger was made impossible after a speech in which he argued that unmarried mothers from lower socio-economic backgrounds should be specifically targeted in contraception campaigns to discourage them from having children. Meanwhile, Thatcher was gaining fans for her ability to challenge the government from her position in the shadow cabinet. When Joseph asked her to stand as the challenger, she agreed. According to Charles Moore, her biographer, Thatcher had decided to run before she was asked, but she still took the party by surprise. Many Conservative MPs, who were the only party members able to vote in the leadership challenge, believed she would lose to 'someone more serious'.[49]

Thatcher's campaign was organized by the MP Airey Neave, but it ran into trouble as an interview with *Pre-Retirement Choice* magazine about her retirement plans led to accusations from the Heath fold that she was hoarding food. 'I resent being called a hoarder,' she said in an interview for the *Daily Express* a day later, before listing the contents of her larder (it included six tins of salmon 'to make salmon mousse', four cans of corned beef, two jars of Bovril and honey bought at Conservative Party bazaars). But Thatcher managed to use it to promote her housewife prudency, adding 'I keep a good stock of food at home for several reasons. The main one is that with prices shooting up, it seems to me to be an eminently prudent piece of housekeeping.'[50] In February 1975 Margaret Thatcher won the leadership election by 130 votes to Heath's 119 in the first round. She lacked a majority, so a second round was needed, but it was enough to force Heath to resign. Willie Whitelaw, Conservative MP and Heath's former secretary of state for employment, was selected to run against her. In that round, Thatcher won by 146 votes to 79. In winning, she became the leader of the Conservative Party, the first woman to lead a parliamentary party in the UK and the first female leader of the opposition. But the battle for power was only just beginning: Thatcher was looked down on by members of her party on account of her gender and her background. Being a woman had made her stand out, but she now had to put up with condescending and misogynist sniggering behind her back, and the remaining assumption that women could not lead political parties, let alone countries. Many Conservative MPs were of a generation that was particularly unused to taking orders from women and took to referring to Thatcher as 'Hilda' (her middle name) or 'milk-snatcher'. The Labour government did not spare its judgement of her either: both Wilson and Callaghan were patronizing in their tone to her at prime minister's questions. Shirley Summerskill remembers that Wilson in particular was 'terribly condescending' at the beginning, 'calling her "my dear" from the front bench. He underestimated her terribly'.[51]

One of only twenty-seven female MPs following the October 1974 election, Thatcher could not have found much strength in female solidarity in Parliament even if she had chosen to look for it. Excluded from many of the parliamentary clubs in which male MPs socialized and networked, female MPs did not form a women's caucus to add strength to their numbers. Thatcher did, however, offer support to other women in the house when she saw fit. Shirley Williams has described how, having faced an hour of parliamentary questions in her role as secretary of state for prices and consumer protection in October 1974, she felt like 'St Sebastian, the target of arrows from every direction. Out of the corner of my eye I could just see a figure behind the Speaker's Chair intently watching my performance. It was Margaret Thatcher, Shadow Environment Secretary. When my ordeal was finished, I retreated to the Lady Members' Room, where she was ironing a dress. "You did well," she said. "After all, we can't let them get the better of us."'[52]

Margaret Thatcher was not going to let people's perceptions of her as a woman hold her back. She set about imposing her will on her unruly fellow MPs and worked on her image with a PR coach. Her voice was also modified as she trained herself to use a lower pitch and softer tone to counter arguments that she was shrill. Thatcher loved being dubbed the 'Iron Lady', a term originally coined by the Soviet press, and hired PR firm Saatchi & Saatchi to work on the Conservative campaign ahead of the next election, cultivating an image of toughness and purpose. As Callaghan failed to call the election for the autumn of 1978 – encouraged by his belief that he could charm trade union leaders and that they could, in turn, charm their members into complying with the government's labour market policies – Thatcher and the Conservatives were encouraged by the polls. The election was scheduled for May 1979 and resulted in a Conservative majority of forty-three. The party's manifesto was vague; the campaign had been won more by the electorate's annoyance with the financial and labour market upheavals during the Winter of Discontent than Conservative promises for the future. Yet, for Thatcher it had worked: emphasizing her ruthlessness and determination to address the UK's economic malaise she had become the UK's first woman prime minister. Margaret Thatcher paraphrased Francis of Assisi's prayer, telling the assembled journalists and the world that 'Where there is discord, may we bring harmony. Where there is error, may we bring truth. Where there is doubt, may we bring faith. And where there is despair, may we bring hope.' The words were jotted down on a small card on the short journey from Buckingham Palace to Downing Street.[53]

The election that gave Britain its first female prime minister also saw the number of women in the British Parliament fall from twenty-seven to just nineteen. Margaret Thatcher later argued that it was more significant that she was the first scientist prime minister than the first female prime minister, and she only appointed one female cabinet minister over the next decade. Having kept her distance from other girls already at school, Thatcher continued to prefer the company of men to that of women.[54] But she did not have a great number of women to choose from in 1979: women held only 3 per cent of the seats – a figure lower than at any point since 1951 – despite the fact that more women than ever had stood as candidates.[55] While the number of Conservative women rose from seven to eight, Labour lost seven women as numbers fell from eighteen to eleven. Among them were Shirley Williams and Margaret Beckett, who lost their seats, and Barbara Castle, who stood down. Of the three, only Castle left the House of Commons for good.

***

The 1970s had been a decade in which rapid changes in society had an impact on Parliament and vice versa. Women were no longer assumed to automatically strive towards looking after children and home at the expense of paid employment, and women in Parliament worked hard to change the legal landscape to give working women access to better salaries and improved workplace rights, and provide role models to inspire future generations of women politicians. The policies pursued by female politicians in the 1960s and 1970s foreshadowed other milestones in the 1980s and 1990s, when minorities and women increasingly had an impact on the political landscape. Britain had a woman prime minister, but the struggle for equality was far from over.

6

Paths to Power: 1979–97

Once you've picked up the flag as a pioneer, you can't easily throw it down. And the whole point is that you are carrying it for others, not for yourself.

HARRIET HARMAN, 2017[1]

The dynamic and revolutionary changes of the 1970s – the legal framework, the feminist campaigning, the increased visibility of women in public and private life – were far from over as that decade drew to a close. The 1980s became a time of clashes and tension in British society with a woman prime minister at the helm. The economy went through boom and bust – more people than ever were in a position to purchase their own homes, but millions were unemployed and vast communities were impoverished as mines in the north of England and Wales were closed. Technological advances coincided with the dismantling of nationalized industries, and income disparities grew. Britain went to war to defend the Falklands and played a significant role in the international community, but the formal empire continued to shrink along with Britain's diplomatic influence.

Settling into Number Ten

Despite the fact that Margaret Thatcher had been leader of the opposition for four years, she seemed ill-prepared for her election as prime minister in 1979. This was partly due to a lack of experience: Thatcher had never held a senior cabinet position; she had never been close to Ted Heath, the prime minister she had served, and she still did not command the respect and solidarity of the men she appointed to her first cabinet. The fact that only three of her chosen ministers – home secretary and deputy prime minister Willie Whitelaw (her former opponent in the Conservative leadership election), chancellor Geoffrey Howe and secretary of state for industry Keith Joseph – could be seen as her allies is an indication of Thatcher's standing in the party at the time of the 1979 election. Surrounded by a cabinet dominated by men originally appointed by Heath, Thatcher did not look like she would last long in the role. As a result, she regarded her cabinet, in the words of her lord privy seal – Heath's secretary of state for defence Ian Gilmour – 'as an obstacle to be surmounted'.[2] In doing so, she proved, once and for all, that she went against the gendered assumption that women were afraid of argument, conflict and hostility.

'The Lady's not for turning'

Thatcher believed that her government should be one of conviction, not compromise. A few months before the election, she told an *Observer* journalist: 'As prime minister, I could not waste time having any internal arguments.'[3] The cabinet meetings were for Thatcher a stage for agreeing on a direction or policy already set; she did not think her policies should be voted down by a group she had selected to advise her. This style of leadership had a deterring effect on discussion and opposition, with Thatcher's wrath brought upon anyone who challenged her views. Her contempt for civil servants was well-known and Peter Hennessy has revealed that some ministers were physically sick before going to cabinet meetings if they thought they were 'likely to be on the receiving end of the most famous handbag in world political history'.[4] On one occasion, Thatcher banged her bag on the table and said: 'Well, I haven't much time today, only enough time to explode and have my way!'[5] Whatever feminine traits her supporters in the leadership election of 1975 had expected, these were surely not those. And perhaps this helped keep her in power for so long: historian David Cannadine has suggested that old-fashioned chivalry – a reluctance to use the dirty methods that are needed to force a prime minister's hand or resignation – on behalf of a generation of cabinet ministers brought up not to be rude to ladies, could have played a part in her longevity. Caroline Slocock, a civil servant and the first female private secretary at Number Ten when she was hired in 1989, has observed that Thatcher's behaviour at cabinet meetings had a lot to do with her being the only woman: 'There was only one thing to do in the battle between the sexes, and that was to win.' Yet, Slocock later told me that Thatcher's career 'wouldn't have ended like that, had she been a man. Her behaviour was driven by the fact she was a woman. What could appear as being bullying was defensive behaviour, not actually aggressive behaviour. She'd learnt a kind of strategy to pick men apart; to find power by grasping the detail.'[6]

It is likely that regardless of her gender, Thatcher's eye for detail, absolute conviction and conflict readiness would have served any man or woman in her position well. Thatcher did have allies, and she made great use of them. According to Slocock, she treated Number Ten as her family not just her official residence, buying personal presents for her staff, inviting those who worked late upstairs for family meals, and creating the most feminine working environment of Slocock's career. 'She could be utterly charming, and really quite empathetic,' Slocock added. 'Thoughtful and polite – more than polite.'[7] Thatcher's policy unit at Number Ten was made up of Centre for Policy Studies colleagues, who helped her keep discussions off the record until policies were presented to the cabinet as finished products. Thatcher's political convictions included that European integration should only be about trade and that it would become a threat to the United Kingdom if it strayed beyond that; that Communism and socialism needed to be fought aggressively at home and abroad; and that, in the words of Conservative MP William Waldegrave, 'a huge dose of radical economic liberalism would reverse the economic collapse'.[8] In this, she found a great many friends and supporters, though many of her cabinet members – One Nation Tories, described by Thatcher as 'wets' – were sceptical about the pace and content of her reforms. Thatcher was also continuously more confrontational with European leaders and the Soviet Union than recommended by the experts in the Foreign and Commonwealth Office.

If Thatcher's style of government seemed revolutionary and a break with the past, her initial policies were ones of continuity with previous Conservative thinking. But already in 1980, one of her lasting legacies was introduced with the Right to Buy scheme, which saw just over two million council tenants become home owners between 1980 and 1995. It was part of Thatcher's plan to establish a property-owning democracy, and it was meant to encourage swathes of formerly Labour-sympathetic working-class tenants into home-owning Conservative supporters. Though there were some positive outcomes, including securing homes and potentially even pension pots for a generation of renters who could afford the heavily subsidized prices, Right to Buy led to a falling number of council properties as councils were not allowed to invest the proceeds of house-sales in building new council homes. It became steadily more difficult to get social housing, a growing problem that hit women, then and indeed now, on low incomes the hardest.

At the extreme, pressures on society caused by the rapid cuts to services sparked riots. In April 1981, 300 members of the police and many members of the public were injured in what became known as the Brixton riots. Cars and buildings were torched as the broken relationship between the locals and the state – in the shape of the police force – gave way to violent protests. For Thatcher's cabinet opponents, it was a sign that her policies were not working. For Thatcher, however, the riots – which spread to Birmingham's Handsworth, London's Southall, Liverpool's Toxteth, Manchester's Moss Side and Nottingham's Hyson Green before the end of the year – were unrelated to the hardships and deprivation caused by economic decline. She had refused to make a U-turn when challenged at the Conservative party conference in 1980 – 'You turn if you want to. The lady's *not* for turning,' she famously told her audience – and she was not about to change course a year later.

Many observers have commented on Thatcher's incredible capacity for work and her rigid convictions. Charles Powell, her private secretary for foreign affairs from 1984, has spoken about Thatcher's Leninist tendencies – her 'absolute determination, the belief that there's a vanguard which is right and if you keep that small, tightly knit team together, they will drive things through'.[9] Peter Hennessy, meanwhile, has written that she was Marxian in her sense of struggle; a claim he illustrates with an anecdote from an advisor who suggested that Thatcher might take a holiday. The response, 'I must govern!', shows both dedication to the office but also a conviction that only she had what it took to get things done.[10]

Boudicca with a handbag: Thatcher at war

Despite Thatcher's bravado in public and cabinet meetings, her government did not seem secure during her first few years as prime minister. Stagflation – high inflation with high unemployment – had set in, and Geoffrey Howe's budgets did not help. In December 1981, opinion polls showed that Thatcher was the least popular prime minister since polling had begun, and in April 1982, the three major parties were at level pegging. Yet when the votes cast in the general election were counted

14 months later, on 9 June 1983, Thatcher won resoundingly, increasing her Commons majority from 43 to 144. It was to some extent due to a partial economic recovery and a divided opposition, which was now a two-party beast with the recently formed Social Democratic Party (SDP) splitting the centre-left vote in two. But the main event that had turned Thatcher's fortunes around was the outbreak of hostilities in the South Atlantic a year earlier. It would also put a spotlight on Thatcher's performance as the first female prime minister at war.

While the pink colour of the British empire continued to fade on the world map as territory by territory sought and gained independence, in the spring of 1982 British forces were deployed to protect the craggy Falklands Islands, home to a population of 1,800 British citizens. The post-mortem to the war did not paint a flattering picture of Thatcher's role in the lead-up to the conflict: her emphasis on protecting Europe from Soviet aggression led to a greater focus on Europe at the expense of the outposts of the empire, and this had left the Falklands with little protection.[11] There were also several blunders, most damningly that intelligence from the area was out of date and scarce despite the fact that there had been concerns that Argentina could be planning an invasion. When the invasion finally took place on 2 April 1982, Thatcher was quick to put the blame on the Foreign Office, annoyed at discussions of diplomacy that she felt were a sign of weakness.[12] She set up a small war cabinet, officially an offshoot of the cabinet committee on overseas and defence policy, consisting of the newly appointed foreign secretary Francis Pym, defence secretary John Nott, home secretary and deputy prime minister Willie Whitelaw, paymaster-general Cecil Parkinson, chief of defence staff Terence Lewin and attorney general Sir Michael Havers.[13]

Thatcher was, again, the only woman at the table and her gender came up time and again in debates in the House of Commons, the House of Lords, and in the press. Enoch Powell, at the time an MP for the Ulster Unionist Party, kicked proceedings off in the House of Commons in March 1982, when he made reference to Thatcher's Iron Lady nickname, stating that 'this House, the nation and the Right Hon. Lady herself will learn of what metal she is made'.[14] On 6 April, Thatcher was interviewed by ITN, whose broadcast showed her saying: 'Do you remember what Queen Victoria once said: "Failure? The possibilities do not exist." That is the way we must look at it.'[15] The next day, James Callaghan – the former Labour leader – told the House of Commons that '[i]t was all very well for Queen Victoria to say that [there was no possibility of defeat] because she was not actually conducting the operations. She could say such a thing, but anyone who is actually in charge of mounting a diplomatic and military operation must contemplate the difficulties ahead, and they are very real in the present circumstances. I beg the prime minister not to take that attitude in the detailed consideration and planning of the operation as she has done in public.'[16]Meanwhile, Labour MPs did not hesitate to express their worry that she was an unsuitable wartime leader because of her gender. On 14 April, former deputy prime minister Lord George Brown felt the need to state: 'If she does not mind (or even if she does), I should like to say publicly that you can get a situation where a prime minister feels that she must appear to be twice as virile as anybody else might feel it necessary to appear in that office, either because she is perhaps overtly conscious of the fact that she is a woman or because she knows that she is in her present office against or despite the wishes of most of her more immediate cousins.'[17] On 29 April, Labour MP Stan Thorne asked if the government intended to use force 'to save the prime minister's face, irrespective of the lives that may be lost in the process? If so, it is the act of a desperate woman and, as such, she has no place in running our affairs in the United Kingdom.'[18] On 20 May, Labour MP Andrew Faulds added: 'What worries me is that the prime purpose [of going to war] I believe is to prove what a man the prime minister is. (. . .) That may lead to a few giggles on the Government Benches, but that is what most of the people in our constituencies who support us and discuss these matters think that the exercise is about – that the prime minister has to prove what a man she is.'[19] In the House of Lords, Labour peer Lord Ardwick concluded: 'I sometimes wonder whether it would not be a good idea to get up a subscription to buy a pair of velvet gloves for the "Iron Lady".'[20]

The press was not to be outdone. After a meeting with the US secretary of state Alexander Haig on 12 April, *The Daily Mail* described Thatcher as 'upset' rather than angered, while *The Sun* argued that she 'dug her heels in'.[21] But Thatcher herself contributed to the amplification of her gender. She was open about her tears for fallen soldiers, telling *Women's Own* in August 1982 that 'You look at the sun and wonder how can it shine. [During the war] I used to go outside to the garden at Chequers and think, isn't it strange how ordinary life goes on?'[22] In the aftermath of the war, it was often pointed out that Thatcher was always impressed by a uniform, and Charles Moore went so far as to call her 'innocent of geography and of the sea' in his authorized biography.[23]

But, despite the criticism, Thatcher emerged victorious, not just in the South Atlantic but in Westminster as her approval ratings soared to 51 per cent.[24] Her stature rose on the international scene too, and her relationship with Ronald Reagan and the American right became closer and friendlier.

A woman's cabinet

It is an often-cited fact that only one woman served in any of Margaret Thatcher's cabinets. She was Baroness Janet Young, born in 1926 and a mother of three. Young was a fervent advocate for traditional family values and Christian society, and led the Conservative support for Section 28, which banned the 'intended promotion of homosexuality'. She also campaigned against the lowering of the age of consent in same-sex relationships. Young's political roots were local: she became a councillor in 1957 and an alderman of Oxford city council in 1967, and was given a peerage by Ted Heath in 1971. Installed in the House of Lords, Young quickly became a government whip. She was promoted to minister of state in the Department for Education by Margaret Thatcher. From 1981, Young served as the leader of the House of Lords for a year before being appointed lord privy seal and a member of Thatcher's cabinet in 1982. She was replaced by John Biffen after only fourteen months in the role. Thatcher later wrote that Young did not 'have the presence to lead the Lords effectively and she was perhaps too consistent an advocate of caution on all occasions'.[25] Others disagreed: colleagues quoted by *The Guardian* after Young's death in 2002 called her a 'competent minister' and a 'bloody tough operator'.[26]

Why were more women not promoted to higher office during Thatcher's years as prime minister? There were a few reasons, the first being that her ideology did not leave any room for preferential treatment. Women did not need her help, Thatcher reasoned. 'A woman must rise through merit', she wrote in her autobiography. 'There must be no discrimination.' In 1982, Thatcher told a children's TV show that 'I think most of us got to our own position in life without Women's Lib and we got here, not by saying "you've got to have more women doing so and so" but saying "look, we've got the qualifications, why shouldn't we have just as much a chance as a man?" And you'll find that so many male bastions were conquered that way, whereas Women's Lib, I think, has been rather strident, concentrated on things which don't really matter and, dare I say it, being rather unfeminine.'[27] Thatcher believed public life was a meritocracy in which women, like men, could rise to the top if they were good enough. Her statement about the women's liberation movement also shows how Thatcher embodied some of the prejudices against women that had threatened to derail her own career before her election to Parliament in 1959. Femininity was key. Having herself talked about the importance of women using their brains in the mid-1970s, a decade later Thatcher suggested on BBC's Woman's Hour that a few hours of work a week would suffice.[28] Although her own children were sent to boarding school, Thatcher felt all other mothers were best placed in a nurturing position at home.

Some observers have also argued that Thatcher found it easier to work with men than women. Edwina Currie said the men in Parliament 'fell about for Thatcher, especially the public school ones.' In her interview with me, Currie said that while at first Thatcher talked about wanting more women in Parliament, this quickly petered out – 'Why weren't women like Lynda Chalker [Conservative MP from 1974–92] and Emma Nicholson [Conservative MP from 1987–97] promoted?' Currie asked. She remembered Thatcher saying that she would not have Heath in her cabinet because he would 'look across the table at me like a woman would'. It suggests, Currie argued, something of the impostor syndrome and a fear that other women might 'find her out' in a way men wouldn't. Gillian Shephard, who was elected in 1987, has also argued that Thatcher should have put Lynda Chalker in the cabinet: 'Lynda had a very senior position as a sort of Deputy Foreign Secretary, and she had worked a lot on her own developing policy on Africa and elsewhere. She was a serious player, loyal to a fault and never put her foot in it – a first class woman.'[29] Chalker herself told me that Margaret Thatcher liked to be the only woman on the horizon.[30] Harriet Harman corroborated this, saying that Thatcher 'didn't want to share the spotlight – it is the Queen Bee syndrome and that was the way women were expected to be. The idea of sisterhood was anathema, women were in competition with each other.'[31]

It is also possible that Thatcher's leadership style made Conservative women reluctant to come forward. However, while Thatcher's disdain for her cabinet colleagues was well known, not everyone faced her steamroller style of management. Shephard later claimed that only senior members of the cabinet were treated aggressively. 'I never suffered myself because I was very junior in Mrs Thatcher's government,' she told *The Daily*

Telegraph in 2013. 'However rude she was in cabinet, she would never raise her voice to a subordinate. To people who couldn't answer back, she was always kind.'[32] Edwina Currie, who was forced to resign as junior health minister in 1988 after claiming that most of Britain's eggs were infected with salmonella, also detailed several instances when Thatcher expressed her concern for Currie's well-being in her later published diaries.[33] Shephard found Thatcher 'terrifically easy when she was in a group of women,' she told me in 2018, adding that Thatcher was 'quite conspiratorial when she worked with women'. Along with other Conservative women MPs, Shephard was regularly invited to her office in the House of Commons where the prime minister would offer them a drink and ask for input on issues to do with women, like child benefit. 'We were there to tell her how it was on the ground, from our point of view, that's what I felt. (. . .) Everybody would tell it like it was. Perhaps slightly deferentially, but nevertheless: if something wasn't going down well, they would say so.'[34] Shephard also remembers Thatcher saying: 'If you want something done, ask a woman. If you want a speech made, ask a man.' And, Shephard said, 'she did mean it. She absolutely did. She felt they didn't master the detail.' Reflecting on Thatcher's rise to power, Shephard told me that the prime minister 'utterly devoted herself to the whole thing from an early age, and that was obviously right for her, especially in her generation. Otherwise she would have never gotten anywhere. She made a lot of sacrifices.'[35]

Under Thatcher's premiership, Shephard was appointed parliamentary under-secretary of state in the Department of Social Security in 1989 and later minister of state at the Treasury. Shephard found it hard to align everything she had heard about Thatcher with what she herself observed: 'She had a very down-to-earth manner one-on-one, with a touch of a Grantham accent.'

Unlike many others, Shephard was quickly promoted once she had been elected an MP. She was a junior minister under Thatcher, and was appointed to a cabinet seat after Thatcher's departure in 1990. Under the premiership of John Major, Shephard served as the secretary of state for employment in 1992–3 – a position that simultaneously made her the UK's first-ever minister for women's issues – before moving to the Ministry of Agriculture, Fisheries and Food 1993–4 and finally becoming secretary of state for education and employment 1994–7. She was joined in the cabinet by Virginia Bottomley, who was promoted from minister of state for health under Thatcher to secretary of state for health (1992–5)

before moving to the National Heritage Department (1995–7). Aware
that the press was looking for an excuse to write about cabinet cat-fights,
Shephard and Bottomley made a deal not to work against one-another.
'We couldn't possibly have been more different,' Shephard told me, 'both
in appearance and manner of working, and past experience. We said
that we would never ever give anybody the chance to say that we were
criticising the other. We would be supportive; end of. And we were.'[36]
Shephard describes Bottomley as a terrific co-conspirator. As employment
secretary, Shephard had responsibility for women's issues, and she
concludes that it was in this area that she made the greatest difference.
When briefing ministers, who were less enthusiastic, Shephard recalls
that the 'terrible ones would come along and kick their feet about and
scuffle and nudge each other'. But then Bottomley would walk in
and said, 'we mean business here'. On employment and access to work,
Shephard was particularly proud of her back-to-work policies and
workplace nurseries.[37]

   Bottomley's relationship with Thatcher also complicates the standard
picture of the prime minister as a woman who pulled up the ladder
behind her. Bottomley only ran as a candidate for the Conservatives in
the 1983 election after receiving a call from Margaret Thatcher imploring
her to stand as the party needed more women in Parliament. Bottomley
lost against the sitting Liberal MP Stephen Ross in the Isle of Wight, but
successfully contested South West Surrey in a 1984 by-election. She had
been devastated in 1983, Bottomley said later. 'The campaign was "Turn
Wight Blue" and Mrs Thatcher even came over to visit. The day after I had
lost she rang me to say, "what bad luck" and I burst into tears.'[38]

Mothers in the House

When Harriet Harman was elected as a Labour MP in 1982, she became
a member of a small group of women in Parliament determined to
challenge structural injustices that kept women from fulfilling their
potential in public and private life. Harman had a particular interest in
improving the lives of working mothers. Born in 1950, she came from a
privileged middle-class background and qualified as a solicitor in London
after graduating from the University of York with a BA in Politics. She
was pulled towards party politics in the 1970s, radicalized by the women's
movement, which made her see the injustices of her experiences of

workplace discrimination and sexual harassment with new eyes. By the time Harman stood for Parliament in 1982, she was a committed feminist.[39] She was also pregnant with a baby that would be born ahead of the 1983 election campaign. But when the incumbent Peckham MP, Harry Lamborn, suddenly died in 1982, a just-married Harman found herself contesting the subsequent by-election while heavily pregnant. She could count on support from many colleagues and friends, and from her obstetrician, whose answer to Harman's question about whether running for a parliamentary seat while pregnant was a good idea was that '[working all hours, going up and down stairs all day and very little sleep] was excellent exercise and that I'd get no sleep when the baby came anyway, so it would be good practice'.[40] Others were less supportive: Harman's Social Democratic Party (SDP) opponent, the former labour minister Dick Taverne against whom Margaret Beckett had lost in the election of February 1974, had his team tell Peckham residents that they should not vote for Harman as she was pregnant and would not be able to do the job. Harman, who lashed out at the SDP in her victory speech, had the opposite experience. She found that her pregnancy positively reinforced her campaign; it marked her out from 'normal politicians' and she gained plenty of solidarity from her female constituents. She even offered to look after a young baby so that a mother would be able to cast her vote on the evening of the election, an offer that was accepted. 'I felt honoured,' Harman later wrote in her memoirs. 'I knew that she would never have left a male candidate alone in her home with her precious children. And, understandably, no male candidate would have offered.'[41]

Arriving in Parliament in late October 1982, Harman walked into a large, male-dominated institution. Women only made up 3.5 per cent of the House of Commons. There were eleven Labour women, and eight Conservative women – including the prime minister. In those days, Harman remembers, it was the women's movement outside Parliament that provided a sisterhood of supporters – the number in Westminster was not great enough and many thought Harman was a 'humourless feminist'. The message from the women's movement was, Harman told me: 'you are in there, in a difficult situation, part of the frontline of delivery for us. We have got your back!' She took her seat wearing a red velvet maternity gown. In December, she was patronized by MPs on all sides when she asked Thatcher to improve holiday childcare facilities for school-age children. It was, Thatcher responded, not for the government to arrange school-holiday provision. The birth of Harman's son in February 1983 was quickly followed by the general election in June and being a mother in Westminster further complicated her relationship to Parliament. It added 'an extra dimension' to her campaigns to improve working life for parents, she later argued, but it also meant that she was torn between the long, inflexible working hours and processes of a rigid institution bound by tradition and male-dominance. Harman did not dare to insist on formal maternity leave for herself, even though she was making the case in Parliament that all women should have the right to maternity leave. She also felt the pressure of needing to represent her constituents and show that women were capable MPs. 'So even when I was scarcely coping,' she wrote in her memoirs, 'I never admitted it but emphasised instead that I was strong, capable and determined in their cause. Presenting that face to the outside world helped me live up to my responsibilities, but it gave many women the false impression that I was, somehow, superhuman, when I was anything but.'[42] Harman was also haunted by accusations that she was an unfit mother and contemplated giving up her seat at times. In the end she could not, feeling that she would be letting down both the party and the women's movement. Harman told me that:

> the biggest challenge was the lack of confidence that it was actually possible. Is it actually possible to be having babies as an MP and to be a decent mother? I had to try, but the fear was that I was letting my constituents down and that I was letting my children down. When I look back at it now, of course, I was overcompensating. I went all around the country, I was in every tenants' association AGM in my constituency. I had five-hour surgeries, I did monthly reports, which detailed all my work. Overcompensating with the kids as well, because I just didn't sleep.

Harman remembers that Tessa Jowell worked in a similar fashion, even forgoing sleep to work through the night twice a week. 'That's how pressurised we felt, because we couldn't not do all these things other mothers were doing, and we couldn't not do all the things we thought other MPs were doing.' But, Harman concluded, 'once you've picked up the flag as a pioneer,' she said, 'you can't easily throw it down. And the whole point is that you are carrying it for others, not for yourself.'[43]

Harriet Harman was a pioneer in many ways, but she was not the first woman to have a child while serving as an MP. Mostly, however, the demands of the job meant that most women MPs had had babies before coming to Westminster, or not at all. One exception was Labour's Helene Hayman, who was elected for Welwyn and Hatfield in October 1974. Hayman was then only twenty-five years old, the youngest MP in the House. She was recently married and had her first child two years later. When I interviewed Hayman in 2017, she said that her constituents were happy for her, but the situation in Parliament was very difficult. Asking the Conservative Party chief whip if Hayman could be paired with one of their MPs [a Conservative MP whose absence at voting meant that Hayman herself did not have to cast her vote] to avoid leaving her ten-day-old baby, she received a negative response. Her own party whips said they could not let her off, so chaperoned by veteran Labour MP Lena Jeger amid a doorstep scrum of photographers and journalists, Hayman made the journey to Westminster. And while she could borrow Shirley Williams's office to breastfeed – there were no other suitable spaces in the whole Palace of Westminster – Hayman remembers a senior female Conservative MP called the police when Hayman left her baby with his nanny in the Lady Members' Room during the vote.[44] Shirley Williams later recalled that the Conservative MP Lady Tweedsmuir – who was born in 1915 and, when elected in 1946, a widow with two daughters[45] – had found her own solution to the problem decades earlier by 'handing over her newest baby in its carrycot to a suitably responsible-looking policeman to care for while she attended a meeting, as to the manner born', and decades later Helene Hayman, Williams added, had to smuggle her son in.[46]

Ann Taylor, who was first elected for Bolton West in 1974 aged twenty-seven, had her first child in 1982. He was born in the summer recess and in the general election the following year she was pregnant with her second child. In language similar to Harriet Harman's, Taylor told me:

> I always took the view that things have got to be possible. It's got to be possible for a young, northern woman to be an MP, obviously. Then it's got to be possible for a young, married northern woman to be a Minister, for a young northern woman on the front bench to have a baby. It has to be possible, the opposite is inconceivable because it's possible for a young, northern man to be on the front bench and have a baby.[47]

In 1983, there were rumours that Harriet Harman had fed her baby in the Chamber, which was untrue; as was the charge that she had taken her son through the Division Lobby, through which MPs walk to have their vote counted. Harman felt particularly angry that the accuser was a fellow Labour MP. 'Why hadn't they said something to me?' she wrote in her autobiography. 'Why did it even matter to them if I *had* taken my baby through under my coat?'[48] It felt, Harman added, like yet another example of the hostility towards mothers in Westminster.

Diane Abbott, first elected in 1987, became a mother in 1992 while serving as MP for Hackney North & Stoke Newington, joining the group of women MPs who struggled to keep their family and work balanced. A single mother, she came in to vote when her son was just eight days old. 'The whips gave no concessions at all,' Abbott says, and she relied on live-in help from a relative from Jamaica who stayed with her for a year. Even so, continuing her work as an MP was a great challenge. 'People weren't understanding,' Abbott said in 2018.

> I had a system: I was in Parliament for four days and hardly saw my son, and then Friday, Saturday and Sunday I spent time with him. I remember being attacked for not being [at work]. It was like 'you've chosen to have this baby, so it's on you'. I always felt that I was either not a good enough mother or that I was not a good enough MP. It was quite stressful, because you didn't feel you were doing either job properly.

In 1994, while giving evidence to the all-male employment select committee, she was asked by Conservative MP Sebastian Coe what qualities mothers brought to the House of Commons. 'First,' Abbott responded, 'I can manage with very little sleep. Secondly, I am very flexible. You have to be flexible with children who one morning will only eat Weetabix and the next morning won't touch Weetabix. And third (. . .) I can put up with a lot of childish babble.' After another question, this time from Conservative MP Harry Greenway, on whether working mothers were trying to square an impossible circle, Abbott retorted 'Even you Mr Greenway, august and distinguished Member of Parliament, might be an even better MP if the way our life is structured enabled you to spend more time with your family.'[49] In 2018, Abbott added that it would not be entirely fair to say that only Conservative MPs had issues with women being in Parliament. 'There was absolutely no accommodation to the situation from the Labour party; I had a pair, but you couldn't pair for specific childcare reasons.' At home, she downplayed being an MP to the extent that her son only fully became aware once her decision to send him to a private school became front-page news. One radio station even phoned Abbott at home, and when her son answered, interviewed him live on air, without parental consent. 'I knew men who sent their kids to private school and got none of that,' Abbott said in 2018. 'It was traumatic for my son. It wasn't nice for me at all, but it was terrible for him. And it was the culmination of the previous eleven years thinking about what a poor mother I'd been. I made a conscious decision to do something that was about him rather than my career; I felt I owed him a difficult decision.'[50] These were experiences shared with many mothers in the House of Commons, including Harriet Harman, who faced a barrage of criticism when she sent her son to a grammar school. Harman also describes ignoring calls from the whips' office when she had promised to take her children to the cinema during the half-term holidays – a truth that she never told her whips or her boss, shadow foreign secretary Robin Cook. Like Abbott, Harman believes that 'the children of a woman are always more exposed than the children of a man, because the mother is regarded as the principal carer by society, usually by the children as well as the mother.'[51]

Leading ladies

Apart from Thatcher, prime minister for eleven years, Shirley Williams was the only woman remotely near to leading a British political party in the 1980s. Having lost her seat in Parliament in 1979 to the Conservative candidate, Williams retained a position of influence on Labour's NEC where she attempted to steer the party away from the left-wing turn it was about to make. Williams had been numbed rather than hurt by the loss of her seat. She wrote in her autobiography that 'By Saturday morning, a good night's sleep and the prospect of freedom from the constraints of being a minister began to cheer me up.' She added: 'I had woken up to a heady sense of freedom, as if I had got my life back after all the years of responsibility and discipline. I didn't know what I would do, but I did know I needed time to think.'[52]

After leaving the UK for the US and a job at the John F. Kennedy School of Government at Harvard University, Williams felt she could objectively assess the issues within the Labour Party on her return: 'Those who live within dysfunctional families rarely regard themselves as dysfunctional,' she wrote, 'and so it was for us.'[53] Inspired by the 1979 Dimbleby Lecture in which the former deputy leader of the Labour Party, Roy Jenkins, stressed the need to break Britain's two-party system, and a hostile party conference in 1981, Williams left Labour to set up the Social Democratic Party (SDP) alongside David Owen, Bill Rogers and Roy Jenkins. The new party was meant to have a collective leadership, but Roy Jenkins' seniority in age and experience meant that Williams deferred the title of leader to him, just like she had in the early 1970s when he returned to the shadow cabinet to take her post as shadow home secretary. David Owen was annoyed at Williams' decision not to challenge Jenkins for the leadership, but she 'readily conceded, publicly and privately, that Roy was a greater person than I was'. She was also nervous about making enemies.[54] But her relationship with Jenkins was not easy; Williams did not trust that he shared the SDP's objectives, and objected to the fact that he did not bear the scars of Labour's infighting that had led to the party's creation. 'I didn't want our new party to be fashioned by someone, however distinguished, who had not been part of our struggle,' she later wrote.[55] It was Williams' refusal to launch the party from Jenkins' house that led to the famous Limehouse Declaration, during which the SDP's formation was announced to the public. The announcement was made from David Owen's home and Williams, who was known for her relaxed attitude to clothes, had to borrow a shirt from Owen's wife, and Matthew (now Lord) Oakeshott, Roy Jenkins' researcher, had to go back to Williams' flat to pick up a skirt, as 'my appearance at that moment was not compatible with a serious attempt to found a new political party'.[56]

It is, perhaps, surprising that Williams did not stand for the leadership when she had the chance. Her new party was male-dominated, and not a single female MP defected to the party from either the Conservatives or Labour. Williams herself returned to the House of Commons in November 1981 as the SDP MP for Crosby, which meant that her stature within the party rose further. Because of that, she became the subject of a campaign masterminded by Jenkins' supporters. There were whispers about Williams being 'disorganized, indecisive and incapable of leadership'. Her name was turned into the anagram 'I whirl aimlessly', which was 'both wounding and clever'.[57] Later, Williams told Peter Hennessy that she agreed with critics who said that she had given up the possibility to lead a party when she left Labour. But, Williams stressed, unlike Thatcher she 'was always more comfortable as a member of a team than as the single leader, whereas in [Thatcher's] case she was much more happy being the single leader than being a member of the team. So it's partly psychological. I don't blame anybody for my not being prime minister except myself.'[58] She also speculated that the support of a loving relationship – she was a single mother when the SDP launched, only remarrying in 1987 – might have given her the courage to stand for leadership.

Internal party divisions were one reason why Williams did not become a party leader, and they also played a great role in Thatcher's eventual downfall. The Conservatives were losing support as the attempted introduction of the poll tax in 1989, a series of insensitive budgets from Nigel Lawson and conflicts about Britain's role in the EU all combined to push the public further away. In 1989, Thatcher survived her first leadership challenge, from Sir Anthony Meyer. A year later, as the Conservatives' divisions on Europe continued and as the economy looked to be stagnating, Michael Heseltine seized the opportunity to stage a second challenge. Thatcher won the first ballot, but lacked a convincing margin and, after consultations with MPs, she resigned. Douglas Hurd later argued that it was Thatcher's failure to make the best of the traditional cabinet system of mutual tolerance and mutual support that caused her downfall. Thatcher herself, meanwhile, described it as a constitutional coup.[59] Tending her resignation to the House of Commons on 22 November 1990, Thatcher put in a barnstorming performance. Defending her record, policies and ideology over the course of thirty-five minutes at the despatch box, Thatcher argued that every British citizen was better off after eleven years of her rule. She was certain, she said, that the Conservatives would win a fourth consecutive election and that the country would continue to prosper. Her speech was her trademark mix of hyperbolic and passionate, unscripted and fluent, exaggerated and inflated. After being interrupted by Labour MP Dennis Skinner she retorted with: 'Now, where were we? I am enjoying this.'[60] But on 28 November, when her successor John Major had been elected leader and taken over as prime minister, a teary Margaret Thatcher left Number Ten, got into a chauffeur-driven car and pulled out through the gates onto Whitehall.

As Britain's first female prime minister, Thatcher left an indelible mark on the British economy and society during her eleven years in office – for good or ill. But she proved that women could lead and reach the highest of political office. Thatcher fought three elections as party leader and won them all.

For a short while in 1994, Labour, too, had a female leader: Margaret Beckett. Beckett had been persuaded to run for deputy leader of the party in 1992, creating a partnership with John Smith, who was elected leader at the same time. The two knew each other well, and Beckett had been particularly incensed by Bryan Gould's claim that he ought to be elected deputy leader to keep 'John Smith in line'. 'I thought that's a very arrogant thing to say,' Beckett told me. 'It's also a pretty stupid thing to say.' Having stood in for Smith on a few occasions when he was absent from Parliament, Beckett became the interim leader of the opposition two years later after Smith's sudden death. Feeling that the party needed someone with their feet on the ground and that she was that person, she decided to run in the leadership election. 'I didn't think that I stood any real chance of winning,' Beckett told me. 'To be perfectly honest, and it's a very old-fashioned thing to say, I thought it might be my duty to stand. I didn't think Tony [Blair] had enough experience.' She expected to lose but was encouraged by her meetings with the public. Still, Beckett's campaign stalled as Tony Blair's accelerated and, in the end, she also lost the deputy leadership to John Prescott. 'I was fond of Tony,' Beckett told me. 'But I didn't want to be his deputy. It was going to be a whole other ball game from being John's deputy.' As the Labour leadership became all-male yet again, Beckett remembers 'looking at the stage with the leader and the deputy leader and their wives, and thinking to myself "normal service has been resumed".' While she felt that the party would have been better served by a more diverse leadership, 'I didn't want particularly to do it'.[61] After the election of a Labour government in 1997, Beckett instead served Tony Blair as a cabinet minister until his resignation in 2007.

Visible women

Britain lost its first female prime minister when Margaret Thatcher resigned, but during the course of John Major's seven years in Downing Street, more women gained senior government positions. They included Gillian Shephard and Virginia Bottomley. Bottomley was perhaps the most visible of the two: her time in charge of the Department of Health coincided with NHS cuts and the fall-out from the AIDS crisis, and she was often in the news. Major also appointed a host of other women, most notably Angela Rumbold as minister of state for home affairs and Baroness Trumpington as minister of state for agriculture, fisheries and food, while Lynda Chalker remained as minister for overseas development. Cheryl Gillan – a cabinet minister as secretary of state for Wales under David Cameron – became an under-secretary of state for education and employment, while Ann Widdecombe held the same title for social security before becoming minister of state for employment and, later, prisons. The cabinet and Parliament remained heavily male-dominated, but Thatcher's departure seemingly opened space for more women in the public eye.

One woman who did not go into Government under John Major was Edwina Currie. Although she was offered a role, Currie told me that she did not think it was the right one, and felt insulted given that Major was handing out jobs to MPs like Jonathan Aitken and Neil Hamilton – both later caught up in the cash for questions scandal. Although not known in 1992, in 2003, Edwina Currie revealed that she had had an affair with Major for four years in the 1980s – until Major was appointed by Thatcher to the cabinet. 'My husband had a demanding job too,' Currie told me. 'We didn't see each other much and our lives began to diverge. Major was encouraging and supportive – he had no enemies, was nice to everyone, and rose to lead the party by friendship.' In politics, Currie added, 'people are separated from their spouses and it can be a very lonely and intense life, a peculiar and shared experience (...) with a miserable week or a big success shared more easily with people there.' She added: 'It was a doddle to have an affair. Loads of people were. If your spouse's head was not on the pillow next to you, someone else's head would be.' The relationship ended because of the risks, and because neither wanted to hurt their families. They remained close, but the relationship did not lead to Currie being offered a job in Government.[62]

On the opposition benches, Labour women had begun to organize with the sole intent of growing their number. Inspired by the women's movement, Harriet Harman sought to build the Labour Party Women's Committee as a parliamentary wing of the many constituency women's groups that were dotted around the country. 'We were so outnumbered in the Commons [in 1982], it was obvious that we had to work collectively as women MPs to raise women's issues in the House, to form a link with women outside Parliament, and to work towards bringing more women into Parliament,' Harman wrote in 2017.[63] Her efforts were greeted with annoyance and fury from male Members of Parliament who thought groups shouldn't be formed that excluded some MPs. It was a charge Harman overcame by pointing out that many other meetings, for example those for Scottish MPs or the miners' group, were closed to her.[64] A decade later, Harman was a member of a dinner club for fellow Labour women – including Margaret Hodge, Anna Coote, Patricia Hewitt and Tessa Jowell – which was regarded with suspicion by men who came across them in the Churchill Room on the parliamentary estate, proving perhaps that women in a group are perceived as a threat despite the fact that all-male tables were the norm on the same premises.[65]

Labour women organizing as women had an immediate impact. Harman noticed a huge growth in the number of delegates at the Labour women's conference from 1981 to 1982, and while the number of women elected onto the Labour benches remained static in 1983, the parliamentary party was in the process of a generational shift that resulted in the increased acceptance of women's movement tactics. One of the new Labour MPs elected in 1983 was Clare Short, who was thirty-seven years old and had plenty of government experience having worked as a civil servant in the Home Office. As the MP for Birmingham Ladywood, Short represented a constituency in which she herself had grown up before going to university in Leeds. She was known for her direct manner, left-wing credentials and quickly gained notoriety when she – against tradition – implied that Alan Clark, the Conservative minister of employment, was drunk at the despatch box. He had been drinking before appearing in the House at 10pm and later recalled the event in his diaries. Clark wrote that: 'A new Labour member whom I had never seen before called Clare Short, dark-haired and serious with a lovely Brummie accent, said something about she'd read that you couldn't accuse a fellow member of being drunk, but she really believed I was incapable.' Her words were followed by shouting in all directions, and a division was quickly called by the speaker. Short later told me that, because of the late hours, the atmosphere in Parliament was often a bit raucous and 'flirty'. She pointed out that it could be intimidating for women, but also for working-class men in that it was 'quite a public school-boy atmosphere'.[66]

According to Harman, Short's arrival galvanized the struggle to push women's issues higher up on Labour's legislative agenda. In 1986, Short slept overnight in Parliament to ensure she was first in the queue to get a ten-minute rule motion for her Indecent Displays (Newspapers) Bill, which sought to ban pictures of women with no clothes on in newspapers. During her speech, male MPs giggled and made noises at her but Short, who received 10,000 letters in support for her stance from women around the country, pressed on. There was a price to pay, however: *The Sun* made their opposition personal with articles about 'Crazy Clare'. The paper also sent a busload of Page 3 girls to her house in Birmingham (where she lived with her mother) and to her flat in London. Years later, the paper's then editor Rebekah Wade apologized for her paper's behaviour in court, but she never apologized to Short personally.[67]

All-women shortlists

Clare Short fought other battles too, often picking up threads left by Jo Richardson who died in 1994 and whom Short replaced as chair of the Women's PLP. In an article she wrote in 1996, Short argued that there had been a 'quiet revolution' taking place in the Labour Party since the late 1980s. In 1986, the Socialist International – an alliance of social democratic parties of which Labour was a member – had endorsed the use of quotas in the selection of prospective parliamentarians. It was an attempt to address the structural imbalances that meant that women were still unlikely to stand in elections, and likely to be selected only for difficult-to-win seats if they did. Inspired by the quota notion and seeing how other parties made great strides in their quest for gender equality (the 1994 Social Democratic government in Sweden, for example, was the first in the world where the number of women equalled the number of men), Labour women wanted to impose quotas for selection in Britain too. Having carefully prepared the ground for it, the Labour conference in 1989 mandated that 40 per cent of all persons elected for Labour at all levels would be women within 10 years, and that 50 per cent of the party's MPs would be women within the same time frame or three elections.[68] That, of course, did not happen. But in 1992, after Labour narrowly lost the election and Labour leader Neil Kinnock resigned, the inquiry into the loss showed that if women had swung to Labour the way that men had, the party would have won and Kinnock would have moved into 10 Downing Street.

Short, as chair of the Women's PLP, lobbied for the introduction of all-women shortlists (AWS) in winnable constituencies to boost women's representation in the parliamentary labour party. In 1990, the Fabian Society published *Quotas Now: Women in the Labour Party*, a pamphlet written by Short, Angela Eagle – who was elected in 1992 – and GMB researcher Rachel Brooks, which called for 40 per cent of all places on party committees and local party delegations to go to women.[69] The unions were surprisingly accommodating. 'We were just at the beginning of the huge shift of women into the labour market,' Angela Eagle told me in 2018. 'The trade union agenda began to change while I was there. A lot of them had begun to change their structures to create women's officers, to create women's places on national executive committees. We were pushing at doors that were beginning to be unlocked at least, [although] you still had to give them a shove.'[70] Eagle found that some of the best allies were 'men who have daughters, who see them go in to the labour market and see what happens, who start thinking "you know what, we've got to do something about it". It was controversial, obviously because it was women-only seats, but you know you can't make an omelette without cracking eggs.' One of the men with daughters was the new leader of the Labour party, John Smith, who proved to be a great ally as AWS were rolled out ahead of the 1997 election. According to Margaret Beckett, that work had begun under Neil Kinnock's leadership when he appointed Jo Richardson to serve as shadow minister for women. 'She worked her socks off,' Beckett told me. 'She just plugged away steadily; it was never acceptable to have something with no women in. And John was very supportive of her. We owe it all to Jo in my opinion.'[71]

Yet, in 1996, two men won an employment tribunal case that declared that AWS contravened the 1975 Sex Discrimination Act.[72] The case had been brought by Roger Dyas-Elliott, who was rejected as a candidate for the marginal seat of Keighley, where Ann Cryer had won the nomination in an AWS. Cryer remembers getting two calls after her selection processes, one telling her that Dyas-Elliott had won his court case, the other that her mum had died. It was a very difficult time for Cryer personally, but in the end the lawsuit did not affect the seats that had already held their selection. As a result, in 1997 the number of Labour women in the House of Commons rose to 101 from 37. Still, according to Clare Short, Tony Blair was more sceptical about AWS than his predecessor, partly because he felt that the policy was unfair to men. 'There were so many talented men or "favourite sons" who might miss out,' Short told me in 2018.[73] Angela Eagle agreed: 'There were inevitably controversies because there always is a favoured son, never a favoured daughter. I don't think [Blair] liked women-only shortlists, I don't think he liked the structure of doing it, I don't think he liked the artificial nature of it. He felt uncomfortable about it. And as soon as he got the chance he ditched it. Arbitrarily.' The Labour Party did not challenge the court ruling. Eagle added: 'I understand why they didn't put it at risk with the election so close, but I'm convinced that it would have been overturned at a higher tribunal.'[74]

The controversies continued long after AWS were restored through the Sex Discrimination (Election Candidates) Act of 2002. In 2005, Welsh Assembly Member Peter Law resigned from the Labour Party and ran as an independent candidate in the safe Labour seat of Blaenau Gwent after the party imposed an all-women shortlist there. Following Law's death just a year later, the Labour Party selected Owen Smith to run as its candidate, but it remained out of Labour's hands until the 2010 election of Nick Smith. Blaenau Gwent has still never had a woman MP.

Despite the set-backs, AWS have transformed the representation of women in Parliament. Harriet Harman said:

> the truth is, you only have successful policies if there's lots of people supporting it, and in different parts of the ecosystem. Angela Eagle was organising with other trade union women, so they would have a caucus before conference to discuss what could be done. There was Ann Pettifor organising the ultra-left in the Labour Women's Action Committee, Clare Short who, ironically, had always regarded the women's movement as a distraction from class struggle, but threw herself into it and brought her resilience and pugnacity to that role.

There was also the Labour Women's Network, set up by Labour women Barbara Follett, Barbara Roche, Hilary De Lyon and Jean Black in response to the disappointing 1987 general election, which saw just twenty-one Labour women elected. Follett's EMILY's List UK, a fundraising organization set up after a US model in 1993 to help female Labour members with the costs of seeking selection as candidates, also distributed over £40,000 in grants to seventeen women ahead of the 1997 elections. Of those, twenty-six were selected and fourteen elected.

Women candidates were pivotal to Labour's success in 1997. 'We were not going to get women's votes as a men-only party,' Harriet Harman told me. 'We didn't look like women, we didn't sound like women, and this was at a time when women were thinking afresh about their lives. And yet we looked like the party representing the world they were trying to escape from. Opening the idea to women that they could have a government that reflected their aspirations for their lives, it was absolutely a landslide.'[75] In 1997, women voters supported Labour to a greater extent than ever before, as the party specifically championed causes that women cared passionately about, particularly education and the NHS. Labour's commitment to a national minimum wage would also vastly improve the incomes of women in low-paid work. Meanwhile, childcare was spoken of as an economic and not just a social policy as it allowed women to return to work and contribute both their skills and tax contributions.

These were policies that were championed by women who had gained seniority in the party between the 1983 and 1997 elections including Harriet Harman, Tessa Jowell, Clare Short and Patricia Hewitt. At first, Harman had to be persuaded by Hewitt to accept a role on the front bench as shadow minister for social security in 1984, but she helped transform the party's policies on women while there. In 1987, she became shadow health minister, followed by shadow chief secretary to the Treasury in 1992–94. She had a permanent place in the shadow cabinet from 1994 as shadow employment minister until 1995, shadow health secretary for a year after that, and shadow social security secretary from 1996. The latter was a role that transformed into her appointment as secretary of state for social security and the first-ever minister for women in 1997.

A fashion House

Fashion and dress were often mentioned by press and colleagues. Thatcher's handbag, used to great effect in cabinet meetings, had the added benefit of allowing her to carry around more things than a male prime minister.[76] Meanwhile, the slowly growing number of women in Parliament meant that many joined Harriet Harman in rethinking their wardrobes. 'I felt my clothes had to send out the message: "I am a competent professional, you can rely on me"', Harman wrote in her memoirs. 'It was a leap of faith for careworn constituents to put their trust in a young woman – and one who didn't at all look like the traditional idea of an MP.'[77] Margaret Hodge recalls the Labour women MPs and candidates being 'Folletted' in the mid-1990s – a term coined after Labour MP Barbara Follett. Follett used the knowledge she had gained as an art history student to 'do' Labour women's colours according to Bauhaus artist Johannes Itten. She recalled to me that 'it had to be done very discretely, and I swore on everything sacred that I wouldn't say who I did or didn't do.'[78] As the 1980s and 1990s progressed, Follett realized that the look of Labour candidates needed to improve so that voters got the right impression.[79] One afternoon, she had a group of eager women to her house – Hodge had her hair tinted and her make-up re-done as a result, but quickly reversed her conversion when told by a friend that she looked much older on the television that night. Others were more easily persuaded. Harriet Harman told me that 'when Marks and Spencer's started doing tailored suits for women and tapered trousers which looked really smart and authoritative but not frumpy, it was like "hallelujah". Adding that there had not been briefcases for women to carry when Harman first entered Parliament in 1982, she said: 'We'd have these ridiculous little handbags and loads of carrier bags making us look slightly deranged'. Going into the House of Commons dressed in a Laura Ashley dress, Harman thought that it was not right 'to be making a speech about the economy, dressed like someone who is on her way to a summer picnic in the countryside. It also affected the way that you felt, because once I'd got the shoulder pads on, and the smart blouse, I felt more authoritative and it made me feel more competent.'[80]

Clothes were also important to Betty Boothroyd, who in 1992 became the first ever woman speaker of the House of Commons. Five years earlier, Labour leader Neil Kinnock had been persuaded to allow Boothroyd to stand as deputy speaker by Gwyneth Dunwoody, who thought that it might one day lead to having a Labour woman speaker. Still, Boothroyd needed to mould the office to fit a woman. She asked to be called 'Madam Speaker' – 'I wasn't going to be called Mr Speaker', Boothroyd told me, 'and it took two weeks to get it done' – and she commissioned Hardy Amies to design something 'distinctive' to wear in the chair, paying for it out of her own pocket. Boothroyd wanted to be formal in a feminine way: 'If Members thought I would look even better in the Speaker's robes, I was already well prepared. I had a half-dozen legal collars made, of the kind Speakers wear, and the rest of the basic kit: white blouse, black skirt and black stockings. I also happened to have a pair of black patent shoes decorated with imitation buckles. It occurred to me that they just might come in useful one day, so I put them at the back of my cupboard,' she wrote in her memoirs. 'Was I being presumptuous? I do not think so. I have always believed in taking life as it comes, but in being ready for it. What I could not do was appear complacent.'[81] Boothroyd later told me that 'the only thing I objected to was the wig. I didn't want to wear it because the job was a huge challenge. I didn't feel inferior, but I felt a bit timid about it. I had no formal education and felt I can't do this big job with a full, heavy wig on. On the more frivolous side, you can't move your head or laugh.' On this too, the House agreed.[82]

When the incumbent speaker, Conservative MP Jack Wetherill, retired in 1992, the newly elected Major government was too distracted to field a candidate until it was too late to oppose Boothroyd's campaign for the speaker's chair. She had been changed by her time as deputy speaker: she had not voted in divisions or made controversial speeches since her 1987 appointment. 'My heart was with Labour as Deputy Speaker,' Boothroyd wrote in her memoirs, 'but my duty was to the whole House and I fulfilled it to the best of my abilities. I would not have found it easy to become partisan again, nor would I have enjoyed trying.'[83] Her back-up plan of becoming a peer did not need to be put in motion as she won one of only six contested speaker's elections since 1800 by a landslide of 372 to 238. Seventy-three of the votes for Boothroyd came from Conservative MPs. Being a woman had given her unlikely supporters: the leader of Northern Ireland's Democratic Unionist Party (DUP), Ian Paisley, said publicly that he would not dare go home to his wife and three daughters had he not voted for Boothroyd.[84] She had been nervous about her lack of academic education, but Boothroyd found that her theatrical training gave her several advantages in the speaker's chair: she exuded confidence and optimism, and her voice carried with authority. In keeping with tradition, Boothroyd was dragged from her seat on the Labour benches to the chair by John Biffen, the Conservative MP who had sponsored her bid, and her Labour seconder Gwyneth Dunwoody.

As she was a very visible woman in Parliament, the press had a very particular way of describing Boothroyd. Satirical magazine *Private Eye* felt that she had the charm of carbon monoxide gas in an airtight room and was thick as the proverbial two planks.[85] Boothroyd's biographer, the *Daily Mirror*'s Paul Routledge, described her as:

A voluptuous figure in a dark red and black dress adorned with a diamond brooch in the shape of the crowned portcullis of Parliament, her thick wavy hair almost as white as the Speaker's wig, she stood, leaned back and stretched out her arms, spread her hands and cried: 'No, no!' She was acting out a drama that is today merely theatrical, but once was only too real: eight of her predecessors had been executed by the sovereign of the day. And as a former professional dancer, Betty knew how to play to the gallery.[86]

Intersections and minority caucus

Other marginalized groups in society were also making progress in their quest for parliamentary representation in the 1980s and 1990s. In the 1987 general election, Diane Abbott became the first black woman to be elected as an MP, after winning Hackney North & Stoke Newington for the Labour

Party. Born in 1953, Abbott came from a working-class background; her parents were immigrants from Jamaica who worked as a welder and a nurse. Abbott's parents were Labour voters, but they were not politically active and could not have imagined that their daughter would become an MP. 'It was way beyond my mother's expectations – if I'd been a staff nurse she would have been very pleased, but MP was way beyond [expectations]; Abbott told me in 2018. She was accustomed to being the odd one out: she attended a grammar school where she was the only black girl, and then went to the University of Cambridge where she studied history. Like Clare Short, Abbott worked as a civil servant in the Home Office: she got the position after a final selection interview chaired by Baroness Warnock, who asked why Abbott wanted to be a civil servant. 'I replied "because I want power", she told me. 'The other people on the panel leant back in amazement; I was this little black girl, wearing a blue flowery dress, bobbly curls and plastic beads. But I met her son years later, and he said that had been the right answer.'[87] Her time at the Home Office was followed by an appointment as race relations officer at the National Council for Civil Liberties in the late 1970s, where Harriet Harman had also worked.

Abbott had been one of only three black students at Newnham College, Cambridge and she was the only black employee at the National Council for Civil Liberties. It was an experience that she found 'very cloying, like walking through glue', she later told the *Times*. 'Full of creepy liberals falling over backwards to be nice to you because you were black. It also gave me a lasting distaste for the race relations industry and the hypocrisy of making a living out of race.' Engaged in the campaign against what was known as the 'sus law', which gave police the power to stop and search individuals, and which showed use of racial profiling, Abbott had first become interested in running for a seat in Parliament when she realized that even when constituencies were diverse, there were no black MPs at all. 'I felt very strongly about women's representation,' she said in 2018, 'but in the end the thing that I was most concerned about was black representation.' Abbott remained the only black woman MP for ten years, until Labour's Oona King was elected in 1997, during which time she was of great interest to the press where any portrayals of her tended to be both gendered and focused on her skin colour. 'When the media interest fell away, it came as a terrific relief,' Abbott later said. 'For the first six months, it was overwhelming.'

Abbott was not the only black parliamentarian, however: Bernie Grant, Keith Vaz and Paul Boateng were also elected in 1987. Abbott remembers: 'Myself and my three colleagues – Bernie, Keith and Paul got stopped all the time because people just couldn't believe we were MPs. They kept stopping the men for quite some time; they stopped stopping me after a bit because I had these long braids. It was a very distinctive look and it was clear that even they understood who I was.'[88] Two years after his election, Bernie Grant established the Parliamentary Black Caucus, which aimed to advance the rights and representation of minorities the way that women MPs were collectively working to advance the rights and representation of women. Although it only existed briefly, with the leadership of the Labour Party keen to see it go as they believed it to be divisive, the Black Caucus helped encourage the election of further minority MPs to the House of Commons.[89]

While there was slight progress on the representation of ethnic minorities in the Houses of Parliament, the growing realization that the LGBTQ community also needed representation proved very hard to put in place. Between the years of 1967, when homosexual acts between men over the age of twenty-one were decriminalized, and 1994 when the age of consent for gay men was lowered to eighteen, great strides were made outside Westminster in the understanding of sexual minority rights. Within Parliament, however, the atmosphere was very different. There had long been rumours about homosexual MPs, but it was not until 1976 that it became public knowledge that a sitting MP lived in a same-sex relationship. She was Maureen Colquhoun, a Labour MP elected in February 1974, and outed by the *Daily Mail* after a journalist contrived his way into a party thrown by Colquhoun and her partner. When elected, Colquhoun – who had two daughters – had been married, but the marriage was dissolved after she left her husband for the editor of *Sappho* magazine in 1975. Between her outing and 1979, Colquhoun fought two attempts to deselect her by her constituency party but finally lost her bid to be re-selected for the 1979 election. Although the official reason was the party's distaste for her feminist politics, the local party chairman added that 'she was elected as a working wife and mother (...) this business has blackened her image irredeemably'.[90] In 1984, Chris Smith became the first openly gay MP when he opened a speech with the words: 'Good afternoon, I'm Chris Smith, I'm the Labour MP for Islington South and Finsbury, and I'm gay.' It was not until 1997 that an already out candidate – Labour's Stephen Twigg – was elected to Parliament. Angela Eagle became the first MP to out herself with a newspaper interview in 1998. She told me in 2018 that 'I didn't hide, I didn't put pictures of fake boyfriends on my leaflets. When I told John Prescott [for whom she worked] about it he said, "tell me something I didn't know already, love". People knew, but I hadn't made it official.' With the treatment of Colquhoun in 1974 fresh in mind, Eagle felt coming out was a big deal, and she engineered a dinner with Chris Smith to talk to him about it. 'A junior minister trying to get a cabinet minister to have a meeting – you can imagine,' she laughed. 'It took all the way until dessert for me to tell him.' Eagle chose to do the interview with Suzanne Moore of *The Independent* because she felt her news would be sensitively handled. The *Daily Mail*, however, splashed the story on their front page with the headline 'Lesbian in the House of Commons'.

It was not until 2010 that the first already out woman – the Conservatives' Margot James – was elected. James told me that she remembers being told by an official in Conservative Central Office in the 1980s that it would not be possible to be an open lesbian and an MP; as a result, she chose a career in business rather than politics. James remembers crying when hearing Chris Smith's speech in 1984 and in the mid-2000s, with attitudes in her party and the country transformed, she sought and then won selection in Stourbridge, where she has been the MP since 2010. 'Being a lesbian was not a barrier, and the woman who was the chairman of my local association was very supportive. One member resigned when I was selected but that was it. People in the Shires are very relaxed,' James reflected.[91] In 2016, Justine Greening – the Conservative MP and secretary of state for international development – joined the group by declaring on Twitter that she was in a same-sex relationship. 'I wanted it to be really positive, because I don't see it as some kind of admission,' Greening told me in 2018. 'It's one of the most amazing moments in my life. I pushed the tweet out and then this swarm of loveliness came back at me. It can only get better for people in the future if people today are willing to stand up and be counted.'[92]

Women in the spotlight

The years between 1979 and 1997 clearly illustrate that there are as many ways to be a female MP as there are individuals with that title. Women who served in the House of Commons came from all sorts of backgrounds, had different ideologies and different trajectories to power. But they all faced similar assumptions about their suitability to hold office, their

priorities and their potential longevity in the House of Commons based
on gendered assumptions in British culture and society.

Margaret Thatcher might have felt that her gender was a secondary
issue, but it was inescapable. The press remarked on the way she dressed
and on her flirtatious style, whether at the despatch box or when meeting
Ronald Reagan. Like Barbara Castle before her, Thatcher used her
femininity to gain support and dazzle her opponents. But it also meant
that she faced opposition of a very particular sort. After removing Lord
Soames from his position as leader of the House of Lords in 1981,
Thatcher described his reaction as 'angry, but in a grander way. I got the
distinct impression that he felt the natural order of things was being
violated and that he was, in effect, being dismissed by his housemaid'.[93]

Assumptions about gender roles and feminine attributes also dogged
the portrayals of other senior women. In 1994, *The Independent on
Sunday* published an article in which Virginia Bottomley was described
as 'a woman, with all the caring connotations that implies, and much
beauty besides'. The reporter went on to say that her

> wide, lipsticked mouth engulfs people in smiles, the eyes are wide and
> concerned-looking, the skin is clear, the shoes sensible; she is an ideal of
> a certain kind of modest, intelligent womanhood. She even, unlike
> Margaret Thatcher, has a lovely voice – melodious, bell-like and
> unstrident. (. . .) She is of the Mary Archer type: controlled, ladylike, and
> beautiful; the type whose composure men frequently long to disturb
> (one Labour MP has called her 'staggeringly sexy'). She listens carefully,
> replying in her caressing, delightfully lulling voice, in little speeches
> larded with statistics and achievements, eschewing the broad sweep.[94]

It is hard to imagine that a male MP and cabinet minister could ever be
described in a similar fashion.

More women than ever before were now Members of Parliament, and
the arrival of a younger generation meant that campaigns on women's
issues grew in intensity and volume. And perhaps most importantly, Britain
had been led for eleven years by its first ever female prime minister in
Margaret Thatcher. Her contested legacy came into sharp focus on her
death in April 2013. A generation of children had grown up assuming that
a female prime minister was the norm. She inspired many – some in
support, some to emulate, others to oppose and to define themselves against
her. But whatever your views, there was no ignoring Margaret Thatcher.

By the 1997 election, issues of women's representation were increasingly talked about as a democratic problem. Labour women had been at the forefront of the struggle, pushing the party into accepting all-women shortlists in order to encourage women to put their names forward and become candidates. With five women in Tony Blair's shadow cabinet prior to the 1997 election – Margaret Beckett, Ann Taylor, Clare Short, Mo Mowlam and Harriet Harman – the future looked promising. It had been a long struggle for these Labour women with few rewards for the individuals at the forefront, but they now had a chance to have a real impact on the country and on ordinary women's lives.

7

New Labour, More Women: 1997–2010

Somewhere inside I'm still genuinely surprised that in 2005 a woman politician has to put up with this.

OONA KING, 2007.[1]

In 1994, John Smith – Labour Party leader and supporter of all-women shortlists – died suddenly from a heart attack. Tony Blair, Margaret Beckett and John Prescott all stood in the subsequent leadership contest, and Beckett and Prescott also sought to become deputy leader. The elections were won by Blair and Prescott respectively, while Gordon Brown remained shadow chancellor after striking a deal with Blair before the campaign to prevent the two from standing against each other. Together, they embarked on a mission to win a general election. Women – both as members of the party and of the electorate – proved key to fulfilling that ambition.

A party for and of women?

Before the 1997 election, there had been a widely held belief among senior members of the Labour Party that the public was too Conservative to vote for them. As the 1990s progressed, it seemed clear that the way to combat this was to offer alternative policies rather than just a running critique of Conservative failures.[2] At the same time, some of the party's leaders recognized that it needed to look more representative of the electorate – that it was far too white and male.[3] These two ideas combined to give some women in the party greater space to formulate policy proposals than before, which had an immediate effect on the 1997 Labour manifesto. After Blair's election in 1994, Harriet Harman was re-elected to the shadow cabinet and promoted to shadow secretary of state for employment. She used her position to instigate research into the measures that would help reduce workplace and salary gender imbalances. In the early days, her most important job was to ensure that Labour did not scrap its commitment to a national minimum wage. Setting up the Low Pay Commission, Harman published a cache of evidence in several working papers that showed just how much struggling sections of society were hit by low pay. The first report, published in March 1995, showed that 300,000 individuals were earning less than £1.50 per hour. Workers in the north, women and ethnic minorities were over-represented within this group, allowing Harman to argue that the introduction of a national minimum wage would go some way to address pay inequality.[4] Although employers were legally obliged to pay women the same as the men with whom they shared their job description, women were – and are still – overrepresented in work that is valued and paid less. Despite some resistance, the Low Pay Commission became a key part of the 1997 Labour manifesto. In government, the National Minimum Wage Bill was introduced by Labour's employment minister Ian McCartney and steered through Parliament by Margaret Beckett, the secretary of state for trade and industry, who later described it as her greatest achievement as an MP. The law came into effect in April 1999, raising the wages of more than one million low-paid workers.[5] 'With the boost it gave to low-paid women,' Harman wrote in 2017, 'it caused the biggest narrowing of the pay gap since the institution of the Equal Pay Act.'[6]

Harman was responsible for another important part of the Labour manifesto: the national childcare strategy, designed to provide all families with affordable, accessible and good-quality childcare, which was usually the preserve of high-income parents and children from troubled families. It was a reiteration of Harman's initial motivation to get into politics: affordable childcare was, she later wrote, 'one of the first demands formulated by the women's movement'.[7] Harman also worked on a New Deal for Lone Parents after research showed that 90 per cent of single mothers wanted to work. Despite this, women with children below the age of sixteen were not classified as jobseekers in the statistics. The New Deal addressed four key areas: childcare for working mothers; the right to flexible working hours; support from special lone-parent advisors at the

Job Centre; and tax credits to top up incomes. It was opposed by the left, who wanted to defend women's right to stay at home until their youngest was sixteen years old, and the right, who still believed a woman's place was in the home.[8] Labour's election campaign in 1997 included women's voices more than ever. Harman describes the women in the team 'putting ourselves out there'. Peter Mandelson, she added, 'seemed to think that he had invented me. They think they promoted us, but they didn't; we barged our way in and then they threw their arms around us. We had slogged for decades, and then the penny dropped, and we were allowed in the picture – but not so much in the room.'[9]

On 1 May 1997, Labour won the general election by a landslide, securing a 179-seat majority. Labour also celebrated its greatest ever number of women MPs: thanks to all-women shortlists being used for selection in safe seats, 101 of Labour's 418 seats were won by women. There were 120 women MPs in total in Westminster, with thirteen Conservative, three Liberal Democrat and two Scottish National Party seats also held by women (the 120th seat was held by the speaker, Betty Boothroyd, who had been a Labour MP but served as a non-partisan after her election in 1992). This amounted to a doubling of the number of women in the House of Commons from the 1992 election, and although women still only held 18.2 per cent of the seats in Parliament, this marked a new era in Westminster. Among the new women were trade unionist Caroline Flint and the former deputy director of the Institute for Public Policy Research, Patricia Hewitt, who had persuaded Harriet Harman to accept a position in the shadow cabinet in 1984. A former researcher at the European Parliament, Oona King, became the second black woman elected as an MP after Diane Abbott. 'These new Labour women MPs weren't just a breath of fresh air,' Harman wrote in her memoirs. 'They were the wind of change. Just by their very presence they embodied the notion that politics, and our government, was now going to represent women as well as men.' Harriet Harman told me that the all-women shortlist was crucial: 'It became the collective of Labour women, so there was a partnership between women inside, where women would be walking through the lobby and seeing other women, and that was an amazing thing.'[10] Clare Short said that the diversity of women was fantastic: 'Young and old, different shapes and sizes, different ages, left and right.' And, she added, the electorate had voted for the women candidates, rendering obsolete the idea that women could not win.[11] Yet women still faced a hostile reception from some in Parliament. Oona King recalls in her diaries that as she entered the Chamber as an MP in May 1997, '[t]hree male Tories walk in. (…) They eye me suspiciously with my brown paper parcel. They're in two minds about calling security, and my presence clearly makes them indignant and worried in equal measure. And then they catch sight of my Member's pass. Their expressions of disdain and disbelief are priceless. They remind me why I worked so hard to get here in the first place. They look at me like I've gatecrashed their private members' club.'[12] Yvette Cooper – who was twenty-eight years old when elected as a Labour MP in 1997 – recalled that when asking for directions to the Chamber, a doorkeeper replied, 'Oh no – you can't go in there, who do you work for?' She added: 'Some of the Members, particularly some of the older Tories, wouldn't say hello, wouldn't talk. They just couldn't cope with the idea of there being so many women. It was a physical reaction, a real discomfort, an unease about the change.'[13]

Despite King and Cooper's experiences, Harman found that they had reached a 'critical mass' and that '[t]here were now so many more women MPs who could be counted on to give vigorous support to Labour's plans for childcare and maternity rights and to tackle domestic violence, it transformed the political dynamic in the PLP'. Politics is never, she added, 'just a question of the strength of your argument, it's about how much support you have for it, too.'[14] Labour MP Jean Corston, who was elected in 1992, did her bit to help the newcomers along by arranging for an instructor from the National Theatre to teach a class on voice projection and speech-making. 'That was very useful,' she told me, 'it made women feel able to play a part.'[15] At a practical level, the House of Commons was an odd working environment for the newly arrived women MPs. Shirley Summerskill remembers following a sign reading 'Members Only' in the 1960s before finding it was for the men's toilets. In 1994, Helen Liddell did the same. But the 1997 women remember the camaraderie most of all. Even Gillian Shephard, whose party had been defeated, recalled that 'it felt at a stroke that it altered the atmosphere. Just the colour and the chat.'[16]

Harman wanted a photo of all the Labour women in Parliament to mark their arrival, in the hope that it would make it clear to the female electorate that change was on the way. As a matter of courtesy, she informed 10 Downing Street, only to find Tony Blair turning up on the day as it had been assumed that he should be part of it. Harman was dismayed; what had been planned as a photograph of powerful women would instead become 'a photograph of a powerful man surrounded by a large group of women'. It was not, however, the done thing to tell a newly elected and extremely popular prime minister that his presence was not wanted, and so the famous 'Blair's Babes' photo was created. Although it has come to capture that moment in history, the term was used in a derogatory fashion by the press to criticize and condescend female politicians. The picture today draws mixed responses from the women it depicts; 'humiliating' is how, Helen Liddell, a cabinet minister under Blair, described it to me, while Yvette Cooper called it 'a complete mistake. It ended up becoming an excuse to patronise a lot of women.' Meanwhile, Jacqui Smith, the first woman to serve as home secretary, said: 'In one way I love it, because it is symbolic of a change. In another way, as somebody said when I did an interview on the anniversary of 1997, there is something a bit handmaiden-ish about it. I still get it now – "you were a Blair's Babe". It's a manifestation of what people think about you as a woman in politics.'[17]

Policies in practice

Many of the women elected for the first time in 1997 went on to have fantastic careers, but it was the parliamentary veterans – Ann Taylor, Harriet Harman, Claire Short and Mo Mowlam who were promoted to their first cabinet positions. Taylor became the first woman appointed leader of the House of Commons and lord president of the council (taking the title 'president' after some debate); Harman the secretary of state for social security and minister for women and equality; Short the secretary of state for international development; and Mowlam the secretary of state for Northern Ireland. Harman played a vital role in pushing for a junior minister for women to be appointed, following on from the Conservatives' Gillian Shephard. Harman felt a junior minister was important as her own civil servants saw Harman's equality brief as 'unimportant and as a distraction from my departmental responsibilities'.[18] Joan Ruddock, who was elected in 1987, was appointed. She describes being 'absolutely thrilled but quickly deflated by adverse comments on the fact that I'm not being paid'. There had been no comment made about the other junior ministers who would not be receiving salaries for their jobs, so why had it been pointed out that Ruddock's position was unpaid? 'I'm pretty sure that I have been deliberately undermined,' Ruddock wrote in her diary.[19] Harman, on the other hand, was grateful that Ruddock in public brushed off 'the embarrassment of being in a role where she had to fight for equal pay for women at a time when her own role was not deemed worthy of being paid at all'. In conversation with me, Harman added: 'There were a number of men already announced as unpaid ministers, I knew it was a practical reality; it was more important to me to take the job.'[20] What happened, I asked Harman? 'They had forgotten about it,' she told me. 'The last thing on anybody's mind was the secretary of state for women and the minister for women.' By the time it was remembered, 'all the junior minister posts had been taken and there was no money left, so they said, "you can have Joan, but she can't be paid".'[21]

There were more obstacles on the way for Harman and Ruddock. Their focus was on domestic violence, childcare and women's representation but, as Harman told me years later, they found that 'you're embattled from the minute you decide your priorities'.[22] Childcare, for example, fell under the Department of Education led by David Blunkett, who was not keen to have Harman and Ruddock step on his turf. He felt that childcare was about children's education rather than empowering women in the workplace. 'David didn't see us as the helpful allies we wanted to be, and his department wanted us out of the way,' Harman wrote.[23] Labour's Margaret Hodge, who entered Parliament in 1994 and became the first minister of state for children within the Department of Education and Skills in 2003, told me in 2018 that SureStart – which is now mostly associated with her colleague Tessa Jowell – was a group effort but with many competing agendas. A programme focusing on the improvement of childcare, early education, health, family support and community development when it launched in 1998, SureStart saw input from the Treasury and the Departments of Health and Education, with Gordon Brown, Yvette Cooper, Tessa Jowell, Margaret Hodge and David Blunkett all weighing in. The great tension was their different visions of early-year education: Brown and Cooper were particularly interested in getting single parents back in the labour market; Jowell and Blunkett were inspired by psychologist John Bowlby's attachment theory and its implications for children's ability to form close relationships; Hodge wanted to put education at the heart of the programme, emphasizing the need for childcare providers to be educated to degree level.

SureStart was launched in 1998 by Tessa Jowell, who replaced Joan Ruddock as minister for women in July 1998. Jowell, who was forty-five years old when she was elected in 1992, had twenty years of professional experience as a psychiatric social worker and later associate director of mental health charity MIND as well as a Labour councillor in Camden from the age of twenty-three.[24] Jacqui Smith described Jowell as 'tough as old boots with her departmental hat on. I thought, that's a lesson learned about how to behave.'[25] Working with Tessa Jowell was Yvette Cooper, then a health minister, who has called her part in the roll-out of SureStart her proudest achievement as an MP.[26] Labour's future shadow secretary of state for education from 2016, Angela Rayner, was one of the beneficiaries of SureStart as a pregnant teenager, and has spoken about the transformative impact it had on her life and those of her children. 'I remember our estate being one of the first to get a community SureStart centre,' Rayner told me an interview in 2019. When she went to the centre, she was put on a parenting course. 'I learned things that might seem simple – that it was important to hug and love your child, and read to them. This might seem obvious, but it wasn't to me at the time', she wrote in an article for *The Guardian* in 2017, having been brought up herself on a council estate 'with a mum who, despite doing everything she could for me, couldn't help me learn to read and write because she had never been taught herself.'[27] Speaking of SureStart, alongside 'childcare, tax credits, things that helped working mums from my background,' Rayner reflected to me, 'I can tell you that it changed my life, and it changed the lives of many of my friends, who had teenage pregnancies, and were living in poverty.'[28]

Harman's deputy, Frank Field, was sceptical about the need for childcare, and has expressed his incredulity that we pay other women to look after children so that mothers go to work somewhere else.[29] But Harman's biggest challenge in 1997 was not childcare but the introduction of welfare cuts that New Labour's spending commitments demanded. The most important and controversial cut was to lone parent benefits, a bill with which Harman herself disagreed and on which she faced strong opposition. While the chancellor was adamant that it was necessary, forty-seven Labour MPs voted against the third reading of the bill, just after midnight on 11 December 1997. Among them were Bernie Grant, John McDonnell and Jeremy Corbyn. Earlier that same evening Diane Abbott, Alice Mahon, Maria Fyfe, Lynne Jones, Ann Clwyd, Ann Cryer, Gwyneth Dunwoody and Audrey Wise – all Labour women MPs – had voted for an amendment that sought to scrap the power to reduce child benefits for lone parents, but that amendment had been defeated.[30] Only seven of the forty-seven opponents to the cuts were women. Mahon was

sacked from her position as an aide to culture secretary Chris Smith for
her rebellion. Yvette Cooper is one of many to argue that the fact that
Harman was in charge of the policy kept many women on board, and that
by keeping a watchful eye on the lives of lone parents after the bill was
passed, the harmful impact of the bill was held at bay by more generous
policies. Still, Cooper added, 'it was a completely stupid thing of the
government to do'.[31] Harman later told me that she should have fought
the cuts: 'It was particularly hard because they were benefits paid to
women. I shouldn't have gone through with it,' she said. 'And I didn't
realize that others were pushing back about their own departments. I just
knew we had to make cuts because we had made promises about our
spending at the election and we had to keep those promises.'[32] In her
memoirs, Harman wrote:

> I should have told Tony that the partnership with Frank was not
> workable and insisted that he reshuffle the team. I should have told
> Gordon that the lone parent cuts were a bridge too far, that I was
> refusing to do them, and I should have insisted he found the
> money from somewhere else. But the idea of standing up against
> either Tony or Gordon was anathema to me. (...) I should have
> listened when I was warned that it was naive to believe that it would all
> be sorted out because Tony was 'my friend'. 'He's not your friend,' was
> the riposte, 'he's the prime minister and the prime minister has no
> friends.'[33]

In 1998, Harman was sacked from the cabinet. Alistair Darling became
secretary of state for social security, and Tessa Jowell became minister for
women. Harman headed to France for a holiday. Next, she cooked her
way through *Delia's Complete Illustrated Cookery Course*.[34] But soon, she
found a position from which she could continue to influence women-
friendly policies in Parliament. As chair of the brand-new Childcare
Commission from 1998, Harman worked closely with Ann Longfield of
4Children, a charity providing after-school care. In 2001, the commission
published a report that called for children's centres to be opened in every
local community across the country; in the summer of 2002, the first
centres opened.[35] In the London borough of Southwark – in which
Harman's Peckham constituency and Jowell's Dulwich constituency were
situated – the number of childcare places rose from under 5,000 to more
than 11,000 between 2001 and 2006.[36]

Maternity leave was another policy Harman had cause to celebrate: in Gordon Brown's 1999 budget, he announced more money for maternity leave, which was reformed with the Maternity and Parental Leave Regulations of 1999. The first maternity leave legislation had been introduced through the Employment Protection Act 1975 and in 1993 all working women had been given the right to maternity leave thanks to a European Commission directive. From 1999, all employees were granted a minimum of three months' unpaid parental leave, while mothers had the right to eighteen weeks' paid leave. Reforms did not stop there: in 2001, the government extended maternity leave to twenty-six weeks and maternity pay to £100 per week, while paternity leave was included in the budget for the first time. In 2003, male employees became eligible for paid statutory paternity leave for the first time and in 2010, a few months before the general election, fathers were granted the right to six months statutory paternity leave. But although women now had the legal right to return to their previous roles and to better financial remuneration during their maternity leave, in practice discrimination in the workplace has remained rife. In her interview with me, Margaret Hodge used maternity rights as an example when stating that one of the great lessons of her political career has been 'that when you think you have a victory, you don't really have it (. . .). It's not a short sprint, it's a long, long marathon.'[37] In 2016, research commissioned by Jo Swinson and Maria Miller through the Equality and Human Rights Commission and the Department for Business, Innovation and Skills showed that 75 per cent of new mothers experience some form of discrimination at work, and 54,000 women each year lose their jobs as a result of having children.[38] In 1999, Yvette Cooper – the minister responsible for maternity services within the Department of Health – struggled to access the rights of other employees when she needed to take maternity leave on the birth of her first child. 'No one knew what maternity arrangements were available for ministers,' she recalled. Cooper was initially told that, as ministers are appointments of the Queen and not employees, there were no maternity rights. The solution was to invent it from scratch. 'The Health Department was incredibly supportive,' Cooper told me. 'They did lots to make it work, to provide support. [But] my responsibilities were shared out between other ministers who ended up being overstretched as a result.' On her return, Cooper felt isolated. 'They had just shifted a whole lot of my responsibilities away, so I was no longer responsible for anything – it was not even clear what job I was coming back into.'[39]

The working families tax credit, which aimed to put more money in the pockets of low-income parents, was also introduced in the 1999 budget. Again, Labour women made sure that the money went to the parent with the greatest care-giving role rather than, as tradition and as the original plan stipulated, the main breadwinner, who was most often the man. 'The money needed to go to the woman,' Harriet Harman told me in 2018. Reminiscent of Eleanor Rathbone's campaign for family allowances to be paid directly to the woman in the 1930s and 1940s, Lorna Fitzsimons – a Labour MP from the 1997 intake and chair of the women's PLP 1997–2001 – petitioned Gordon Brown about it along with Yvette Cooper. Cooper remembers that 'we raised it with Treasury ministers, and the initial response from the Treasury was that it can't be done, it's not possible to separate this out into two payments, it's not possible to pay this to the main carer, and it's going to have to be paid to the main earner. We then had strong lobbying over a series of months to try and get it sorted out.' The lobbying involved asking questions in Parliament, particularly on the topic of the distributional impact on women and men of Labour's budgets. 'We did eventually persuade the Treasury to completely redraw its plans,' Cooper told me. 'They had to change the whole design of the tax credits system in order to do it – but they did end up with the child tax credit being paid to the main carer.'[40] According to Harriet Harman, this was one area in which 'it made a huge difference having so many women in Parliament at last. And now you had for the first time the women's movement inside Parliament offering support and encouragement and sharing the campaigning and lobbying.'[41]

Another sign of the strength in numbers was the 2002 introduction of the statutory right to flexible working, which qualifying employees could use to petition their employers about the hours, times or locations that they were contracted to work. It was originally aimed at parents and others with caring responsibilities but has since seen its scope widen. According to Margaret Hodge, this reform was a direct result of the large number of women together in Parliament. 'Blair and Brown were both hostile,' Hodge told me, 'because they worried it was anti-business. But there was (...) [an] alliance of women, both as ministers and together with women at Number Ten who absolutely bludgeoned them until they caved in.'[42]

Back as a minister, as solicitor general for England and Wales between 2001 and 2005, Harriet Harman also built on Jo Richardson's legacy on tackling domestic violence, particularly where the treatment of victims was concerned. Harman put forward the Domestic Violence, Crime and Victims Act of 2004, which sought greater penalties for offenders, more support for victims and to address the bias that saw 'good' men receive lenient sentences for their violence. In 2007, victim impact statements were allowed in court proceedings for the first time, and in 2009 the law allowing for offenders to plead provocation as a means to get a lower sentence was abolished. One of the lawyers involved in making that happen was Vera Baird, Mo Mowlam's successor as Labour MP for Redcar from 2001 to 2010. By the time the bill passed, Harman was at last back in the cabinet, appointed minister for women and equality along with leader of the House of Commons when Gordon Brown became prime minister in 2007.

Courage and controversy

There were two major areas of military conflict that defined the Tony Blair era: Northern Ireland and Iraq. Both involved and affected women serving in the House of Commons.

Northern Ireland

Women MPs had long been involved in the Northern Ireland conflict. Going back to 1969, the 21-year-old Bernadette Devlin, a community activist and republican, was elected as MP for Mid Ulster. The youngest woman elected to Parliament, Devlin emerged as one of the leaders of the three-day Battle of the Bogside in August 1969. She subsequently served a nine-month prison sentence but was still re-elected as an independent socialist in 1970. On 30 January 1972 Devlin was back in Bogside, in the city of Derry, as the events that would later be called 'Bloody Sunday' took place. On that day, twenty-eight unarmed civilians were shot by British forces; fourteen died. According to a witness at the Saville Inquiry into the events in 2001, Devlin had been a target for the bullets.[43] When published in 2010, the Saville report stated that the killings had been unjustified and unjustifiable, and prime minister David Cameron issued a formal apology. But on 31 January 1972, the Conservative home secretary Reginald Maudling told the House of Commons that British troops had only fired to protect themselves from earlier shots from the

IRA. 'That is the second time the Minister has stood up and lied to the House,' Devlin responded. 'Nobody shot at the paratroops, but somebody will shortly.'[44] As the speaker, Selwyn Lloyd, declined her the right to speak further, Devlin rose from her seat, walked over to Maudling and slapped him. To journalists gathered outside the Houses of Parliament, Devlin stated that it had not been an emotional act, but that it was 'coldly and calmly done'. When asked if she would apologize, she said: 'I'm just sorry I didn't get him by the throat.'[45] In the general election of February 1974, Devlin lost her seat to John Dunlop, a Unionist. Reflecting on her time as an MP, she later said: 'I look back on myself then and I am astounded I survived. I took risks and made mad decisions no one else would.'[46]

There were several attempts at a political solution to the Troubles in the following decades and when a peace agreement was finally signed on 10 April 1998, it was with much thanks to the hard work of Labour MP Marjorie Mowlam, better known as Mo. Having been elected in 1987, Mowlam was appointed secretary of state for Northern Ireland the day after the election in 1997. Keen for the first photos of her in office to be of her in conversation with people on the street, rather than the behind-the-desk images that her all-male and predominantly Conservative predecessors had been associated with, Mowlam's first act in office was to head straight to Belfast. 'I wanted to say as clearly as I could to the people of N. Ireland that they were what was going to be important to me in this job,' Mowlam later wrote in her memoirs.[47]

Mowlam's appointment as Northern Ireland secretary had been welcomed by both sides, but trust had to be established ahead of negotiations.[48] Mowlam was certain that 'we had to take risks to get the talks going. If folk are constantly waiting for someone to make a move, you can wait till the violence starts up again.'[49] She was frustrated by the slow pace of negotiations, and by the civil service who deemed many of her ideas too 'dodgy'.[50] Nevertheless, Mowlam somehow managed to get approval for her visit to the Maze prison in the wake of the Irish National Liberation Army's murder of loyalist prisoner Billy Wright in December 1997. A few days after Wright's death, the loyalist prisoners at the Maze voted to abandon the peace process, and Mowlam was asked by the Ulster Democratic Party's Gary McMichael to pay them a visit. Mowlam reflected that her 'gut immediately told me this was the right thing to do'. On Friday 9 January, she woke up at her house in Islington, dressed herself in neutral colours (no orange or green), put on the wig that covered the hair she lost having cancer treatment a couple of years earlier, and set off for Belfast. She had decided to meet prisoners from both factions, and had a clear agenda of points to discuss, of which one was new and very controversial: in the event of a successful peace treaty, prisoner releases would be considered. 'Had I been manipulated?' she later asked. 'Were the loyalists politicians using me to shore up their position among their own side? Yes, I think that's probably true, and we knew it at the time. But it didn't matter. If that's what it took, that's what needed to be done.'[51] A few hours later, the loyalist prisoners reinstated their support for the peace process.

Being a woman marked Mowlam out as different in the Northern Ireland context: it contributed to her success and how she dealt with negotiations, but also how she has been remembered. Some observers have argued that the novelty and shock of having to deal with a woman meant that the unionists were moved to accelerate the process.[52] Mowlam herself recalled comments about having a woman in charge being exactly what Northern Ireland needed, as all the men before her had been unsuccessful. Seamus Mallon, a member of the Social Democratic and Labour Party (SDLP) who went on to serve as deputy first minister of Northern Ireland from 1998 to 2001, later said that 'The North of Ireland was used to grey men in grey suits coming and doing a grey job for a grey period of time. No grey suits with Mo. She came attired as she usually did – in what she could find at the last moment.'[53] Mowlam had her own way of rallying support from people on the street: not content with just talking to them, she became famous for throwing her arms around everyone she met. Mowlam also understood the need to include women in the peace process in order to make a lasting change in a divided society. To do so, Mowlam sought to amplify the voices of women's organizations in Northern Ireland, including the recently established non-partisan Women's Coalition, which campaigned to get women's voices represented in the multi-party talks.[54]

Mowlam was very popular, but her unusual approach also made her enemies who felt she was too careless with the 600-year history on which the Troubles were built. She did not get on with her civil servants, who resented her resistance to making decisions and her broad-brushed approach. She was also prone to making the wrong decision at the spur of the moment: in 1997, Mowlam shook hands with Sinn Féin's Gerry Adams, an incident that allowed the loyalist parties to portray her as too friendly with the nationalists. Tony Blair was less than impressed and increasingly stepped in above Mowlam. As a result, it was Blair and the Irish Taoiseach Bertie Ahern who were captured by the cameras at the Stormont negotiations. When the Good Friday Agreement was signed in 1998, Mowlam was absent from the photos. Harriet Harman has called this 'one of the best examples of a woman being written out of history'.[55] In October 1999, Mowlam was replaced as secretary of state for Northern Ireland by Peter Mandelson and she spent the last two years of her time in Parliament as minister for the cabinet office. Mowlam stood down in the 2001 election because of ill health; four years later, she died from the same brain tumour that she had had treatment for in the mid-1990s. Her doctor later revealed that the tumour had been malignant despite Mowlam having claimed it had been benign.[56]

Iraq: Crises and conflicts

While the Labour government could take a large part of the credit for negotiating a lasting peace deal in Northern Ireland, it would also lead the country to war in the Middle East.

The lead-up to the invasion of Iraq on 20 March 2003 saw months of fraught debates as the country and MPs questioned and tried to understand the intelligence dossier that made the government so certain that an invasion was necessary. At the Department for International Development (DfID), Clare Short attempted to prepare for the humanitarian needs of war, and during cabinet meetings before the invasion, she argued that there ought to be a UN resolution for reconstruction as well as one for intervention.[57] On 15 February 2003, people took to the street to march against the war. In London, the BBC estimated that one million people attended the rally in Hyde Park – making it the largest protest march on record in the UK. Yet, on 18 March, the House of Commons voted to support Tony Blair's proposition that military force should be used in Iraq. Harriet Harman, then the deputy solicitor general, voted in favour as she felt the risk of Saddam Hussein using weapons of mass destruction (WMD) again was too high. 'If I'd have known that there were no WMD in Iraq, I wouldn't have voted for the use of force,' Harman later wrote. 'But no one knew for sure.'[58] Clare Short, who had decided that war was unstoppable a few weeks earlier, had made a public statement that she would resign in the absence of a second UN resolution authorizing war. Yet, in the end, she too supported the government in the vote, making clear that it was the attorney general's support for the invasion that had changed her mind.[59]

A quarter of the PLP voted against the government.[60] The war effectively ended the honeymoon period that had started when Labour first came to power in 1997. As Blair failed to curb the American rush to war, Short felt he broke the promises he had made her on the reconstruction of Iraq. On 12 May, Short informed the prime minister that she was resigning. While at DfID, Short had experienced the golden age of international development, between the Cold War and the War on Terror. Although there had been a feeling that DfID was a department concerned with 'soft' issues – perhaps encouraging male prime ministers to appoint women to it, including Barbara Castle, Judith Hart and Lynda Chalker, before Short – she found that 'it is an area at the heart of global economic inequalities'.[61] Short, along with Blair and Brown, helped shape the global Millennium Development Goals (MDGS) to reduce poverty in some of the world's poorest countries.

The Iraq War dented the Labour Party's impressive electoral run of landslide victories, but the party still won its third consecutive election in 2005, albeit with a majority of 66 in comparison to the 167 it had secured in 2001. One of the most keenly-felt losses was that of Bethnal Green and Bow, which had been represented by Oona King. George Galloway, the MP for Glasgow Kelvin who had left Labour for the newly formed anti- war party Respect-Unity Coalition in 2003 (later to become the Respect Party), used both King's record of voting for the war and her Jewish background to sway the electorate his way. In her diary, King described Galloway as

> all over me like a rash. He's bought a house in the constituency; he is often at the mosque bad-mouthing me. And then the Respect lot go out and imply to my Muslim community that I shoot Muslim babies between the eyes. They've even super-imposed my head onto a photograph of a man driving a tank on a mission to kill. It's gone through everyone's letter box. And they point out that I'm Jewish, and there's a Jewish world conspiracy, and I must be part of it. They shout 'Murderer! Murderer!' all the time.[62]

Throughout the campaign, King felt that her being a woman mattered less than her having a Jewish mother. Although King had always made clear her pro-Palestinian stance and called for sanctions against the Israeli government for breaking the fourth Geneva Convention in the

Occupied Territories, Galloway and his supporters repeatedly insinuated that she was a supporter of Israeli aggression.[63] By the time the election came around, Galloway took the seat, beating King by just 823 votes.

Critical moments

Aside from some misogynistic press patronizing the new women MPs, there were also clashes between veteran women and the new intake. Diane Abbott, who had already been an MP for ten years by 1997, was very pleased to see the number of women rise dramatically. 'I wrote to every single new woman who had come in, and only one of them responded,' she told me in 2018. When Labour MPs rebelled against the lone parent benefit cut later in the year, Abbott was not surprised that more men than women voted against it. '[The 1997 newcomers] were women who as a group very much saw themselves as Blairite fangirls,' Abbott said. 'So you didn't get a lot of sisterhood, really.'[64]

Research by political scientist Sarah Childs has confirmed that the new women MPs were less likely to rebel against the party whip. Many of them explained their actions by saying that they were bringing in a new style of politics, one of consensus where discussions were held behind closed doors. Childs concurred, as her findings showed that new women MPs' voices were often more present in agenda setting and policy formulation than voting.[65] In 2018, Jean Corston agreed with that statement: 'Men make speeches and go on telly a lot – what I've always felt about women is that the lobby system works better, you reach consensus behind the scenes. Women did politics differently: more consensual, talking to people outside, working out who to speak to.' Still, she added, their way of working meant that journalists then called them useless, because they did not speak up in public.[66]

Childs found that, among the new MPs, Ann Cryer and Betty Williams were the most rebellious. There was also an element of self-interest involved: MPs who voted against the government were likely to be hindering their career progress. Oona King was certain that turning down the opportunity to work as a PPS in favour of sitting on a select committee, voting against the government on bombing Iraq in 1998, and refusing to pen a letter to the press denouncing Ken Livingstone's candidacy for mayor of London in 1998 cost her promotions and support. 'It's not the end of your career, Oona,' Alastair Campbell allegedly told

King when she held firm on Livingstone. 'Just the next five years.'[67] Regarding herself as a socialist firebrand and feeling less than supported by the New Labour leadership, King did not recognize her portrayal as an arch loyalist Blairite in the press.[68]

King also struggled as her family life was subsumed by the demands put on MPs. During the first few years, she rarely saw her husband – who threatened to leave her at several points.[69] When she sought to conceive through IVF, King went through multiple traumatic rounds. She was devastated when she had to represent the secretary of state, John Reid, on a visit to a family planning clinic just as her fifth round of IVF failed.[70] Some of King's struggles might have been helped by the introduction of family-friendly hours in the Commons, which would put an end to the all-night votes that often meant that MPs could go for days without seeing their families.

But reform of Parliament was controversial. During her time as speaker, Betty Boothroyd had resisted calls for shorter hours. In 2018, Boothroyd told me that she received applause when, in her valedictory speech in 2000, she said 'that when there was work to do here and domestic things too, then the work here must come first. Because I always feel that this house takes priority, quite frankly, and you don't come here to work family-friendly hours. You go to Marks & Spencer if that's what you want, you don't come here to do that.'[71] As a member of the modernisation select committee from 2002, Joan Ruddock had a different agenda, as she worked hard to move the hours of business forward three hours on Tuesdays and Wednesdays so that voting would start at 7pm rather than 10pm. The committee also proposed returning in September rather than October after the summer recess. 'We started the campaign for the simple reason that life was intolerable,' Ruddock told me. 'Seven members died in the 1987–1992 Parliament. We really felt we were going to go on losing people, because 40 per cent of the sittings went to midnight or beyond and we sat five days a week. There was a huge amount of alcoholism and family breakdown.'[72] Working together with Conservative MPs, their suggestions were adopted in 2003, but in 2005 the House of Commons voted to return to 10pm sittings on Tuesdays. Ruddock despaired, angry that those who wanted normal hours were portrayed as workshy. Reformed hours were not, she said, 'about MPs' convenience or preferences' but 'efficiency, keeping sane and trying to have some semblance of a normal life'.[73] Harriet Harman, who in 1991 wrote a pamphlet called 'Time, Gentlemen, Please' to highlight and complain about the hours, told me that:

If you add the exhaustion of babies waking up all night with working all night, with constituents needing you to be around during the day, being on the front bench and having team meetings and shadow cabinet meetings, the hours were an absolute killer. Of course, for the men, the hours were absolutely charming, with hanging out in the bars on the House of Commons terrace.[74]

In 2011, the hours were reformed again so that the House of Commons now sits until 10pm on Monday, 7pm on Tuesday and Wednesday, 5pm on Thursdays and on some Friday mornings. These reforms make balancing parliamentary and family responsibilities a bit easier. A Hansard Society survey in 2011 found that the average working week for a new MP was sixty-seven hours plus travel, with 63 per cent of their time being spent in Westminster. The hours, the division of time between Parliament and constituency, and the expense system were found to make family life a struggle.[75]

Conservatives in opposition

Some of the opposition to Labour's women-friendly policies show just how diverse a group of women MPs can be. One example was the attempt to curb the twenty-four-week time limit on abortions by Ann Widdecombe through an amendment to the draft Human Tissue and Embryos Bill in 2007. Born in 1947, Widdecombe is a committed Christian who converted to Catholicism in 1993 in opposition to the Anglican Church's decision to ordain women bishops. Elected as a Conservative MP in 1987, she stood down at the 2010 election. Before then, she served as a minister of state for prisons under John Major and as shadow secretary of state for health and shadow home secretary under William Hague (the first woman in that role since Shirley Williams' appointment in 1971). Widdecombe – who only supported abortions if the mother's life was at risk – told the BBC that although there was little support for the amendment in the Commons, the public wanted a discussion on the topic.[76] Widdecombe said: 'What does it say for our moral compass that you can have two children of exactly the stage in gestation, one is in a cot with all the resources of medical science being poured in to look after it – the other is being taken from the womb?'[77] Opponents to the amendment also welcomed the discussion, as it was a rare opportunity to discuss the legal restrictions on women's agency within the Abortion Act of 1967, and the fact that abortions were illegal in Northern Ireland. Widdecombe did not succeed, but neither did the pro-choice MPs succeed in changing the legislation concerning abortions in Northern Ireland.

Widdecombe was also opposed to all-women shortlists. In an interview with *The Times* in October 1998, she argued that many of the women elected in 1997 were less qualified and not up to the job. 'Serious politicians arrive in the House already battle-hardened,' Widdecombe told the reporter.

> Blair's Babes have arrived with starry eyes and a pager, shielded by positive discrimination from any real competition. They nod in unison behind the front bench (...) Some of the dear little souls have even whinged that Madam Speaker is too hard on them and indeed has caused more than one to burst into tears. Can anyone imagine Bessie Braddock, Barbara Castle or Margaret Thatcher dissolving at a ticking off from the Speaker?[78]

Yet many of the New Labour women have described the challenges they had to confront that men did not: 'It was rough for some of the women who were making their maiden speech,' Helen Liddell told me. 'Some of the Tories would make lewd comments (...) and by 10pm lots of people had been in the bars and were well refreshed and making comments about people's figures and loud asides. (...) It was just awful.' Gillian Shephard agreed with Liddell: although she described herself as 'not intimidated', she recalls her coping strategy: 'if they behaved a bit absurdly, one just waited until they finished, and then started again'.[79]

Labour leaders

In 1994, Margaret Beckett had become the first woman to lead the Labour Party between the death of John Smith and Tony Blair's election as leader, as she had been elected deputy leader in 1992. She then stood in both the deputy and the leadership elections, losing both. Many of the women in the party supported her: Joan Ruddock later wrote that she had sacrificed John Prescott's patronage by supporting Beckett, only to find that 'Margaret was no sister and would never repay my support'.[80] Harriet Harman wanted Beckett to hold on to the deputy role as it would mean a woman in the top leadership team, but she also felt Beckett had reduced her chances of success by standing for leader at the same time.[81] In 2006, Beckett's own loyalty to the leadership paid off as she was promoted to secretary of state for foreign and commonwealth affairs, becoming the first woman to head the Foreign Office. She was surprised when she was appointed, and she was thrown in at the deep end immediately. 'I was appointed on Friday, and on Monday I was in the States meeting Condi Rice, Sergey Lavrov, the German and French foreign ministers, and the Chinese foreign minister, all to talk about Iran,' Beckett told Peter Hennessy in 2014.[82] Clearly capable and in control of her new brief, Beckett's arrival at the Foreign Office still caused controversy. She later told me that the media coverage was particularly bad, and that women journalists – who had wanted a female foreign minister, but not Beckett – 'tore me limb from limb'. As for parliamentary colleagues, Malcolm Rifkind – a Conservative cabinet minister under Thatcher and Major – claimed that she was an unsuitable choice as she had no experience of negotiations.[83] 'I think he meant I'd never been in the Foreign Office as a junior minister,' Beckett told me. 'I think I'd done more negotiating than Malcolm had had hot dinners.'[84]

On Blair's resignation in 2007, Gordon Brown succeeded him as leader of the Labour Party and prime minister. The race for deputy was more complicated with six candidates: Alan Johnson, Jon Cruddas, Harriet Harman, Hilary Benn, Peter Hain and Hazel Blears. Harman had originally not intended to run as she did not want to go back to frontline politics, but she was dismayed when she saw the lack of women in Brown's top team. Having had pressure put on her by her family and Margaret Hodge, Harman agreed, though she still thought her chances of actually winning were very slim. 'Women in the party were starting to urge me to run,' Harman wrote in 2017, 'and, though it was gratifying, it seemed inconceivable that I should. I had been downwardly mobile in government. This hardly seemed an auspicious base from which to challenge the big and popular men in the cabinet. And it would do nothing to advance the cause of women in the party if my candidature attracted derision.'[85] Still, over the years, she had come to realize that 'it doesn't necessarily become apparent what leadership qualities someone has until the mantle of responsibility falls on their shoulders. When Tony [Blair] decided to stand for leader it was like one of those TV cartoons where a cat peels back his skin and a tiger jumps out.'[86] As it turned out, Harman's strength was her gender and the impression she gave of not being a leadership contender, i.e. not a threat to Brown. With the help of her team – which included Joan Ruddock – Harman commissioned a YouGov poll that

PLATE 17 Women MPs from various parties in 1988.

PLATE 18 Labour MP Diane Abbott, the first black woman to be elected as an MP, in 1987.

PLATE 19 Labour MP Margaret Beckett in 1997. She later became the first woman foreign secretary.

PLATE 20 Labour's Betty Boothroyd, in 1994, two years after having been elected as the first woman Speaker of the House of Commons.

PLATE 21 The infamous 'Blair's Babes' photo, taken shortly after the 1997 Labour landslide at which a record of 101 Labour women were elected.

PLATE 22 Labour MPs Caroline Flint and Hazel Blears among others in their dance group, 'The Division Belles'.

PLATE 23 Labour MP Tessa Jowell in 1998.

PLATE 24 Conservative MP Gillian Shephard in 1998.

PLATE 25 Mo Mowlam, the first woman secretary of state for Northern Ireland.

PLATE 26 Labour MP Clare Short in 2008.

PLATE 27 New Labour women MPs in the Downing Street White Room in July 2007.

PLATE 28 A photograph taken in 2010 to celebrate the record number of sitting Labour women MPs who had held the position of secretary of state.

PLATE 29 Labour women Harriet Harman, Gloria De Piero and Yvette Cooper with the pink bus.

PLATE 30 Theresa May on the day she took office as the second woman prime minister in 2016.

PLATE 31 Labour MP Jo Cox at a Macmillan Cancer fundraising event in 2016.

PLATE 32 Me with Jo Cox's sister Kim Leadbeater and Conservative MP Seema Kennedy.

showed that the public favoured her out of the six candidates and that she was particularly popular with women and swing voters. A significant 29 per cent of swing voters said that with Harman installed as deputy leader, they would be more likely to vote Labour. As the party's electoral success was on the wane, that was a very important piece of information.[87] Glenys Kinnock made that clear as she announced her support for Harman's campaign in May 2007, stating to the press that 'It's unthinkable that the Labour Party should elect a deputy leader who wasn't a woman [and] that woman has to be Harriet!'[88]

Harman's campaign picked up pace. She accepted every invitation offered, made personal phone calls across the country, and took out a second mortgage on her home in order to pay for campaign leaflets.[89] Ruddock told Harman to wear lipstick at the hustings, as her paleness was amplified by spotlights. Her efforts – both in terms of content and image – paid off: on 27 June 2007 Harman was elected deputy leader of the Labour Party, narrowly beating Alan Johnson.[90] When the result was announced, Johnson proved to be a gracious loser, stating that 'I was the best man, but as is so often the case, along came a better woman'. 'It was so gracious,' Harriet Harman told me. 'It gave me space to win over the nearly 50 per cent of members who didn't support me. It also signalled to Alan's supporters that they should support me and if they briefed against me, it was not in his name.'[91] John Prescott, Harman's predecessor as deputy leader who had served in that role for thirteen years, was less generous. He told Harman on the same night that he would not give her advice and support.[92] It was, Harman believed, a result of her declaring that she would not use Dorneywood, the official residence where Prescott had been photographed by the press while playing croquet on the lawn.

The deal made between Tony Blair and Gordon Brown in 1994 had allowed Blair to win the leadership election of that year, and Brown to stand unopposed in 2007. As a result, there was next to no chance that a woman would lead the party between 1994 and 2010 – a period in which the number of Labour women in Parliament dramatically rose. Yet, there were other ways of exercising power. In comparison to the Thatcher (nil) and Major (two) governments, Blair promoted fifteen women to his cabinet, while seven served under Brown. One of Brown's key appointees was Jacqui Smith, who had been elected in 1997 and who became only the third woman to hold one of the great offices of state as home secretary 2007–09. Selected on an all-women shortlist and supported by EMILY's

List in 1997, Smith was a mother of two with children born in 1993 and 1998, and her career as a minister was enabled by her husband taking the main carer role. 'I had the advantage in 1997 of being pretty sure that I was going to win,' Smith told me. 'We'd talked it all through; we'd worked out how we were going to organize ourselves.' Hers was, she added, a very different experience to some of those in the 1997 cohort: 'Things went very bad for some people, especially women who were elected when their husbands didn't expect them to be.' Smith's youngest son was born at the beginning of the summer after her election, allowing her to take a few months off before returning to Parliament in October. 'I thought that was quite generous,' Smith said. 'Looking back on it, it wasn't.' The worst moment was when she had to leave her four-month-old to go to London for three days a week. 'I don't quite know how I did it. But what other people have said to me was that there was a sort of sisterhood effort to recognize how difficult it would be, and on a Monday night they would make sure that somebody was keeping an eye on me, which was just splendid of them.'

Unlike some of her predecessors, Smith was never worried that the path to ministerial power might be closed to women. 'The women in the cabinet and minister of state level were some of the people I had looked up to as I was coming into Parliament,' Smith told me. 'You can't be what you don't see, and the implication was that if you got on, you would be a minister.' But Smith's appointment as home secretary in 2007 still came as a surprise: 'I was a bit shocked when it happened, but I think other people weren't expecting me to have it either, which is an interesting position to be in.' On her second day at the Home Office, a terrorist incident took place. 'The interesting thing was the number of people that went with "oh she actually handled that quite well, she appeared quite calm",' Smith told me. 'The implication being: you make a woman home secretary, there's a terrorist attack and she's going to come running out of Number Ten Downing Street shouting "I can't manage it, I can't manage it".'[93]

Window dressing

Jacqui Smith believes one reason she became home secretary was because Gordon Brown wanted a woman in a top role.[94] Yet, despite their number, despite the progress and despite the public's support for women politicians, even the most senior of Labour women who had secured the top jobs hit glass ceilings. Harriet Harman is one example: she made clear before her election as deputy leader that she would not want to combine the role with a departmental position. Instead, she became chair of the Labour Party.[95] Yet, she was bitterly disappointed when Gordon Brown decided to break with tradition and not appoint her deputy prime minister. It was 'a golden opportunity for Gordon (. . .) and, if it had been any other woman in the position of Deputy Labour Leader, I would have recognised that in an instant. I'd have fought for her to be Deputy Prime Minister and I'm sure I would have succeeded,' Harman wrote in 2017. In conversation with me, she added: 'I should have insisted on it.' Explaining why she did not, Harman cited the sense of loyalty that caused her dilemma with lone parent benefits in 1997. 'I didn't want to be disloyal or cause difficulties to Gordon, who was already beleaguered.'[96]

Harman also found herself located far away from the prime minister in both cabinet meetings (where Jack Straw had been allocated the chair next to Brown) and the first formal photograph of the Brown cabinet, both sure signs that Harman was being marginalized. The lack of formal acknowledgement of her position did not mean that Harman was not expected to fill in when Brown was away: in March 2008, she became the first woman to do prime minister's questions since Margaret Thatcher in 1990. It was, she wrote in her memoirs, a moment of triumph and enhanced her standing in the party.[97]

But although more women had been elected and promoted, their power was limited. In 2018, Harman told me that Gordon Brown 'objectively deliver[ed] for women [with] childcare, maternity [leave] and tax credits. But he didn't really work with them.'[98] She was not the only woman MP to criticize Brown's working practices. On 5 June 2009, Caroline Flint, a Labour MP from the 1997 intake, resigned from the government with a letter accusing Brown of having 'a two-tier Government. Your inner circle and then the remainder of cabinet'. She had been the minister of state for Europe for eight months and 'worked her socks off,' she told me in 2018. Having been told that she would be attending cabinet when Europe was on the agenda, Flint was subsequently uninvited. Flint tried to flag up her concerns about the European elections taking place that year, but these fell on deaf ears. The election proved a disaster for Labour, as they received just 15.2 per cent of the vote.[99] In her resignation letter, Flint argued that few women were allowed into the prime minister's inner circle despite their positions in the cabinet. She also stated that several of them – herself included – had 'been treated by you as little more than female window dressing. I am not willing to attend cabinet in a peripheral capacity any longer.'[100] Harman was asked to defend Brown in the press. Making a point not to criticize Flint directly, Harman told journalists that while she understood Flint's frustrations, Brown had overseen lots of policies that had improved women's lives as both chancellor and prime minister. 'I didn't want to deny what Caroline Flint said about window dressing, but I had made a different choice,' Harman told me. She sympathized with Flint and knew she had a point but felt Flint's approach 'wasn't going to get us anywhere'.[101] These were among the tensest days of Harman's relationship with Brown, coming as they did in the middle of her battle to prevent Peter Mandelson from becoming deputy prime minister, a job which Harman's elected position should have given her entitlement to. Confronting Brown about the rumours that were circulating in-between her meetings with the press to defend his record with women, Harman told him that the appointment would be over her dead body. She pointed out the great irony of having to defend Brown in the press against Flint's accusations, only to find that he was trying to appoint a man over her head. In the end, Brown appointed Mandelson first secretary of state. Harman soon discovered that 'it was an office which puts the holder above all other cabinet ministers and is always held by the deputy prime minister. [...] Just in case anyone was to miss the point, Number Ten briefed the media that Peter Mandelson was now "deputy prime minister in all but name"'. It was a terrible affront to Harman.[102]

There were other kinds of marginalization that would have been familiar to earlier generations of women MPs. In 2009, Harriet Harman's office was aghast when she was invited to join the G20 wives' dinner rather than the summit dinner itself. The meeting was organized by the government and held in London; whoever sent the invitations must have known who Harriet Harman was. The need to reply led to a great debate among her staff. 'Should I refuse to go, reminding them that, although I am a woman, that did not make me a G20 wife? Or would that be an insult to all the women who were there and make it look as if I thought I was somehow above them? Should I therefore go and show sisterly solidarity? In the end, we decided that there was nothing for it but for me to go, and with good grace. I sat next to the wife of the conservative prime minister of Canada and there was a lively discussion at the table about a new diet.'[103]

Press attention on what women wore in Parliament also continued. On Jacqui Smith's first time at the despatch box as home secretary, she wore a low-cut top, resulting in a 'Minister for Melons' headline in a newspaper. 'I don't think men would have had the same problem [but] I did think quite carefully about what I wore after that,' Smith told me. 'I don't think you want to be the home secretary in a pink jacket when something shit happens and you have to front that up. That is about being a woman, because you have a wider range of things to wear, but it's also about feeling responsibility towards the role.' In the end, it was press intrusion following the expenses scandal in 2009 – with revelations that Smith listed her sister's house in London as her primary residence and claimed expenses for the constituency home where her children lived, and that her husband had been reimbursed for watching two adult films – that made Smith step down after two years as home secretary. 'On the whole, I didn't read [the newspapers]; they were removed from my office,' she told me. 'I just don't think I would've been able to get up and put one foot in front of the other, had I read it. And the allegations had a sexist element to them – people couldn't believe that I spent more time at the home where my children weren't than where they were. I'm not sure that would've been the same for a man. And obviously the whole porn thing, that was always going to be a massive nightmare.' With her husband badly affected by the revelations, Smith resigned. 'I was only able to do the job because he cared for the family,' she told me. 'When he was no longer able to do that', Smith concluded, she couldn't either.[104]

***

The New Labour era marked a distinct shift towards women-focused policies thanks to the hard work of women's activists within the party who dared provoke conflict with the male leadership over issues close to their hearts. Over the space of thirteen years, Labour women were able to influence and make policies that greatly enhanced women's rights and opportunities, whether in the workplace or at home. Their strength in numbers fell in 2010, when the party lost the general election to the Conservative–Liberal Democrat coalition led by David Cameron and Nick Clegg. Forty-nine Conservative women were elected in 2010, while the number of Labour women MPs fell to eighty-one from ninety-eight. At the dawn of one era and the end of another, women held 22 per cent of the seats in the House of Commons. It was a greater proportion than ever before, but their number had only risen by twenty-three in thirteen years. New challenges would be faced by the coalition government and the women MPs in the new Parliament.

8

More in Common: 2010–19

We are far more united and have far more in common with each other than things that divide us.

JO COX, 2015[1]

At the 2005 election, just seventeen Conservative women had been elected. By 2010, that number had nearly trebled to forty-nine, after decades of stagnation. The Conservative Party also expanded their appeal to women, especially among middle-class mothers dubbed 'the Mumsnetters' who supported Cameron's modernizing approach. The party had begun a shift away from Theresa May's label of the 'nasty party', made at the 2002 party conference, and it was bringing women voters and candidates with it. By 2016, Theresa May had steadily made her way through the ranks of the cabinet and, in the reverberations of the Brexit vote, emerged unscathed to become the second female prime minister in British history, but by 2019 she had been replaced by Boris Johnson.

The huge improvements in Conservative female representation and engagement over the last decade have gone hand-in-hand with increases in the total number of women MPs. In 2016, the total number of women MPs ever elected finally equalled the number of male MPs in a single Parliament (454), and in 2019, they broke the 500 barrier, increasing to 556 women MPs. But success also came with a sobering reminder that the battle for representation was not over: the Liberal Democrats, who had been the third largest party and the junior member of the coalition government from 2010–2015, elected no women MPs whatsoever in 2015. The following year, they were compelled to introduce all-women shortlists. Among the seven Lib Dem women to lose their seats in 2015 was Jo Swinson, who would go on to become leader of the party in 2019, having returned to Parliament in 2017. Her seat of East Dunbartonshire, like many, fell to the SNP in 2015, and again in 2019, who made sweeping gains across Scotland under the leadership of Nicola Sturgeon. The SNP's Mhairi Black, a twenty-year-old student at Glasgow University, became the youngest MP ever to be elected, beating the record of Bernadette Devlin who had been elected forty-six years previously.

The 2017 general election, which delivered Theresa May a minority government in place of the landslide she had anticipated, again saw the total number of women inch upwards from 191 to 208. There were also significant improvements for other marginalized groups. The number of Black, Asian and Minority Ethnic (BAME) women MPs increased from twenty to thirty. Labour's Preet Kaur Gill became the first female Sikh MP in Birmingham Edgbaston, while Marsha de Cordova, who is registered blind, overturned a large Conservative majority in Battersea.

The following year – 2018 – saw celebrations of the centenary of women's suffrage and of women being able to stand as MPs. The difference in women's status between now and then is huge: we had no women in Parliament in 1918 before Nancy Astor took her seat, and now we have 220.

After losing her majority in the 2017 general election, Theresa May's position looked increasingly precarious. By the summer of 2019 her failure to secure a Brexit deal that could find a parliamentary majority in the House of Commons ushered her out of, and Brexiteer Boris Johnson into, Downing Street. In a huge cull of his Cabinet, Johnson made notable appointments of Brexiteer women to senior cabinet posts – most noticeably Priti Patel as home secretary and Andrea Leadsom as business secretary. In doing so, Priti Patel became the first BAME woman home secretary. She recounted to me how 'It was such a big moment ... it's a really big vote of confidence in you, that you have that ability ... so when you have that coming from the most senior person, the prime minister, that's a really significant moment. And I think being a woman as well, that's doubly significant.'[2] A few MPs who campaigned for Remain were also appointed by Johnson: Nicky Morgan as secretary of state for digital, culture, media and sport, who stood down at the December 2019 election, and Amber Rudd as secretary of state for work and pensions (who was replaced by Thérèse Coffey when Rudd quit the Cabinet and resigned the Conservative whip and then her seat in protest at Johnson's treatment of MPs who opposed a 'no deal' Brexit).

From 'Blair's Babes' to 'Cameron's Cuties'

But the fact that Boris Johnson had a choice of senior women to appoint to the Cabinet, and indeed that he was expected to do so, went back to decisions made in the Conservative Party more than a decade ago. By 2005, with all-women shortlists having been implemented by the Labour Party and the number of Labour women MPs having expanded, it was seen that the women-friendly culture of the Labour Party had contributed towards its electoral fortunes. It began to occur to senior Conservatives, including Iain Duncan Smith and David Cameron, that the same could be true for their own party.

The problem was that Conservative women weren't being selected by local parties. Former Conservative MP Caroline Spelman, who served in the cabinet under David Cameron, was rejected by twenty-seven constituencies before finally being selected. Spelman recalls that at one selection interview, the panel asked her the age of her children, and she remembers 'you could just feel people disengage when I said six, four and two'.[3] She was also asked to set out her own childcare plans in detail, a demand which would never have been made of a man at a selection interview. During one of Penny Mordaunt's selection attempts, a man 'stood up and gave me a speech about how it was totally inappropriate that someone like me was doing this,' she told me. 'His parting shot was "Will we be having children?"' Mordaunt responded wryly, 'Well, you're very attractive, but we've only just met'.[4] Anne Jenkin, co-founder of Women2Win, remarked to me that Conservative associations are systematically biased against women: 'you'll show them three great women and they'll say, "those women were fantastic", and in walks a bloke and they'll say, "but there's our MP"', Jenkin laughs. 'Especially if he's got a nice labrador and a lovely wife on his arm'.[5] Laura Sandys, who became a Conservative MP in 2010, once overheard a selection panel say of her successful opponent: 'Well, he may be a homosexual, but at least we didn't get a woman'.[6] Similarly, the Labour Party selection process, despite AWS, still suffers from these institutional biases. As Rushanara Ali, the first British-Bangladeshi woman MP, who has served as MP for Oona King's former seat of Bethnal Green and Bow since 2010, told me: 'There is something about selection processes that just brings out the worst in people'.[7] One of Emily Thornberry's first attempts at selection was in Dagenham, where in 2001 the MP Judith Church was standing down after serving the constituency for seven years, having struggled to combine being an MP with being a mother of two children. Thornberry revealed to me that the leader of the Dagenham council wrote to her advising her not to bother since 'we already have three excellent candidates, and in my opinion, given the behaviour of our previous MP, it would be impossible for any woman, let alone the mother of children, to be elected for this seat'. Describing herself as one of the so-called 'Dagenham survivors', Thornberry was not the only woman who was treated in this way.

Even when women do manage to be selected, it is often for seats the party doesn't expect to win because it is only then that local parties feel they have nothing to lose. But as Jess Phillips puts it, when you are fighting in a no-hope seat against an incumbent MP, 'you are essentially taking a jelly to a knife fight.'[8]

Theresa May was at the forefront of attempts to solve these problems within the Conservative Party. In 2001, she proposed what would become known as the 'A-list' as an alternative to AWS. The A-list consisted of 100 candidates selected as having the greatest potential, with 50 per cent reserved for women. Though Ken Clarke and Iain Duncan Smith – the two final candidates in the leadership election of 2002 – disagreed with the proposal, David Cameron took it up in 2005 as part of his mission to modernize his party. In the same year, the modernizing May joined Anne Jenkin to create Women2Win. Inspired by the Labour Women's Network, Women2Win set out to encourage Conservative women to stand for selection. It ran an 'Ask Her to Stand' campaign from 2005 to 2010, with panel events targeted at talented women featuring MPs, candidates, councillors and party activists along with headhunters to provide support and explain the selection process. May told me that Women2Win was an attempt to solve the situation in which 'women think they're in competition with other women – whereas men don't think they're in competition, the men all think they're the greatest'.[9] I interviewed May the day after Johnson – then foreign secretary in her government – had written an article for *The Telegraph* in which he described Muslim women who wear a veil as looking like bank robbers or letter boxes. I expect she was thinking of him.

Women2Win was an institutional extension of some of the advice that Margaret Thatcher had given to women in politics, despite the fact that she has been criticized for failing to support female colleagues. Back in 1979, Thatcher told Cheryl Gillan, Conservative MP from 1992, 'We need women like you.'[10] Penny Mordaunt also told me that Thatcher continued to write to Conservative candidates – though not exclusively women – long after she left Parliament. Thatcher wrote to Mordaunt in 2005 when she first stood to say 'get back on the horse, you'll be great when you get here'.[11]

Remembering the early days of Women2Win, Jenkin recalls that May was the 'in the driving seat', providing the vision and influence, while Jenkin described herself as 'plodding about doing the photo-copying and the calling'.[12] May provided continual support and encouragement to many Conservative women candidates. Anna Soubry recalls May phoning her up on the night before her selection to wish her luck and ask if there was anything she could do to help.

When Cameron adopted the A-list in 2005, it was predominantly due to the work of Women2Win and Theresa May. Having been elected as leader of the party in December 2005, Cameron and his team immediately contacted Women2Win with a view to implementing the A-List and did so within a week. Amber Rudd, who was herself on the A-list, said it was a 'a smart approach' that 'stopped the business of all men short-lists'; acknowledging how crucial it was as a springboard into politics, she told me: 'It was amazing to get on that list.' Rudd added that the A-list brought 'dramatic, permanent change to the Conservative Parliamentary party'.[13] Andrea Leadsom, who was also on the A-list, told me that it 'definitely was what made the difference, because it just gave the female candidates the chance to be looked at'.[14] In 2010, as the number of Conservative women increased, the pressure for the maintenance of the A-list waned and it was later discontinued.

Cameron's further attempts to modernize his party hit the headlines in 2014 in a cabinet reshuffle that replaced many older male ministers with women including Esther McVey, Nicky Morgan and Liz Truss who, at thirty-eight, became the youngest ever female cabinet minister. The number of women in the cabinet rose to five (24 per cent of the total), with an additional three attending cabinet. As the new women strode into Number Ten, the press branded it the 'Downing Street catwalk'. With Priti Patel having been promoted to the position of treasury minister, *The Daily Mail* commented that she 'must be the first person in that post to wear giant polka dots'.[15] Esther McVey, who had been appointed as employment secretary, responded to the focus on her own sartorial choices by saying, 'I hope our Downing Street catwalk inspires young girls to go into politics'. Penny Mordaunt had appeared on the television diving programme *Splash!* that year; consequently, every news story about her was accompanied by a photo of her in a red swimming costume.

Mordaunt responded to the Downing Street catwalk frenzy by saying that 'I'm actually feeling pretty good, because it's the first time the Mail have run a picture of me with my clothes on.'[16] While Cameron's reshuffle provoked frenzied objectification from the press, it elicited hysterical accusations of a matriarchy from his parliamentary party. Many male MPs angrily alleged that Cameron was biased towards women, to the detriment of men. Conservative MP Richard Drax contemptuously dubbed Cameron's reshuffle as 'the night of the petticoats', in a parody of Harold Macmillan's 'night of the long knives' of 1962.[17] Meanwhile, former Conservative MP Jerry Hayes tweeted: 'Bad weekend for any ambitious Tory MP with a penis.'

While more women had now entered the cabinet, Cameron's inner circle was still dominated by men and the nature of coalition government naturally meant that power was concentrated among a few figures – men such as Cameron, Osborne, Clegg and Cable. When Cameron's small business ambassador and judge of the BBC television series *The Apprentice*, Karren Brady, met a group of Conservative women MPs to ask them about their life at Westminster, she compared being a woman MP today to working in 'football in the 1990s'. At the 2015 Conservative Party conference, female Conservative MPs were put on an 'arm candy rota' to walk around the Manchester conference venue with Cameron. The incident provoked mixed responses from senior Conservative women: some viewed it as a way of boosting their own image and prestige; others felt it was condescending and objectifying. One female cabinet member told Isabel Hardman at *The Spectator*: 'I didn't get into Parliament to be a bit of fucking arm candy'. Meanwhile, Nicky Morgan joked that her female colleagues would 'flatten' any journalist who called them by that name.[18]

Policies for women?

Just as the inclusion of women in Cameron's cabinet did not entail their treatment as equals within it, so too the party's electoral positioning towards the 'Mumsnetters' in 2010 did not necessarily translate into benefits for women across the country. The coalition government's economic programme of austerity attracted significant opposition. Social security benefits were cut, public sector pay was frozen, and all government departments excluding health and international development saw deep cuts of up to 51 per cent.[19] Labour's then shadow foreign secretary and minister for women, Yvette Cooper, highlighted the gendered impact of austerity by commissioning the House of Commons Library to estimate the proportion of austerity borne by women, something that she had first started doing in the late 1990s. The figure was 86 per cent, reflecting the fact that women earn less, do more of the childcare, are more likely to work in the public sector, and rely more on public services. However, many Conservative women have disputed this analysis: preferring to view economic distribution in terms of households rather than individuals, they sometimes argue that the reduction in child benefit, for example, cannot be seen as a gendered policy. Jess Phillips expressed frustration to me at the passivity of Conservative women on issues such as these:

> The thing that annoys me about it is that they leave being radical to people like me and they go on their processions and wave their green, white and purple flags and they show up for the photo events about Millicent Fawcett but they still expect the tough stuff, the difficult conversations to be had by people like me.[20]

Jo Swinson, who served as a Liberal Democrat minister in the Coalition, conceded that 'There's a kind of basic truth when you're cutting public spending' that women will be disproportionately harmed, but she also felt that positive reforms were achieved.[21] These included shared parental leave, the right to request flexible working, greater state support within the tax system for childcare, and measures to tackle violence against women. Policies for women were in large part achieved because of a new type of Conservative woman in Parliament, one who was not ashamed to call herself a feminist and who explicitly positioned herself away from figures such as Margaret Thatcher. Nicky Morgan told me that 'After the 2010 election, because there were more of us, a number of backbench Conservative female MPs decided that we wanted to do more on women's issues, which traditionally the party has not been good at talking about.'[22] In 2011, before she had entered the cabinet, Amber Rudd wrote an article for *The Telegraph* entitled 'We are not Thatcher's children'. Referring to the 2010 intake, including many who had been supported by Women2Win and the A-list, she wrote that: 'We grew out of the ground that Margaret Thatcher ploughed, but in our approach to supporting women, we are not her children.'[23] Conservative women MPs were 'determined to take ownership of women's issues back' from the hands of Labour.[24] Nicky Morgan told me that 'you would never expect a Conservative Treasury to have a big thing about [improvements in access to childcare]. And it was there.'[25]

One success of huge symbolic and practical importance to women, and a further chapter in the equal pay story, was mandatory gender pay gap reporting, a personal campaign of Jo Swinson's. Despite Barbara Castle's Equal Pay Act in 1970, which made it illegal to pay men and women different wages for the same work, today there is still a large gender pay gap of 18.4 per cent – the difference in the average hourly earnings of women compared to men. This is mostly due to occupational segregation (the process by which women and men are concentrated in different types of job), with lower wages for occupations that are perceived as 'women's work'. The idea behind mandatory reporting of businesses' gender pay gaps was that it would shine a light on where the largest gaps existed and embarrass employers into treating women more equally. 'It is precisely because so much gender bias is unconscious and unintentional,' Swinson later argued, 'that it persists without challenge, even from companies and individuals committed to rooting it out. Looking at the numbers in black and white helps to pierce this bubble of complacency.'[26] However, the Conservatives were initially reluctant to support what was seen as a 'nanny state' policy of interference with businesses and preferred a voluntary approach. 'Everything was so anti-regulation, anti-regulation, anti-regulation,' Swinson reflected.[27] Yet under the incumbent system of voluntary reporting, only *five* companies had reported their pay levels for men and women within a five-year period.

In 2010, an amendment to Harriet Harman's Equality Act had legislated for mandatory reporting, but there was a delay on implementation and the general election enabled the issue to be kicked into the long grass. With the Conservatives' flagship Small Business Bill going through Parliament, Swinson and Liberal Democrat leader Nick Clegg lobbied the Lords to push through an amendment requiring all businesses with 250 or more employees to report their gender pay gaps. With it being undesirable politically for the Conservatives to whip the vote against the amendment just before a general election, the amendment passed. As Swinson put it, 'I figured they'd blink first, which they did.'[28] In passing the amendment, the UK became the second country in the world to establish gender pay gap transparency, after Iceland.

When the 2015 election brought an end to the coalition, the new Conservative government had a choice: it could either implement mandatory reporting or overturn it. It was a testament to Swinson's agenda-setting capabilities that 'they tried to make a virtue out of necessity and pretend that it was their idea.'[29] In April 2018, Conservative minister

Victoria Atkins was able to report to the House that 10,055 employers had reported their gender pay gaps. The figures from 2018 suggest that 78 per cent of businesses pay men more than women.

Theresa May: last woman standing

When Thatcher came to power in 1979, a young Oxford geography student and member of the university's Conservative association named Theresa Brazier was slightly disappointed. She had been beaten to the post of being the first woman prime minister of Britain, an ambition of hers since she was twelve years old. But thirty-seven years later, she too entered Number Ten, as Theresa May.

Prior to her election as MP for Maidenhead in 1997, May had worked at the Bank of England and had served as a councillor in Merton. A vicar's daughter whose childhood was steeped in family tradition, public service and discipline, May has had a political career that demonstrates a clear sense of independence, determination and duty. When she was elected in 1997 as Conservative MP for Maidenhead, she was often mistaken for one of 'Blair's Babes', arriving as she did alongside a wave of New Labour women. Although she says that she didn't mind, May certainly sought to set herself apart from the Labour women, particularly in the earlier years of her career. Harriet Harman described her as a 'drag anchor' on attempts to legislate for feminist reforms, including AWS and the Equality Act. But May prided herself on doing politics her own way, with a sense of purpose and direction that defied clubbishness – whether with the feminist movement or with the various groupings within the Conservative Party. When I interviewed her in the summer of 2018, May reflected on this individual approach by recalling a story told to her by a female colleague: 'she felt she had to go into the smoking room and had to be part of that kind of clubby culture in order to be seen to be doing the job the way the men did it. Whereas I didn't do that. Some people would say of course that's been one of my problems over the years, I haven't done it in the way that the men did it', she laughed.[30]

Home secretary

May's disavowal of clubbishness created a distaste, which grew over time, for Cameron's cabal of male, Eton-educated, self-professed modernizers. She worked her way through multiple shadow cabinet roles by quietly getting on with her job and eschewing the peacocking camaraderie of her male colleagues. Unlike most MPs, May was reluctant to network and was hardly ever spotted in the tea-rooms; this meant that unlike others she did not have a natural group of supporters in Parliament. It was therefore a surprise both to herself and to the political elite that Cameron offered May one of the great offices of state in 2010 – home secretary.

The press leapt on May's alleged lack of experience for the role, although she had been in Parliament for longer than both Cameron and Osborne (as well as having been an active and modernizing party chairman from 2002 to 2003), and cast doubt on her ability to succeed. With the Home Office regarded as the 'traditional graveyard of political ambition', the press portrayed May as 'totty set up to fail'.[31] She proved them wrong when she became the longest-serving home secretary and used her position as a launchpad into Downing Street.

As home secretary, May took an active lead on the issues of domestic violence and sexual exploitation. Many of her supporters see her time as home secretary as foreshadowing the promise she would make on the steps of Number Ten in 2016 to tackle the 'burning injustices' of British society. '[T]o me,' May said when I interviewed her, 'it's about fundamentally an equality of saying, men and women we're all human beings and we should all be treated properly and fairly, and the concept that women can be treated as commodities or in a different way, simply because you're a woman – I think it's social injustice.'[32] May prioritized action on female genital mutilation (FGM), introduced domestic violence protection orders, and introduced a law against coercive control, so that emotional abuse could be punished as well as physical abuse. But her proudest achievement as home secretary, she told me, was the Modern Slavery Act, which sought to act against slavery and human trafficking (of particular significance for women and girls). When I asked May why she felt so strongly about the legislation, she said that it was 'an issue which most people felt was non-existent, that had just gone away and been dealt with 200 years ago – but is happening in towns and cities around our country and around the world every day'.[33] A year after my interview with May, when she had left Downing Street and Priti Patel was installed as home secretary, Patel paid tribute to May's legacy: 'I would say credit to Theresa May,' Patel reflected, 'what she did with modern slavery. She showed international leadership.'[34]

Alongside her Home Office brief, in 2010 May was appointed the first Conservative minister for women and equalities. She was a controversial figure for the equalities brief: she had opposed the repeal of Section 28 in

2000 (legislation banning the so-called 'promotion' of homosexuality in schools), voted against same-sex adoption, and opposed same-sex marriage. A petition demanding her removal from the role attracted 70,000 signatures. However, two weeks later, she went on BBC Question Time and said that she had 'changed [her] mind' on same-sex marriage. She explained her change of heart to me in terms of a realization

> that again this was about equality of treatment, and this was about seeing individual human beings as individuals . . . you take one view at one time, and you have a look at it and you think, 'Well actually, you know what, was that really the right approach – do I really think that this is going to be such a problem?'[35]

Lynne Featherstone was a Liberal Democrat minister at the Home Office and May's deputy for the women and equalities brief. Featherstone was encouraged by May's statement and seized the opportunity by drafting a proposal for legislation to legalize same-sex marriage. May approved the proposal, as did all but two cabinet members. Despite its huge controversy within the Commons and a slightly uneasy fit with May's own Christian faith, she worked with Featherstone to push same-sex marriage onto the statute book. It was a relationship more of mutual admiration than affection but 'we got on very well', May told me. 'I think it was that ability, and in a sense two women coming from slightly . . . different approaches and experiences and being able just to share that together and come up with proposals and solutions that we felt were the right ones.'[36] The bill passed through the House in July 2013. When I asked today's home secretary Priti Patel why she voted against the bill in 2013, she claimed that it was purely due to legal issues and the legislative detail of the bill, rather than any opposition to the principle of same-sex marriage: 'I'm not anti-same-sex-marriage. It's always wrong to assume because of how one's voted that you're anti-this or anti-that. That's absolutely not the case.'[37] At midnight on 29 March 2014, when the legislation took effect for the first time, dozens of same-sex couples took their marriage vows. A year later, over 15,000 same-sex couples were married. Justine Greening, then a Conservative MP and secretary of state for education from 2016 to 2018, who came out in 2016 as being in a same-sex relationship, said that 'for women like me, [the legislation] was really important'.[38]

During her time as home secretary, May experienced tension with her male cabinet colleagues, ranging from grudge-forming disagreements to what Cameron described as a 'fucking car crash' in her battle with Nick Clegg over immigration and civil liberties.[39] She came into conflict not only with Liberal Democrats such as Nick Clegg, Vince Cable and Chris Huhne, but also David Cameron, George Osborne, Michael Gove and Ken Clarke. The latter famously described May as a 'bloody difficult woman', a description which she embraced in her 2016 leadership campaign. Lynne Featherstone attributed May's tendency to provoke tension with male cabinet colleagues to her resoluteness, bordering on stubbornness, and her distinct lack of clubbability: they 'just weren't used to someone who stood their ground the way that she did'.[40] While political differences between Clegg and Cameron, for example, could sometimes be ironed out over a drink or chat, May intentionally set herself apart from this style of politics. By and large, she concealed her discontent under a veneer of professionalism until the day she became prime minister.

The second woman prime minister

In the summer of 2016, May's path to Number Ten was cleared by her colleagues (David Cameron, George Osborne, Michael Gove, Boris Johnson and Andrea Leadsom) inadvertently jeopardizing their political careers in their pursuit of power, where she remained cool-headed. As Yvette Cooper, who shadowed May for nearly five years while she was home secretary, admits, 'I think she's a grown-up, which compared to Boris Johnson and Michael Gove is quite an important thing'.[41] With Johnson and Gove cancelling themselves out of the race, by the second round of the leadership contest it had become clear that, whatever the result, Britain would have a second female prime minister. The question was whether it would be Theresa May or Andrea Leadsom, a key Leave campaigner and environment secretary under Cameron.

The odds were in May's favour: she had a solid track record and was well-respected among Conservative members. But in the end it turned out that May hardly had to fight at all. Leadsom gave an interview for *The Times* in which she declared herself to be more in touch with voters than May because, as a mother, she had a special stake in the country's future. Leadsom's comments would have been unfair regardless of whether May's childlessness was a matter of choice or not. But the fact that May and her husband Philip had been unable to have children made the comments particularly unkind and foolish. Amid a whirlwind of media criticism, Leadsom phoned May to inform her that she had decided to withdraw her candidacy: the premiership was May's. Leadsom was distraught at the fallout from the incident and believes that her comments had been taken out of context: 'I was pressed to say how my children had formed my views. I didn't want it to be used as an issue. Having children has no bearing on the ability to be PM. I deeply regret that anyone has got the impression that I think otherwise,' she told *The Telegraph*.[42]

When I interviewed Leadsom and asked about the incident, she reiterated how the coverage of the interview was misleading, and stated that she had in fact already decided to stand down from the race due to May's clear lead in the polls: 'people say it was why I pulled out; it was actually the strongest reasons to not withdraw ... it was a reason to keep going because I could have sort of set the record straight'.[43] But withdraw she did.

May was the last woman standing. The fact that she had not fallen foul of the gaffes and self-destructive behaviour of her colleagues, during a very turbulent fortnight in politics, was indicative of a calm and determined individual who did not let ambition cloud her judgment. Even in the closing moments of the contest, May did not rise to Leadsom's comments about not being a mother. She has understandably proved reluctant to talk about not having children, saying in 2002: 'I don't think it's an issue. And I don't think it should become an issue.'[44] It was only in 2012 as home secretary that she divulged more about her sadness at the situation: 'It just didn't happen ... You look at families all the time and you see there is something there you don't have.'[45] Characteristically, she emphasized that she doesn't like to dwell on it, however: 'you just get on with things. There are lots of problems people have.'[46] May has adopted a similar attitude in response to her diagnosis with late-onset Type I Diabetes in 2013. She has insulin injections four times a day and has to monitor her blood sugar levels, a challenging feat for anyone, let alone someone with the hectic calendar of a prime minister.

Within an hour of entering Number Ten as prime minister, May was able to turn the tables on the Cameroons. First, she sacked Osborne not only from his role as chancellor but from the cabinet. In all, she swiftly dispatched thirteen of twenty-two cabinet members who had served under Cameron. It was a decisive blow to the male establishment who had hitherto dominated the party. May appointed eight women to her cabinet, matching the total in Tony Blair's final cabinet in 2007. With the exceptions of herself and Baroness Evans, all of those women had been mentored by Women2Win. Notably, she promoted Amber Rudd to be her successor at the Home Office. It was the first time that two of the top cabinet roles had been held by women simultaneously. In 2019 after May dismissed defence secretary Gavin Williamson over a leak to the National Security Council, she appointed Penny Mordaunt in his place, who became the first woman defence secretary in history – notable not least due to historically masculine connotations of the role. Mordaunt, who serves as a Royal Naval Reservist and whose father was a paratrooper, brought a wealth of experience to her new role, having served as minister of the armed forces previously. When she arrived at the ministry of defence, 'my office was full of flowers', she told me, 'from the Navy Women's Network and other women'. Mordaunt felt that the armed forces were happy at her appointment 'because I'd worn uniform' and had extensive experience and knowledge of defence – more, for example, than her predecessor.[47]

It is widely acknowledged that a sense of purpose, moral mission and public service has orientated May's work in Parliament. Justine Greening told me that May demonstrates 'a level of fortitude and persistence that most people find bewildering, because they don't know how she does it. I think that's great. That she's out there, just plugging away'.[48] She continued to prioritize her constituency as prime minister, as she told me it is important 'to listen to people at the grassroots rather than just getting embedded in the Whitehall and Westminster and Downing Street bubble'.[49] Rudd emphasized that May's main goal was to tackle injustice, and believes that in government 'where we've spotted injustice, where it's been glaring, we've tried to address it'.[50] May's premiership was significant for the women's movement. Unlike Margaret Thatcher, Theresa May identifies as a feminist and was photographed wearing a Fawcett Society t-shirt with the print 'This is what a feminist looks like'.

Many attributed the surge in female Conservative candidates in the 2017 general election to the 'Theresa factor' and predicted that the party could trump Labour's 1997 record.[51] However, the Conservatives' unexpectedly poor performance in the election – not least due to May's weak campaign – dashed those hopes. When I interviewed Amber Rudd in 2018, she maintained that May's role model status had been immense, and that 'people now think of the Home Office [and Downing Street] as a job that women can do'.[52] She was also positive about the permanence of this change – 'that's all you need . . . I think that once that glass ceiling has been broken, it's completely swept away'.[53] Nevertheless, Anne Jenkin told me that 'There are a lot of people that think because we've had the two women prime ministers – job done. But we're very weak underneath and very vulnerable.'[54] As a country, we are yet to have a woman chancellor of the exchequer, a role which is often gendered as masculine. Labour MP Stella Creasy told me that she finds it frustrating that many Conservatives still have a tokenistic attitude towards May and Thatcher of 'We had a lady, there's been a whole lady there, and then we found another lady, so that's your lot.'[55] Amber Rudd confirmed this, telling me that in response to speculation about Rudd standing to succeed May, a male Conservative colleague informed her 'the only thing is I think you'd be great but I'm not sure that the party wants another woman.'[56]

The impact of the May government's policies on women has led to notable criticism, especially from women on the Labour benches. A recurrent criticism is that she has failed to prioritize women's refuge services in spite of her claims to tackle domestic violence. As Labour MP Sarah Champion pointed out in 2017, 17 per cent of specialist refuges for domestic violence victims in England have been closed since 2010, leaving a third of women turned away from refuges when they seek help or flee domestic violence.[57] Harriet Harman is particularly sceptical of May's feminist credentials: 'Theresa May has never been ideologically sympathetic to the feminist movement. I think she's recognised that exposes the Conservative party as old-fashioned, so for vote-getting reasons she's changing her tune, but she's no sister.'[58]

Ultimately and undoubtedly, the defining issue of May's premiership was Brexit – and, in the eyes of many, it is an issue on which she failed to provide leadership. In many ways, that was true: her downfall was caused by setting out early red lines that prevented consensus-building and calling an unnecessary election that led to the disappearance of her majority. But to watch the final few weeks of Theresa May's time as prime minister was often painful. To see male Conservative MPs repeatedly attack her in the Chamber – from Mark Francois to Iain Duncan-Smith to Johnny Mercer – was undignified at best and motivated by a contempt of powerful women at worst. Whatever your criticism of May as prime minister – I voted against her Brexit deal on all three occasions – it was clear that she was trying to get a deal and to find a way through the Brexit chaos, which was not of her causing. In the end, her premiership and her attempt to deliver Brexit were brought down by Brexiteers in her own party. It is interesting that Boris Johnson's deal is remarkably similar to Theresa May's, and yet all of May's critics are now wholeheartedly backing Johnson.

When I interviewed Jo Swinson after she was elected as leader of the Liberal Democrats, she reflected that 'I think that not bringing the country together after 2016 was . . . the missed opportunity of her [May's] leadership'.[59] However, Swinson reflected that 'What's really fascinating of course, is all these blokes saying they could do a better negotiation than Theresa May. I mean, I think the deal that she brought is rubbish, but that's because I think that Brexit itself is a huge mistake, and damaging for our country full stop. If you support Brexit, the thought that there's some nirvana Brexit that Theresa May just didn't manage to find is, I think rather fanciful.' In Swinson's first PMQs as leader of her party– which was May's last – Swinson asked May with a heavy dose of humour what advice she would have for women across the country on 'how to deal with men who think they can do a better job but are not prepared to do the actual work'.[60] The following week, Boris Johnson was at the despatch box as prime minister.

The new prime minister's reputation with regard to women is well rehearsed. Police were called to his house during the Conservative party leadership contest in concern over a loud altercation with his girlfriend Carrie Symonds; there have been allegations by Charlotte Edwardes of Johnson groping her under a dinner table; and there has been speculation about the inappropriate use of public funds and influence to benefit American businesswoman Jennifer Arcuri, with whom it is alleged Johnson had a close relationship. Famously, Johnson has refused to answer questions about how many children he has. However, as Penny Mordaunt reflected, 'it is not just a Boris problem, it's a problem my party has'.[61]

Leaders of the future

If the summer of 2019 saw the fall of one female leader in Theresa May, it saw the ascent of another in Jo Swinson, who was elected as the first female leader of the Liberal Democrats. Swinson had decided against standing for leader in 2017: 'it didn't feel right at the time' both from a political and a personal perspective, as she was a new mum and planning to have another baby. When I re-interviewed Swinson in September 2019 after her successful election as leader, she said 'It sort of felt right, this time round . . . the task we have now is one where I'm very clear about where I need to take the party'.[62]

Under Swinson's leadership, the Liberal Democrats' opposition to Brexit has shifted from advocating a second referendum to revoking Article 50 altogether, a bold move which has sparked strong feelings on both sides of the debate. The combined force of a record membership of over 115,000, success in the Brecon and Radnorshire by-election and a strong showing in the European Elections had led to talk of a 'Swinson surge' for the Liberal Democrats – but it was not to be. After the splintering of the Independent Group which was formed in February 2019, Luciana Berger, Angela Smith, Chuka Umunna, Sarah Wollaston and Heidi Allen all defected to the Liberal Democrats. Disaffected Conservatives Phillip Lee and Sam Gyimah also joined the them in September 2019.

When I spoke to Swinson ahead of the December 2019 election, she was clear that she would not form a coalition with the Labour Party led by Jeremy Corbyn – instead she advocated a national government led by the mother or father of the House, Harriet Harman or Ken Clarke. This is in part due to Swinson's claim that Corbyn has not been a sufficiently active campaigner for Remain, but she also expressed concern that 'for a party that's supposed to stand for equality,' Corbyn has 'fundamentally failed' to 'stamp down on anti-Semitism'. While she stated that she had never found Corbyn difficult personally, she felt 'quite a disconnect between the polite gentleman who at cross-party meetings will offer you a tea and a biscuit' and 'what, through his inaction, he's allowing to continue'.[63]

Labour is, at the end of 2019, the only political party represented at Westminster that has never had a woman leader. The Green Party has always been led by a woman or co-led by a woman. This is no small feat given fact that, until Caroline Lucas' time, the Green Party was 'suspicious of leadership' and so a very strong case had to be made for adopting an alternative type of leadership model, by showing that 'leadership didn't have to be a very top-down, clunking-fist kind of leadership, that it could be a much more bottom-up, inspiring, engaging, listening type of leadership'. Sinn Féin, Plaid Cymru and the SNP have all had women leaders. Even the DUP under Arlene Foster, and indeed UKIP under Suzanne Evans, have managed it. But not, yet, the Labour Party.[64]

Labour's poor record on electing women to lead the party contrasts with the much larger numbers of women MPs elected. At the end of 2019, the Labour Party could point to 50 percent of its MPs being women, albeit in a depleted parliamentary Labour party, compared to just 24 percent of the Conservative Party.

Why has Labour never elected a woman leader? Some maintain that it is due to blatant sexism incarnated into the Labour Party through the historically male-dominated trade union movement and conceptions of leadership: '[It's] because we are basically utterly bloody sexist,' Labour MP Margaret Hodge told me.[65] However, it hardly seems as if the Conservative party is exempt from sexism. To a certain extent, the explanation for Thatcher and May's rise to power was that the party underestimated both of them: as Anne Jenkin admits, 'Lady T was obviously the disruptive option and nobody ever thought she would win. Theresa was, because she was the last woman, last person standing.'[66] Jo Swinson speculated that Labour's success in boosting the number of women MPs and AWS may have led to complacency and masked underlying sexism within the party: 'celebrating having lots of women MPs has resulted in less introspection about whether or not the culture is one where women are genuinely regarded on an equal basis'. 'Embarrassment', Swinson declared, 'is one of the things that drives this up the priority list, and I think perhaps by removing that, it's made it easier for other Labour leaders not to do some of the intensive work that other parties have had to do.'[67] Jess Phillips and Harriet Harman have argued that it is because Labour women have been feminist activists and established themselves as critics of the establishment rather than executors of its will. Phillips suggested to me that 'the reason a Tory woman can rise is because a Tory woman doesn't threaten the established order, she agrees to hold the line on issues like welfare regardless of how it affects women, and immigration regardless of how it affects women, and to keep the people in power in power.'[68]

In a similar vein, shadow secretary of state for education Angela Rayner attributed part of the problem to the fact that 'Women get criticized for being pushy, for being more ambitious than a man is, because culturally, that's not seen as the norm for women.'[69] Emily Thornberry had to be chased down the corridor by Harriet Harman to be persuaded to stand for the shadow cabinet in 2010, yet she is now one of Labour's most senior women as shadow foreign secretary. Thornberry corroborated the idea that women sometimes have to be pushed to stand and to be given the confidence to think they can stand.

Thornberry's explanation for the lack of Labour women leaders was less convincing: 'I think we're quite a grown-up party,' she told me, 'and I don't think we're into gestures. And I think that the Tories are ... We've got nearly half of the PLP women, we've won the argument, I think, in terms of all-women shortlists, the political argument, we're half the shadow cabinet – I think it's like a wave coming up through the party. I don't think we could have done it just by plonking someone in as leader.'[70] Whether the 'wave' coming through the Labour party will ensure a woman leader reaches the shore at the next opportunity is still unknown.

Putting attempts at explanation aside, the fact that the Labour Party is yet to elect a female leader is a source of shame and embarrassment, and must change. As Angela Rayner told me: 'it's long overdue. We can't have had two Tory Prime Ministers who are female, and not have had a Labour leader [who is female]. And I think our politics needs it. I think our country needs it.'[71] When I asked Rayner whether she would consider standing, she said 'if I don't stand, I'll be pushing and supporting another woman to do it. Put it that way. If it ain't me, it'll be another woman!'[72] Harman has led the call for Labour men to 'sit out' of the next leadership election. 'But they won't, of course,' Phillips told me with a wry smile.'[73] Angela Eagle concurred: 'Don't hold your breath is all I'm going to say!'[74]

Abuse of women MPs

Boris Johnson's approach to politics, to Europe and to managing Parliament are a far cry from the approach of his predecessor, Theresa May. He stripped twenty-one of his MPs of the party whip, others have joined the Liberal Democrats and even more did not stand again in the December 2019 general election. As his parliamentary majority evaporated, Boris Johnson's attempt to call a general election was originally thwarted by the majority of MPs who feared that with Parliament dissolved, we could crash out of the EU without a deal. Instead, Johnson asked the Queen to prorogue Parliament for an unprecedented five weeks. He was taken to court in Scotland and England by campaigners led by Gina Miller. On 24 September, the President of the Supreme Court Baroness Brenda Hale judged Johnson's prorogation of Parliament as unlawful, null and void. When forced back to Parliament by the Supreme Court, Johnson did not modify his approach, but instead doubled down on it. In the Commons chamber, he referred to the MPs trying to block a 'no deal' Brexit as 'betraying' the will of the British people, and the Benn Act, which legally requires Johnson to seek an extension from the EU if he does not achieve a deal, the 'Surrender Act'. Its supporters countered that it was in fact a 'Safeguarding Act', to protect

British interests against the whims of the prime minister. After two hours of intense debate, Paula Sherriff and Tracy Brabin (who represents Jo Cox's former constituency of Batley and Spen) called out Boris Johnson for his use of inflammatory language and the abuse of MPs that follows. In reference to Jo Cox, Sherriff addressed the House: 'We stand here, Mr Speaker, under the shield of our departed friend. Many of us in this place are subject to death threats and abuse every single day. Let me tell the Prime Minister that they often quote his words – Surrender Act, betrayal, traitor – and I, for one, am sick of it.' Johnson responded by declaring that he had 'never heard such humbug in all my life'.[75] He also claimed that 'the best way to honour the memory of Jo Cox ... would be, I think, to get Brexit done'.[76] Sherriff reflected to me a couple of weeks later that 'I had no intention of speaking,' but 'I was listening to what he had to say, and it became very evident that he was deliberately using almost the language of war – "surrender" and "capitulation" and "betrayal". I was sitting amongst a group of female MPs, and we were saying "Oh God, this is what's going to be in my inbox tomorrow."'[77]

When I asked Jo's sister, Kim Leadbeater, how she felt about Johnson's reference to Jo, she said 'I was sort of mixed between feeling disbelief, dismay, and just sort of numbness really at seeing Jo's name brought into the middle of such a heated discussion'. Kim also reiterated that 'words have consequences and language does matter'. Yet, as Anna Soubry reflected to me, language is 'used so cheaply now'.

When I asked Priti Patel about the use of language in the Commons, she did not criticize Johnson's language directly but neither did she defend it, saying that 'we owe it to the public to show leadership, and that means, yes, professionalism, that means moderation in language, what we do, but also how MPs behave'.[78] Penny Mordaunt – a Leave supporter who was sacked by Johnson after she backed Jeremy Hunt in the leadership campaign – similarly said that whilst she does not have a problem with 'dramatic language being used for political purpose', she does 'have an issue when people imply from that that people are traitors'.[79]

Abuse and intimidation of women MPs is not new – one hundred years ago, Nancy Astor was ridiculed in the press and physically blocked from taking her seat in Parliament by male colleagues – but the intensity of the abuse has unquestionably increased in the digital age. In 2017, research by Amnesty International revealed that in just six months, 25,000 abusive Twitter messages were sent to female MPs in the UK.[80] Half of those were directed towards Diane Abbott, shadow home secretary and the first black woman to become an MP. Abbott said to me that social media has a role to play in the escalation of abuse: 'When I was a new MP if you wanted to write an abusive letter to an MP you literally had to write it out, put it in an envelope, put a stamp on it, walk to the letterbox, and so maybe we got one racist letter a month or something. Now you can press a button to send all of this abuse.'[81] Theresa May echoed this:

> It's the chap who used to sit on the corner end of the bar every night muttering into his beer, who can now mutter on social media, and people pick it up and believe it and send it round. Suddenly, there's a thing about social media that people don't feel any inhibitions at all on what they're saying, they almost don't feel that it is directed to another person. But of course, it is; it can hugely affect somebody.[82]

Abbott now receives so many threatening messages that her office simply do not have time to report them to the police every day, so they pile them up and send them in a weekly batch. Jess Phillips explains in her book *Everywoman* that there are two main variants of abuse via social media. First, there is the 'dog-piling attack', in which hundreds or thousands of people flood a woman's account with abusive and intimidating messages. Jess Phillips' worst dog-piling attack was initiated by a man who tweeted that he 'wouldn't even rape her'.[83] Second, there is the 'isolation tactic', in which trolls strategically abuse the people to whom the targeted woman is close, to put them off from associating with her.

The most harrowing aspect of the abuse is that it is not confined to the web. Rape and death threats on Twitter – of which they are many – can become all too real, as they did when my friend and Labour MP Jo Cox was murdered by a neo-Nazi activist on 16 June 2016. When Cox was elected for her home constituency of Batley and Spen in 2015, it was the fulfilment of her two lifelong ambitions – to fight for social justice, and to represent and support her local area. While Cox was only in Parliament for just over a year, she made her mark immediately and threw herself into campaigns regarding Syria, the refugee crisis and combatting loneliness. Her strong and principled stance on three issues in particular – the need for intervention in Syria, the leadership of Jeremy Corbyn, and as a Remainer in the EU referendum – led to a significant backlash online from both the far right and the far left. When Cox co-wrote an article for *The Guardian* with Neil Coyle criticizing Corbyn in early June 2016, Cox attracted five times as much online abuse as Coyle, according to

Cox's husband Brendan. When I interviewed him, he made it clear that this was rooted in nothing more than misogyny: 'neither of them were more high-profile than each other, it was exactly the same text . . . so there was no good reason for it at all.'[84] One particularly foreboding tweet read: 'Jo Cox and Neil Coyle sign their political death warrants. Tick tock, scabs.' Brendan told me that Jo, who had previously worked for Oxfam and never encountered this kind of abuse, found it incredibly difficult at first. However, she gradually found ways to cope with it – including delegating her social media to her staff so that she wouldn't have to be confronted with the personal abuse every moment of every day.

On 16 June, as Cox stepped out of her car to attend her constituency surgery at a local library, a 52-year-old white man stepped out in front of her and shouted 'Britain First' as he shot and stabbed her multiple times. Cox was rushed to hospital but she died of her injuries.

Her husband Brendan told me that, although there is little evidence to say whether Cox's gender had a part to play in her murder, 'I think all the evidence suggests that women with opinions are more likely to be attacked than men with opinions.'[85] Her murder has made many women MPs more alert to the possibility of intimidation spiralling into violence. Previously, Diane Abbott always thought that the chance of abusers following through with rape or death threats was slim. 'I've always said it'll never happen,' she told me. 'But when Jo Cox was killed, that was really shocking to me because I had to face the fact that it could happen.' When Abbott met a policeman assigned to the Cox case, he told her that the suspect had a whole room papered with photos of Cox. Abbott thought to herself: 'I have no doubt that there's someone out there with a whole wall papered with pictures of me.'[86] The level of threat to women MPs remains high despite the public outpouring of anger and sadness at Cox's murder. A 23-year-old man pleaded guilty to buying a machete with which he planned to kill Labour MP Rosie Cooper in the summer of 2017. In 2019, Anna Soubry was harassed outside Parliament by pro-Brexit supporters, who chanted 'Nazi and scum' as she tried to go to work on multiple occasions; in September a pro-Brexit protestor was arrested after trying to break into Jess Phillips' constituency office, shouting 'fascist'. Former Independent MP Heidi Allen described to me the worst threat she has received, from a man who lived about 300 yards away from her, who posted photographs and details of her house on social media as well as declaring that he planned to climb up to her bedroom window using a rope. 'I was absolutely terrified,' Allen relayed to me. 'I was a jibbering wreck. Every noise in the house – if there was a creak, or a bump . . .'[87]

In the wake of Cox's murder and these developments, there has been an increase in office, constituency and home security for MPs, particularly women. In my own constituency, I have additional security in my home and my office. The police visit the office at least weekly to check on my movements and at times to be present for events. It is not how I want to do my job, but it would be foolish to ignore the warnings of the police. Many MPs who stood down during 2019 were women who cited the daily abuse they received as a significant reason for quitting. These resignations shouldn't be a surprise when MPs are subjected to death and rape threats on a daily basis. Some claim that the number of women MPs standing down is proportional with the percentage of women MPs in Parliament. However, the true picture is that departing female MPs are younger and have spent less time in Parliament than their male counterparts. According to one analysis, the average age of Tory male MPs retiring is 64 with an average of 20 years service. That compares to an average age of 51 for female Conservative MPs who are leaving with an average of ten years service. It is not hard to see why they are leaving. Culture Secretary Nicky Morgan is standing down after enduring many threats including phone calls telling her that her "days were numbered". [88]

The Amnesty analysis clearly shows that abuse is most frequently directed at women MPs with marginalized identities – for example those who are BAME, LGBTQ, Jewish, or working class. Even if you exclude Diane Abbott, BAME female MPs received 35 per cent more abusive tweets than their white colleagues. The abuse includes regular rape and death threats, with shocking racist language. Tulip Siddiq, a Muslim Labour MP, has been asked 'why aren't you wearing a Hijab' and threatened 'if I could kill you, I would'.[89] Luciana Berger, a Jewish (former Labour, then Liberal Democrat) MP, was continually subject to anti-Semitic abuse: online trolls sent her photos of gas chambers and photoshopped her face onto a picture of a rat with the Star of David on it. A '"filthy Jew bitch" campaign' against Berger trended on Twitter during 2014–15.[90] During its worst period, Berger received over three thousand hate messages in just one day. Four men, at least three of whom were identified with far-right groups, have received prison sentences for threatening her. One of the men threatened that she was 'going to get it like Jo Cox'.[91]

Although a lot of the abuse comes from the far right, several Labour women MPs have told me that some of the worst abuse comes from the hard left. Moderate Labour women are often confronted with vitriol and violent condemnation. In the 2015 leadership election the moderate candidate Liz Kendall, who was elected in 2010, was called Tory Scum, a witch and a cow. In 2014, John McDonnell described Esther McVey as a 'bitch' who should be 'lynched'.[92]

Just weeks after Jo Cox's murder, Angela Eagle launched a leadership bid against Labour leader Jeremy Corbyn and was forced to cancel a constituency surgery after the police warned her that her safety was at risk. A brick had been thrown through her constituency office window, 'which apparently [according to some on the hard left], I threw, even though I was in London at the time,' she told me.[93] A 'kind of siege' by Corbyn's supporters took hold, with 'serious attacks on all my output, to cripple it. So phones, emails, the lot . . . the phone went every 30 seconds and there were silences, or heavy breathing, or threats or nastiness.'[94] One email received on the day after her leadership launch read: 'if you become leader of the Labour party, you will split it and make Labour lose . . . you will die you Bitch . . . this is my one and only warning. Next time you see me I'll be with a real gun or knife cutting your life to an end.'[95]

The infighting within the Labour Party has also taken its toll on women MPs who supported Corbyn. Diane Abbott feels that 'I was a sort of lightning rod for Jeremy', and that 'the amount of abuse we received went up when Jeremy put me on the frontbench and it continued to climb'.[96] Angela Rayner, was called 'thick' by hard right Twitter users due to her Northern, working-class accent in a torrent of online abuse after she appeared on the Andrew Marr Show.[97] Rayner told me that she feels resilient against this kind of abuse because 'I was the ginger kid on the council estate . . . I'm used to being dissed because of the way I speak. I'm used to being dissed because of the way I look. And therefore, that doesn't feel unusual to me.' However, she said she feels more sensitive when she is criticized or abused for the content of her policies, 'because I feel like I've let the people who elected me down' – 'I still have moments, like everyone else.' But the thing that frustrates her most is that that the party infighting detracts from the party's mission to get into government. Rayner described this as 'self-indulgent, because it's easy for me to have a factional fight, but what about the Angela Rayners of today who can't get Sure Start because they've all gone, or to university . . . or to adult education because courses have closed down, who can't get a council house now because they're on the waiting list, who can't get those opportunities and support that were available to me.'

While Rayner is often sneered at for being working class, Emily Thornberry is ridiculed for her marriage to a high court judge, Sir Christopher Nugee: both Boris Johnson and Theresa May have inaccurately referred to her as 'Lady Nugee' to discredit her (similarly, Yvette Cooper is sometimes referred to as 'Mrs Balls' for being married to Ed Balls, former shadow chancellor). In 2017, Johnson referred to Thornberry as 'the noble and learned Lady, the Baroness, whatever it is – I cannot remember what it is. Nugee' and was reprimanded by the Speaker for being sexist.[98] Thornberry claimed that she receives a particularly high level of abuse because 'not only am I a woman, I am also middle-aged and overweight, and it is an affront that I should think so much of myself, that I should be as mouthy as I am, that I wouldn't shut up.'[99]

How do women MPs cope with the abuse? There seem to be a range of coping mechanisms, but there is no way to abstract from it completely. May suggested to me that 'I suppose ... you get used to it,'[100] but many other women are understandably less philosophical about it. 'You don't get inured to it, it's very painful,' Abbott said. 'You get on and do the job, but it's immensely personally corrosive.'[101] Jess Phillips resorts to what she calls 'Dog-piling with love': in advance of a media appearance, she will request supportive messages and pictures of cats from her friends and followers so that they will flood her inbox and counter some of the negative dog-piling she will receive.[102] Many women MPs, including myself, also delegate much of their social media work to their staff and have periods of disconnecting from social media, to avoid being confronted with abuse every time we check our phones.

Towards the end of 2015, Yvette Cooper launched a cross-party campaign to crack down on the online abuse of women, Reclaim the Internet. It was inspired by the Reclaim the Night marches of the 1970s and 80s, on the basis that 'The internet is our new street'.[103] Supporters included Maria Miller, Jo Swinson and Jess Phillips. The campaign was also supported by an array of organizations, including the Fawcett Society as well as Facebook, Twitter and Google. A two-month online debate was launched, followed by a conference in July 2016 to crowdsource ideas on what the police and prosecutors should do in response to allegations of abuse. The suggestion that social media companies should censor abusive posts provoked allegations of curbing free speech. Stella Creasy has rebutted this allegation powerfully, saying it 'isn't about restricting free speech. Quite the opposite. Right now, young activists are deciding not to speak out, or campaign online, because of the onslaught of abuse they receive.'[104] Yvette Cooper and Stella Creasy have both been prominent campaigners for social media companies to take more responsibility, and a hate crime inquiry is imminent. 'I think social media companies can do a much better job of enforcing and living up to their own community standards,' Cooper commented to me. 'A lot of their own community standards are very good, but they never actually take the practical steps to implement them.' Both Cooper and Abbott emphasized that tackling anonymity is a key part of this. 'Social media companies should know who is on their platforms,' Cooper said, so that they can be prosecuted for abuse.[105]

After the 2017 election, Theresa May set up a commission to investigate the abuse faced by politicians and candidates. On the centenary of women's suffrage, May announced that the government would consult on the prospect of making abuse of MPs a criminal offence. However, Diane Abbott criticized this as 'a thoroughly misguided intervention' on the grounds that MPs do not deserve special treatment above other women who receive abuse.[106]

In the meantime, women MPs are determined to continue practising their politics in the same way as normal. Abbott felt that 'if I was to say I'm going to step down from Parliament because I can't take the abuse, then they would have won.'[107] Rayner viewed it similarly, that 'there is an obligation on us to continue to be who we are ... lead by example and not let those people force you off social media, and not make you change the way you speak ... but equally to try and fix it structurally, to make it easier for the sisters who come along, and you create that space for them.'[108] This feeling lies behind the concern of many women MPs that the abuse they receive will put younger women off the idea of standing for Parliament. Rushanara Ali said that this concern causes her to hesitate from publicizing the abuse she receives, because 'there was a part of me that didn't want particularly women to feel frightened about going into politics. I wanted them to feel confident about it.'[109] Thornberry explained that she tries to avoid talking about the abuse because 'I want 15-year-old girls to look at Emily Thornberry to go "Look at Emily Thornberry, she's having a whale of a time, she's really good, I can be like that". And I'm very conscious that I have a responsibility in that way.' Phillips described the abuse as being 'like childbirth: it's horrible but once you've been through it you know you'll cope ... I don't let [Jo's murder] change the way in which I'm a Member of Parliament. I have an open office, I have my surgery, I carry on just as I did before.'[110] The only thing that has changed, for her among others including Yvette Cooper and indeed myself, is that whereas previously we might tweet in advance of an event, now we only tweet retrospectively about where we have been.

Creating a female- and family-friendly Parliament

Parliament is not only a workplace that was originally designed to cater to the needs of an exclusively male workforce, but it also values tradition and can be reluctant to modernize. Former Labour MP Laura Pidcock's maiden speech in 2017 was an indictment of the often backwards nature of Westminster and a timely call for modernization. '[T]his building is intimidating,' she reflected.

> It reeks of the establishment and of power; its systems are confusing— some may say archaic—and it was built at a time when my class and my sex would have been denied a place within it because we were deemed unworthy. I believe that the intimidating nature of this place is not accidental. The clothes, the language, and the obsession with hierarchies, control and domination are symbolic of the system at large.[111]

Angela Rayner speculated that 'Jacob Rees Mogg probably feels it's quite chill for him', but for her, like Pidcock, Parliament was a completely different world from the one she knew, having grown up in poverty on a council estate. While working as a care worker as a single parent, Rayner's colleagues urged her to be their union rep and she progressed rapidly through the union movement into Labour politics (she recalls meeting Gordon Brown when he was prime minister and being told off by her mum for calling him by his first name). Eventually, some of her friends and colleagues were urging her to become an MP. 'And I was like, "People like me can't be MPs." And so, I stood to prove that people like me can't be elected.' In 2015, she was; in 2016 she was appointed shadow secretary of state for education. But as with political parties, in Parliament, the inclusion of women and other marginalized groups does not necessarily imply the integration of them into it as an institution. Rayner describes Parliament as 'deliberately created to make you feel like this place isn't for you ... The whole thing is just very masculine, and very institutional. It's basically like Hogwarts, it's like a private school.'[112]

To fully integrate women and women's concerns into Parliament requires reforms to make it a welcoming place for women on their own terms. The period from 2010 has seen significant progress in this respect, with the reintroduction of more family-friendly sitting hours, the introduction of the parliamentary nursery, the gradual introduction of 'baby leave' for MPs with new children and increasing awareness about Westminster's endemic bullying and sexual harassment problems. Those reforms are the result of the rising numbers of women in Parliament in all parties. Westminster journalist Rachel Sylvester said that over her twenty-year career, she has seen that the increase in numbers of women MPs has made a 'real difference to the atmosphere' in Parliament.[113]

'I'm not a cleaner. I'm an MP': Continuing sexism in the Commons

In 2014, the all party parliamentary committee on women's equality published a report entitled 'Improving Parliament: Creating a Better and More Representative House', which found that 58 per cent of the women MPs surveyed had experienced discrimination during their time in Parliament, compared with only 40 per cent of men.[114] Just as Ellen Wilkinson was stopped from entering the Smoking Room in the 1920s, so too women today are often made to feel unwelcome in Parliament. I was asked in 2010 who I worked for by a male SNP MP, on the assumption that I must be a researcher. Stella Creasy recalled that on one occasion when she was using the lift while the division bell was ringing, a Conservative MP told her off for using it, as lifts are reserved for MPs when the bell rings (and evidently she did not look like a typical MP on account of her gender). In a lift with fellow MPs, Labour MP Dawn Butler, who is of African-Caribbean heritage, was told by one Conservative that it was inappropriate for a cleaner to be in the lift with them.[115] Butler responded, 'Number one, it's rude. It doesn't matter who uses the lift ... And number two, I'm not a cleaner. I'm an MP.'[116] Yet such instances are all too common for Butler and she is regularly made to feel unwelcome in Parliament. Once, a male Conservative MP stopped her as she approached the Members' Section of the Terrace and asked her where she thought she was going. When she informed him that she was going to have lunch with her team, he responded: 'This place is going to rack and ruin, they're letting anyone in nowadays.'[117] Butler reported the incident to the Conservative chief whip to no avail.

Despite the huge increase in the number of women in the House of Commons, the scrutiny of women's bodies and wardrobes continues. Former Liberal Democrat leader Jo Swinson, who became 'Baby of the House' aged twenty-five when she was elected in 2005, was asked by the *Daily Mail* if she would pose for them in school uniform. She was also asked to do a bikini shoot for a lad's magazine.[118] On appearances and fashion, former Labour MP Caroline Flint concluded that 'you're damned if you do and damned if you don't'.[119] It is a theme that resonates across the one hundred years of women in Parliament. If women dedicate too much attention to their appearances, they are trivialized and portrayed as shallow or even provocative. If women do not dedicate enough attention to it, they are portrayed as unattractive and spinster-like. Caroline Lucas – who dresses very smartly but has a distinctive alternative style – said that 'as soon as you do something that's even a little bit unusual, something that's not just the stereotypical suit, quite a lot of rubbish comes back [in the media] . . . I learnt the hard way to modify what I was wearing. There were a couple of times where I was wearing probably something a bit like this,' she said, gesturing to her beige-coloured linen suit, 'and they were saying "It looks like she's from the Taliban".'[120] Lucas is not the only woman MP to have deliberately modified her style in order to be taken seriously. Penny Mordaunt said that she 'learnt quite quickly' that in order to focus attention on what she was saying rather than how she looked, you need to make sure 'you are not doing anything that distracts from that. So I chopped off my hair, I wore dark clothes. My glorious wardrobe of reds and purples I shall not be seeing again.'[121]

In 2007, when May was shadow leader of the House, the *Daily Mail* snapped a photograph of her in what it described as 'a bright pink wrap dress with its fetching dashes of orange and green', while also pointing out that 'as if the dress was not eye-catching enough, Mrs May also had a serious amount of cleavage on show'.[122] On another occasion, Labour MP Alison McGovern received a letter from a Newsnight viewer who objected to her 'prominent cleavage' during her appearance on the show, which 'distracted your male observers from hearing what you were saying'.[123] The press often prefix Luciana Berger's name with 'raven-haired' and they have commented on the colour of her nail polish no less than five times.[124]

The relationship between clothing, objectification and admiration is particularly interesting for Theresa May. Theresa May told me that she has had 'both a double-page spread on "am I the new Cara Delavigne", and a double-page spread on "how not to dress over 50"' in the same newspaper.[125] From her shoulder-pads and mini-skirts as a Conservative candidate, to her leopard print kitten heels as party chairman, to her lavender leather jacket as home secretary and brown leather trousers as prime minister, May has always been fascinated by fashion. She uses clothing, and shoes in particular, as a way of expressing herself and refusing to fit the masculine mould of an MP. But if May's embrace of fashion is refreshingly distant from many of the early women MPs trying to 'undo' their gender and emulate male MPs, there is a risk that others fixate on it. May's campaign manager for the 2005 election reported that the famous leopard-print kitten heels which May wore during her 'nasty party' speech became a nuisance. Whenever she turned up to a meeting, people would ask, 'Where are the shoes, Theresa?'[126]

Some latched onto May's embrace of fashion and used it to undermine her politically on several occasions. In 2016, May posed for a photo shoot in a pair of chocolate leather trousers, designed by Amanda Wakeley and costing £995. Nicky Morgan, who had been sacked by May the same year, told *The Times* that the trousers had been 'noticed and discussed' in Conservative circles. 'I don't have leather trousers. I don't think I've ever spent that much on anything apart from my wedding dress,' she added. The drama of what came to be known as 'Trousergate' escalated further and became a debate about the sexist attitudes that people demonstrate towards women MPs' choice of clothing. It even turned out that the trousers did not belong to May, but had been loaned to her for the shoot.[127] Nadine Dorries criticized Morgan's comments as sexist, 'because she never criticized David Cameron's extremely expensive suits'.[128] Dorries attributed Morgan's comments to her Remainer sympathies and an alleged determination to undermine May's Brexit plans. Morgan was then lambasted for hypocrisy, having been photographed on a number of occasions carrying a leather bag from the luxury brand Mulberry, which the press estimated to have cost £950. Ken Clarke told the *Sunday Politics*: 'I feel sorry for women in politics. I'm glad to say men in politics don't have great news stories about what they are wearing.'

Baby steps: Reforms for MPs with families

Women in politics also face a huge challenge in combining family life with being an MP. Women are still generally expected to perform more domestic labour and childcare than their male counterparts, making the job of being an MP more demanding. According to a 'Parents in Parliament' survey from 2013, mothers are significantly underrepresented in the House of Commons, more so than women as a whole. While just 28 per cent of male MPs do not have children, 45 per cent of women MPs do not.[129] This statistic is significantly higher than the national average for women.[130] Women are often made to feel that they will either be a bad mother, a bad MP, or both. When I asked home secretary Priti Patel, whose son was young when she entered Parliament, how she achieved a work-life balance, she answered simply: 'There is no balance.'[131] Caroline Spelman recalled canvassing while pregnant in the rainy 1992 election wearing a big blue raincoat which conveniently concealed her bump. On a rare, sunny day of campaigning, it was suggested to her that she should take her coat off. 'No, no, I've worn it all these days and it's brought me luck,' she insisted. Spelman was concerned that her pregnancy would 'worry people about how you're going to manage.'[132]

When Spelman was elected in 1997, she was the only female Conservative MP with school-age children. Her local party made it a condition of her selection that her children had to be educated in the constituency, which meant that she spent a lot of time away from them. 'I pined for my children and lost a lot of weight,' she told me. 'I think my children were fine, but I wasn't.'[133] Meanwhile, Labour MP Jo Cox was incredibly frustrated by the late votes in the Commons and the way it prevented her being able to say goodnight to her children. She managed to do it on most nights regardless. Her parliamentary researcher, Ruth Price, told me that she would vote in her cycling gear and pedal home as fast as she could to make it in time for the children's bedtime. Cox's husband, Brendan, said that the thing that irritated her the most was 'the inefficiency of it; there was no reason why their day can't start at the same time as everyone else's day and finish an hour earlier.'[134] Emily Thornberry explained to me how she wanted her children to have their own surname (her husband's name, Nugee) and to go to school outside her borough 'so that they could have their own lives'. This worked less well, however, when she was trolled as 'Lady Nugee' and scrutinized for not choosing a school in her borough. Thornberry also relayed to me how, amidst a hectic parliamentary diary, she committed to 'Birthday breakfasts' with her children at 6.30 in the morning: the policy was 'if it's your birthday, you can have whatever you want, so we'd have these ridiculous things, and because the kids had to go a long way to school, it would mean cooking extraordinary food at half past six in the morning,' she laughed. Former Labour MP Caroline Flint's children lived in her Doncaster constituency when they were younger, which she found hard when she had to be in Westminster for half the week. She recalled that the whips office never asked her whether she would like to get away early, and that they were more likely to do so for London-based MPs.

For Angela Rayner, the main issue in balancing work as an MP with having children is 'not knowing whether we're going to [need to] be here ... having a three-line whip just to safeguard business all the time, and not knowing when it will drop – that's pretty brutal ... More certainty around the week would be helpful'. However, Andrea Leadsom – leader of the House of Commons from 2017 to 2019 – rebutted Rayner's frustrations in an interview with me, arguing that unpredictability was inevitable in a hung parliament and 'To be perfectly honest ... that is the job .... We do have important business to get done, and so from Monday afternoon until Thursday 5pm colleagues need to make themselves available.'[135]

But there have been baby steps towards reforms in the last decade which make it easier for women MPs to combine a career and a family. In 2010, speaker John Bercow introduced a parliamentary nursery despite fervent opposition, as Mary Beard emphasizes in her foreword to this book. The nursery provides childcare for up to forty children, aged three months to five years, for the use of the children of MPs, staff, lobby journalists and civil servants. When the nursery was first built, occupancy rates were naturally low and took time to increase, which caused the media to claim that it was a waste of public money. But today, occupancy rates are high, and it is relied on by many MPs, particularly women. This, combined with the move to allow MPs to take their children through the division lobbies, has done a great deal to facilitate women MPs' family lives.

In 2018, women MPs turned their attention to maternity leave in Westminster. Until 2019 there was no formal system in place for MPs who have children. Instead, pregnant women had to request time off from the whips. This works through a pairing system in which, for example, a Labour MP might be paired with a Conservative MP who also needs time off, to ensure the party balance of numbers in votes. This antiquated and patronage-based system is far from ideal: as Harriet Harman put it in an article for *The Telegraph*, 'there's still no system or rules to rely on. You shouldn't have to ask. It shouldn't need two whips offices to agree.'[136] It also means that your vote is left unrecorded and your constituency unrepresented in Parliament. Consequently, having a baby risks a woman MP's reputation where it often does not for a man.

The pairing system is subject to the whims of whips and has proven to be unreliable. During the long votes on the Lords amendments to the EU Withdrawal Bill in 2018, the government refused to allow pairing, or even for pregnant or sick MPs to be 'nodded through' so that they didn't have to enter the chamber. Consequently, two heavily pregnant female MPs – Jo Swinson and Laura Pidcock – were forced to come in and go through the division lobbies when they should have been at home. Jo Swinson was just five days away from her due date. Naz Shah and Laura Pidcock were pushed through the division lobby in wheelchairs, with Shah stooped over a sick bucket in extreme discomfort after complications from a car accident, and Pidcock with her baby pressing against her sciatic nerve. In July 2018, the unreliable nature of the current system was highlighted further when Jo Swinson's pair, Brandon Lewis, was instructed to vote in a particularly tight Brexit division, in violation of the pairing agreement. Swinson was furious.

The incident gave real momentum to the campaign for baby leave via proxy voting, led by a cross-party group of women MPs consisting of Harriet Harman, Maria Miller, Jo Swinson and Hannah Bardell. This would work by MPs nominating another MP to vote on their behalf for six months. Theresa May told me that baby leave was an important right that should apply to any job, including being an MP: 'I think there's been a sense in Parliament for a long time that people who are MPs are somehow very special . . . Actually, we're doing a job for the public, and in any job you'd expect to be able to have time[off].'[137]

But despite May's and then leader of the house, Andrea Leadsom's, support of baby leave, the government were slow to commit to the implementation of proxy voting. Leadsom told me that she 'was trying to get this through for a long time, and I was really committed to it', but that she had to broker debates about whether proxy voting should extend to cases of sickness, bereavement or other family events. In the end, she pushed through a year-long trial of proxy voting on the condition that it was strictly limited to baby leave. When she received criticism for not going far enough, she responded, 'it's baby steps. You have to do these things one step at a time. With parliamentary conventions, if you want to eat an elephant, you have to take it one bite at a time – you can't try to stuff the whole thing in your mouth at once.'[138]

Labour MP Tulip Siddiq became the first MP to benefit from proxy voting in January 2019 – though it was not in time for the birth of her baby so she had to vote just days after, which Leadsom said she was 'heartbroken' about. At the time of writing, a total of sixteen male and female MPs have voted by proxy. Many of those were women – including Tulip Siddiq, Luciana Berger, Chloe Smith, Emma Reynolds, Suella Braverman and Kemi Badenoch – but, strikingly, some of them were men, such as Darren Jones, who used a proxy vote for a crucial Brexit vote the day after his wife gave birth.

But of course, voting is just one part of the job – casework, surgeries and select committees all need attention even if an MP has had a baby. When Stella Creasy announced that she was pregnant in June 2019, she wrote an article for *The Guardian* entitled 'I'm pregnant and forced to choose between being an MP and a mum',[139] protesting at the fact that the Independent Parliamentary Standards Authority (IPSA) did not 'recognise' that women MPs go on maternity leave. Creasy movingly detailed how the responsibilities of an MP do not make any allowances for the responsibilities of being a mother and a parent: 'During my first miscarriage, aching and bleeding, I joined a protest for the extradition of a man who had raped and murdered a constituent. The day after I found out that another baby's heartbeat had stopped, I led a public meeting on gang crime. I even scheduled the procedure to remove the body on a day I didn't have a constituency advice surgery'. The parliamentary authorities have now agreed for the first time to provide maternity cover, beyond proxy voting, funding a 'locum MP' for seven months of maternity leave in her Walthamstow constituency. When I asked Creasy how she managed to persuade IPSA to fund the role, she said, 'I shamed them into justifying a position that's completely untenable'. On previous occasions when women MPs such as Tulip Siddiq had enquired about the possibility of maternity cover, IPSA had responded by saying that 'this just doesn't happen very often, it's not usually something we have to deal with, as if women MPs were creating the problem',[140] Creasy told me. However, with funding finally having been provided by IPSA, Creasy was able to hire a locum MP who started work in November 2019. Stella Creasy's baby was born on 27th November, two weeks before the general election, while Ellie Reeves, MP for Lewisham West and Penge gave birth earlier in the campaign. Both took their newborns on the campaign trail.

These developments are hugely encouraging, and a testament to the cross-party campaigning by women MPs for baby leave. However, there is no guarantee that either the trial of proxy voting or Creasy's locum MP initiative will be extended, formalized and implemented in full for all MPs who have a baby or adopt. Only time will tell whether these baby steps of reform will progress into larger strides for equality.

*

Over the last decade, the status of women MPs has risen significantly, particularly in the Conservative Party. We have now had two women prime ministers. But both of them have been from the Conservative Party. It is crucial that the Labour Party catches up, and it now has the opportunity to do so. There has been undeniable progress in recent years: mainstreaming what were previously regarded as 'women's issues'; women MPs rising to the top jobs; and reforms making it easier to balance work and family life. The election has seen a fresh intake of young female MPs including Nadia Whittome for Labour and Sara Britcliffe for the Conservatives. But in a digital age women MPs particularly are victims of abuse, both online and in person. As the number of women MPs continues to grow, we must challenge and root out abuse whenever we find it, and stand together as women in defiance against its attempt to silence us. Boris Johnson's government now needs to deliver on commitments made in the manifesto on childcare, domestic violence and NHS funding. His newly elected MPs, and indeed opposition MPs, must hold his feet to the fire.

Epilogue: A Century of Parliamentary Sisterhood

In the one hundred years that women have taken seats as MPs in the House of Commons, vast progress has been made for women's rights both within and outside of Parliament. At the beginning of 1919, no women MPs sat in the Commons, despite legislation being passed in the previous year enabling women to serve as MPs, and despite the election of Sinn Féin's Constance Markiewicz. At the time of writing, one hundred years on, 220 women MPs sit in the Commons. In 1919, women were banned from some spaces in Parliament and were often confined to a small dingy room in the basement which served as their communal office. Today, both female and male MPs have their own offices and we even have a parliamentary nursery which replaced one of its bars.

The battles fought by the early women MPs – including Nancy Astor, Ellen Wilkinson and Eleanor Rathbone – were fought painstakingly on the back of the sacrifices made by women involved in the suffrage campaign. Wilkinson paid tribute to this in her speech during the debate on equal franchise in 1928: 'Women have worked very hard. They have starved in prison, they have given their lives, or have given all their time, in order that women might sit in this House and take part in the legislation of the country', she told the Chamber.[1] Women MPs over the hundred years have used their hard-won position to carry forward the work of the suffragettes and suffragists by championing the rights of women. The list of achievements they have driven is staggering and simply too long to be fully encapsulated in a book, let alone a sentence, but it includes: equal guardianship of children, equal compensation, equal pay for equal work, family allowances and child benefit, SureStart nurseries, the right to abortion, same-sex marriage and action against domestic violence. Yet women MPs have also refused to be pigeonholed into 'women's issues' and have ventured into stereotypically 'masculine' policy areas and leadership positions. Margaret Bondfield became the first woman to enter the cabinet in 1929, but I expect it would have been difficult for her to anticipate that we could have a woman prime minister or that we could have seven women in the cabinet, as we do today. As Theresa May summed it up, while 'it's important that people don't feel in Parliament that the men do "men's issues" and the women do "women's issues", it is undoubtedly the case that having more women in Parliament has meant that "women's issues" have been given a greater prominence.'[2]

Throughout the one hundred years of women in the House of Commons, a striking theme prevails: that women have often worked together, in sisterhood, towards common goals: from Astor and Wintringham on equal guardianship and clean milk in the 1920s; to Wilkinson, Rathbone and Atholl on appeasement in the 1940s; to Stella Creasy's cross-party campaign on Northern Irish women's rights to abortion today. The variety of parties represented by women has also widened. Impressively, the only Green Party MP, Caroline Lucas, is a woman. There are a raft of SNP women MPs including Mhairi Black, Joanna Cherry and Hannah Bardell, and also Liz Saville-Roberts for Plaid Cymru. Within this context, women have been able to exert considerable pressure by working together, across parties, for change. While there are notable exceptions in this cross-party approach – with former Labour MP Laura Pidcock having expressed a strong aversion to working or socializing with Conservatives, calling them 'the enemy' – non-partisan partnership and friendship is prevalent among women MPs.[3]

As stories of sexual harassment in Westminster accumulated in late 2017, women MPs came together to highlight the problems of sexism and misogyny. In the Commons debate on harassment, sixty-five women MPs and fifty-six men attended: for once, women MPs outnumbered their male counterparts. The cross-party solidarity was instrumental in pressurizing the government and parliamentary authorities to reform parliamentary procedures for reporting harassment. Since there is no HR department in Parliament, all too often the only person that a member of staff could report abuse or harassment to is their boss – who might well be the culprit. Then leader of the house, Andrea Leadsom, described to me how she convened all the party leaders to push for an independent complaints commission, with a strictly confidential hotline so that staff and MPs can report bullying or harassment without fear of jeopardizing their career. This was a mammoth task that faced a great deal of opposition from MPs who objected to being scrutinized in this way. 'I used to joke,' Leadsom commented, 'you think leaving the EU is hard – you want to try negotiating the complaints procedure.'[4]

The sense of cross-party sisterhood that catalyzed this reform was also strongly expressed in the campaign against 'upskirting' – the act of taking a photograph up someone's skirt without their permission – spearheaded by Liberal Democrat MP Wera Hobhouse's private member's bill which aimed at the criminalization of the deed. Despite the attempts of Conservative MP Christopher Chope to filibuster her bill, the parliamentary pressure was so significant that the government adopted the bill themselves, and legislation was successfully passed in September 2018. Chope's office in the Commons was festooned with homemade knicker bunting the following week.

Why is cross-party work and friendship so common between women MPs? Part of it rests on the fact that, as a minority in Parliament, women have to work harder to build influence; bringing in a range of voices is an effective way to do that. There is also less of what Caroline Flint described as 'a very male sort of politics' of 'playing one off against the other' among women MPs.[5] Margaret Hodge emphasized to me that women are much 'better at building consensus.'[6] Theresa May echoed this idea during her speech on the centenary of suffrage. In a clear jibe to male cabinet colleagues such as Boris Johnson, who had briefed the press on their own personal opinions on Brexit while serving in her cabinet, May stated that: 'For women, politics can be as much about listening and learning from others as it is about broadcasting your own views and opinions.'[7]

Caroline Lucas' call for an all-female 'emergency cabinet' to sort out Brexit was received with criticism, on grounds that it rested on a problematic stereotyping of women and that it seemed to exclude BAME women. Lucas told me that it 'was the worst 48 hours of my political life' due to the backlash on social media – 'I just felt sick'. Lucas confessed that her 'mistake' was to 'use the word "cabinet" in inverted commas . . . what I wasn't proposing was a formal cabinet, all being women that would be there for months and months . . . I was simply saying that in my experience . . . when you get a group of women together, ideas that haven't been thought of can arise.'[8] However, Lucas' contribution speaks to a clear and observable tendency for pragmatism and cooperation to be key features of interactions between women MPs.

One notable feature of the formation of The Independent Group in February 2019 was the large number of women who felt they had to abandon their party ties in order to work for progress – whether against anti-Semitism or Brexit. Sarah Wollaston and Heidi Allen, for example, were unconventional Conservatives from the start and made strong critiques of Conservative policy on health and welfare respectively. Heidi Allen told me how she has never been a party animal: 'I have never got the whole ideology [thing], of what colour your rosette is. I couldn't give a damn. I just want the right brains and the right skills to come up with solutions.'[9]

Although Jo Cox's time in Parliament was cut brutally short, her style of doing politics has had a major influence on the work of women MPs after her death. When I paid tribute to her in the Commons after her death, I said that 'it now falls on all our shoulders . . . to carry on Jo's work: to combat and guard against hatred, intolerance and injustice and to serve others with dignity and love. That is the best way we can remember Jo and all she stood for.'[10] According to Jo's husband Brendan, she found the tribal nature of politics baffling and frustrating, and felt that it was 'often an impediment to making good policy and progress'.[11] Having worked as a campaigner against poverty for years and having had to build consensus across a range of stakeholders, he told me that she was always thinking in terms of 'what are the alliances we need to create?'[12] On her main projects, she set out to find the people whom she respected and would be best to work with. On Syria, Cox approached Conservative MPs with a track record of campaigning on the issues she cared about, particularly Tom Tugendhat and Andrew Mitchell. On loneliness, she set up a commission with a Conservative co-chair from her intake in 2015, Seema Kennedy. Cox was approachable and kind-hearted, and people warmed to her effortlessly. As Brendan emphasizes, her focus 'on the issue, not the angle' and her lack of a 'crusade to get her name in the papers' helped to facilitate a cooperative style of politics. After Cox's death, her family along with Seema Kennedy approached me and asked me to take forward the cross-party work in the form of the Jo Cox Commission on Loneliness. Working with Kennedy has been an absolute privilege and I believe we have carried Cox's spirit of cross-party work forwards in a way that has raised awareness about this important issue. Seema Kennedy and I have also formed a strong friendship. In December 2016, we were invited on Woman's Hour to speak about our work on loneliness, and we received as much positive feedback for the nature of our cross-party approach as for the topic itself.

Cox's way of doing politics reflected her maiden speech from 2015. With reference to her hometown constituency of Batley and Spen, she said:

> While we celebrate our diversity, what surprises me time and time again as I travel around the constituency is that we are far more united and have far more in common with each other than things that divide us.[13]

This spirit among women MPs lives on.

Domestic violence is one of the most prominent policy areas on which women MPs have cooperated during my time in Parliament. This is due to the scale and severity of the problem and the fact that it is something that MPs, whatever their 'politics', care passionately about. On average, two women in England and Wales are killed by their current or former partner every single week.[14] Jess Phillips has been a long-time campaigner on the issue and has been at the forefront of the cross-party work. On International Women's Day in 2016, she stood up in the Commons and read out the names of the 120 women who had been murdered by men in the UK in the previous year. In doing so, she became the first woman MP in history to draw applause in the Chamber. She regards it as the 'proudest moment' of her parliamentary career.[15] Phillips's cross-party work has led her to work collaboratively with Thangam Debbonaire, Baroness Jean Corston and Fiona MacTaggart on the Labour benches, as well as Maria Miller, Flick Drummond and Caroline Nokes on the Conservative side. Phillips sees engagement with Conservative women as fundamental to achieving change for victims of domestic abuse: 'They've got the power. They've got more chance to be listened to. When I worked at Women's Aid, I didn't refuse it when Theresa May offered to come and see us. I opened my arms.'[16]

One of the many egregious impacts of Boris Johnson's unlawful prorogation of Parliament in September 2019 was to halt the progression of the Domestic Abuse Bill, an historic piece of legislation championed across the House and spearheaded by the former prime minister Theresa May. However, after the Supreme Court's ruling, the second reading of the bill took place on 22 October 2019. There will be huge pressure on the new government to take forward this work. During May's time as prime minister, she worked collaboratively across the party divide to achieve consensus on the bill, particularly with Labour MPs Jess Phillips and Harriet Harman, who lobbied robustly for the inclusion of certain issues such as a legal obligation for the provision of refuge beds per thousand women. Amber Rudd, who was May's home secretary at the time, told me that she felt the process was building momentum by the time she resigned from the role: 'I was very keen to take the opportunity the prime minister gave me to bring forward a new bill ... I think we were beginning to get there and get quite a lot of commitment from the prime minister and a bit more money from the Treasury.'[17] The result was a wide-ranging raft of provisions: the creation of the first all-purpose statutory definition of domestic abuse (which includes economic abuse and coercive control), the appointment of a domestic abuse commissioner to champion victims and survivors, the establishment of new domestic abuse protection orders so that the police can intervene earlier, and the prohibition of cross-examination of victims by their abusers in family courts.

The contributions of women MPs across the House during the second reading of the bill in October 2019 were a testament to the competence and compassion that can be achieved when we work together on the issues that matter regardless of your political colours. In what was Theresa May's first speech in the chamber since standing down as prime minister, she described the bill as 'a landmark piece of legislation' that gave a 'once-in-a-lifetime opportunity' to tackle domestic abuse.[18] MPs across the House paid tribute to the impact that May had on prioritizing the bill, as well as minister for women Victoria Atkins (who was pivotal in pushing the government to make parliamentary time for the bill after Parliament returned from prorogation). But most powerful of all, Labour MP Rosie Duffield gave a heartbreakingly moving account of her own recent experience of living in an abusive relationship. Duffield explained how 'Abuse is not just about noticeable physical signs. Sometimes there are no bruises. Abuse is very often all about control and power.'[19] She concluded her speech by saying that 'the brightest and most precious thing of all is realizing that you are loved and believed by friends, family and colleagues who believe in you and support you.'[20] As she finished her speech, she crumpled in tears as she resumed her seat, with friends and colleagues around embracing her and the chamber applauding her. When I interviewed home secretary Priti Patel on the day of the Queen's Speech in October 2019 when the government announced its legislative agenda including a promise to bring back the Domestic Abuse Bill, she was unequivocal on her support for the bill. She described it as 'long overdue and so welcome', and said that she would 'pray, as it goes through the committee stage, that unity of purpose remains there'. But despite this implicit call for critics to lay further demands aside and back the bill, when I asked Patel whether she would consider supporting the calls of MPs including Jess Phillips to extend the three months of destitution funding currently available to migrant women without a spousal visa, she agreed to 'look at that fully'. Patel described the various speeches by women MPs during the second reading of the bill as 'incredible, absolutely incredible'. She also paid tribute to the cross-party work that had led to the bill, arguing that 'when there are issues of that nature, when there's a sense of injustice, MPs really do work together, and I think that is one of the best things about being a member of Parliament'.[21]

Meanwhile, Labour MP Stella Creasy has led on the cross-party campaign to increase access to abortion services for Northern Irish women. The 1967 Abortion Act does not extend to Northern Ireland, so abortion there remains illegal and punishable by a prison sentence. In summer 2017, Creasy tabled an amendment to allow women from Northern Ireland to access an abortion for free in England and Wales through the NHS in England and Wales, thus forcing a vote in the Commons. Her amendment received substantial cross-party support and the government was forced to retract its opposition in order to ward off imminent defeat, agreeing within twenty-four hours to fund abortions for Northern Irish women on the NHS. The change was implemented by a supportive Justine Greening (then women and equalities minister): 'We all felt we had an opportunity to do something constructive and positive', Greening has said.[22] Greening added that working with Creasy 'was a complete meeting of minds in terms of trying to get some progress' and that 'it was a really constructive piece of work together across the two parties'.[23] On International Women's Day in 2018, Creasy gathered the support of over 100 cross-party MPs and peers to lobby the home secretary, Amber Rudd, to allow women in Northern Ireland access to abortions locally rather than having to travel to England and Wales.

Creasy's campaign was propelled further when, on 26 May 2018, the Republic of Ireland voted decisively to decriminalize abortion in an historic referendum. This prompted a debate about the 1861 Offences against the Person Act (OPA), the piece of legislation which made it a crime for a woman to have an abortion both in the UK and in Ireland, since it was passed prior to the partition of Ireland. In June 2018, Creasy struck while the iron was hot. She proposed an amendment to repeal the OPA. This was a clever strategy which engaged a diverse set of supporters. In removing criminalization from all parts of the UK, it would remove the barrier to Northern Ireland making its own legislation on abortion, without violating devolution. With the support of then secretary of state for international development (and minister for women) Penny Mordaunt and secretary of state for Northern Ireland Karen Bradley, Creasy also managed to win a bid for an emergency debate, in which women MPs made important contributions, drawing from the experiences of constituents and themselves. Heidi Allen gave an incredibly moving account of her own experience of needing an abortion when she was severely ill with daily seizures. Making the speech 'wasn't something I planned to do,' Allen told me, but 'if you're an MP, it's not just about trotting out party lines, it's about trying to shift the debate on things . . . but I didn't quite expect it to have quite the impact it did. And people still come up to me now and thank me for doing it.'[24] Meanwhile, the former Conservative MP Anna Soubry challenged male DUP MP Sammy Wilson, asking the Commons 'what's the Right Hon. Gentleman going to do about it? That's what I would ask him. What about the 724 women who came to this country to have an abortion? What are you going to do? Make them stay in Northern Ireland to have children they do not want? What's your solution?'[25]

Creasy's amendment to extend abortion rights to Northern Ireland attracted wide parliamentary support from nationalist MPs, such as the SNP's Hannah Bardell and Alison Thewliss, and Sinn Féin's leader, Michelle O'Neill. A letter to the government demanding the repeal of the OPA was signed by Creasy and Diana Johnson from Labour, Jo Swinson from the Lib Dems, Caroline Lucas from the Greens, Liz Saville Roberts from Plaid Cymru and Sarah Wollaston, then from the Conservatives (chair of the Commons health and social care select committee). Creasy's amendment was passed with resounding Commons support in July 2019 and came into force at the end of October on the condition that the Stormont Assembly had not recalled by then. Anti-abortion unionist parties did in fact recall the Assembly to try to thwart Creasy's amendment, but their attempts failed when it was unable to elect a speaker with cross-community backing. Just two months later, an anti-abortion campaign group initiated a billboard campaign after Creasy's amendment passed in the Commons in Creasy's constituency, depicting nine-week living fetuses on billboards alongside the slogan 'Stop Stella', who was eight months pregnant after having suffered multiple miscarriages in the past. Creasy reflected that

> on a practical level, I will say "bullies don't waste my time, they waste their own time." But of course on a human level, when you put a picture of my head, twenty-foot high and wide, next to a picture of a baby roughly the same age as the one I'm carrying and tell me that I want to kill them ... I defy anyone to not be completely floored by it.

Creasy also relayed to me how the campaign's use of the slogan 'Stop Stella' has whipped up further abuse and intimidation against her and her office: 'if they're saying stop somebody, what do they think is going to happen?,' she emphasised. 'And now the threats have started rolling into my office ... I mean they didn't put a target on my head, but they might as well have done'.[26]

Women MPs have been underestimated time and again, but with more than one hundred years of experience we continue to make our mark. And even though there is much despair about Parliament and politics today, I believe that women over the last century have changed politics and policy for the better. Many of these changes would have been impossible if women MPs hadn't decided to take hands in sisterhood across political divides, all the stronger for building on the things we have in common with one another.

The stories in this book of collaboration, commitment and, at times, conflict, demonstrate that the parliamentary sisterhood is alive and well. Yet if the history of the last hundred years tells us anything, it is that there is always more to be done, and that we must stride forwards rather than looking back at our achievements. As Angela Rayner put it when I interviewed her, 'We stand on the shoulders of giants – people who fought for our holiday pay, people who fought for trade unions, people who fought for the suffragette movement'.[27] Just as the first women MPs stood on the shoulders of the suffragettes and suffragists, so too current women MPs stand on the shoulders of their predecessors, and so too will future women MPs. Who knows what the next hundred years will bring. I hope it is greater opportunity and equality for us all.

Afterword: The Right Honourable Harriet Harman MP

The past one hundred years have seen nothing less than a transformation in women's legal rights, in their role in the home and the family, their involvement in the world of work and their participation in politics.

We have gone from a situation where a woman was defined by her marital status in a household headed by a man. It was expected that her primary role would be in the home, supporting him and in particular caring for the children and older relatives. Many women did work outside the home but their employment was regarded as for 'pin money'. Most professions were barred to women and though women were allowed to stand for Parliament the percentage of women MPs remained stuck at 3 per cent. Women were wholly absent from the public policy decisions which affected their lives.

We are now in a situation where women, and most men, believe that women are equal with men, not inferior or subordinate to them, that marriage should be a partnership of equals, that women should be treated equally at work and should have an equal say in decision-making.

But just because there's broad agreement now on the principle of women's entitlement to equality, that shouldn't blind us to the fact that this progress did not happen by amicable agreement. Far from it. It was hard fought for by women over the decades and in particular by women working together, and with women MPs, in the women's movement which gathered force in the 1960s, 70s and 80s. Those women who fought against oppressive laws and attitudes of men, against patriarchy and male violence and for equality at work were not listened to by a respectful and responsible establishment. Far from it. Obstacles were thrown in their path. They were vilified as subversive, unnatural, or even dangerous.

Women who argued for childcare were accused of harming children by encouraging their mothers to go out to work. Women who set up refuges for women fleeing domestic violence were accused of undermining the family by encouraging the notion that a woman could leave her husband. Women who argued for equal pay were accused of undermining men at work by challenging the notion that he, as the breadwinner, was entitled to the 'family wage'. So while we should be gratified by how far we've come, we should not be grateful because we were only ever fighting for what should always have been ours – our right to equality.

We have learnt many lessons from this decades-long fight. Change is not accepted with equanimity by those who hold power. There will be backlash which is often very personal and threatening in nature. It is not possible to make change as a woman acting alone. It is the solidarity of women working together which has forced progress. Women have not progressed by having a few inspirational leaders but by working together. Change, no matter how well argued for and justified takes years to achieve. Persistence is essential. Women who propose change cannot expect to be popular with the vested interests but will be criticized as awkward, aggressive and abnormal. But women sticking their neck out for change will always have the support of millions of women who, like them, rail against unfairness and face discrimination in their own lives.

Now, not only have attitudes changed but there are women working and making progress in every field of endeavour. Women are working in engineering, in law, on the shop floor and in the board room. Women are now 32 per cent of MPs. But though women have pushed their way into what were hitherto men only spheres, we are as yet not on equal terms.

Though we should be gratified by how far we have progressed we need to be realistic about how much more still needs to change before equality becomes a reality.

We need further progress on equal pay. It was clear when the Equality Act provisions on gender pay gap reporting were made public in April 2018 the extent to which women remain unequal in the world of work. Eight out of ten employers still pay their men more than their women. This is the case in all sectors including those such as retail which would not exist without women's work. It is the case in trade unions, who are pledged to fight for equality for their women members, yet do not achieve it in their own offices. Unite, our biggest union, pays their men employees 30 per cent more than their women and the teachers union, NASUWT, pays their men 40 per cent more than their women. The situation is even starker when it comes to the payment of bonuses. In Facebook UK the men get bonuses which are 60 per cent higher than the women.

We need further progress on tackling domestic violence and in particular domestic homicide. We need to protect the funds going to tackle domestic violence and in particular ensure that we sustain and improve refuge provision.

We need to ensure that women are not only in Parliament in equal numbers but that we are, as MPs, sharing power on equal terms. We need to be so we are able to deliver the progressive change that women in our country need.

At the outset of the women's movement our determination to increase the number of women MPs was seen very much as a left of centre political movement. So as feminists we made our home in the Labour Party which had always seen itself as the party of women and equality. And indeed when it came to 1997 our policy of women-only shortlists for selection in constituencies which we expected to win delivered over 100 Labour women MPs and changed not only the face of Parliament but also what was seen as the political agenda. Demands for childcare and for the tackling of domestic violence advanced onto the political agenda. But they are still not mainstream.

As we press for further progress we draw on our experience but also recognize that new times bring new issues and offer new opportunities.

In the age of the internet social media is a great opportunity for women to campaign together. But it is also the vehicle for misogyny and for threats and abuse against women who have the temerity to take leading positions or venture into public life. We need to challenge this misogyny and not believe that by complaining about it we will be seen as weak.

In the past the few women in Parliament relied heavily on solidarity and support from women in the wider women's movement. And that is still strongly there. And then when there was a big increase in Labour women MPs we were able to work together within Parliament to make progress. Now there is starting to be an increase in the number of women Conservative MPs. It is not just that their numbers are new, they have new attitudes too. Many of them are what I describe as the 'daughters of the women's movement'. They have been brought up by women who espoused the notion of equality for women. It is to be hoped that despite our deep party loyalties and wide division between the parties, we will, nonetheless, be able to work across parties on issues of concern to women. We have already seen that on the move to allow women MPs proxy votes when they are on maternity leave and on extending abortion rights to women in Northern Ireland.

And there is new opportunity in the changing attitudes of men. There are far fewer men openly espousing the notion that women are inferior to men and should stay at home to look after the children. There are many more men who are 'sons of the women's movement' who have seen their mothers work, support their wives as they go out to work and believe they should play an equal part in the home. We now have men in Parliament supporting women's causes and we have had, in John Bercow, a speaker eager to support changes which help women's equality.

We need to ensure that we end male dominance in the leadership of the Labour Party. We have, in 2018, a male leader and deputy and men lead the party in Wales and in Scotland. We have never had a woman Labour prime minister or deputy prime minister. That is wrong for a party which espouses equality and is an embarrassment when the Conservative Party have managed two women leaders and prime ministers. The next leader of the Labour Party simply must be a woman and there are many brilliant and committed women in Parliament for the party to choose from.

The women's movement has always been internationalist in outlook and we are in solidarity with our sisters around the world who have the same commitment to equality, who face the same obstacles as us and often many more. We must strengthen those links and that solidarity as we all make progress.

As we mark the centenary of the first British women winning the right to vote and stand for Parliament, we face many of the old battles and also some new ones. But we have new allies and opportunities. The women's movement has been one of the most successful movements for change in modern times. We have won the battle of ideas. Now we must win the battle for the reality of the change.

Appendix

List of all women MPs to be elected, 1918–2019 (in order of taking the oath of allegiance)

Number	Name	Party	Constituency	Dates as an MP
1	Constance MARKIEVICZ	Sinn Féin	Dublin, St Patrick's	1918–22
2	Nancy ASTOR	Conservative	Plymouth, Sutton	1919–45
3	Margaret WINTRINGHAM	Liberal	Lincolnshire, Louth	1921–24
4	Mabel PHILIPSON	Conservative	Berwick-upon-Tweed	1923–29
5	Dorothea JEWSON	Labour	Norwich	1923–24
6	Arabella Susan LAWRENCE	Labour	East Ham, North	1923–24; 1926–31
7	Margaret BONDFIELD	Labour	Northampton; Wallsend	1923–24; 1926–31
8	Vera TERRINGTON	Liberal	Buckinghamshire, Wycombe	1923–24
9	Katharine (Duchess of) ATHOLL	Conservative	Perth & Kinross, Kinross & Western	1923–38
10	Ellen WILKINSON	Labour	Middlesbrough, East; Jarrow	1924–31; 1935–47

11	Gwendolen (Countess of) IVEAGH	Conservative	Southend-on-Sea	1927–35
12	Hilda RUNCIMAN	Liberal	Cornwall, St Ives	1928–29
13	Florence DALTON	Labour	Durham, Bishop Auckland	1929
14	Jennie LEE	Labour	Lanarkshire, Northern; Staffordshire, Cannock	1929–31; 1945–70
15	Edith PICTON-TURBERVILL	Labour	Shropshire, The Wrekin	1929–31
16	Mary HAMILTON	Labour	Blackburn	1929–31
17	Ethel BENTHAM	Labour	Islington, East	1929–31
18	Megan LLOYD GEORGE	Liberal	Anglesey; Carmarthen	1929–51; 1957–66
19	Marion PHILLIPS	Labour	Sunderland	1929–31
20	Cynthia MOSLEY	Labour	Stoke-on-Trent, Stoke	1929–31
21	Eleanor RATHBONE	Independent	Combined English Universities	1929–46
22	Lucy NOEL-BUXTON	Labour	Norfolk, North; Norwich	1930–31; 1945–50
23	Leah MANNING	Labour	Islington, East; Essex, Epping	1931; 1945–50
24	Helen SHAW	Conservative	Lanarkshire, Bothwell	1931–35
25	Mavis TATE	Conservative	Willesden, West; Somerset, Frome	1931–35; 1935–45
26	Ida COPELAND	Conservative	Stoke-on-Trent, Stoke	1931–35
27	Sarah WARD	Conservative	Staffordshire, Cannock	1931–35
28	Thelma CAZALET-KEIR	Conservative	Islington, East	1931–45
29	Irene WARD	Conservative	Wallsend; Tynemouth	1931–45; 1950–74
30	Norah RUNGE	Conservative	Bermondsey, Rotherhithe	1931–35

31	Florence HORSBURGH	Conservative	Dundee; Manchester, Moss-Side	1931–45; 1950–59
32	Marjorie GRAVES	Conservative	Hackney, South	1931–35
33	Mary PICKFORD	Conservative	Hammersmith, North	1931–34
34	Frances Joan DAVIDSON	Conservative	Hertfordshire, Hemel Hempstead	1937–59
35	Agnes HARDIE	Labour	Glasgow, Springburn	1937–45
36	Edith SUMMERSKILL	Labour	Fulham; Warrington	1938–55; 1955–61
37	Jennie ADAMSON	Labour	Dartford; Bexley	1938–45; 1945–46
38	Beatrice WRIGHT	Conservative	Cornwall, Bodmin	1941–45
39	Lady Violet APSLEY	Conservative	Bristol, Central	1943–45
40	Barbara CASTLE	Labour	Blackburn; Blackburn East; Blackburn	1945–50; 1950–55; 1955–79
41	Jean MANN	Labour	Lanarkshire, Coatbridge; Coatbridge and Airdrie	1945–50; 1950–59
42	Grace COLMAN	Labour	Tynemouth	1945–50
43	Margaret HERBISON	Labour	Lanarkshire, North	1945–70
44	Barbara GOULD	Labour	Hendon, North	1945–50
45	Alice BACON	Labour	Leeds, North East; Leeds, South East	1945–55; 1955–70
46	Muriel NICHOL	Labour	Bradford, North	1945–50
47	Florence PATON	Labour	Nottinghamshire, Rushcliffe	1945–50
48	Freda CORBET	Labour	Camberwell, North-West; Camberwell, Peckham	1945–50; 1950–74
49	Mabel RIDEALGH	Labour	Ilford, North	1945–50
50	Caroline GANLEY	Labour	Battersea, South	1945–51
51	Bessie BRADDOCK	Labour	Liverpool, Exchange	1945–70

52	Clarice SHAW	Labour	Ayrshire & Bute, Kilmarnock	1945–46
53	Edith WILLS	Labour	Birmingham, Duddeston	1945–50
54	Lucy MIDDLETON	Labour	Plymouth, Sutton	1945–51
55	Priscilla TWEEDSMUIR	Conservative	Aberdeen, South	1946–66
56	CULLEN	Labour	Glasgow, Gorbals	1948–69
57	Dorothy REES	Labour	Glamorgan, Barry	1950–51
58	Eirene WHITE	Labour	Flintshire, East	1950–70
59	Elaine BURTON	Labour	Coventry, South	1950–59
60	Patricia HORNSBY-SMITH	Conservative	Kent, Chislehurst	1950–66; 1970–74
61	Eveline HILL	Conservative	Manchester, Wythenshawe	1950–64
62	Harriet SLATER	Labour	Stoke-on-Trent, North	1953–66
63	Patricia FORD	Ulster Unionist	Down, North	1953–55
64	Edith PITT	Conservative	Birmingham, Edgbaston	1953–66
65	Lena JEGER	Labour	Holborn & St Pancras, South	1953–59; 1964–79
66	Joan VICKERS	Conservative	Plymouth, Devonport	1955–74
67	Joyce BUTLER	Labour	Wood Green	1955–79
68	Patricia McLAUGHLIN	Ulster Unionist	Belfast, West	1955–64
69	Evelyn EMMET	Conservative	East Sussex, East Grinstead	1955–64
70	Mervyn PIKE	Conservative	Leicestershire, Melton	1956–74
71	Muriel GAMMANS	Conservative	Hornsey	1957–66
72	Mary McALISTER	Labour	Glasgow, Kelvingrove	1958–59
73	Betty HARVIE ANDERSON	Conservative	Renfrewshire, East	1959–79

74	Judith HART	Labour	Lanark; Clydesdale	1959–83; 1983–87
75	Margaret THATCHER	Conservative	Finchley	1959–92
76	Joan QUENNELL MBE	Conservative	Petersfield	1960–74
77	Anne KERR	Labour	Rochester & Chatham	1964–70
78	Shirley WILLIAMS	Labour; Social Democratic Party	Hertfordshire, Hitchin; Hertford & Stevenage; Crosby	1964–74; 1974–79; 1981–83
79	Shirley SUMMERSKILL	Labour	Halifax	1964–83
80	Renée SHORT	Labour	Wolverhampton, North-East	1964–87
81	Margaret McKAY	Labour	Wandsworth, Clapham	1964–70
82	Jill KNIGHT	Conservative	Birmingham, Edgbaston	1966–97
83	Joan LESTOR	Labour	Eton & Slough; Eccles	1966–83; 1987–97
84	Gwyneth DUNWOODY	Labour	Exeter; Crewe; Crewe & Nantwich	1966–70; 1974–83; 1983–2008
85	Winifred EWING	Scottish National Party	Lanarkshire, Hamilton; Moray & Nairn	1967–70; 1974–79
86	Bernadette DEVLIN	Independent Unity	Mid-Ulster	1969–74
87	Elaine KELLETT-BOWMAN	Conservative	Lancaster	1970–97
88	Constance MONKS	Conservative	Chorley	1970–74
89	Doris FISHER	Labour	Birmingham, Ladywood	1970–74
90	Sally OPPENHEIM	Conservative	Gloucester	1970–87
91	Peggy FENNER	Conservative	Rochester & Chatham; Medway	1970–74 and 1979–83; 1983–97

92	Janet FOOKES	Conservative	Merton & Morden; Plymouth, Drake	1970–74; 1974–97
93	Joan HALL	Conservative	Keighley	1970–74
94	Mary HOLT	Conservative	Preston, North	1970–74
95	Betty BOOTHROYD	Labour	West Bromwich; West Bromwich, West	1973–74; 1974–2000
96	Margo MACDONALD	Scottish National Party	Glasgow, Govan	1973–74
97	Maureen COLQUHOUN	Labour	Northampton, North	1974–79
98	Lynda CHALKER	Conservative	Wallasey	1974–92
99	Audrey WISE	Labour	Coventry, South-West; Preston	1974–79; 1987–2000
100	Jo RICHARDSON	Labour	Barking	1974–94
101	Millie MILLER	Labour	Ilford North	1974–77
102	Margaret JACKSON (later BECKETT)	Labour	Lincoln; Derby, South	1974–79; 1983–
103	Helene HAYMAN	Labour	Welwyn & Hatfield	1974–79
104	Ann TAYLOR	Labour	Bolton, West; Dewsbury	1974–83; 1987–2005
105	Joan MAYNARD	Labour	Sheffield, Brightside	1974–87
106	Margaret BAIN (later EWING)	Scottish National Party	East Dunbartonshire; Moray	1974–79; 1987–2001
107	Oonagh McDONALD	Labour	Thurrock	1976–87
108	Sheila FAITH	Conservative	Belper	1979–83
109	Sheila WRIGHT	Labour	Birmingham, Handsworth	1979–83
110	Angela RUMBOLD	Conservative	Merton, Mitcham and Morden; Mitcham and Morden	1982–83; 1983–97
111	Harriet HARMAN	Labour	Peckham; Camberwell & Peckham	1982–1997; 1997–
112	Helen McELHONE	Labour	Glasgow, Queen's Park	1982–83

113	Edwina CURRIE	Conservative	South Derbyshire	1983–97
114	Marion ROE	Conservative	Broxbourne	1983–2005
115	Anna McCURLEY	Conservative	Renfrew West & Inverclyde	1983–87
116	Elizabeth PEACOCK	Conservative	Batley & Spen	1983–97
117	Ann WINTERTON	Conservative	Congleton	1983–2010
118	Clare SHORT	Labour	Birmingham, Ladywood	1983–2010
119	Virginia BOTTOMLEY	Conservative	South West Surrey	1984–2005
120	Ann CLWYD	Labour	Cynon Valley	1984–2019
121	Elizabeth SHIELDS	Liberal	Ryedale	1986–87
122	Llin GOLDING	Labour	Newcastle-under-Lyme	1986–2001
123	Rosie BARNES	Social Democratic Party	Greenwich	1987–92
124	Joyce QUIN	Labour	Gateshead, East; Gateshead East and Washington West	1987–97; 1997–2005
125	Ann WIDDECOMBE	Conservative	Maidstone; Maidstone and the Weald	1987–97; 1997–2010
126	Gillian SHEPHARD	Conservative	South West Norfolk	1987–2005
127	Dawn PRIMAROLO	Labour	Bristol South	1987–2015
128	Joan WALLEY	Labour	Stoke-on-Trent, North	1987–2015
129	Maria FYFE	Labour	Glasgow, Maryhill	1987–2001
130	Maureen HICKS	Conservative	Wolverhampton, North East	1987–92
131	Alice MAHON	Labour	Halifax	1987–2005
132	Marjorie ('Mo') MOWLAM	Labour	Redcar	1987–2001
133	Hilary ARMSTRONG	Labour	North West Durham	1987–2010

134	Teresa GORMAN	Conservative	Billericay	1987–2001
135	Mildred GORDON	Labour	Bow & Poplar	1987–97
136	Joan RUDDOCK	Labour	Lewisham, Deptford	1987–2015
137	Emma NICHOLSON	Conservative	Devon, West & Torridge	1987–97
138	Diane ABBOTT	Labour	Hackney North & Stoke Newington	1987–
139	Ray MICHIE	Liberal Democrat	Argyll & Bute	1987–2001
140	Kate HOEY	Labour	Vauxhall	1989–2019
141	Sylvia HEAL	Labour	Mid-Staffordshire; Halesowen and Rowley Regis	1990–92; 1997–2010
142	Irene ADAMS	Labour	Paisley North	1990–2005
143	Jane KENNEDY	Labour	Liverpool, Broad Green; Liverpool, Wavertree	1992–97; 1997–2010
144	Rachel SQUIRE	Labour	Dunfermline West; Dunfermline and West Fife	1992–2005; 2005–06
145	Liz LYNNE	Liberal Democrat	Rochdale	1992–97
146	Estelle MORRIS	Labour	Birmingham, Yardley	1992–2005
147	Helen JACKSON	Labour	Sheffield, Hillsborough	1992–2005
148	Angela KNIGHT	Conservative	Erewash	1992–97
149	Jacqui LAIT	Conservative	Hastings & Rye; Beckenham	1992–97; 1997–2010
150	Olga MAITLAND	Conservative	Sutton & Cheam	1992–97
151	Lynne JONES	Labour	Birmingham, Selly Oak	1992–2010
152	Ann COFFEY	Labour; Change UK	Stockport	1992–2019
153	Barbara ROCHE	Labour	Hornsey & Wood Green	1992–2005
154	Janet ANDERSON	Labour	Rossendale & Darwen	1992–2010

155	Glenda JACKSON	Labour	Hampstead & Highgate; Hampstead and Kilburn	1992–2010; 2010–15
156	Jean CORSTON	Labour	Bristol East	1992–2005
157	Angela BROWNING	Conservative	Tiverton; Tiverton & Honiton	1992–97; 1997–2010
158	Anne CAMPBELL	Labour	Cambridge	1992–2005
159	Cheryl GILLAN	Conservative	Chesham & Amersham	1992–
160	Judith CHAPLIN	Conservative	Newbury	1992–93
161	Bridget PRENTICE	Labour	Lewisham East	1992–2010
162	Tessa JOWELL	Labour	Dulwich; Dulwich & West Norwood	1992–97; 1997–2015
163	Angela EAGLE	Labour	Wallasey	1992–
164	Diana MADDOCK	Liberal Democrat	Christchurch	1993–97
165	Margaret HODGE	Labour	Barking	1994–
166	Judith CHURCH	Labour	Dagenham	1994–2001
167	Helen LIDDELL	Labour	Monklands East; Airdrie and Shotts	1994–1997; 1997–2005
168	Roseanna CUNNINGHAM	Scottish National Party	Perth & Kinross; Perth	1995–97; 1997–2001
169	Anne McINTOSH	Conservative	Vale of York; Thirsk and Malton	1997–2010; 2010–15
170	Jenny TONGE	Liberal Democrat	Richmond Park	1997–2005
171	Christine BUTLER	Labour	Castle Point	1997–2001
172	Helen JONES	Labour	Warrington North	1997–2019
173	Joan HUMBLE	Labour	Blackpool North and Fleetwood	1997–2010
174	Judy MALLABER	Labour	Amber Valley	1997–2010
175	Linda GILROY	Labour	Plymouth, Sutton	1997–2010
176	Christine RUSSELL	Labour	Chester, City of	1997–2010

177	Jenny JONES	Labour	Wolverhampton South West	1997–2001
178	Ann KEEN	Labour	Brentford and Isleworth	1997–2010
179	Eleanor LAING	Conservative	Epping Forest	1997–
180	Melanie JOHNSON	Labour	Welwyn Hatfield	1997–2005
181	Phyllis STARKEY	Labour	Milton Keynes South West	1997–2010
182	Jacqui SMITH	Labour	Redditch	1997–2010
183	Hazel BLEARS	Labour	Salford; Salford and Eccles	1997–2010; 2010–15
184	Beverley HUGHES	Labour	Stretford and Urmston	1997–2010
185	Linda PERHAM	Labour	Ilford North	1997–2005
186	Louise ELLMAN	Labour	Liverpool, Riverside	1997–2019
187	Jackie LAWRENCE	Labour	Preseli Pembrokeshire	1997–2005
188	Candy ATHERTON	Labour	Falmouth and Camborne	1997–2005
189	Fiona MACTAGGART	Labour	Slough	1997–2017
190	Gillian MERRON	Labour	Lincoln	1997–2010
191	Theresa MAY	Conservative	Maidenhead	1997–
192	Barbara FOLLETT	Labour	Stevenage	1997–2010
193	Gisela STUART	Labour	Birmingham, Edgbaston	1997–2017
194	Patricia HEWITT	Labour	Leicester West	1997–2010
195	Julie MORGAN	Labour	Cardiff North	1997–2010
196	Claire WARD	Labour	Watford	1997–2010
197	Debra SHIPLEY	Labour	Stourbridge	1997–2005
198	Charlotte ATKINS	Labour	Staffordshire Moorlands	1997–2010
199	Margaret MORAN	Labour	Luton South	1997–2010

200	Oona KING	Labour	Bethnal Green and Bow	1997–2005
201	Caroline FLINT	Labour	Don Valley	1997–2019
202	Eileen GORDON	Labour	Romford	1997–2001
203	Fiona JONES	Labour	Newark	1997–2001
204	Joan RYAN	Labour; Change UK	Enfield North	1997–2010; 2015–19
205	Anne BEGG	Labour	Aberdeen South	1997–2015
206	Chris McCAFFERTY	Labour	Calder Valley	1997–2010
207	Caroline SPELMAN	Conservative	Meriden	1997–2019
208	Claire CURTIS-THOMAS	Labour	Crosby	1997–2010
209	Maria EAGLE	Labour	Liverpool, Garston; Garston and Halewood	1997–2010; 2010–
210	Rosie WINTERTON	Labour	Doncaster Central	1997–
211	Kali MOUNTFORD	Labour	Colne Valley	1997–2010
212	Geraldine SMITH	Labour	Morecambe and Lunesdale	1997–2010
213	Jackie BALLARD	Liberal Democrat	Taunton	1997–2001
214	Tess KINGHAM	Labour	Gloucester	1997–2001
215	Diana ORGAN	Labour	Forest of Dean	1997–2005
216	Angela SMITH	Labour	Basildon	1997–2010
217	Helen BRINTON (later CLARK)	Labour	Peterborough	1997–2005
218	Betty WILLIAMS	Labour	Conwy	1997–2010
219	Ann CRYER	Labour	Keighley	1997–2010
220	Janet DEAN	Labour	Burton	1997–2010
221	Karen BUCK	Labour	Regent's Park and Kensington North; Westminster North	1997–2010; 2010–
222	Dari TAYLOR	Labour	Stockton South	1997–2010

223	Helen SOUTHWORTH	Labour	Warrington South	1997–2010
224	Liz BLACKMAN	Labour	Erewash	1997–2010
225	Laura MOFFATT	Labour	Crawley	1997–2010
226	Julia DROWN	Labour	South Swindon	1997–2005
227	Yvette COOPER	Labour	Pontefract and Castleford; Normanton, Pontefract and Castleford	1997–2010; 2010–
228	Sandra OSBORNE	Labour	Ayr; Ayr, Carrick and Cumnock	1997–2005; 2005–15
229	Lynda CLARK	Labour	Edinburgh, Pentlands	1997–2005
230	Rosemary McKENNA	Labour	Cumbernauld and Kilsyth; Cumbernauld, Kilsyth and Kirkintilloch East	1997–2005; 2005–10
231	Sally KEEBLE	Labour	Northampton North	1997–2010
232	Jane GRIFFITHS	Labour	Reading East	1997–2005
233	Julie KIRKBRIDE	Conservative	Bromsgrove	1997–2010
234	Valerie DAVEY	Labour	Bristol West	1997–2005
235	Siobhain McDONAGH	Labour	Mitcham and Morden	1997–
236	Shona McISAAC	Labour	Cleethorpes	1997–2010
237	Ruth KELLY	Labour	Bolton West	1997–2010
238	Anne McGUIRE	Labour	Stirling	1997–2015
239	Lorna FITZSIMONS	Labour	Rochdale	1997–2005
240	Sandra GIDLEY	Liberal Democrat	Romsey	2000–10
241	Meg MUNN	Labour	Sheffield, Heeley	2001–15
242	Iris ROBINSON	Democrat Unionist	Strangford	2001–10
243	Ann McKECHIN	Labour	Glasgow Maryhill; Glasgow North	2001–05; 2005–15

244	Anne PICKING (later MOFFAT)	Labour	East Lothian	2001–10
245	Sue DOUGHTY	Liberal Democrat	Guildford	2001–05
246	Vera BAIRD	Labour	Redcar	2001–10
247	Angela WATKINSON	Conservative	Upminster; Hornchurch and Upminster	2001–10; 2010–17
248	Annette BROOKE	Liberal Democrat	Mid Dorset & North Poole	2001–15
249	Patsy CALTON	Liberal Democrat	Cheadle	2001–05
250	Sylvia HERMON	Ulster Unionist	North Down	2001–19
251	Annabelle EWING	Scottish National Party	Perth	2001–05
252	Michelle GILDERNEW	Sinn Féin	Fermanagh & South Tyrone	2001–15; 2017–
253	Sarah TEATHER	Liberal Democrat	Brent East; Brent Central	2003–10; 2010–15
254	Siân JAMES	Labour	Swansea East	2005–15
255	Anne MILTON	Conservative; Independent	Guildford	2005–19
256	Anne MAIN	Conservative	St Albans	2005–19
257	Katy CLARK	Labour	North Ayrshire and Arran	2005–15
258	Julia GOLDSWORTHY	Liberal Democrat	Falmouth & Camborne	2005–10
259	Alison SEABECK	Labour	Plymouth, Devonport; Plymouth, Moor View	2005–10; 2010–15
260	Kitty USSHER	Labour	Burnley	2005–10
261	Lynda WALTHO	Labour	Stourbridge	2005–10
262	Justine GREENING	Conservative; Independent	Putney	2005–19
263	Theresa VILLIERS	Conservative	Chipping Barnet	2005–
264	Madeleine MOON	Labour	Bridgend	2005–19

265	Maria MILLER	Conservative	Basingstoke	2005–
266	Jenny WILLOTT	Liberal Democrat	Cardiff Central	2005–15
267	Lorely BURT	Liberal Democrat	Solihull	2005–15
268	Lyn BROWN	Labour	West Ham	2005–
269	Jo SWINSON	Liberal Democrat	East Dunbartonshire	2005–15; 2017–19
270	Anne SNELGROVE	Labour	South Swindon	2005–10
271	Mary CREAGH	Labour	Wakefield	2005–19
272	Susan KRAMER	Liberal Democrat	Richmond Park	2005–10
273	Sarah McCARTHY-FRY	Labour	Portsmouth North	2005–10
274	Helen GOODMAN	Labour	Bishop Auckland	2005–19
275	Meg HILLIER	Labour	Hackney South and Shoreditch	2005–
276	Linda RIORDAN	Labour	Halifax	2005–15
277	Lynne FEATHERSTONE	Liberal Democrat	Hornsey and Wood Green	2005–15
278	Natascha ENGEL	Labour	North East Derbyshire	2005–17
279	Roberta BLACKMAN-WOODS	Labour	Durham, City of	2005–
280	Angela SMITH	Labour; Change UK; Independent; Liberal Democrat	Sheffield, Hillsborough; Penistone and Stocksbridge	2005–10; 2010–
281	Celia BARLOW	Labour	Hove	2005–10
282	Kerry McCARTHY	Labour	Bristol East	2005–
283	Jessica MORDEN	Labour	Newport East	2005–
284	Diana JOHNSON	Labour	Kingston upon Hull North	2005–

285	Nadine DORRIES	Conservative	Mid Bedfordshire	2005–
286	Dawn BUTLER	Labour	Brent South; Brent Central	2005–10; 2015–
287	Emily THORNBERRY	Labour	Islington South & Finsbury	2005–
288	Barbara KEELEY	Labour	Worsley; Worsley and Eccles South	2005–10; 2010–
289	Sharon HODGSON	Labour	Gateshead East & Washington West; Washington and Sunderland West	2005–10; 2010–
290	Rosie COOPER	Labour	West Lancashire	2005–
291	Nia GRIFFITH	Labour	Llanelli	2005–
292	Chloe SMITH	Conservative	Norwich North	2009–
293	Valerie VAZ	Labour	Walsall South	2010–
294	Catherine McKINNELL	Labour	Newcastle upon Tyne North	2010–
295	Pat GLASS	Labour	North West Durham	2010–17
296	Priti PATEL	Conservative	Witham	2010–
297	Charlotte LESLIE	Conservative	Bristol North West	2010–17
298	Mary MacLEOD	Conservative	Brentford and Isleworth	2010–15
299	Claire PERRY	Conservative	Devizes	2010–19
300	Anna SOUBRY	Conservative; Change UK	Broxtowe	2010–19
301	Fiona BRUCE	Conservative	Congleton	2010–
302	Angie BRAY	Conservative	Ealing Central and Acton	2010–15
303	Esther McVEY	Conservative	Wirral West; Tatton	2010–15; 2017–
304	Sarah WOLLASTON	Conservative; Change UK; Independent; Liberal Democrat	Totnes	2010–19

305	Tracey CROUCH	Conservative	Chatham and Aylesford	2010–
306	Mary GLINDON	Labour	North Tyneside	2010–
307	Julie ELLIOTT	Labour	Sunderland Central	2010–
308	Heather WHEELER	Conservative	South Derbyshire	2010–
309	Pauline LATHAM	Conservative	Mid Derbyshire	2010–
310	Caroline NOKES	Conservative; Independent	Romsey and Southampton North	2010–
311	Caroline DINENAGE	Conservative	Gosport	2010–
312	Lorraine FULLBROOK	Conservative	South Ribble	2010–15
313	Julie HILLING	Labour	Bolton West	2010–15
314	Yasmin QURESHI	Labour	Bolton South East	2010–
315	Kate GREEN	Labour	Stretford and Urmston	2010–
316	Rachel REEVES	Labour	Leeds West	2010–
317	Lilian GREENWOOD	Labour	Nottingham South	2010–
318	Cathy JAMIESON	Labour	Kilmarnock and Loudoun	2010–15
319	Thérèse COFFEY	Conservative	Suffolk Coastal	2010–
320	Jessica LEE	Conservative	Erewash	2010–15
321	Nicky MORGAN	Conservative	Loughborough	2010–19
322	Bridget PHILLIPSON	Labour	Houghton and Sunderland South	2010–
323	Eilidh WHITEFORD	Scottish National Party	Banff and Buchan	2010–17
324	Penny MORDAUNT	Conservative	Portsmouth North	2010–
325	Chi ONWURAH	Labour	Newcastle upon Tyne Central	2010–
326	Heidi ALEXANDER	Labour	Lewisham East	2010–18
327	Yvonne FOVARGUE	Labour	Makerfield	2010–

328	Gloria De PIERO	Labour	Ashfield	2010–19
329	Jenny CHAPMAN	Labour	Darlington	2010–19
330	Liz KENDALL	Labour	Leicester West	2010–
331	Luciana BERGER	Labour; Change UK; Independent; Liberal Democrat	Liverpool, Wavertree	2010–19
332	Anne Marie MORRIS	Conservative	Newton Abbot	2010–
333	Elizabeth TRUSS	Conservative	South West Norfolk	2010–
334	Sheryll MURRAY	Conservative	South East Cornwall	2010–
335	Helen GRANT	Conservative	Maidstone and the Weald	2010–
336	Andrea LEADSOM	Conservative	South Northamptonshire	2010–
337	Jackie DOYLE-PRICE	Conservative	Thurrock	2010–
338	Margot JAMES	Conservative; Independent	Stourbridge	2010–19
339	Jane ELLISON	Conservative	Battersea	2010–17
340	Nicola BLACKWOOD	Conservative	Oxford West and Abingdon	2010–17
341	Harriett BALDWIN	Conservative	West Worcestershire	2010–
342	Karen LUMLEY	Conservative	Redditch	2010–17
343	Gemma DOYLE	Labour	West Dunbartonshire	2010–15
344	Lisa NANDY	Labour	Wigan	2010–
345	Margaret CURRAN	Labour	Glasgow East	2010–15
346	Susan Elan JONES	Labour	Clwyd South	2010–19
347	Rebecca HARRIS	Conservative	Castle Point	2010–
348	Caroline LUCAS	Green	Brighton, Pavilion	2010–
349	Louise BAGSHAW (later MENSCH)	Conservative	Corby	2010–12

350	Teresa PEARCE	Labour	Erith and Thamesmead	2010–19
351	Pamela NASH	Labour	Airdrie and Shotts	2010–15
352	Laura SANDYS	Conservative	South Thanet	2010–15
353	Amber RUDD	Conservative; Independent	Hastings and Rye	2010–19
354	Sarah NEWTON	Conservative	Truro and Falmouth	2010–
355	Rushanara ALI	Labour	Bethnal Green and Bow	2010–
356	Shabana MAHMOOD	Labour	Birmingham, Ladywood	2010–
357	Naomi LONG	Alliance	Belfast East	2010–15
358	Emma REYNOLDS	Labour	Wolverhampton North East	2010–19
359	Sheila GILMORE	Labour	Edinburgh East	2010–15
360	Fiona O'DONNELL	Labour	East Lothian	2010–15
361	Margaret RITCHIE	Social Democratic and Labour Party	South Down	2010–17
362	Tessa MUNT	Liberal Democrat	Wells	2010–15
363	Karen BRADLEY	Conservative	Staffordshire Moorlands	2010–
364	Stella CREASY	Labour	Walthamstow	2010–
365	Alison McGOVERN	Labour	Wirral South	2010–
366	Debbie ABRAHAMS	Labour	Oldham East and Saddleworth	2011–
367	Seema MALHOTRA	Labour	Feltham and Heston	2011–
368	Lucy POWELL	Labour	Manchester Central	2012–
369	Sarah CHAMPION	Labour	Rotherham	2012–
370	Emma LEWELL-BUCK	Labour	South Shields	2013–
371	Liz MCINNES	Labour	Heywood and Middleton	2014–19

372	Amanda SOLLOWAY	Conservative	Derby North	2015–17
373	Judith CUMMINS	Labour	Bradford South	2015–
374	Liz SAVILLE-ROBERTS	Plaid Cymru	Dwyfor Meirionnydd	2015–
375	Victoria BORWICK	Conservative	Kensington	2015–17
376	Kate HOLLERN	Labour	Blackburn	2015–
377	Nusrat GHANI	Conservative	Wealden	2015–
378	Anne-Marie TREVELYAN	Conservative	Berwick-Upon-Tweed	2015–
379	Rebecca POW	Conservative	Taunton Deane	2015–
380	Mims DAVIES	Conservative	Eastleigh Mid Sussex	2015–19 2019–
381	Antoinette SANDBACH	Conservative; Independent	Eddisbury	2015–19
382	Angela RAYNER	Labour	Ashton-Under-Lyne	2015–
383	Rupa HUQ	Labour	Ealing Central and Acton	2015–
384	Maggie THROUP	Conservative	Erewash	2015–
385	Suella FERNANDES (later BRAVERMAN)	Conservative	Fareham	2015–
386	Sue HAYMAN	Labour	Workington	2015–19
387	Melanie ONN	Labour	Great Grimsby	2015–19
388	Catherine WEST	Labour	Hornsey and Wood Green	2015–
389	Angela CRAWLEY	Scottish National Party	Lanark and Hamilton East	2015–
390	Mhairi BLACK	Scottish National Party	Paisley and Renfrewshire South	2015–
391	Philippa WHITFORD	Scottish National Party	Central Ayrshire	2015–17
392	Joanna CHERRY	Scottish National Party	Edinburgh South West	2015–

393	Michelle THOMSON	Scottish National Party	Edinburgh West	2015–17
394	Lisa CAMERON	Scottish National Party	East Kilbride, Strathaven and Lesmahagow	2015–
395	Hannah BARDELL	Scottish National Party	Livingston	2015–
396	Kate OSAMOR	Labour	Edmonton	2015–
397	Paula SHERRIFF	Labour	Dewsbury	2015–19
398	Naz SHAH	Labour	Bradford West	2015–
399	Corri WILSON	Scottish National Party	Ayr, Carrick and Cumnock	2015–17
400	Carol MONAGHAN	Scottish National Party	Glasgow North West	2015–
401	Patricia GIBSON	Scottish National Party	North Ayrshire and Arran	2015–
402	Helen HAYES	Labour	Dulwich and West Norwood	2015–
403	Vicky FOXCROFT	Labour	Lewisham, Deptford	2015–
404	Kirsten OSWALD	Scottish National Party	East Renfrewshire	2015–17
405	Marion FELLOWS	Scottish National Party	Motherwell and Wishaw	2015–
406	Tasmina AHMED-SHEIKH	Scottish National Party	Ochil and South Perthshire	2015–17
407	Marie RIMMER	Labour	St Helens South and Whiston	2015–
408	Thangam DEBBONAIRE	Labour	Bristol West	2015–
409	Holly LYNCH	Labour	Halifax	2015–
410	Kirsty BLACKMAN	Scottish National Party	Aberdeen North	2015–
411	Jess PHILLIPS	Labour	Birmingham, Yardley	2015–
412	Victoria PRENTIS	Conservative	Banbury	2015–

413	Flick DRUMMOND	Conservative	Portsmouth South	2015–17
414	Colleen FLETCHER	Labour	Coventry North East	2015–
415	Catherine SMITH	Labour	Lancaster and Fleetwood	2015–
416	Deidre BROCK	Scottish National Party	Edinburgh North and Leith	2015–
417	Natalie McGARRY	Scottish National Party	Glasgow East	2015–17
418	Rebecca LONG BAILEY	Labour	Salford and Eccles	2015–
419	Maria CAULFIELD	Conservative	Lewes	2015–
420	Alison THEWLISS	Scottish National Party	Glasgow Central	2015–
421	Margaret FERRIER	Scottish National Party	Rutherglen and Hamilton West	2015–17
422	Jo COX	Labour	Batley and Spen	2015–16
423	Rachael MASKELL	Labour	York Central	2015–
424	Louise HAIGH	Labour	Sheffield, Heeley	2015–
425	Lucy ALLAN	Conservative	Telford	2015–
426	Jo STEVENS	Labour	Cardiff Central	2015–
427	Lucy FRAZER	Conservative	South East Cambridgeshire	2015–
428	Victoria ATKINS	Conservative	Louth and Horncastle	2015–
429	Seema KENNEDY	Conservative	South Ribble	2015–19
430	Karin SMYTH	Labour	Bristol South	2015–
431	Wendy MORTON	Conservative	Aldridge-Brownhills	2015–
432	Margaret GREENWOOD	Labour	Wirral West	2015–
433	Amanda MILLING	Conservative	Cannock Chase	2015–
434	Andrea JENKYNS	Conservative	Morley and Outwood	2015–
435	Jo CHURCHILL	Conservative	Bury St Edmunds	2015–

436	Helen WHATELY	Conservative	Faversham and Mid Kent	2015–
437	Julie COOPER	Labour	Burnley	2015–19
438	Tulip SIDDIQ	Labour	Hampstead and Kilburn	2015–
439	Anne McLAUGHLIN	Scottish National Party	Glasgow North East	2015–17
440	Anna TURLEY	Labour	Redcar	2015–19
441	Ruth CADBURY	Labour	Brentford and Isleworth	2015–
442	Carolyn HARRIS	Labour	Swansea East	2015–
443	Christina REES	Labour	Neath	2015–
444	Tania MATHIAS	Conservative	Twickenham	2015–17
445	Mary ROBINSON	Conservative	Cheadle	2015–
446	Ruth SMEETH	Labour	Stoke-On-Trent North	2015–19
447	Kelly TOLHURST	Conservative	Rochester and Strood	2015–
448	Caroline ANSELL	Conservative	Eastbourne	2015–17
449	Heidi ALLEN	Conservative; Change UK; Independent	South Cambridgeshire	2015–19
450	Michelle DONELAN	Conservative	Chippenham	2015–
451	Gill FURNISS	Labour	Sheffield, Brightside and Hillsborough	2016–
452	Rosena ALLIN-KHAN	Labour	Tooting	2016–
453	Tracy BRABIN	Labour	Batley and Spen	2016–
454	Sarah OLNEY	Liberal Democrat	Richmond Park	2016–17 2019–
455	Caroline JOHNSON	Conservative	Sleaford and North Hykeham	2016–
456	Trudy HARRISON	Conservative	Copeland	2017–
457	Fiona ONASANYA	Labour	Peterborough	2017–19
458	Kirstene HAIR	Conservative	Angus	2017–19

459	Eleanor SMITH	Labour	Wolverhampton South West	2017–19
460	Marsha DE CORDOVA	Labour	Battersea	2017–
461	Wera HOBHOUSE	Liberal Democrat	Bath	2017–
462	Jo PLATT	Labour	Leigh	2017–19
463	Tonia ANTONIAZZI	Labour	Gower	2017–
464	Laura SMITH	Labour	Crewe and Nantwich	2017–19
465	Christine JARDINE	Liberal Democrat	Edinburgh West	2017–
466	Anneliese DODDS	Labour	Oxford East	2017–
467	Emma HARDY	Labour	Hull West and Hessle	2017–
468	Thelma WALKER	Labour	Colne Valley	2017–19
469	Ruth GEORGE	Labour	High Peak	2017–19
470	Laura PIDCOCK	Labour	North West Durham	2017–19
471	Ellie REEVES	Labour	Lewisham West and Penge	2017–
472	Stephanie PEACOCK	Labour	Barnsley East	2017–
473	Liz TWIST	Labour	Blaydon	2017–
474	Emma LITTLE PENGELLY	DUP	Belfast South	2017–
475	Rachel MACLEAN	Conservative	Redditch	2017–
476	Vicky FORD	Conservative	Chelmsford	2017–
477	Julia DOCKERILL	Conservative	Hornchurch and Upminster	2017–
478	Gillian KEEGAN	Conservative	Chichester	2017–
479	Anna McMORRIN	Labour	Cardiff North	2017–
480	Preet GILL	Labour	Birmingham Edgbaston	2017–

481	Lesley LAIRD	Labour	Kirkcaldy and Cowdenbeath	2017–19
482	Danielle ROWLEY	Labour	Midlothian	2017–19
483	Kemi BADENOCH	Conservative	Saffron Walden	2017–
484	Layla MORAN	Liberal Democrat	Oxford West and Abingdon	2017–
485	Karen LEE	Labour	Lincoln	2017–19
486	Sarah JONES	Labour	Croydon Central	2017–
487	Rosie DUFFIELD	Labour	Canterbury	2017–
488	Emma DENT COAD	Labour	Kensington	2017–19
489	Elisha McCALLION	Sinn Féin	Foyle	2017–19
490	Órfhlaith BEGLEY	Sinn Féin	West Tyrone	2018–
491	Janet DABY	Labour	Lewisham East	2018–
492	Ruth JONES	Labour	Newport West	2019–
493	Lisa FORBES	Labour	Peterborough	2019–2019
494	Jane DODDS	Liberal Democrat	Brecon and Radnorshire	2019–2019
495	Nickie AIKEN	Conservative	Cities of London and Westminster	2019–
496	Fleur ANDERSON	Labour	Putney	2019–
497	Sarah ATHERTON	Conservative	Wrexham	2019–
498	Siobhan BAILLIE	Conservative	Stroud	2019–
499	Paula BARKER	Labour	Liverpool, Wavertree	2019–
500	Apsana BEGUM	Labour	Poplar and Limehouse	2019–
501	Olivia BLAKE	Labour	Sheffield, Hallam	2019–
502	Sara BRITCLIFFE	Conservative	Hyndburn	2019–
503	Felicity BUCHAN	Conservative	Kensington	2019–
504	Amy CALLAGHAN	SNP	East Dunbartonshire	2019–

505	Miriam CATES	Conservative	Penistone and Stocksbridge	2019–
506	Wendy CHAMBERLAIN	Liberal Democrat	North East Fife	2019–
507	Feryal CLARK	Labour	Enfield North	2019–
508	Theo CLARKE	Conservative	Stafford	2019–
509	Daisy COOPER	Liberal Democrat	St Albans	2019–
510	Claire COUTINHO	Conservative	East Surrey	2019–
511	Virginia CROSBIE	Conservative	Ynys Môn	2019–
512	Alex DAVIES-JONES	Labour	Pontypridd	2019–
513	Dehenna DAVISON	Conservative	Bishop Auckland	2019–
514	Sarah DINES	Conservative	Derbyshire Dales	2019–
515	Ruth EDWARDS	Conservative	Rushcliffe	2019–
516	Natalie ELPHICKE	Conservative	Dover	2019–
517	Florence ESHALOMI	Labour	Vauxhall	2019–
518	Laura FARRIS	Conservative	Newbury	2019–
519	Katherine FLETCHER	Conservative	South Ribble	2019–
520	Mary FOY	Labour	City of Durham	2019–
521	Jo GIDEON	Conservative	Stoke-on-Trent Central	2019–
522	Kate GRIFFITHS	Conservative	Burton	2019–
523	Claire HANNA	SDLP	Belfast South	2019–
524	Sally-Ann HART	Conservative	Hastings and Rye	2019–
525	Rachel HOPKINS	Labour	Luton South	2019–
526	Jane HUNT	Conservative	Loughborough	2019–
527	Kim JOHNSON	Labour	Liverpool, Riverside	2019–
528	Fay JONES	Conservative	Brecon and Radnorshire	2019–
529	Alicia KEARNS	Conservative	Rutland and Melton	2019–

530	Carla LOCKHART	DUP	Upper Bann	2019–
531	Cherilyn MACKRORY	Conservative	Truro and Falmouth	2019–
532	Julie MARSON	Conservative	Hertford and Stortford	2019–
533	Joy MORRISSEY	Conservative	Beaconsfield	2019–
534	Holly MUMBY-CROFT	Conservative	Scunthorpe	2019–
535	Charlotte NICHOLS	Labour	Warrington North	2019–
536	Lia NICI	Conservative	Great Grimsby	2019–
537	Abena OPPONG-ASARE	Labour	Erith and Thamesmead	2019–
538	Kate OSBORNE	Labour	Jarrow	2019–
539	Taiwo OWATEMI	Labour	Coventry North West	2019–
540	Sarah OWEN	Labour	Luton North	2019–
541	Bell RIBEIRO-ADDY	Labour	Streatham	2019–
542	Nicola RICHARDS	Conservative	West Bromwich East	2019–
543	Angela RICHARDSON	Conservative	Guildford	2019–
544	Selaine SAXBY	Conservative	North Devon	2019–
545	Jane STEVENSON	Conservative	Wolverhampton North East	2019–
546	Zarah SULTANA	Labour	Coventry South	2019–
547	Laura TROTT	Conservative	Sevenoaks	2019–
548	Suzanne WEBB	Conservative	Stourbridge	2019–
549	Claudia WEBBE	Labour	Leicester East	2019–
550	Nadia WHITTOME	Labour	Nottingham East	2019–
551	Munira WILSON	Liberal Democrat	Twickenham	2019–
552	Beth WINTER	Labour	Cynon Valley	2019–

Notes

1 Seats for women: 1919–31

1 Notes for an Equal Franchise Meeting, 8 March 1928. Nancy Astor Papers. Special Collections, University of Reading. MS1416/1/1/264,

2 'The Ladies' Gallery', Living Heritage, Parliament UK. Available at: www. parliament.uk/about/living-heritage/transformingsociety/electionsvoting/womenvote/overview/the-ladies-gallery/ [Accessed 4/10/18].

3 Arthur Gronno, 'The Woman MP', 1909, pp. 32–3.

4 HC Debs, vol. 110, c. 839, 23 October 1918.

5 Collis, *Nancy Astor: An informal biography* (New York, 1960), pp. 77–8.

6 *Western Morning News*, 4 November 1919.

7 Astor, *My Two Countries* (New York), p. 5.

8 Nancy Astor, Woman's Hour, BBC 1956.

9 Nancy Astor, BBC TV Interview, 7 October 1962.

10 *Edinburgh Evening News*, 4 April 1932.

11 Interview with Lady Jean Weatherall, Norah Runge's granddaughter, 19 May 2017.

12 Baroness Irene Ward Interview by Brian Harrison, LSE Women's Library, 8SUF/B/159, Tape 59, Box 1, Disc 33.

13 Interview with Dr Jacqui Turner, 25 January 2017.

14 Fort, Adrian, *Nancy: The Story of Lady Astor* (London, 2012), p. 132.

15 Harrison, Brian, 'Women in a men's house: the women M.P.s, 1919–1945', *The Historical Journal*, 29/3 (1986), pp. 623–54.

16 Notes from my political diary, by the Viscountess Astor, LSE Women's Library, 7BSH/5/1/1/1.

17 Nancy Astor to Millicent Fawcett, 15 June 1920, LSE Women's Library, 7MGF/A/1/210.

18 Wilkinson, Ellen, *Peeps at Politicians* (London, 1930), p. 103.

19 As referred to in Labour's 1918 manifesto.

20 Fort, Adrian, *Nancy*, p. 198.

21 Masters, Anthony, *Nancy Astor: A Life* (London, 1981), p. 225.

22 Notes from my political diary, by the Viscountess Astor, LSE Women's Library, 7BSH/5/1/1/1.

23 *The Times*, 24 September 1921.

24 Women's Hour 1956 interview with Nancy Astor.

25 Letter from Lord Astor to Mrs Wintringham, 16 November 1923. Nancy Astor Papers, Special Collections, University of Reading MS 1416/1/1/1747.

26 Nancy Astor Papers, Special Collections, University of Reading MS1416/1/2/62.

27 Panorama interview, with Nancy Astor, BBC, 1959.

28 *Manchester Guardian*, 2 December 1944.

29 HC Debs, vol. 148, cc466–7, 9 November 1921.

30 HC Debs, vol. 163, c.1759 et seq., 13 July 1923.

31 *Manchester Guardian*, 21 November 1927.

32 A term coined by Brian Harrison in Harrison, Brian, *Prudent Revolutionaries: Portraits of British feminists between the wars* (Oxford, 1987), p. 79.

33 Interview with Anne Jenkin, 24 May 2018.

34 Bondfield, Margaret, *A Life's Work* (London, 1948), p. 246.

35 Hamilton, Mary, *Margaret Bondfield* (London, 1924), p. 95.

36 Hamilton, *Margaret Bondfield*, p. 153.

37 Hamilton, *Margaret Bondfield*, p. 156.

38 Bondfield, *A Life's Work*, p. 245.

39 Bondfield, *A Life's Work*, p. 251.

40 The term was used in the eighteenth century to refer to a literary or intellectual woman, who perhaps might have worn blue worsted stockings rather than the more chic and fashionable black silk stockings. It developed an almost derogatory connotation.

41 Wilkinson, *Peeps at Politicians*, p. 26.

42 *Women's Leader*, 3 November. 1924. Nancy Astor Papers, Special Collections, University of Reading MS 1416/1/1/758.

43 HC Debs, vol. 149, c. 242, 10 December 1924.

44 Beers, Laura, *Red Ellen*, p. 131.

45 Vernon, Betty, *Ellen Wilkinson, 1891–1947* (London, 1982), p. 75.

46 Bartley, Paula, *Ellen Wilkinson: From Red Suffragist to Government Minister (Revolutionary Lives)* (London, 2014), p. 28.

47　*Daily Express*, 11 December 1924. People's History Museum LP/WI, Ellen Wilkinson Press Cuttings.

48　*Evening Standard*, 28 January 1926.

49　Beers, *Red Ellen*, p. 157.

50　*Sydney Morning Herald*, Obituary of Ellen Wilkinson.

51　*The Daily Herald*, 12 May 1929.

52　HC Debs, vol. 197, cc 1359–1475, 1 July 1926.

53　Pedersen, Susan, *Eleanor Rathbone and the Politics of Conscience*, (New Haven, 2004) p. 224.

54　Perry, Matt, '*Red Ellen' Wilkinson: Her Ideas, Movements and World* (Manchester, 2014), p. 3.

55　Beers, *Red Ellen*, p. 242.

56　In Wilkinson's novel, *The Division Bell Mystery*, a murder mystery set in the Commons, Wilkinson's fictional female MP (Gracie Richards) is often mistaken for a secretary or an MP's daughter. This still happens to women MPs today.

57　Interview with Mark Collins, 23 May 2018.

58　*John Bull*, 30 January 1932.

59　Wilkinson, Ellen, *The Division Bell Mystery* (London, 1932) p. 91.

60　Howell, David, 'Lawrence, (Arabella) Susan (1871–1947)', *Oxford Dictionary of National Biography*, Oxford University Press, 2004; online edn, May 2015.

61　*People*, 12 April 1925.

62　'A Lady in the House', *The Times*, 29 November 1919, p. 7.

63　HC Debs, vol. 245, c. 1710, 28 November 1930.

64　HC Debs, vol. 500, c. 1646, 22 Feb 1928.

65　Atholl, *Working Partnership* (London, 1958), p. 139.

66　Beers, *Red Ellen*, p. 135.

67　*Labour Magazine*, Feb 1924, Women's Library, LSE, London ILP/7/2/2.

68　*Evening Star*, 9 April 1937.

69　HC Debs, vol. 215, cc 1406–07, 29 March 1928.

70　HC Debs, vol. 125, c. 1631, 24 February 1920.

71　HC Debs, vol. 166, c. 1768, 13 July 1923.

72　HC Debs, vol. 171, c. 2660, 4 April 1924.

73　HC Debs, vol. 181, c. 541, 4 March 1925.

74　*Leeds Mercury*, 15 Dec. 1924. Labour Party Archive, People's History Museum, Manchester LP/W1/1.

75　HC Debs, vol. 180, cc 1500–1503, 20 February 1925.

76　HC Debs, vol. 215, c. 1415, 29 March 1928.

77   HC Debs, vol. 215, cc 1452–1453, 29 March 1928.

78   NUSEC annual report 1928. LSE Women's Library 2NSE/C/11.

79   Unnamed and undated newspaper clipping, The Open University, JL/4/2/1/7.

80   *Daily Record and Mail*, 10 March 1931, The Open University, JL/4/2/1/3.

81   Lee, Jennie, *This Great Journey* (London, 1963), p. 52.

82   *Manchester Guardian*, 23 March 1929.

83   Unnamed and undated newspaper clipping, The Open University, JL/4/2/2/2.

84   *The Wishaw Press and Advertise*, 29/03/1929, The Open University, JL/2/1/1/2.

85   HC Debs, vol. 215, cc1452–3, 29 March 1928.

86   A Parliamentary Private Secretary (PPS) is a backbench MP who is selected to assist a minister with their parliamentary duties, usually by being their 'eyes and ears' in Parliament. It is generally considered as the first rung on the ministerial ladder.

87   Wilkinson, *Peeps at Politicians*, p. 66.

88   Hetherington, S.J., *Katharine Atholl, 1874–1960: against the tide* (Aberdeen, 1989), p. 109.

89   Beers, *Red Ellen*, p. 222.

90   Hamilton, *Margaret Bondfield*, p. 164.

91   Bondfield, *A Life's Work*, p. 279.

92   HC Debs, vol. 237, c. 856, 28 March 1930.

93   Bondfield, *A Life's Work*, pp. 276–7.

2 Women at war: 1931–45

1   HC Debs, vol. 365, c. 1932, 19 November 1940.

2   November 1933 Conservative pamphlet, 'From Chaos to Confidence: A great record', Nancy Astor Papers, Special Collections, University of Reading MS1416/1/1/1041.

3   *Evening Standard*, 9 February 1932.

4   Cited in Langley, Helen (2015) 'Irene Ward MP (1895–1980), doughty parliamentarian and campaigner', Speaker's Advisory Committee on Works of Art, International Women's Day Lecture.

5   *Sunday Chronicle*, 17 April 1932.

6   *The Daily Mail*, 16 December 1933.

7   HC Debs, vol. 317, c. 15, 3 November 1936.

8   *Morning Post*, 4 November 1936, Churchill Archive Centre, Horsbrugh
    Papers, HSBR 1/3.

9   *The National*, 4 November 1936, Churchill Archive Centre, Horsbrugh
    Papers, HSBR 1/3.

10 HC Debs, vol. 314, c. 1269, 8 July 1936.

11 Wilkinson, Ellen, *The Town that was Murdered: The Life-Story of Jarrow*
    (London, 1939), p. 283.

12 *The Labour Woman*, Mar./Apr. 1947.

13 HC Debs, vol. 317, c. 1024, 12 November 1936; HC Debs, vol. 317, c. 1895,
    19 November 1936.

14 *Evening Express*, 10 November 1922. University of Liverpool, Eleanor
    Rathbone Papers, RP XIV.3.90.

15 Quoted in Rathbone, Eleanor, *The Case For Family Allowances*
    (Harmondsworth, 1940), p. 101.

16 *The Guardian*, 21 December 1940.

17 Pedersen, *Eleanor Rathbore and the Politics of Conscience*, p. 223

18 Ministry of Information poll, 1943.

19 HC Debs, vol. 380, cc 1876–78, 23 June 1942.

20 HC Debs, vol. 380, c. 1913, 23 June 1942.

21 HC Debs, vol. 404, c. 1123, 3 November 1944.

22 HC Debs, vol. 408, c. 2326, 8 March 1945.

23 HC Debs, vol. 408, c. 2268, 8 March 1945.

24 HC Debs, vol. 408, c. 2283, 8 March 1945.

25 'A most independent member: Eleanor Rathbone MP', *Vote 100*. Available at:
    www.parliament.uk/documents/parliamentary-archives/Curators-Eleanor-
    Rathbone-Exhibition-Leaflet.pdf [Accessed 12/09/18].

26 HC Debs, vol. 301, c. 638, 2 May 1935.

27 HC Debs, vol. 314, c. 1270, 8 July 1936.

28 *Daily Mirror*, 4 September 1935.

29 HC Debs, vol. 339, c. 360, 5 October 1938.

30 Letter from Chamberlain to his sister, 25 June 1938. Cited in Fort, p. 260.

31 Nancy Astor Papers, Special Collections, University of Reading,
    MS1416/1/1/1585–1591.

32 Letter from Mary Downes, 29 April 1938, Astor Papers MS1416/1/1/1585.

33 Notes for a speech on the National Government, Astor Papers MS
    1416/1/1/1041.

34 Interview with Viscount William Astor, 24 January 2017.

35 Gottlieb, Julie, *'Guilty Women', Foreign Policy, and Appeasement in Inter-war
    Britain* (Basing-Stoke, 2015), 200; 'Pale Cast of Thought', *Manchester
    Guardian*, 4 November 1938.

36 Gottlieb, '*Guilty Women*', *Foreign Policy, and Appeasement in Inter-war Britain* (Basing-Stoke, 2015), p. 200, 244.

37 Dalton, Hugh, *The Fateful Years* (London, 1957), p. 108.

38 HC Debs, vol. 318, c. 1114, 1 December 1936.

39 'British Women MPs under Fire', *The Times,* 19 April 1937.

40 Referring to Dolores Ibárruri, a Spanish anti-fascist woman known in Spain as 'La Pasionara' whom Wilkinson and Atholl met.

41 Bartley, Paula, *Ellen Wilkinson: From Red Suffragist to Government Minister (Revolutionary Lives)*, p. 81.

42 Atholl to EFR, 23 April 1933; EFR to Atholl, 27 April 1933. University of Liverpool Special Collections, Rathbone Papers, Dec. 2002 accession (being catalogued).

43 Beers, *Red Ellen*, p. 361.

44 Cazalet-Keir, Thelma, *From the Wings* (London, 1967), p. 139.

45 Bew, John, *Citizen Clem: A Biography of Attlee* (London, 2017), p. 241.

46 HC Debs, vol. 332, c. 736, 28 February 1938.

47 HC Debs, vol. 351, c. 50, 24 August 1939.

48 Harrison, '*Women in a men's house*', p. 648.

49 HC Debs, vol. 351, c. 50, 24 August 1939.

50 Eleanor Rathbone to Churchill, 10 September 1938, from Garthdale. Churchill Archive Centre, Churchill Papers, CHAR 2/331/60.

51 *Manchester Guardian*, 25 February 1939.

52 Ball, Stuart, 'The Politics of Appeasement: The Fall of the Duchess of Atholl and the Kinross and West Perth By-Election, December 1938', *The Scottish Historical Review*, 69, (1990), p. 49.

53 Gottlieb, '*Guilty women*', Foreign Policy, and Appeasement in Inter-war Britain (Basing-Stoke, 2015), p. 226.

54 Gottlieb, '*Guilty women*', Foreign Policy, and Appeasement in Inter-war Britain (Basing-Stoke, 2015), pp. 225–6.

55 Pedersen, *Eleanor Rathbone and the Politics of Conscience*, p. 294.

56 'Labour Majority of 4,200', *Manchester Guardian*, 8 November 1938.

57 HC Debs, vol. 343, c. 1472, 13 February 1939.

58 'A summary of the refugee problem', by Eleanor Rathbone, 1940, p. 6. LSE Women's Library, 5BFW/11/04/05, Box 84.

59 *Daily Herald*, 5 September 1938.

60 *The Observer*, 9 February 1947.

61 'German Atrocities 1945', British Pathé. Available at: www.britishpathe.com/video/german-atrocities/query/mavis+tate [Accessed 12/09/18].

62 Harrison, Brian, '*Women in a men's house*', p. 639.

63 Quoted in Vernon, Betty, *Ellen Wilkinson, 1891–1947* (London, 1982), 184.

64 *Daily Telegraph*, 15 July 1939. Churchill Archive Centre, Horsbrugh Papers, HSBR 2/10.

65 HC Debs, vol. 357, cc. 1413–4, 21 February 1940.

66 HC Debs, vol. 378, cc 873–4, 5 March 1942.

67 HC Debs, vol. 372, c. 259, 11 June 1941.

68 *Sunday Graphic and Sunday News*, 30 July 1939. Churchill Archive Centre, Horsbrugh Papers, HSBR 2/10.

69 *Tribune*, 24 May 1940.

70 Beers, *Red Ellen*, p. 387.

71 Hollis, Patricia, *Jennie Lee: a life* (Oxford, 1998), p. 152.

72 *Western Morning News*, 9 August 1943.

73 *Nottingham Evening Post*, 15 October 1940.

74 Beers, *Red Ellen*, p. 106.

75 *News Chronicle*, 30 October 1941.

76 *Birmingham Gazette*, 5 November 1942.

77 *Western Daily News*, 7 March 1941.

78 The title of a pamphlet produced by Edith Summerskill in 1941 encouraging women into war work.

79 Mass-Observation. *The Journey Home*, 1944, p. 58.

80 Dame Irene Ward interview by Brian Harrison at House of Lords, 6 July 1977. LSE Women's Library, 8SUF/B/159.

81 Cazalet-Keir, *From the wings*, p. 127.

82 Cazalet-Keir, *From the wings*, p. 127.

83 PRO LAB 26/59, Wilkinson to Bevin, 3 July 1940. Cited in Smith, Harold L., 'The Womanpower Problem in Britain during the Second World War', *The Historical Journal*, 27/4 (1984), p. 930.

84 PRO LAB 26/59, Ethel Wood to Ernest Bevin, 11 January 1941. Cited in Smith, p. 928.

85 HC Debs, vol. 370, cc 315–400, 20 March 1941.

86 Interview with Shirley Summerskill, 9 November 2017.

87 HC Debs, vol. 378, c. 848, 5 March 1942.

88 HC Debs, vol. 373, c. 2096, 7 August 1941.

89 Parliamentary Archives, HC/CL/CO/AA/AI/1/01, Fighting Services, 13 January 1942.

90 Brookes, Pamela, *Women at Westminster: An Account of Women in the British Parliament 1918–1966* (London, 1967), p. 140.

91 Dame Irene Ward interview by Brian Harrison at House of Lords, 6 July 1977. LSE Women's Library, 8SUF/B/159.

92 HC Debs, vol. 307, c. 619, 9 December 1935.

93 Cazalet-Keir, *From the wings*, p. 123.

94 *The New York Times*, 2 December 1944.

95 Plymouth Papers 1944–1945, Nancy Astor Papers, Special Collections, University of Reading. MS 1416/1/2/30.

96 Fort, Nancy, p. 301.

97 *The Daily Telegraph*, 16 June 1934.

98 HC Debs, vol. 408, c. 2332, 8 March 1945.

99 Copy of the Address by The Right Hon. Sir Arthur Salter, M.P. on the occasion of the Memorial Service to Miss Eleanor Rathbone, M.P. University of Liverpool, Eleanor Rathbone papers, RP XIV.5.84.

3 Let us face the future: 1945–59

1   Election address headline, Bill, Ron and Newens, Stan, *Leah Manning* (Harlow, 1991), p. 49.

2   The Labour Party, Report of the Forty-Fourth Annual Conference, 1945.

3   Interview with Baroness Helen Liddell, 11 September 2017.

4   Interview with Baroness Patricia Hollis, 4 December 2017.

5   Mann, Jean, *Woman in Parliament*, (London, 1962), p. 11.

6   Castle, Barbara, *Fighting All The Way*, (London, 1993), p. 126.

7   Castle, *Fighting All the Way* p. 126.

8   Manning, Leah, *A Life for Education*, (London, 1970), p. 205.

9   Brookes, Pamela, *Women at Westminister*, p. 191.

10 Hollis, Patricia, *Jennie Lee*, p. 121.

11 Summerskill, Edith, A Woman's World: Her Memoirs (Heinemann, 1967), p. 61.

12 Mann, *Woman in Parliament*, p. 10.

13 Mann, *Woman in Parliament*, p. 11.

14 Manning, *A Life for Education*, pp. 202–03.

15 HC Debs, vol. 530, c. 1429, 21 July 1954.

16 *The Yorkshire Post*, 1950.

17 Mann, Woman in Parliament, p. 18.

18 *The Manchester Guardian*, 15 February 1946.

19 Mann, Woman in Parliament, p. 37.

20 Mann, Woman in Parliament, p. 36.

21 Jeger, Lena, 'The Missing Women', draft essay (1972). Jeger papers, LSE Women's Library, JEGER 6/36.

22 Summerskill, *A Woman's World: Her Memoirs*, p. 139.

23 Jeger, Lena, 'The Missing Women', draft essay (1972). Jeger papers, LSE Women's Library, JEGER 6/36.

24 *Cannock Courier*, 27 January 1950, 3, 17, 24 February 1950.

25 Hollis, *Jennie Lee*, p. 172.

26 The Labour Party Report on the 42nd Annual Conference, 1943.

27 See Conservative MP Sir Arnold Grindley speaking in HC Debs, vol. 404, cc 1151–2, 3 November 1944.

28 You can watch her speech here: www.unesco.org/archives/multimedia/? pg=34&prs=Ellen+Wilkinson [Accessed 04/09/17].

29 *New York Times*, 7 February 1947.

30 Cabinet Minutes, Thursday, August 23, 1945, 11:00am, The National Archives, London, CAB 128/1/8.

31 Beers, *Red Ellen*, 423. Eleanor Rathbone's family motto, 'What ought to be done, can be done' comes to mind.

32 Summerskill, *A Woman's World*, p. 107.

33 Hennessy, Peter. *Never Again: Britain 1945–51*. (London, 1992), p. 162.

34 Attlee Papers, Bodleian Library, University of Oxford, MS. Attlee dep. 23, fols 171–2.

35 Economic Survey for 1947: Proposed postponement of the raising of the school leaving age, 14 January 1947. The National Archives, London, CAB/129/16/29.

36 *Manchester Guardian*, 7 February 1947.

37 Summerskill, *A Woman's World*, p. 59.

38 Gillard, Derek. *Food for Thought: Child nutrition, the school dinner and the food industry* (2003).

39 Crosland, Anthony, *The future of socialism*, (London, 1956), p. 258.

40 Mann, *Woman in Parliament*, p. 40.

41 London – Ellen Wilkinson (1947), British Pathé. Available at: www.youtube.com/watch?v=j-cFuHo4WD4 [Accessed 15/06/17].

42 Cabinet Minutes, Thursday, 6 February 1947, 11:00am, The National Archives, London, CAB 128/9/17.

43 Mann, *Woman in Parliament*, p. 12.

44 Interview with Baroness Patricia Hollis, 4 December 2017.

45 Jennie Lee interview by Sue McGregor, Woman's Hour, 13 November 1980.

46 Brookes, Pamela, 181–183.

47 HC Debs, vol. 498, c. 248, 25 March 1952.

48 HC Debs, vol. 498, cc 264–5, 25 March 1952.

49 *The Sunday Times*, 3 February 1952.

50 Interview with Ben Summerskill, 6 December 2017.

51 HC Debs, vol. 338, c. 3402, 28 July 1938.

52 Interview with Ben Summerskill, 6 December 2017.

53 Interview with Ben Summerskill, 6 December 2017.

54 HC Debs, vol. 342, c. 1704, 12 December 1938.

55 The Labour Party, Report of the Forty-Second Annual Conference, 1943; Report of the Forty-Fourth Annual Conference, 1945.

56 Hollis, *Jennie Lee*, p. 169.

57 The Labour Party, Report of the Forty-Second Annual Conference, 1943.

58 Zweiniger-Bargielowska, Ina, 'Rationing, Austerity and the Conservative Party Recovery after 1945', *The Historical Journal*, 37/1 (1994), p. 179.

59 HC Debs, vol. 450, c. 1722, 10 May 1948; HC Debs vol. 473, c. 17, 27 March 1950.

60 HC Debs, vol. c. 16, 21 October 1947.

61 HC Debs, vol. 498, c. 130W, 2 April 1952; HC Debs, vol. 516, c. 967, 17 June 1953; HC Debs, vol. 498, c. 1197, 31 March 1952; HC Debs vol. 547, c. 12, 5 December 1955.

62 HC Debs vol. 547, c. 12, 5 December 1955.

63 Mann, *Woman in Parliament*, p. 17.

64 Summerskill, *A Woman's World*, p. 96.

65 Summerskill, *A Woman's World*, p. 92.

66 Brookes, *Woman at Westminster*, p. 161.

67 Mann, *Woman in Parliament*, p. 16.

68 HC Debs, vol. 457, c. 1552, 10 November 1948.

69 Castle, *Fighting All The Way*, p. 136.

70 Toole, Millie, *Bessie Braddock M.P.*, (London, 1957), p. 143.

71 C.R.D., *All the answers*, second edn, April 1949.

72 *Home Truths*, February 1951.

73 Zweiniger-Bargielowska, 'Rationing, Austerity and the Conservative Party Recovery after 1945', p. 181.

74 The Labour Party Report of the 44th Annual Conference, 1945, 79.

75 HC Debs, vol. 523, c.1974, 17 February 1954.

76 HC Debs, vol. 546, c. 1465, 23 November 1955.

77 HC Debs, vol. 546, c. 1556, 23 November 1955.

78 HC Debs, vol. 551, c. 1108, 18 April 1956.

79 HC Debs, vol. 598, c. 1267, 29 January 1959.

80 HC Debs, vol. 598, c. 1320, 29 January 1959.

81 HC Debs, vol. 598, c. 1267, 29 January 1959.

82 HC Debs, vol. 598, c. 1322, 29 January 1959.

4 Stilettos and springboards: 1959–70

1   Jeger Papers, LSE Women's Library, JEGER 6/36.

2   Williams, Shirley, *Climbing the Bookshelves*, (London, 2009 & 2010),
    p. 147.

3   *The Times*, 28 May 1962.

4   *The Sunday Express*, 1960.

5   Ridge, Sophy, *The Women who Shaped Politics* (London, 2017), p. 142.

6   Interview with Shirley Summerskill, 9 November 2017.

7   HC Debs, vol. 620, 31 March 1960, c. 1648.

8   Castle, *Fighting All The Way*, p. 127.

9   HC Debs, vol. 618, c. 20, 23 February 1960.

10 HC Debs, vol. 620, c. 1533, 31 March 1960.

11 HC Debs, vol. 620, c. 1546, 31 March 1960.

12 Brookes, *Women at Westminster*, p. 217.

13 Campbell, John, *The Iron Lady: Margaret Thatcher*, (London, 2012), p. 44.

14 Perkins, *Red Queen: The Authorized Biography of Barbara Castle* (London,
    2003), pp. 177–179.

15 Mann, *Woman in Parliament*, p. 31.

16 HC Debs, vol. 616, c. 1358, 5 February 1960.

17 Black, Amy and Brooke, Stephen, The Labour Party, Women, and the
    Problem of Gender, 1951–1966', *Journal of Political Studies* 36 (1997), 436.

18 Notes on headed note paper, Jeger papers, LSE Women's Library, JEGER
    6/36.

19 Brooke, Stephen, *Sexual Politics: Sexuality, Family Planning, and the British
    Left from the 1880s to the Present Day* (Oxford, 2011), p. 165.

20 Ibid.

21 HC Debs, vol. 724, c. 293, 17 February 1966.

22 ALRA, May 1965, Wellcome Collection, SA/ALR/A.15/19.

23 HC Debs, vol. 795, c. 985, 9 February 1970.

24 Brookes, *women at westminster*, p. 236.

25 Castle, *Fighting All The Way*, p. 164.

26 Manning, *A Life for Education*, p. 166.

27 Castle, Barbara. *Fighting All The Way*, p. 62.

28 Currie, Edwina, 'Dame Irene Ward', in Dale, Iain and Smith, Jacqui (eds), The Honourable Ladies: Volume I: Profiles of Women MPs 1918–1996. London: Biteback, 99.

29 Perkins, Anne, *Red Queen*, p. 356.

30 Jenkins, Roy, *A Life at the Centre*, (London, 1991), p. 226.

31 Crossman, Richard, *The Diaries of a cabinet minister, Volume 1: minister of housing, 1964–66* (London, 1975), 14 November 1965.

32 Castle, *Fighting All The Way*, pp. 163–4.

33 Castle, Barbara, The Castle Diaries 1969–1970 (London, 1984), 21 December 1965.

34 Despite the previous attempts of Michael Foot, a close friend of hers, to teach her.

35 Castle, *Fighting All The Way*, p. 365.

36 Letter from Mrs Mildred K Brown 23 December 1963, Castle Papers, Bodleian Library, MS Castle 262.

37 Wilson, Harold, *The Labour Government 1964–1970: A Personal Record*. (London, 1971), p. 191.

38 BBC interview, 1 October 1967.

39 Castle, *Fighting All The Way*, p. 375.

40 Fighting All the Way, Castle p. 375.

41 Letter from Joan Wake, 7 May 1968, Castle Papers, Bodleian Library, Castle 267.

42 HC Debs, vol. 724, c. 745, 10 February 1966.

43 Castle, *Fighting All The Way*, p. 388.

44 Phillips, Melanie, *The Divided House: Women at Westminster* (London, 1980), p. 160.

45 *London Daily Telegraph*, 8 October 1964.

46 *Evening Standard*, 7 September 1959.

47 Castle, *Fighting All The Way*, p. 398.

48 Wilson, The Labour Goverment (1964–1970): A Personal Record, p. 521.

49 Letter from Harriet Slater 6 April 1968, Castle Papers, Bodleian Library, MS Castle 267.

50 Letter dated 7 April 1968, Castle Papers, Bodleian Library, MS Castle 267.

51 Perkins, *Red Queen*, p. 262.

52 Castle reply to Leah Manning, Castle Papers, Bodleian Library, MS Castle 267.

53 Castle, The Castle Diaries 1964–1970, 5 April 1968.

54 Perkins, *Red Queen*, p. 296.

55 *Daily Telegraph*, 1 May 1970.

56 HC Debs, vol. 779, c. 41, 3 March 1969.

57 Perkins, *Red Queen*, p. 267.

58 Perkins, *Red Queen*, p. 98.

59 Perkins, *Red Queen*, p. 99.

60 Pimlott, Ben, *Harold Wilson*, (London, 1992), p. 337.

61 Crossman, Richard, *The Diaries of a cabinet minister, Volume 3: secretary of state for Social Services, 1968–70* (London, 1977), 3 July 1969.

62 Letter from Joan Lestor, 5 May 1969. Castle Papers, Bodleian Library, MS Castle 274.

63 Castle, *Fighting All The Way*, p. 420.

64 Wilson, *The Labour Government 1964–1970*,p. 662.

65 Hollis, Jennie Lee, p. 252.

66 *Times Educational Supplement*, 19 September 1969.

67 Hollis, Jennie Lee, p. 251.

68 *The Sunday Times*, 20 February 1966.

69 Hollis, Jennie Lee, 278; HC Debs, vol. 725, 3 March 1966, c. 1477.

70 Weinbren, Daniel, *The Open University: A History* (Manchester, 2015), pp. 6–7.

71 The Independent Labour Party (ILP) was founded in 1893 by Keir Hardie and established the Labour Representation Committee in 1900, which subsequently became the Labour Party in 1906. The ILP was affiliated with the Labour Party from 1906 to 1932, but its MPs tended to be more left-wing than their Labour colleagues.

72 HC Debs, vol. 709, 2 April 1965, c. 2062.

73 Hollis, Jennie Lee, p. 317.

74 HC Debs, vol. 776, c. 1513, 30 January 1969.

75 Hollis, Jennie Lee, p. viii.

76 Weinbren, The Open University, p. 50.

77 Weinbren, The Open University, p. 51.

78 Hollis, Jennie Lee, p. 321.

79 HC Debs, vol. 795, cc 613–4, 5 February 1970.

80 Letter from Jennie Lee to Frank Soskice, 18 August 1970, Parliamentary Archives, STH/FS/1/LEE.

81 HL Debs, vol. 361, c. 969, 18 June 1975.

82 Hollis, Jennie Lee, p. 303.

83 Hollis, Jennie Lee, p. 305.

84 HC Debs, vol. 795, c. 614, 5 February 1970.

85 HC Debs, vol. 732, c. 1877, 28 July 1966.

86 HC Debs, vol. 795, c. 975, 9 February 1970.

87 Lena Jeger notes for a *New Statesman* article on equal pay. Jeger Papers, LSE Women's Library, JEGER/6/13.

88   Cazalet-Keir to Churchill, 6 March 1949, Cazalet-Keir Papers, LSE Women's Library.

89   This is the Road: The Conservative and Unionist Party's Policy, 1950.

90   Summerskill, Edith, *Letters to my daughter* (London, 1986), p. 138.

91   HC Debs, vol. 524, c. 1911, 9 March 1954.

92   HC Debs, vol. 524, cc 1909–11, 9 March 1954.

93   R.A. Butler to Florence Horsbrugh, 20 March 1954, PRO, T 171/439. Cited in Smith, Harold L., 'The Politics of Conservative Reform: The Equal Pay for Equal Work Issue, 1945–1955', *The Historical Journal*, 35/2 (1992), p. 412.

94   Butler to Iain Macleod, 20 March 1954, PRO, T 171/439 (vol III of 1954 Budget). Cited in Smith, 'The Politics of Conservative Reform', p. 414.

95   *News Chronicle*, 8 April 1954.

96   Article by Lena Jeger on equal pay. *The Scottish Monthly Business Review*, September 1968, pp. 26–8.

97   Castle, *Fighting All the Way*, p. 427.

98   Wilson, *The Labour Government* 1964–1970, p. 623.

99   Cohen, Sheila, 'Equal pay – or what? Economics, politics and the 1968 Ford sewing machinists' strike', *Labor History*, 53/1(2012), p. 56.

100 HC Debs, vol. 795, c. 918, 9 February 1970.

101 HC Debs, vol. 795, c. 914, 9 February 1970.

102 See Cohen, 'Equal pay – or what? and Castle, *Fighting All The Way*, p. 409.

103 HC Debs, vol. 795, c. 971, 9 February 1970.

104 Ridge, The Women Who Shaped Politics, p. 117.

105 HC Debs, vol. 795, c. 975, 9 February 1970.

106 Letter from Shirley Williams to Barbara Castle, 17 April 1976. Castle Archives, MS Castle 262.

107 Perkins, *Red Queen*, pp. 377, 378, 379.

108 Leapman, Michael, 'Mrs Castle chides Women's Lib in US' *The Times*, 16 February 1972, p. 8.

109 Hennessy, Peter and Shepherd, Robert, *Reflections: Conversations with politicians* (London, 2016), p. 55.

110 Barbara Castle diary (unpublished), 3 July 1976.

111 Martineau, Lisa, *Politics & Power: Barbara Castle – A Biography* (London, 2000), pp. 315–16.

5 Leaders and losses: 1970–79

1   Letter from Shirley Williams to Barbara Castle, 17 April 1976. Castle Papers, Bodleian Library, MS Castle 262.

2   Betty Harvie Anderson (1913–79) was a Conservative MP for East Renfrewshire 1959–79. She was made a life peer in 1979 and died within a week of her introduction to the House of Lords as Baroness Skrimshire of Quarter.

3   *Sunday Graphic*, 17 February 1952.

4   Young & Sloeman, *The Thatcher Phenomenon* (London, 986), p. 17.

5   Charles Moore, *Margaret Thatcher: The Authorized Biography – Volume One* (London, 2013) p. 5; David Cannadine, *Margaret Thatcher: A Life and Legacy* (Oxford, 2017), p. 12.

6   Moore, *Margaret Thatcher*, p. 9.

7   Cannadine, *Margaret Thatcher*, p. 5.

8   Haessly, Katie, 'British Conservative women MPs and "women's issues" 1950–1979'. PhD thesis, University of Nottingham (2010), pp. 44–7.

9   Moore, *Margaret Thatcher*, p. 135.

10 Cannadine, *Margaret* Thatcher, p. 16.

11 Thatcher, Margaret, *The Path to Power*, (London, 1995), p. 166.

12 Moore, *Margaret Thatcher*, p. 218.

13 Moore, *Margaret Thatcher*, p. 223.

14 Cannadine, *Margaret Thatcher*, p. 18.

15 *Daily Mail*, 9 March 1974.

16 BBC2 Argument, 21 March 1974.

17 Smith Wilson, Dolly, 'Gender: Change and Continuity' in Addison and Jones (eds) *A Companion to Contemporary Britain 1939–2000* (Oxford, 2005), p. 254.

18 Gregg P., Gutierrez-Domenech M., & Waldfogel J., 'The Employment of Married Mothers in Great Britain, 1974–2000', *Economica*, 74 (296) (November 2007), pp. 843–64.

19 Boothroyd, Betty, *The Autobiography* (London, 2001), p. 92.

20 Reeves, Rachel, *Alice in Westminster: the Political Life of Alice Bacon* (London, 2017), p. 80.

21 Boothroyd, *The Autobiography*, p. 33.

22 Boothroyd, *The Autobiography*, pp. 34, 35.

23 Interview with Betty Boothroyd, 16 May 2018.

24 Boothroyd, *The Autobiography*, p. 26.

25 Boothroyd, *The Autobiography*, p. xiv.

26 Boothroyd, *The Autobiography*, p. 98.

27 Boothroyd, *The Autobiography*, pp. 99–102.

28 Joyce Gould, 'Jo Richardson' in Iain Dale & Jacqui Smith, *The Honourable Ladies, Vol. 1* (London, 2018), pp. 350–5.

29 Hennessy and Shepherd, *Reflections: Conversations with Politicians*, pp. 91, 92, 93.

30 Hennessy & Shepherd, *Reflections*, pp. 186, 188.

31 Hennessy & Shepherd, *Reflections*, pp. 193, 194.

32 Interview with Margaret Beckett, 5 September 2018.

33 Williams, *Climbing the Bookshelves*, p. 234, 237.

34 Interview with Steve Hart, 2 October 2017.

35 Interview with Steve Hart, 2 October 2017.

36 'Explosive device sent to Mrs Judith Hart', *The Times* (22 January 1972).

37 Benn, Tony, *The Benn Diaries 1940–1990* (London, 2005), p. 301.

38 Interview with Steve Hart, 2 October 2017.

39 Williams, *Climbing the Bookshelves*, p. 190.

40 Williams, *Climbing the Bookshelves*, p. 203.

41 Hennessy & Shepherd, *Reflections*, p. 25.

42 Interview with Shirley Summerskill, 9 November 2017.

43 Williams, *Climbing the Bookshelves*, pp. 212, 213.

44 Williams, *Climbing the Bookshelves*, pp. 214, 215.

45 Williams, *Climbing the Bookshelves*, pp. 225, 226.

46 Williams, *Climbing the Bookshelves*, pp. 237, 238.

47 Williams, *Climbing the Bookshelves*, p. 227.

48 Moore, *Margaret Thatcher*, pp. 254, 255.

49 Moore, *Margaret Thatcher*, p. 271.

50 Birkett, Peter, 'Margaret lifts the lid off her larder', *Daily Express*, 29 November 1974.

51 Interview with Shirley Summerskill, 9 November 2017.

52 Williams, *Climbing the Bookshelves*, p. 148.

53 Remarks on becoming prime minister (St Francis's prayer), Margaret Thatcher Foundation.

54 Cannadine, *Margaret Thatcher*, p. 5.

55 Women MPs and parliamentary candidates since 1945, UK Political Info database.

6 Paths to power: 1979–97

1 Harman, Harriet, *A Woman's Work* (London, 2017), p. 103.

2 Hennessy, Peter, *The prime minister: The Office and Its Holders Since 1945* (London, 2001), p. 400.

3   Interview with Kenneth Harris, *Observer*, 25 February 1979. Cited in Hennessy, *The prime minister*, p. 401.

4   Hennessy, *The prime minister*, p. 401.

5   Hennessy, *The prime minister*, p. 402.

6   Slocock, Caroline, *People Like Us: Margaret Thatcher and Me* (London, 2018), pp. 160, 189; interview with Caroline Slocock, 4 September 2018.

7   Slocock, *People Like Us*, p. 60; interview with Caroline Slocock, 4 September 2018.

8   Cannadine, *Margaret Thatcher*, p. 37.

9   Hennessy, *The prime minister*, p. 397.

10 Hennessy, *The prime minister*, p. 402.

11 Ball, Simon, 'British Defence Policy' in Addison, Paul & Jones, Harriet (eds.) *A Companion to Contemporary Britain 1939–2000* (Oxford 2005), p. 546.

12 Hennessy, *The prime minister*, pp. 413, 415.

13 Hennessy, *The prime minister*, p. 416.

14 HC Debs, vol 21, c. 644, 3 March 1982.

15 TV Interview for ITN (Falklands) 5 April 1982. Transcript available via the Margaret Thatcher Foundation – www.margaretthatcher.org/document/104913 [accessed 4 April 2018].

16 HC Debs, vol 21, c. 1000, 7 April 1982.

17 HL Debs, vol 429, cc 316–17, 14 April 1982.

18 HC Debs, vol 22, c. 1014, 29 April 1982.

19 HC Debs, vol 24, cc 513–14, 20 May 1982.

20 HL Debs, vol 430, c. 826, 20 May 1982.

21 'No Deal!', *The Sun*, 13 April 1982; 'Maggie Digs Her Heels In', *Daily Mail*, 13 April 1982.

22 'Whatever I go through now can't be as terrible', *Women's Own*, 28 August 1982.

23 Moore, *Margaret Thatcher*, pp. 666–7.

24 Cannadine, *Margaret Thatcher*, p. 49.

25 Thatcher, Margaret, *The Downing Street Years* (London, 1993), p. 307; 'Profile: Baroness Young' BBC News, 29 November 2000.

26 Langdon, Julia, 'Obituary: Lady Young of Farnworth', *The Guardian*, 7 September 2002.

27 TV Interview for Thames TV, *CBTV* (children's television), 13 December 1982. Transcript available at www.margaretthatcher.org/document/105071 [Accessed 4 April 2018].

28 Murray, Jenni, 'What did Margaret Thatcher do for women?', *The Guardian*, 9 April 2013.

29 Interview with Gillian Shephard, 6 June 2018.

30 Interview with Lynda Chalker, 12 November 2018.

31 Interview with Harriet Harman, 26 July 2018.

32 Grice, E., 'Gillian Shephard: Maggie Thatcher didn't rate me at all!' *The Daily Telegraph*, 17 March 2013.

33 Currie, Edwina, *Diaries 1987–1992* (London, 2002), pp. 108, 118.

34 Interview with Gillian Shephard, 6 June 2018.

35 Interview with Gillian Shephard, 6 June 2018.

36 Interview with Gillian Shephard, 6 June 2018.

37 Interview with Gillian Shephard, 6 June 2018.

38 White, Peter, 'Virginia Bottomley: my passion for Island', *Island Life Magazine*, 1 October 2012.

39 Harman, *A Woman's Work*, p. 45.

40 Harman, *A Woman's Work*, p. 64.

41 Harman, *A Woman's Work*, p. 66.

42 Harman, *A Woman's Work*, p. 102.

43 Harman, *A Woman's Work*, p. 103; interview with Harriet Harman, 26 July 2018.

44 Interview with Helene Hayman, 13 November 2017.

45 Ewan E L., Innes S., Reynolds S., & Pipes R. (eds.) *The Biographical Dictionary of Scottish Women* (Edinburgh, 2006), p. 51.

46 Williams, *Climbing the Bookshelves*, pp. 152–3.

47 Interview with Ann Taylor (Baroness Taylor of Bolton), 5 June 2018.

48 Harman, *A Woman's Work*, p. 89.

49 Goodwin, Stephen, 'Inside Parliament: Woman MP gives "facts of life" to inquiry on working mothers', *The Independent*, 16 March 1994.

50 Interview with Diane Abbott, 27 February 2018.

51 Interview with Harriet Harman, 26 July 2018.

52 Williams, *Climbing the Bookshelves*, pp. 255, 256.

53 Williams, *Climbing the Bookshelves*, p. 261.

54 Williams, *Climbing the Bookshelves*, p. 300.

55 Williams, *Climbing the Bookshelves*, p. 281.

56 Williams, *Climbing the Bookshelves*, p. 282.

57 Williams, *Climbing the Bookshelves*, pp. 299, 300.

58 Hennessy & Shephard, *Reflections*, pp. 39.

59 Hennessy, *The prime minister*, pp. 398, 405.

60 HC Debs, 22 November 1990, vol 181, col 446–54.

61 Interview with Margaret Beckett, 5 September 2018.

62 Interview with Edwina Currie, 21 June 2018.

63 Harman, *A Woman's Work*, p. 72.

64 Harman, *A Woman's Work*, p. 73.

65 Harman, *A Woman's Work*, p. 131; interview with Margaret Hodge, 2 July 2018.

66 Interview with Clare Short, 31 July 2018.

67 Interview with Clare Short, 31 July 2018.

68 Short, Clare, 'Women and the Labour Party', *Parliamentary Affairs*, 49 (1) (1996), p. 19.

69 Brooks, Rachel, Eagle, Angela & Short, Clare, *Quotas Now: Women in the Labour Party* (London 1990).

70 Interview with Angela Eagle, 5 September 2018.

71 Interview with Margaret Beckett, 5 September 2018.

72 Breitenbach, Esther and Thane, Pat (eds.) *Women and Citizenship in Britain and Ireland in the 20th Century: What Difference Did the Vote Make?* (London, 2010), p. 145.

73 Interview with Clare Short, 31 July 2018.

74 Interview with Angela Eagle, 5 September 2018.

75 Interview with Harriet Harman, 26 July 2018.

76 Hennessy, *The prime minister*, p. 401.

77 Harman, *A Woman's Work*, p. 55.

78 Interview with Barbara Follett, 12 September 2018.

79 Interview with Barbara Follett, 12 September 2018.

80 Interview with Harriet Harman, 26 July 2018.

81 Boothroyd, *The Autobiography*, pp. 136–7.

82 Interview with Betty Boothroyd, 16 May 2018.

83 Boothroyd, *The Autobiography*, p. 141.

84 Boothroyd, *The Autobiography*, p. 143.

85 Boothroyd, *The Autobiography*, p. 121.

86 Routledge, Paul, *Madam Speaker: the Life of Betty Boothroyd* (London, 1995), p. 1.

87 Interview with Diane Abbott, 27 February 2018.

88 Interview with Diane Abbott, 27 February 2018.

89 Interview with Diane Abbott, 27 February 2018.

90 McVeigh, Tracy, 'Heckled but happy: the graceful star of gay marriage debate', *The Guardian*, 26 May 2013.

91 Interview with Margot James, 5 July 2018.

92 Interview with Justine Greening, 12 September 2018.

93 Thatcher, *The Downing Street Years*, p. 151.

94 Bedell, Geraldine, 'Ginny knows best', *The Independent on Sunday*, 27 February 1994.

7 New Labour, more women: 1997–2010

1   King, Oona, *House Music: The Oona King Diaries* (London, 2007), p. 333.

2   Harman, *A Woman's Work*, p. 172.

3   Harman, *A Woman's Work*, p. 173.

4   Harman, *A Woman's Work*, p. 177.

5   Rhodes, Mandy, 'Nothing like a dame: interview with Dame Margaret Beckett', *Holyrood*, 14 March 2018 (www.holyrood.com/articles/inside-politics/nothing-dame-interview-dame-margaret-beckett).

6   Harman, *A Woman's Work*, p. 180.

7   Harman, *A Woman's Work*, p. 187.

8   Harman, *A Woman's Work*, pp. 188, 187.

9   Interview with Harriet Harman, 26 July 2018.

10 Interview with Harriet Harman, 26 July 2018.

11 Interview with Clare Short, 31 July 2018.

12 King, *House Music*, p. 78.

13 Interview with Yvette Cooper, 18 September 2018.

14 Harman, *A Woman's Work*, p. 193.

15 Interview with Baroness Corston, 18 June 2018.

16 Interview with Gillian Shephard, 6 June 2018.

17 Harman, *A Woman's Work*, pp. 193–4; interview with Helen Liddell, 11 September 2017; interview with Yvette Cooper, 18 September 2018; interview with Jacqui Smith, 5 September 2018.

18 Harman, *A Woman's Work*, p. 197.

19 Ruddock, Joan, *Going Nowhere: A Memoir* (London, 2016), p. 190; Interview with Joan Ruddock, 11 September 2018.

20 Harman, *A Woman's Work*, p. 198.

21 Interview with Harriet Harman, 26 July 2018.

22 Interview with Harriet Harman, 26 July 2018.

23 Harman, *A Woman's Work*, p. 199.

24 Jowell, Tessa & D'Souza, Frances, *The Power of Politicians* (London, 2018), pp. 18, 19.

25 Interview with Jacqui Smith, 5 September 2018.

26 Interview with Yvette Cooper, 18 September 2018.

27 Rayner, Angela. 'How Labour took me from teenager mother to shadow education secretary', *The Guardian*, 1 June 2017.

28 'Indian Summer or Winter Chill: what's in store for the Autumn Budget?', Resolution Foundation, Monday 13 November 2017 with Frank Field and Nicky Morgan.

29 HC Deb 10 December 1997, vol. 302 col. 1146; HC Deb 10 December 1997, vol. 302 col. 1124; BBC News 'Blair suffers in benefits revolt', 11 December 1997.

30 Interview with Yvette Cooper, 18 September 2018.

31 Interview with Harriet Harman, 26 July 2018.

32 Harman, *A Woman's Work*, p. 207

33 Harman, *A Woman's Work*, p. 211.

34 Harman, *A Woman's Work*, p. 214.

35 Harman, *A Woman's Work*, p. 215.

36 Interview with Margaret Hodge, 2 July 2018.

37 www.equalityhumanrights.com/en/managing-pregnancy-and-maternity-workplace/pregnancy-and-maternity-discrimination-research-findings

38 Interview with Yvette Cooper, 18 September 2018.

39 Interview with Yvette Cooper, 18 September 2018.

40 Interview with Harriet Harman, 26 July 2018.

41 Interview with Margaret Hodge, 2 July 2018.

42 BBC News, 'Former soldier "provided IRA cover"', 1 May 2001.

43 HC Debs, vol. 830, c. 37, 31 January 1972.

44 BBC 24 Hours, 31 January 1972.

45 Holland, Kitty, 'Bernadette McAliskey: "I am astounded I survived. I made mad decisions"', *Irish Times*, 22 September 2016.

46 Mowlam, Mo, *Momentum* (London, 2003), pp. 51–2.

47 Mowlam, *Momentum*, pp. 71, 72.

48 Mowlam, *Momentum*, p. 78.

49 Mowlam, *Momentum*, p. 86.

50 Mowlam, *Momentum*, pp. 183–9.

51 Langdon, *Julia, Mo Mowlam: The Biography* (London, 2000), pp. 269–70.

52 Langdon, *Mo Mowlam*, p. 270.

53 Langdon, *Mo Mowlam*, p. 284.

54 Interview with Harriet Harman, 26 July 2018.

55 Dejevsky, Mary, 'Mo Mowlam lied to Blair about her brain tumour', *Independent on Sunday*, 17 January 2010.

56 Short, Clare, *An Honourable Deception? New Labour, Iraq and the Misuse of Power* (London, 2005), pp. 142, 144, 159, 168–9, 175.

57 Harman, *A Woman's Work*, pp. 253–4.

58 Short, *An Honourable Deception?*, pp. 177, 180, 189, 193.

59 Ruddock, *Going Nowhere*, p. 324.

60 Interview with Clare Short, 31 July 2018.

61 King, *House Music*, p. 261.

62 King, *House Music*, pp. 265–6.

63 Interview with Diane Abbott, 27 February 2018.

64 Cowley, Philip and Childs, Sarah, 'Too Spineless to Rebel? New Labour's Women MPs' *British Journal of Political Science*, 33 (3) (July 2003), pp. 345–65.

65 Interview with Baroness Corston, 18 June 2018.

66 King, *House Music*, p. 115.

67 King, *House Music*, p. 120.

68 King, *House Music*, p. 129.

69 King, *House Music*, pp. 277, 340.

70 Interview with Baroness Boothroyd, 16 May 2018.

71 Interview with Joan Ruddock, 11 September 2018.

72 Ruddock, *Going Nowhere*, pp. 313, 360, 363.

73 Interview with Harriet Harman, 26 July 2018.

74 Ruddock, *Going Nowhere*, p. 537.

75 Widdecombe, Ann, *Strictly Ann: The Autobiography* (London, 2013), p. 121.

76 'MPs prepare for abortion debate', BBC News, 11 June 2007.

77 Cowley, Childs, 'Too Spineless to Rebel? New Labour's Women MPs', p. 353.

78 Interviews with Helen Liddell, 11 September 2017 and Gillian Shephard, 6 June 2018.

79 Ruddock, *Going Nowhere,* p. 249.

80 Harman, *A Woman's Work*, p. 163.

81 Hennessy & Shepherd, *Reflections: Conversations with Politicians*, pp. 201–02.

82 Interview with Margaret Beckett, 5 September 2018.

83 Interview with Margaret Beckett, 5 September 2018.

84 Harman, *A Woman's Work*, p. 256.

85 Harman, *A Woman's Work*, p. 161.

86 Ruddock, *Going Nowhere*, p. 399.

87 Ruddock, *Going Nowhere*, p. 412.

88 Harman, *A Woman's Work*, pp. 262, 270.

89 Ruddock, *Going Nowhere*, p. 414.

90 Interview with Harriet Harman, 26 July 2018.

91 Harman, *A Woman's Work*, pp. 270, 271, 272.

92 Interview with Jacqui Smith, 5 September 2018.

93 Interview with Jacqui Smith, 5 September 2018.

94 Ruddock, *Going Nowhere*, p. 418.

95 Interview with Harriet Harman, 26 July 2018.

96 Harman, *A Woman's Work*, pp. 276 280, 287, 289.

97 Interview with Harriet Harman, 26 July 2018.

98 Interview with Caroline Flint, 12 June 2018.

99 'Caroline Flint: resignation letter in full', *The Daily Telegraph*, 5 June 2009.

100 Interview with Harriet Harman, 26 July 2018.

101 Harman, *A Woman's Work*, pp. 309–10.

102 Harman, *A Woman's Work*, p. 306.

103 Interview with Jacqui Smith, 5 September 2018.

104 NOTE TEXT TO BE SUPPLIED.

8 More in common: 2010–19

1 HC Debs, vol. 596, c. 675, 3 June 2015.

2 Interview with Priti Patel, 14 October 2019.

3 Interview with Caroline Spelman, 10 July 2018.

4 Interview with Penny Mordaunt, 14 October 2019.

5 Interview with Anne Jenkin, 24 May 2018.

6 Interview with Anne Jenkin, 24 May 2018.

7 Interview with Rushanara Ali, 3 July 2018.

8 Phillips, Jess, *Everywoman: One Woman's Truth about Speaking the Truth* (London, 2017), p. 146.

9 Interview with Theresa May, 6 August 2018.

10 Interview with Cheryl Gillan, 4 September 2018.

11 Interview with Penny Mordaunt, 14 October 2019.

12 Interview with Anne Jenkin, 24 May 2018.

13   Interview with Amber Rudd, 26 June 2018.

14   Interview with Andrea Leadsom, 8 October 2019.

15   '"I hope our Downing Street catwalk inspires young girls to go into politics": Esther McVey says the cabinet's new women ministers can be "role models"'. *The Daily Mail*, 15 July 2014.

16   Interview with Penny Mordaunt, 14 October 2019.

17   Barnett, Emma. 'Tory MP petticoat row: What right-minded woman would want to be a British politician?' *The Telegraph*, 21 July 2014.

18   Syal, Rajeev, Female MPs complain of being Cameron's conference 'arm candy', *The Guardian*, 6 October 2015.

19   Whittaker, M. (2017) 'Ending austerity? The priorities, price tags and practicalities for a government changing course on spending cuts'. *The Resolution Foundation*.

20   Interview with Jess Phillips, 12 June 2018.

21   Interview with Jo Swinson, 6 June 2018.

22   Interview with Nicky Morgan, 23 July 2018.

23   Rudd, Amber. 'We are not Thatcher's children'. *The Telegraph*, 26 April 2011.

24   Rudd, Amber. 'We are not Thatcher's children'. *The Telegraph*, 26 April 2011.

25   Interview with Nicky Morgan, 23 July 2018.

26   Swinson, Jo. 'Gender pay reporting is just the start of a drive to transparency'. *Financial Times*, 31 March 2018.

27   Interview with Jo Swinson, 6 June 2018.

28   Brooks, Cody, 'British MP says people confuse equal pay and gender pay gap', *Wiki Tribune*, April 2018.

29   Brooks, Cody, 'British MP says people confuse equal pay and gender pay gap', *Wiki Tribune*, April 2018.

30   Interview with Theresa May, 6 August 2018.

31   Perkins, Anne, 'Theresa May will be nobody's stooge'. *The Guardian*, 12 May 2010.

32   Interview with Theresa May, 6 August 2018.

33   Interview with Theresa May, 6 August 2018.

34   Interview with Priti Patel, 14 October 2019.

35   Interview with Theresa May, 6 August 2018.

36   Interview with Theresa May, 6 August 2018.

37   Interview with Priti Patel, 14 October 2019.

38   Interview with Justine Greening, 12 September 2018.

39   'James Slack on Politics and Power', *Daily Mail*, 8 January 2011.

40 Prince, Rosa, *Theresa May: The Enigmatic Prime Minister* (London, 2017), pp. 222–3.

41 Interview with Yvette Cooper, 18 September 2018.

42 Elgot, Jessica. 'Andrea Leadsom apologises to Theresa May for motherhood remarks'. *The Guardian*, 11 July 2016.

43 Interview with Andrea Leadsom, 8 October 2019.

44 D'Ancona, Matthew. 'Diana Rigg meets Sybil Fawlty in her first newspaper interview as the Conservative chairman.' *Sunday Telegraph*, 28 July 2002.

45 Pearson, Alison. 'Theresa May Interview: "I probably was Good Two Shoes at school"'. *The Telegraph*, 21 December 2012.

46 Prince, *Theresa May*, p. 61.

47 Interview with Penny Mordaunt, 14 October 2019.

48 Interview with Justine Greening, 12 September 2018.

49 Interview with Theresa May, 6 August 2018.

50 Interview with Amber Rudd, 26 June 2018.

51 'Theresa factor' credited with surge in women candidates as party looks set to make history by securing more women MPs than ever before. *The Telegraph*, 6 May 2017.

52 Interview with Amber Rudd, 26 June 2018.

53 Interview with Amber Rudd, 26 June 2018.

54 Interview with Anne Jenkin, 24 May 2018.

55 Interview with Stella Creasy, 6 June 2018.

56 Interview with Amber Rudd, 28 June 2019.

57 Mason, Rowena. 'Theresa May: I want to transform how we think about domestic violence'. *The Guardian*, 17 February 2017.

58 Silver, Laura, 'Here's How Some MPs Have Put Aside Party Politics To Force Change on Women's Issues'. *Buzzfeed News*, 8 March 2018.

59 Interview with Jo Swinson, 19 September 2019.

60 HC Debs, vol. 663, c. 1305, 24 July 2019.

61 Interview with Penny Mordaunt, 14 October 2019.

62 Interview with Jo Swinson, 19 September 2019.

63 Interview with Jo Swinson, 19 September 2019.

64 Interview with Caroline Lucas, 10 September 2019.

65 Interview with Margaret Hodge, 2 July 2018.

66 Interview with Anne Jenkin, 24 May 2018.

67 Interview with Jo Swinson, 19 September 2019.

68 Interview with Jess Phillips, 12 June 2018.

69 Interview with Angela Rayner, 18 September 2019.

70 Interview with Emily Thornberry, 16 September 2019.

71 Interview with Angela Rayner, 18 September 2019.

72 Interview with Angela Rayner, 18 September 2019.

73 Interview with Jess Phillips, 12 June 2018.

74 Interview with Angela Eagle, 5 September 2018.

75 HC Debs, vol. 664, c. 794, 25 September 2019.

76 HC Debs, vol. 664, c. 802, 25 September 2019.

77 Interview with Paula Sherriff, 14 October 2019.

78 Interview with Priti Patel, 14 October 2019.

79 Interview with Penny Mordaunt, 14 October 2019.

80 'Female MPs were sent 25,000 abusive Twitter messages in just six months – with half of them directed at Diane Abbott.' *The Telegraph*, 4 September 2017.

81 Interview with Diane Abbott, 27 February 2018.

82 Interview with Theresa May, 6 August 2018.

83 Phillips, *Everywoman*, p. 216.

84 Interview with Brendan Cox, 24 May 2018.

85 Interview with Brendan Cox, 24 May 2018.

86 Interview with Diane Abbott, 27 February 2018.

87 Interview with Heidi Allen, 11 September 2019.

88 Reeves, Rachel, '100 years since Nancy Astor took her seat, what would she make of today's abuse of female MPs?', *The Telegraph*, 1st December 2019, https://www.telegraph.co.uk/women/politics/100-years-since-nancy-astor-took-seat-would-make-todays-abuse/

89 Griffiths, Sian, 'Trolls may frighten female MPs but they won't be silenced', *The Times*, 5 June 2016.

90 Interview with Luciana Berger, 24 July 2018.

91 Interview with Luciana Berger, 24 July 2018.

92 'Theresa May demands John McDonnell apologises for "lynching" comments about Esther McVey', *Politics Home*, 7 February 2018.

93 Interview with Angela Eagle, 5 September 2018.

94 Interview with Angela Eagle, 5 September 2018.

95 Waugh, Paul. 'Angela Eagle Interview: On Homophobia, Brick-Throwing, Tory Cuts And Labour's Future.' *HuffPost*, 31 October 2016.

96 Interview with Diane Abbott, 27 February 2018.

97 'Labour MP Angela Rayner: "I'm proud of my accent"', *BBC News*, 10 July 2017.

98   HC Debs, vol. 638, c.640, 27 March 2018.

99   Interview with Emily Thornberry, 16 September 2019.

100   Interview with Theresa May, 6 August 2018.

101   'Diane Abbott interview: "Why am I abused so much? I'm both black and a woman."' *The Times*, 28 April 2018.

102   Phillips, *Everywoman*, p. 227.

103   Cooper, Yvette. 'Why I'm campaigning to reclaim the internet from sexist trolls.' *The Telegraph*, 26 May 2016.

104   Cooper, Yvette. 'Why I'm campaigning to reclaim the internet from sexist trolls.' *The Telegraph*, 26 May 2016.

105   Interview with Yvette Cooper, 18 September 2018.

106   Abbott, Diane, 'I've had plenty of online abuse, but I still don't think MPs deserve special treatment'. *The Guardian*, 6 February 2018.

107   Interview with Diane Abbott, 27 February 2018.

108   Interview with Angela Rayner, 18 September 2019.

109   Interview with Rushanara Ali, 3 July 2018.

110   Interview with Jess Phillips, 12 June 2018.

111   HC Debs, vol. 626, c. 527, 27 June 2017.

112   Interview with Angela Rayner, 18 September 2019.

113   Sylvester, Rachel, 'The hard left makes a mission of misogyny'. *The Telegraph*, 31 October 2017.

114   All Party Parliamentary Group on Women's Equality, 'Improving Parliament: Creating a Better and More Representative House', July 2014. Available at: http://appgimprovingparliamentreport.co.uk/download/ APPG-Women-In-Parliament-Report-2014.pdf [Accessed 15 October 2018].

115   'Dawn Butler: As a female, working-class, Afro-Caribbean, trade unionist MP I want to smooth the way for those who follow', *LabourList*, 20 December 2016.

116   Interview with Dawn Butler, 24 July 2018.

117   Interview with Dawn Butler, 24 July 2018.

118   Interview with Jo Swinson, 6 June 2018.

119   Interview with Caroline Flint, 19 June 2018.

120   Interview with Caroline Lucas, 10 September 2019.

121   Interview with Penny Mordaunt, 14 October 2019.

122   Mavin, Sharon, Bryans, Patricia and Cunningham, Rosie 'Fed-up with Blair's babes, Gordon's gals, Cameron's cuties, Nick's nymphets: Challenging gendered media representations of women political leaders, *Gender in Management: An International Journal*, 25/17(2010), p. 562.

123 Sanghani, Radhika, 'The Labour MP's breasts are 'distracting' to TV viewers. Apparently.' *The Telegraph*, 25 August 2015.

124 Interview with Luciana Berger, 24 July 2018.

125 Interview with Theresa May, 6 August 2018.

126 Day, Elizabeth. 'Theresa May – what lies beyond the public image?' *The Observer*, 27 July 2014.

127 Wilford, Greg 'Theresa May didn't want to wear £995 trousers but was forced into it by aide, report claims', *The Independent*, 15 July 2017.

128 'Grandee Sir Nicholas Soames blasts "impertinent" Nicky Morgan for her "unacceptable" jibe at PM's £995 trousers because it "trivialises" their soft Brexit case.' *The Daily Mail*, 11 December 2016.

129 Campbell, Rosie and Childs, Sarah, 'Parents in Parliament: "Where's Mum?"', *The Political Quarterly*, 85/4 (2014), pp. 487–92.

130 Proportion of women who never have children has doubled in a generation, ONS figures show, *The Telegraph*, 24 November 2017.

131 Interview with Priti Patel, 14 October 2019.

132 Interview with Caroline Spelman, 10 July 2018.

133 Interview with Caroline Spelman, 10 July 2018.

134 Interview with Brendan Cox, 24 May 2018.

135 Interview with Andrea Leadsom, 8 October 2019.

136 Harman, Harriet. 'It's 35 years too late for me, but MPs must get baby leave.' *The Telegraph*, 1 February 2018.

137 Interview with Theresa May, 6 August 2018.

138 Interview with Andrea Leadsom, 8 October 2019.

139 Creasy, Stella, 'I'm pregnant and forced to choose between being an MP and a mum', *The Guardian*, 17 June 2019.

140 Interview with Stella Creasy, 14 October 2019.

Epilogue: A century of parliamentary sisterhood

1 HC Debs, vol. 215, cc 1405–06, 29 March 1928.

2 Interview with Theresa May, 6 August 2018.

3 One of Labour's new rising stars talks class, Westminster and 'the enemy', *Squawkbox*, 11 August 2017.

4 Interview with Andrea Leadsom, 8 October 2019.

5 Interview with Caroline Flint, 19 June 2018.

6   Interview with Margaret Hodge, 2 July 2018.

7   'Theresa May women's suffrage speech hides dig at male colleagues.' *The Guardian*, 6 February 2018.

8   Interview with Caroline Lucas, 10 September 2019.

9   Interview with Heidi Allen, 11 September 2019.

10   HC Debs, vol. 611, c. 1887, 20 June 2016.

11   Interview with Brendan Cox, 24 May 2018.

12   Interview with Brendan Cox, 24 May 2018.

13   HC Debs, vol. 596, c. 675, 3 June 2015.

14   Mason, Rowena. 'Theresa May: I want to transform how we think about domestic violence.' *The Guardian*, 17 February 2017.

15   Phillips, *Everywoman*, p. 49.

16   Interview with Jess Phillips, 12 June 2018.

17   Interview with Amber Rudd, 26 June 2018.

18   HC Debs, vol. 664, cc 1261–1262, 2 October 2019.

19   HC Debs, vol. 664, cc 1272–1273, 2 October 2019.

20   HC Debs, vol. 664, cc 1274–1275, 2 October 2019.

21   Interview with Priti Patel, 14 October 2019.

22   Silver, Laura, 'Here's how some MPs have put aside party politics to force change on women's issues'. *Buzzfeed News*, 8 March 2018.

23   Silver, Laura, 'Here's how some MPs have put aside party politics to force change on women's issues'. *Buzzfeed News*, 8 March 2018.

24   Interview with Heidi Allen, 11 September 2019.

25   HC Debs, vol. 642, c. 241, 5 June 2018.

26   Interview with Stella Creasy, 14 October 2019.

27   Interview with Angela Rayner, 18 September 2019.

Select Bibliography

Archival material

Bodleian Library, University of Oxford (BOD): Barbara Castle (BCP), Clement Attlee (CRA), Conservative Party Archive (CPA).

Churchill College, University of Cambridge (CUC): Florence Horsburgh (FHP), Winston Churchill (WCP), Margaret Thatcher (THCR).

London School of Economics (LSE): Millicent Fawcett (7MGF), Edith Summerskill (ECL), William Beveridge (BEVERIDGE), Equal Pay Campaign Committee (6EPC), British Federation of University Women (5BFW), Lena Jeger (JEGER).

National Archives, Kew, London (TNA): Cabinet Papers (CAB).

Open University: Jennie Lee (JL).

People's History Museum, Manchester (PHM): *The Labour Woman 1914–1970*, Ellen Wilkinson Press Cuttings (LP/WI), Judith Hart (LP/HART).

Parliamentary Archives, Westminster (PARL): Norah Runge Scrapbooks (RUN), Jennie Lee (JLE), Peggy Herbison (HER), Graham White (WHI), Parliamentary Committee on Refugees (HC/LB/1/122), Sub-Committee on Women's Medical Services (HC/CL/CO/AA/AN), Sub-Committee on Fighting Services (HC/CL/CO/AA/AI), Lloyd George Papers (LG), Ernest Brown (BRO), Stow Hill (STH).

University of Liverpool (UL): Eleanor Rathbone (RP XIV).

University of Reading (UR): Nancy Astor (NAP).

Wellcome Collection: Abortion Law Reform Association (SA/ALR).

Margaret Thatcher Foundation www.margaretthatcher.org

Interviews and correspondence

Diane Abbott, 27 February 2018.
Rushanara Ali, 3 July 2018.
Heidi Allen, 11 September 2019.
Viscount William Astor, 24 January 2017.

Margaret Beckett, 5 September 2018.
Dr Laura Beers, 7 April 2017.
Speaker John Bercow, 23 July 2018.
Luciana Berger, 24 July 2018.
Betty Boothroyd, 16 May 2018.
Tracy Brabin, 10 October 2019.
Chris Bryant, 14 May 2018.
Dawn Butler, 24 July 2018.
Lynda Chalker, 12 November 2018.
Dr Sarah Childs, 17 April 2018.
Joe Clinch, 4 December 2017.
Mark Collins (Parliament's Estates Archivist and Historian), 23 May 2018.
Yvette Cooper, 18 September 2018.
Jean Corston, 18 June 2018.
Brendan Cox (Jo Cox's husband), 24 May 2018.
Stella Creasy, 6 June 2018 and 14 October 2019.
Edwina Currie, 21 June 2018.
Angela Eagle, 5 September 2018.
Caroline Flint, 12 June 2018.
Barbara Follett, 12 September 2018.
Cheryl Gillan, 4 September 2018.
Dr Julie Gottlieb, 13 July 2017.
Justine Greening, 12 September 2018.
Harriet Harman, 26 July 2018.
Steve Hart, 2 October 2017.
Helene Hayman, 13 November 2017.
Margaret Hodge, 2 July 2018.
Margot James, 5 July 2018.
Anne Jenkin, 24 May 2018.
Kim Leadbeater, 10 October 2019.
Andrea Leadsom, 8 October 2019.
Helen Liddell, 11 September 2017.
Caroline Lucas, 10 September 2019.
Theresa May, 6 August 2018.
Penny Mordaunt, 14 October 2019.
Nicky Morgan, 23 July 2018.
Priti Patel, 14 October 2019.
Professor Susan Pedersen, 9 October 2017.
Anne Perkins, 6 December 2017.
Jess Phillips, 12 June 2018.
Angela Rayner, 18 September 2019.
Dr Charlotte Lydia Riley, 9 October 2017.
Amber Rudd, 26 June 2018.
Joan Ruddock, 11 September 2018.
Gillian Shephard, 6 June 2018.
Paula Sherriff, 14 October 2019.

Clare Short, 31 July 2018.
Caroline Slocock, 4 September 2018.
Jacqui Smith, 5 September 2018.
Sam Smethers (Chief Executive of the Fawcett Society), 21 May 2018.
Caroline Spelman, 10 July 2018.
Jack Straw, 18 October 2017.
Ben Summerskill (Edith Summerskill's grandson), 6 December 2017.
Shirley Summerskill, 9 November 2017.
Jo Swinson, 6 June 2019 and 19 September 2019.
Dr Mari Takayanagi, 16 January 2017.
Ann Taylor (Baroness Taylor of Bolton), 5 June 2018.
Emily Thornberry, 16 September 2019.
Baroness Trumpington (correspondence 27 January 2017 via her son, Adam
    Barker).
Dr Jacqui Turner, 25 January 2017.
Lady Jean Weatherall (Norah Runge's granddaughter), 19 May 2017.
Jaselle Williams (great-great-niece of Nye Bevan), 10 August 2017.
Shirley Williams, 9 November 2017.

Published Diaries and Memoirs

Astor, Nancy, *My Two Countries* (New York, 1923).
Atholl, Katharine, *Working Partnership* (London, 1958).
Benn, Tony, *The Benn Diaries 1940–1990* (London, 2005).
Bondfield, Margaret, *A Life's Work* (London, 1948).
Boothroyd, Betty, *The Autobiography* (London, 2001).
Castle, Barbara, *The Castle Diaries 1964–70* (London, 1984).
Castle, Barbara, *Fighting All The Way* (London, 1993).
Cazalet-Keir, Thelma, *From the Wings* (London, 1967).
Crossman, Richard, *The diaries of a cabinet minister, Volume 1: minister of
    housing, 1964–66*, (London, 1975).
Crossman, Richard, *The diaries of a cabinet minister, Volume 3: secretary of state
    for Social Services, 1968–70* (London, 1977).
Currie, Edwina, *Diaries 1987–1992* (London, 2002).
Dalton, Hugh, *The Fateful Years* (London, 1957).
Jenkins, Roy, *A Life at the Centre* (London, 1991).
Jowell, Tessa & D'Souza, Frances, *The Power of Politicians* (London, 2018).
Harman, Harriet, *A Woman's Work* (London, 2017).
King, Oona, *House Music: The Oona King Diaries* (London, 2007).
Lee, Jennie, *This Great Journey* (London, 1963).
Mann, Jean, *Woman in Parliament* (London, 1962).
Manning, Leah, *A Life for Education* (London, 1970).
Mowlam, Mo, *Momentum* (London, 2003).
Ruddock, Joan, *Going Nowhere: A Memoir* (London, 2016).

Short, Clare, *An Honourable Deception? New Labour, Iraq and the Misuse of Power* (London, 2005).
Slocock, Caroline, *People Like Us: Margaret Thatcher and Me* (London, 2018).
Summerskill, Edith, *A Woman's World: Her Memoirs* (Heinemann, 1967).
Summerskill, Edith, *Letters to my daughter* (London, 1986).
Thatcher, Margaret, *The Downing Street Years* (London, 1993).
Thatcher, Margaret, *The Path to Power* (London, 1995).
Widdecombe, Ann, *Strictly Ann: The Autobiography* (London, 2013).
Wilkinson, Ellen, *Peeps at Politicians* (London, 1930).
Wilkinson, Ellen, *The Town that was Murdered: The Life-Story of Jarrow* (London, 1939).
Wilkinson, Ellen, *The Division Bell Mystery* (London, 1932).
Williams, Shirley, *Climbing the Bookshelves* (London, 2009 & 2010).
Wilson, Harold, *The Labour Government 1964–1970: A Personal Record.* (London, 1971).

Films

To Be a Woman. Dir. Jill Craigie. Outlook, 1951. Film.
Made in Dagenham. Dir. Nigel Cole. Paramount Pictures, 2010.
Suffragette. Dir. Sarah Gavron. Pathé, 2015. Film.
'German Atrocities 1945', British Pathé. Available at: www.britishpathe.com/video/german-atrocities/query/mavis+tate [Accessed 12/09/18].
London – Ellen Wilkinson (1947), British Pathé. Available at: www.youtube.com/watch?v=j-cFuHo4WD4 [Accessed 15/06/17].
Mrs Dr MP Pathe Close-Up Of Dr Edith Summerskill (1945), British Pathé. Available at: www.youtube.com/watch?v=wMbXCnje7Hs [Accessed 05/10/18].
BBC2 Argument, 21 March 1974. Available at: www.bbc.co.uk/archive/70sfeminism/10409.shtml [Accessed 25/09/17].
'Creation of UNESCO', UNESCO Multimedia Archives. Available at: www.unesco.org/archives/multimedia/?pg=34&prs=Ellen+Wilkinson [Accessed 04/09/17].
Margaret Thatcher TV Interview for Thames TV *CBTV* (children's television) 13 December 1982.
BBC 24 Hours, 31 January 1972. Available at: www.bbc.co.uk/programmes/p00nm166 [Accessed 05/10/18].

Lectures

Langley, Helen (2015) 'Irene Ward MP (1895–1980), doughty parliamentarian and campaigner', Speaker's Advisory Committee on Works of Art, International Women's Day Lecture.

Reports

Childs, Sarah 'The Good Parliament', July 2016. Available at: www.bristol.ac.uk/
 media-library/sites/news/2016/july/20%20Jul%20Prof%20Sarah%20
 Childs%20The%20Good%20Parliament%20report.pdf [Accessed 01/11/16].
Equality and Human Rights Commission 'Pregnancy and Maternity
 Discrimination Research Findings', www.equalityhumanrights.com/en/
 managing-pregnancy-and-maternity-workplace/pregnancy-and-maternity-
 discrimination-research-findings [Accessed 11/12/18].
'Women in Parliament: a guide to the history of women's participation in
 Parliament and their representation in the historical collections', Houses of
 Parliament, March 2015. Available at: www.parliament.uk/documents/
 works-of-art/Women%20in%20Parliament%20Catalogue.pdf [Accessed
 27/10/16].
'Women MPs and parliamentary candidates since 1945', UK Political Info database.
 Available at www.ukpolitical.info/FemaleMps.htm [Accessed 20/09/17].

Secondary sources: Books

Bartley, Paula, *Ellen Wilkinson: From Red Suffragist to Government Minister
 (Revolutionary Lives)* (London, 2014).
Beers, Laura, *Red Ellen* (London, 2016).
Bew, John, *Citizen Clem: A Biography of Attlee* (London, 2017).
Bill, Ron and Newens, Stan, *Leah Manning* (Harlow, 1991).
Braybon, Gail and Summerfield, Penny, *Out of the Cage: Women's experiences in
 two world wars* (London, 2013).
Breitenbach, Esther & Thane, Pat (eds.) *Women and Citizenship in Britain and
 Ireland in the 20th Century: What Difference Did the Vote Make?* (London,
 2010).
Brooke, Stephen, *Sexual Politics: Sexuality, Family Planning, and the British Left
 from the 1880s to the Present Day* (Oxford, 2011).
Brookes, Pamela, *Women at Westminster: An Account of Women in the British
 Parliament 1918–1966* (London, 1967).
Bryant, Chris, *Parliament: The Biography. Volume 2: Reform.* (London, 2014).
Cannadine, David *Margaret Thatcher: A Life and Legacy* (Oxford, 2017).
Childs, Sarah and Lovenduski, Joni, 'Political Representation', in Waylen,
 Georgina, Celis, Karen, Kantola, Johanna and Weldon, S. Laurel (eds) *The
 Oxford Handbook of Gender and Politics* (Oxford, 2013), pp. 489–513.
Childs, Sarah, *Women and British Party Politics: Descriptive, substantive and
 symbolic representation* (Abingdon, Oson, 2008).
Childs, Sarah and Campbell, Rosie 'What the Coalition did for women: a new
 gender consensus, coalition division and gendered austerity', 2015, Seldon,
 Anthony and Finn, Mike (eds), *The Coalition Effect 2010–2015* (Cambridge,
 2015), pp. 397–429.

Collis, Maurice. *Nancy Astor: An informal biography* (New York, 1960).

Cox, Brendan, *Jo Cox: More in Common* (London, 2017).

Ewan, E. L., Innes, S., Reynolds, S. & Pipes, R. (eds.) *The Biographical Dictionary of Scottish Women* (Edinburgh, 2006).

Fort, Adrian, *Nancy: The Story of Lady Astor* (London, 2012).

Gillard, Derek. *Food for Thought: Child nutrition, the school dinner and the food industry* (2003).

Gottlieb, Julie, *'Guilty Women', Foreign Policy, and Appeasement in Inter-War Britain* (Basingstoke, 2015).

Hamilton, Mary, *Margaret Bondfield* (London, 1924).

Harrison, Brian, *Prudent Revolutionaries: Portraits of British feminists between the wars* (Oxford, 1987).

Hennessy, Peter & Shepherd, Robert, *Reflections: Conversations with politicians* (London, 2016).

Hennessy, Peter. Never Again: Britain 1945–51. (London, 1992).

Hetherington, S.J., *Katharine Atholl, 1874–1960: against the tide* (Aberdeen, 1989).

Hollis, Patricia, *Jennie Lee: A life* (Oxford, 1997).

Honeyball, Mary, *Parliamentary Pioneers: Labour Women MPs 1918–1945* (Chatham, 2015).

Langdon, Julia, *Mo Mowlam: The Biography* (London, 2000).

McDougall, Linda, *Westminster Women* (London, 1998).

Marr, Andrew, *The Making of Modern Britain* (London, 2009).

Martineau, Lisa, *Politics & Power: Barbara Castle – A Biography* (London, 2000).

Masters, Anthony, *Nancy Astor: A Life* (London, 1981).

Moore, Charles, *Margaret Thatcher: The Authorized Biography – Volume One* (London, 2013).

Sones, Boni, Moran, Margaret and Lovenduski, Joni, *Women in Parliament: The new suffragettes* (London, 2005).

Pedersen, Susan, *Eleanor Rathbone and the Politics of Conscience* (New Haven, 2004).

Perkins, Anne, *Red Queen: The Authorized Biography of Barbara Castle* (London, 2003).

Perry, Matt, *'Red Ellen' Wilkinson: Her Ideas, Movements and World* (Manchester, 2014),

Phillips, Anne, *The Politics of Presence* (Oxford, 1995).

Phillips, Jess, *Everywoman: One Woman's Truth about Speaking the Truth* (London, 2017).

Phillips, Melanie, *The Divided House: Women at Westminster* (London, 1980).

Pimlott, Ben, *Harold Wilson* (London, 1992).

Prince, Rosa, *Theresa May: The Enigmatic prime minister* (London, 2017).

Pugh, Martin, *Women and the Women's Movement Since 1914* (Basingstoke, 2015).

Reeves, Rachel, *Alice in Westminster: The Political Life of Alice Bacon* (London, 2016).

Ridge, Sophy, *The Women Who Shaped Politics* (London, 2017).

Routledge, Paul *Madam Speaker: the Life of Betty Boothroyd* (London, 1995)
Toole, Millie, *Bessie Braddock M.P.* (London, 1957).
Vallance, Elizabeth, *Women in the House: A Study of Women Members of Parliament* (London, 1979).
Vernon, Betty, *Ellen Wilkinson, 1891–1947* (London, 1982).
Weinbren, Daniel, *The Open University: A History* (Manchester, 2015).
Young, Hugo & Sloman, Anne *The Thatcher Phenomenon* (London, 1986).
Zweiniger-Bargielowska, Ina, *Austerity in Britain: rationing, controls and consumption 1939–1955* (Oxford, 2000).

Secondary sources: Journal articles and book chapters

Baldwin, M. Page, 'Subject to Empire: Married Women and the British Nationality and Status of Aliens Act', *Journal of British Studies*, 40/4 (2001), pp. 522–56.
Ball, Simon 'British Defence Policy' in Paul Addison & Harriet Jones (eds.) *A Companion to Contemporary Britain 1939–2000* (Oxford: Blackwell, 2005), pp. 539–55.
Ball, Stuart, 'The Politics of Appeasement: The Fall of the Duchess of Atholl and the Kinross and West Perth By-Election, December 1938', *The Scottish Historical Review*, 69, (1990), pp. 49–83.
Baxter, Kenneth, 'Florence Gertrude Horsbrugh: The Conservative Party's forgotten first lady', *Conservative History Journal*, 8/21 (2009/10), pp. 21–3.
Black, Amy and Brooke, Stephen, 'The Labour Party, Women, and the Problem of Gender, 1951–1966', *Journal of Political Studies* 36/4 (1997), pp. 419–52.
Beers, Laura, 'A Model MP? Ellen Wilkinson, gender, politics and celebrity culture in interwar Britain', *Cultural and Social History*, 10/2 (2013), pp. 231–50.
Brooke, Stephen, 'Gender and Working Class Identity in Britain during the 1950s', *Journal of Social History*, 34/4 (2001), pp. 773–95.
Campbell, Rosie and Childs, Sarah, 'Parents in Parliament: "Where's Mum?"', *The Political Quarterly*, 85/4 (2014), pp. 487–92.
Cowley, Philip and Childs, Sarah 'Too Spineless to Rebel? New Labour's Women MPs', *British Journal of Political Science*, 33/3 (Jul. 2003), pp. 345–65.
Cohen, Sheila, 'Equal pay – or what? Economics, politics and the 1968 Ford sewing machinists', strike' *Labor History*, 53/1 (2012), pp. 51–68.
Colwill, Jeremy, 'Beveridge, women and the welfare state', *Critical Social Policy*, 14/41 (1994), pp. 53–78.
Gould, Joyce 'Jo Richardson' in Iain Dale & Jacqui Smith *The Honourable Ladies, Vol. 1* (London: Biteback Publishing, 2018), pp. 350–55.
Gregg, P., Gutierrez-Domenech, M. & Waldfogel, J. 'The Employment of Married Mothers in Great Britain, 1974–2000', *Economica*, 74/296 (November 2007), pp. 842–64.

Harrison, Brian, 'Women in a men's house: the women M.P.s, 1919–1945', *The Historical Journal*, 29/3 (1986), pp. 623–54.

Keen, Richard et al. (2018). Women in Parliament and Government. *House of Commons Library*, Briefing Paper SN01250.

Kelan, Elisabeth, 'Gender Logic and (Un)doing Gender at Work', *Gender, Work and Organization*, 17/2 (2010), pp. 174–94.

Kelly, Richard (2018). Women Members of Parliament. *House of Commons Library*, Briefing Paper 06652.

Lowe, Rodney, 'The Second World War, Consensus, and the Foundation of the Welfare State', *Twentieth Century British History*, 1/2 (1990), pp. 152–82.

Mavin, Sharon, Bryans, Patricia and Cunningham, Rosie, 'Fed-up with Blair's babes, Gordon's gals, Cameron's cuties, Nick's nymphets: Challenging gendered media representations of women political leaders', *Gender in Management: An International Journal*, 25/7 (2010), pp. 550–69.

Neale, R.S. 'Working-Class Women and Women's Suffrage', *Labour History*, 12 (May 1967), pp. 16–34.

Pedersen, Susan 'The Failure of Feminism in the Making of the British Welfare State', *Radical History Review*, 43 (Winter 1989), pp. 86–110.

Potter, Alan, 'The Equal Pay Campaign Committee: A Case Study of a Pressure Group', *Political Studies*, 5/1 (1957), pp. 49–64.

Short, Clare 'Women and the Labour Party' *Parliamentary Affairs*, 49/1 (1996), pp. 17–25.

Smith, Harold L., 'The Politics of Conservative Reform: The equal pay for equal work issue, 1945–1955', *The Historical Journal*, 35/2 (1992), pp. 401–15.

Smith, Harold L., 'The problem of 'Equal Pay for Equal Work' in Great Britain during World War II', *The Journal of Modern History*, 53/4 (1981), pp. 652–72.

Smith, Harold L., 'The Womanpower Problem in Britain during the Second World War', *The Historical Journal*, 27/4 (1984), pp. 925–45.

Smith Wilson, Dolly 'Gender: Change and Continuity', in Addison and Jones (eds) *A Companion to Contemporary Britain 1939–2000* (Oxford: Blackwell, 2005), pp. 245–62.

Tomlinson, Jim, 'Managing the economy, managing the people: Britain c. 1931–70', *Economic History Review*, 58/3 (2005), pp. 555–85.

Weldon, Laurel, 'Beyond Bodies: Institutional Sources of Representation for Women in Democratic Policymaking', *Journal of Politics*, 64/4 (2002), pp. 1153–74.

Zweiniger-Bargielowska, Ina, 'Rationing, Austerity and the Conservative Party Recovery after 1945', *The Historical Journal*, 37/1 (1994), pp. 173–97.

Online resources

Oxford Dictionary of National Biography

Academic theses

Haessly, Katie, 'British Conservative women MPs and "women's issues" 1950–1979', PhD Thesis, University of Nottingham, 2010.

Parker, Kristy, 'Women MPs, feminism and domestic policy in the Second World War', PhD Thesis, University of Oxford, 1994.

Takayanagi, Mari 'Parliament and Women, c. 1900–1945', PhD Thesis, King's College London, 2012.

Contemporary publications

Hansard (HC Debs – Commons, HL Debs – Lords)
The Times
The Guardian
The Observer
The New Statesman
The Telegraph
The Evening Standard
HuffPost
The Daily Mail
Financial Times
The Independent
Buzzfeed News
Daily Express
Sunday Graphic
The Sun
Women's Own
Island Life Magazine
Holyrood
BBC News
Contemporary Fabian Society pamphlets
Thompson, Joan, *Next Steps in Education* (1951).
Gaitskell, Hugh, *Socialism and Nationalisation* (1956).
Crosland, Tony, *Can Labour Win?* (1960).
Crossman, Richard, *Labour in the Affluent Society* (1960).
Brooks, R., Eagle, A. & Short, C. *Quotas Now: Women in the Labour Party* (1990).

Index